EARLY
CHILDHOOD
STUDIES

SAGE was founded in 1965 by Sara Miller McCune to support the dissemination of usable knowledge by publishing innovative and high-quality research and teaching content. Today, we publish more than 750 journals, including those of more than 300 learned societies, more than 800 new books per year, and a growing range of library products including archives, data, case studies, reports, conference highlights, and video. SAGE remains majority-owned by our founder, and after Sara's lifetime will become owned by a charitable trust that secures our continued independence.

Los Angeles | London | Washington DC | New Delhi | Singapore

4th Edition

EARLY CHILDHOOD STUDIES

An introduction to the study of children's
lives and children's worlds

EDITED BY

ROD PARKER-REES *&* CAROLINE LEESON

Los Angeles | London | New Delhi
Singapore | Washington DC

Learning Matters
An imprint of SAGE Publications Ltd
1 Oliver's Yard
55 City Road
London EC1Y 1SP

SAGE Publications Inc.
2455 Teller Road
Thousand Oaks, California 91320

SAGE Publications India Pvt Ltd
B 1/I 1 Mohan Cooperative Industrial Area
Mathura Road
New Delhi 110 044

SAGE Publications Asia-Pacific Pte Ltd
3 Church Street
#10–04 Samsung Hub
Singapore 049483

Editor: Amy Thornton
Development editor: Jennifer Clark
Production controller: Chris Marke
Project management: Deer Park Productions
Proofreader: Alison Wilson
Marketing manager: Lorna Patkai
Cover design: Wendy Scott
Typeset by: C&M Digitals (P) Ltd, Chennai, India
Printed by: CPI Group (UK) Ltd, Croydon, CR0 4YY

Library of Congress Control Number: 2015937415

A catalogue record for this book is available from
the British Library

ISBN 978-1-47391-592-3 (pbk)
ISBN 978-1-47391-591-6

Contents

Part 5 Researching practice: developing critical engagement 249

Contributors

Mandy Andrews lectures in Early Childhood Studies at Plymouth University and was recently a senior lecturer at the University of Worcester where she led the Early Years Teacher Status programme. Formerly a youth worker and a play officer for a local authority, she has worked in arts contexts, environmental project development and PVI projects in the arts, and community development. She has experience of supporting children's play in many contexts, from running an adventure playground and environmental play activities and community arts events to community-led play projects and Children's Centre management, and she has been a playwork trainer for over 20 years. Mandy is the author of *Exploring Play for Early Childhood Studies* and regularly participates on the Kidz Field at Glastonbury Festival.

Dr Verity Campbell-Barr is a lecturer in Early Childhood Studies at Plymouth University where she teaches on both undergraduate and postgraduate courses. Prior to joining Plymouth she worked as a researcher and gained experience of conducting both national and local level policy evaluations. She continues to research and write about early childhood education and care policy and has developed a particular interest in the quality of early childhood education and care services, with a more specific interest in the role of the workforce in delivering quality provision. She has recently completed research on the quality of early years services for two-year-olds and a European project on the attitudinal competences which early childhood practitioners are expected to demonstrate.

Victoria Bamsey is a part-time lecturer in Early Childhood Studies on both the BA and BEd programmes at Plymouth University. She also works as an Associate Early Years Consultant supporting and mentoring Early Years Leaders across her local authority, supporting the continued professional development of this early years workforce as part of the continuing work to raise quality in early years settings.

Dr Sofia Chanda-Gool is a lecturer in Early Childhood Studies at Plymouth University. Her ethnographic research has focused on cross-cultural issues in education, developmental psychology and inclusive practice. She has worked closely with diverse minority ethnic communities in the UK, families in South Asia and the indigenous communities of Australia. Her work with Bristol Education Action Zone, developing relationships between schools and communities and designing an inclusive curriculum, was the focus of her PhD and was inspired by the communities' values and beliefs. As a BACP-accredited counsellor and lecturer she is interested in group-work research with students to enhance collaborative learning styles, in contrast with the more individualistic focus of academic learning, and to integrate the socioemotional dimension into the academic experience.

Dr Ulrike Hohmann is an associate professor in Early Childhood Studies. She worked as a research associate at the University of Newcastle on a number of social policy projects before she joined Plymouth University. She holds a German childcare qualification and has worked in a wide range of childcare settings in Germany. Her research interests include children and social policy, childcare settings and the relationships that develop between children and their adult carers. She is interested in comparative, cross-national research, has worked on a number of comparative research projects and acts as supervisor for national and international Masters dissertations and doctoral theses.

Dr Valerie Huggins is an experienced lecturer in Early Childhood Studies at Plymouth University, with a lead role in early years teacher education and professional studies. Before taking up her current post, she spent many years working as an early years teacher and consultant and some time with VSO, training teacher educators in Ethiopia. Her research interests centre on approaches to promoting Early Care and Education for sustainability, both in the UK and in Majority World contexts, through the professional development of practitioners. Valerie has recently completed a Doctorate in Education with a focus on interculturalism.

Dr Marie Lavelle is a lecturer in Early Childhood Studies at Plymouth University. She originally trained as a nurse and then a midwife, practising in some of the most disadvantaged areas of the country. Later she worked for the family support charity, Home-Start. Her research interests have focused predominantly on parents and families. Her PhD study explored parental participation in Sure Start Children's Centres and she is currently exploring reflections on parenting from across the lifespan.

Dr Caroline Leeson is an associate professor and joint programme leader on the BA (Hons) Early Childhood Studies degree at Plymouth University. She has particular interests in the welfare of looked-after children, children's centre leadership and reflective practice. Her research interests include social justice; children with a parent in prison; children who go missing and/or are vulnerable to sexual exploitation; as well as the involvement of children in decision-making processes. Before working in higher education she worked as a social worker in child protection, fostering and adoption.

Dr Christoforos Mamas is a lecturer in Early Childhood Studies and Education at Plymouth University. His main research interests lie in the area of inclusive and special education and he is particularly interested in using mixed methods within comparative and cross-cultural studies. He is about to embark on a three-year research fellowship to examine the social interactions, peer relationships and friendship networks of primary school children with an emphasis on those identified as having additional support needs and disabilities.

Dr Rebecca McKenzie is a developmental psychologist specialising in research with families of children with autism. She also has a research interest in cultural influences on intervention and diagnosis of developmental disorders. Dr McKenzie is the organiser of the Plymouth Autism Network, bringing people with an interest in autism together. She initially trained as a primary school teacher specialising in early years and taught in a range of inner city and rural schools and settings. Dr McKenzie is currently a lecturer in Early Childhood Studies at Plymouth University.

Dr Julia Morgan is a lecturer in Early Childhood Studies at Plymouth University. She has worked as a health professional in various NHS hospitals, taught on an online Masters in Public Health (MPH) and worked as a researcher on studies for organisations including The Children's Society, Sure Start and Home-Start. She has also worked with 'street children' in Mongolia, Southern Africa and Romania. Her research has focused on support offered by schools to children with a father in prison, children's experiences of visiting their parent in prison, the children of military families project and a project on services for children who 'go missing'. Her research interests include social justice and inequality, children's perspectives, participatory research, child and maternal health, criminal justice and cross-cultural perspectives.

Rod Parker-Rees is an associate professor (senior lecturer), coordinator of Early Childhood Studies and joint programme leader for the BA (Hons) Early Childhood Studies degree at Plymouth University. He taught three- to five-year-old children in Bristol and was a researcher with the National Primary Centre (South West) before working at Plymouth. His research interests centre on very early communication, playfulness and the role of young children as active social agents. He co-edited *Early Years Education: Major Themes in Education* (2006) and edited *Meeting the Child in Steiner Kindergartens* (2011) and since 1999 he has been a co-editor of *Early Years: An International Research Journal*.

Philip Selbie is a lecturer in Early Childhood Studies at Plymouth University. He is a qualified primary teacher with an MA in Early Childhood Education and has taught young children in international schools as well as schools in the UK. He currently teaches students on BEd, BA and MA programmes as well as students studying to be teachers at universities in Central Eastern Europe. Philip is a school governor and is particularly interested in researching children's spirituality and the contribution of Jan Amos Comenius (1592–1670) to early childhood education and care.

Karen Wickett lectures on the BA and BEd Early Childhood Studies programmes. Originally she qualified as an NNEB and later trained as an early years teacher. Between 2003 and 2012 she worked in a Sure Start Local Programme/Children's Centre. During this period she created learning environments with children, parents and ECEC practitioners. This was a space for all to learn and grow. Motivated by the need to construct a local definition of school readiness she embarked on her Professional Doctorate in Education (EdD). She designed the research so that parents, ECEC practitioners and teachers could share their experiences and understandings of school readiness and the process of transition to school. Her teaching and research interests are transitions, co-constructed curriculum and learning environments.

Preface

The preface to the first edition of this book, by Lesley Abbott (2004), emphasised the excitement associated with rapidly expanding integrated services and the opportunity to develop a new multiprofessional discourse in early years provision. Lesley's preface identified the value of this book in clearly setting out the field to a new lecturer setting out to teach in the rapidly emerging field of Early Childhood Studies. This fourth edition of the book underlines its enduring value to the subject's canon of texts. The book offers students, both experienced and new to the field, a clear and accessible overview of the key topics, debates and attitudes. With each edition, the growing team at Plymouth have taken account of developments in thinking, research and the ever-changing context for those working with young children and their families.

This fourth edition of the book is also forged in exciting times that lend it new weight and purchase. Public services, which had fully acknowledged the value of early development and accepted a greater role in developing integrated family, health, education and play provision through Children's Centres, have been decimated by the austere economic climate and a neoliberal ideology. The number of children involved in preschool activities continues to rise with the increasing offer of two-year-old places but so too do concerns over the impact of poverty and social inequality. While the economic situation may improve, the implications of neoliberal policy are profound. Its impact is not just on the structures of provision but on the way we see ourselves and others. Personal responsibility and personal choice are core values of neoliberalism and while they are also clearly values that are central to young children's development, they may be damaging if taken to extremes. Early childhood studies increasingly document the importance of supportive social structures as the cradle of positive long-term attitudes to self and society. Neoliberal policies, such as offering choice from a range of commercial baseline assessment systems for Reception classes without providing accompanying guidance on what is in the best interests of children, emphasise the importance of having a sound understanding of the field. Graduates from Early Childhood Studies degrees *will* be challenged to do more with fewer resources. Those concerned with the well-being of young children need, more than ever before, to be well informed, thoughtful and smart in their thinking. They will need to be able to defend what they believe to be in the best interests of the children in their care.

The authors continue to offer sound principles and insights into children's development and well-being, as well as encouraging readers to be enquiring and reflective practitioners. If the proof of the pudding is in the eating, then I have had the great privilege to read students' writing in response to the Plymouth team's teaching, thinking and way of being. The strength of their students' work is the insights that they identify, through enquiry, into how children's development is nurtured and challenged by policy. This book highlights the authors' passion and their understanding of the interplay between these issues and their deep desire to promote social justice for children and families in national and international contexts.

Martin Needham
Education and Social Research Institute,
Manchester Metropolitan University

Introduction

Rod Parker-Rees

Early Childhood Studies (ECS) occupies a particularly interesting boundary space among other areas of study. It has obvious links with Childhood Studies programmes, some of which may include opportunities to focus on early childhood, but it is more than just a sub-section of this broader area. What sets it apart is the breadth of its scope, including the areas addressed in Childhood Studies programmes, such as history, sociology, philosophy and the arts, but also addressing the practical knowledge required for working with young children and their families. Many ECS programmes are located in education departments where they may sit alongside Initial Teacher Education programmes such as a BEd and PGCE Primary Education (Early Years) and Early Years Initial Teacher Training (EYITT) which focus on preparing students to take on a particular professional role and which confer a practice qualification; others sit in social science departments alongside programmes in social work and health care. What is distinctive about ECS is that it provides rich opportunities for students to explore the border areas between thinking and doing, between examining how and why *communities* come to do things as they do and reflecting on how and why we do what we do when we actively engage with children and their families. The Childhood Studies elements of an ECS programme enrich our learning about the 'how' and 'what' of practical work with children by adding a focus on 'why' and the Early Childhood elements ground these wider reflections in the embodied and felt experience of engaging directly with other people and with our own responses.

This book has been written by members of the ECS team at Plymouth University, where we introduced an Early Childhood Studies degree in 2000. The first edition was published in 2004 and much has changed since then, both in the worlds and lives of young children and in the worlds and lives of students. Our thinking about the scope and purpose of our ECS degree has been informed by what we describe as a 'core of care', reflecting our aim of encouraging students to become passionate advocates for children; professionals who care about policies and processes as well as practitioners who are able to provide sensitive care for children. We also believe that studying for an ECS degree provides valuable opportunities for students to play an active role in extending the core of care beyond what they are learning and the way they are treated by tutors to include the way they support and encourage each other. Engaging with other students, working in groups, studying together and contributing to a learning community will require students to deal with disagreements, cope with clashes of personalities and notice when others may need a bit of care and encouragement. In several of the chapters in this book we have written about the benefits of difference, how children's worlds and lives are enriched by opportunities to engage with different experiences, different ways of doing things, different people and different cultures. We believe that it is particularly important that people who will be working with young children and their families should develop a core of care which will enable them to engage respectfully with people who do not share their own background, experiences and assumptions. This core of care will also encompass a strong and principled ethical stance – engaging respectfully with people who hold different views does not mean agreeing with everything they say!

We hope to show, in this book, how ECS can lead you into fascinating areas of social and cultural enquiry which will help you to develop your own critical capabilities as you learn to challenge and question what you care most about and why this may be. Developing a critical perspective involves more than just challenging everything (though this is a good start!); it requires a willingness and ability to subject other people's ideas to careful scrutiny, matching them against our own developing values, beliefs and principles and following up on any interesting discrepancies. Developing a personal understanding of complex issues also requires much more than just accumulating knowledge (though, again, this is a good start). Knowledge can only be woven into personal understanding when the common framework of 'what everyone knows' is 'coloured in' with the complex significance and unique richness of our own personal experience.

The study of early childhood presents us with frequent opportunities to reflect on how our own feelings and concerns relate to those experienced by young children: How would I feel if someone treated *me* like that? Would I talk like that to another adult? What would it be like if we, as adults, could only study alongside others of our own year group or if we had no say in what we had to study? How do I feel when I enter a situation in which I don't know anyone and I don't know how I'm supposed to behave?

This introduction cannot hope to represent the full range of ideas which this book will address but it should give you a feel for what you will find in each chapter by showing how the different themes and topics which make up the rich mix of Early Childhood Studies can provide opportunities to learn about yourself as well as about the lives and worlds of young children.

Part 1 – What can children do? Sociocultural factors in development

The title of this section – 'What can children do?' – addresses the question of what children are *able* to do, acknowledging and respecting their capabilities, but it also touches on what children are *allowed* to do. Whenever we talk about children's developing abilities we must recognise that what they can do is influenced by the tools, opportunities and support which we provide for them. While it has always been tempting to look for ways to accelerate children's development, to hurry them along in particular areas, we must also recognise that encouraging children to devote more time to improving one skill may limit their opportunities to grow in other ways. The fact that children *could* do something, given a particular set of environmental factors, does not mean that they *should* be expected to do this. We have to be prepared to question and challenge assumptions about what children need and what is best for them.

In Chapter 1, 'An introduction to child development', Rebecca McKenzie outlines the relationships between what children's bodies and brains enable them to do and how other people, cultures and artefacts open or close off opportunities for particular kinds of development. This complex interaction is sometimes reduced to a simple question: Which is most important in human development, nature or nurture? Behind this simplification, however, there are many fascinating issues which we are still only just beginning to explore. We can clearly recognise the signs of neglect in children who have been deprived of the attentive, loving relationships which we know children need but it is much more difficult to imagine how children's lives might be further enriched if we were to provide for them in ways which we currently do not consider. Our cultures support and enable the development of children but they can also create the conditions, such as Early Childhood Studies degree programmes, which allow us to study and develop our understanding of development itself.

In Chapter 2, 'Children at play: evolution, playfulness and creativity', Mandy Andrews examines ethological, psychological and sociocultural accounts of the role and importance of play, not only in childhood but also in the shaping of human societies. Play is one of several key concepts in early childhood studies which appear straightforward and 'obvious' until we subject them to careful scrutiny, when they slip through our fingers and defy definition. Mandy argues that free-flow play, when children (or adults) are able to pursue their own interests in a rich environment with a wide variety of flexible materials and without externally imposed goals or restrictive time constraints, nurtures and develops our 'play instinct' in a way which cannot be matched by adult-led 'learning activities' however much we try to make these look 'playful'. Although we tend to associate play with young children (and other young animals), playfulness continues to have an important function in professional decision making and behaviour. We have to be prepared to be creative when we explore ways of adapting policy requirements to make them appropriate for different settings, families and children.

In Chapter 3, 'Developing communication: getting to know each other', I argue that a narrow focus on the importance of language development risks distracting us from careful examination of the earliest stages of communication. The special pleasure derived from sharing attention with other people may be more important than we realise. While gossip and idle chat may appear 'unprofessional', this kind of unstructured, social interaction is what allows us to get to know other people as individuals, with their own interests, perspectives and priorities. You will have experienced the difference in 'feel' between conversations with tutors who engage with students and lectures from tutors who are 'delivering' information. You will also be aware of the very different *feel* of settings where practitioners talk *with* colleagues, parents and children rather than *to* them or *at* them (see Chapter 11).

In Chapter 4, 'Spirituality and young children's well-being', Philip Selbie argues that our understanding of well-being as a broad, holistic term may be diminished if we fail to acknowledge its spiritual component. Philip outlines the history of interest in aspects of education which go beyond the simple transmission of knowledge and skills to consider how children can be helped to develop as whole, rounded and caring people. It is particularly difficult to put into words what we mean by 'spirituality' because this concept encompasses modes of being and relating to the world and other people which are intangible and which resist definition. The long history of associations between spirituality and religion may also make it difficult for some people, in an increasingly secular society, to recognise that they have a responsibility to nurture the spiritual life as well as the physical and emotional well-being of the children with whom they work. The increasingly critical engagement with personal values, principles and beliefs which is encouraged in higher education may also remind us of the need to engage with our own spirituality, to explore and question why we care passionately about certain aspects of our work with children. Spending time with children and engaging fully with their interests and questions often presents us with rich opportunities to further our own spiritual development.

Part 2 – Working with children: extending opportunities for participation

Any study of early childhood must include substantial experience of spending time with children, both working with them in a professional capacity and enjoying their company. Direct, experiential learning offers special opportunities and challenges. Learners must always acknowledge their responsibility for the effects of their actions on the children and while they tiptoe among the eggshells of professional sensitivities (see Part 3) they also have to become increasingly aware of how their own assumptions, preconceptions and prejudices may affect the way they engage with different children and families. When we are dealing with people our mistakes have real consequences which can be difficult to put right. On the other hand, when we spend time in the company of young children we are forced to refine our ability to 'read' subtle cues which can tell us what matters to a particular child at a particular time. The kinds of learning which are available to us in our interactions with children (and with members of their families) are importantly different from the learning which can be expressed in words, talked *about*, written *about* and read *about* outside any particular context.

In Chapter 5, 'Observing children: the importance of personal insight and reflective action', Mandy Andrews and Karen Wickett encourage you to think carefully about *why* we observe children. After charting the history of approaches to observing children, from Darwin, Montessori, Steiner, MacMillan and Isaacs to Carr, Malaguzzi and Deleuze and Guattari, they set out six key principles which can inform a critical, reflective and, above all, respectful approach to observation. It is important to remember that what we notice is shaped as much by our own interests and priorities (including policy guidelines and schedules of developmental goals) as by what is 'out there'. It is too easy to put on observational blinkers and see only what we are looking for but Karen and Mandy argue that an extended form of documentation, involving dialogue with colleagues and family members as well as the children themselves, can help us to become aware of the lenses through which we see children and to recognise that other lenses are available. Karen and Mandy remind us that we should *enjoy* our observation of children's play and work, not just because this makes our work more agreeable but also because this can allow us to engage affective responses which can enrich our understanding of how different children actively make sense of their worlds.

In Chapter 6, 'Providing an enabling environment', Karen Wickett and Philip Selbie remind us that there is much more to children's worlds than just physical spaces and resources. If we aim to create conditions in which children are enabled, not merely allowed, to explore, learn and develop, then our understanding of the environment must extend to the people, ethos and principles which frame the opportunities available to them. We can learn from other countries and other traditions, recognising some of the ways in which different environments enable children in different ways but it is important that our 'borrowing' from other traditions involves more than just collecting 'features', like souvenirs from our travels. Every environment extends into time as well as space. Like a story, an environment has meanings which are built on what has happened in the past; practitioners draw from traditions which have been shaped and refined by the experience of many others and children draw on experiences shared with their peers. A community with a shared history is enabling because it allows people to feel comfortable and supported enough to take on challenges which would otherwise appear too daunting. Students may initially feel disabled in the new environment of lectures and seminars but as friendships, trust and relationships develop, it may become easier to participate more fully.

In Chapter 7, 'Children, inequality and risk', Caroline Leeson and Julia Morgan examine the ways in which social inequalities, and particularly the widening gap between the rich and the poor, influence the way we think about risk in the lives of children. While very young children are often assumed to be precious, innocent and at risk from adults, older children, especially those who inhabit marginal social spaces, may come to be seen *as* risk. Older children who do not conform to our expectations of how children are meant to behave may even be thought of as deserving the disadvantages they experience. Thus children may be 'contaminated' with the blame attached to a parent who is in prison; 'street children' may be vilified as thieving drug abusers who threaten the civilised order of a city and child victims of sexual abuse may be seen as being at least partly responsible for what happens to them. When we work with children from disadvantaged families we may need to be particularly alert to the risk that we may, even unconsciously, attach personal blame to these children and families and not recognise that structural inequalities often have a major part to play in the position in which they find themselves.

Chapter 8, 'Tackling inequality in early years settings', by Ulrike Hohmann, also focuses on inequality, especially as it affects younger children. Much as health cannot be understood simply as the absence of illness, so equality of opportunities implies much more than just avoiding discriminatory practices. Where 'integration' has sometimes been interpreted as helping 'different' children to be absorbed among their 'normal' peers, 'inclusive' approaches acknowledge the need for settings to provide an environment in which children with different abilities, needs and interests can thrive together and learn from each other. The focus on inclusion is driven by changes in policies concerning provision for children with special educational needs but it fits comfortably within an early years philosophy which insists that every child (and every parent) must be respected as an individual, with particular needs, concerns and capabilities. Tackling inequality means actively identifying and addressing aspects of practice which can distort the opportunities we provide for different children and families. Those who work with young children have a special responsibility, not only to ensure that their practice will promote equality of opportunity but also to provide environments in which children learn to value and enjoy the diversity which an inclusive group can offer.

Part 3 – Multiprofessional practice: developing empowering communities

Anyone who considers a career working with children because they get on better with children than with other adults will soon discover that virtually every possible kind of work will necessarily involve working with parents and families as well as colleagues and professionals from other agencies. Learning how to get on with other adults and how to help them to achieve their full potential is an essential part of any professional training and fortunately we all have plenty of experience of working with others in different kinds of groups and teams, collaborating, submitting to leadership and also, perhaps, leading. We each have a considerable stockpile of both positive and negative examples of factors which affect how people get on, both with each other and with the task in hand. In the early stages of any career our main priority will be to survive being led by others (drawing on our creative ability to interpret what we are expected to do) but sooner or later (and this is alarmingly soon for most early years professionals), we will find ourselves leading other adults as well as children. The experiences we can gain while studying alongside a range of other adults of different ages, with different backgrounds and, possibly with different career interests, as well as our experiences of working in real early years settings, on placements, in a voluntary capacity or in part-time work, can also help us to deepen our understanding of what makes people tick and how to oil the wheels when friction between individuals prevents a team from working together smoothly.

Chapter 9, 'Language, cultural identity and belonging', developed out of conversations between its authors, Sofia Chanda-Gool and Mandy Andrews, about their different understandings of the word 'integration'. The chapter addresses some of the ways in which language can be used to bind people into a community of shared understandings or to marginalise people who are different in some way. Changes in the words we use to identify people and in the way we feel about the labels attached to us by others reflect shifting power relations in people's struggles to own how they are known. Sofia and Mandy point out that the best way to avoid inadvertently using language which others may find offensive is to 'seek the other', to engage with people and ask them how they feel about words that may be used to identify them. By actively entering into dialogue with the people we encounter in our work we can enrich and extend the range of perspectives available to us. We can also make an important contribution to strengthening our local community, both inside our setting and beyond it.

Chapter 10, 'Working in partnership: encounters with colleagues in the third space' by Valerie Huggins and Caroline Leeson, addresses the increasing emphasis on 'joined-up' planning and delivery of services for children following several well publicised cases of children's deaths which might have been prevented if the various agencies involved in their care had worked together in more coordinated ways. Professional partnerships are complex, social relationships which must be forged between individual practitioners, not just between 'services' or 'roles'. In working relationships between adults there will always be a mix of person-to-person and role-to-role forms of interaction but an emphasis on the latter at the expense of the former can lead to fragile and insincere forms of partnership. Martin Buber (2004) has written powerfully about this difference between 'I-thou' relationships and 'I-it' relationships and you will be well aware of the difference between tutors or placement staff who take the trouble to engage with you as a person and those for whom you remain 'a student'. Work with young children is an area which requires high levels of intercultural sensitivity, not only to meet the needs of different families and children but also to collaborate sensitively with colleagues who may come from very different professional cultures.

In Chapter 11, 'Parenting in trouble?' Marie Lavelle examines relationships between parents and early years practitioners through the lenses of power and trust. In children's centres, where practitioners are specifically charged with working to support the development of parents' relationships with their children, this 'top down' function can sometimes get in the way of the development of trusting and mutually supportive relationships. Where there is a simplistic equation between being poor, in terms of access to resources, and being a 'poor parent', it is difficult for parents to buy into the aims of centres and professionals who want to 'improve' them. Drawing on the work of Michel Foucault, Marie shows how power operates through the regulation of apparently trivial events such as whether parents are 'allowed' to have a cup of tea and a chat, defining relationships and influencing the ways in which people are willing to engage with each other. Marie argues that the kinds of care demonstrated in interactions between parents and professionals form an important part of the affective 'climate' of a setting, informing the development of children's understanding of how people can be expected to respect each other.

In Chapter 12, 'Leadership in early childhood settings', Caroline Leeson points out that much research on effective leadership draws on models derived from studies of businesses or big organisations which have tended to be led by men. Most early years settings, on the other hand, will be led by women, whose preferred leadership style is often more collaborative than competitive. This style may prove particularly appropriate for graduate leaders of complex, multiprofessional settings, where practitioners from a wide range of backgrounds and professional cultures must be encouraged to support and learn from each other if they are to develop and improve the quality of provision. Leadership can be learned and practised by all members of an early years team and distributed leadership can support flexible and sustainable ways of working together and learning from each other. Caroline makes the important point that studies of generalised features of the role of the leader can only go so far. All leaders are individuals, with unique personal histories and cultures, which will influence their style, their decisions and their priorities. Effective leaders cannot refer to an instruction manual to decide how to respond in a particular situation; they have to exercise professional judgement and acknowledge the individuality of each of the children, parents and colleagues with whom they work.

Part 4 – Comparing children's worlds: making the familiar strange

The fact that we have all been children may, at first, appear to give us a good foundation for studying childhood but this familiarity can also make it more difficult for us to notice what is right under our noses. However, as soon as we begin to introduce some distance between our own experience and the children and childhoods we study, we are more able to recognise that what children do is heavily shaped and constrained by what adults want, expect, allow and even need children to do. What we see children doing or not doing, in a particular context, should not be taken as evidence of the limits of what they *could* do, if we were to change aspects of the culture which shapes their lives.

In Chapter 13, 'Concepts of childhood: meeting with difference', I focus on the place of childhood in the dynamic co-construction of both individuals and communities. By adopting a historical perspective we can recognise that the relationship between childhood and adulthood has not always been understood in the same way and this can help us to notice the assumptions which inform our own attitudes to childhood and children. Looking more closely at the processes involved in the co-construction of our memories of our 'own' childhood helps us to recognise how our adult, concept-based ways of thinking differ from the more immediate, 'innocent' experience of young children. In order to be able to live together in large numbers we have had to negotiate a degree of consistency in how we expect people to behave and adulthood is largely defined in terms of 'knowing the ropes'. Throughout history this social requirement to *fit in* has developed in a dynamic relationship with a desire to *stand out* and we have learned to value the creative, transformative energy of childhood which helps to keep individuals and communities flexible and adaptable. I argue that while we acknowledge the contribution of the 'inner child' to the life of a balanced individual, the increasing segregation of children's worlds and adults' worlds is reducing opportunities for children to contribute to the life of balanced communities.

In Chapter 14, 'The benefits of comparison: recent developments in the German early years workforce', Ulrike Hohmann shows how debates in Germany about changes to training for early years practitioners can help to provide a bit of perspective on arguments in the UK about the education, training and accreditation of early years teachers. It may be particularly difficult for students on an ECS course to stand back from their own motives, experiences and aspirations enough to be able to consider what kind of preparation would be best for people who intend to work with young children. Do we need relatively short, low-cost, competence-focused training to equip students with the skills they will need to work safely and effectively with young children, or should we focus on more extensive, and more expensive, degree-level education programmes which support the development of students' abilities to evaluate policy initiatives and interpret them creatively in different contexts? Should we expect an individual to master all of the skills required for work with children and families or should we develop a range of specialist roles which will contribute to the team around the child? Awareness of some of the cultural, social and policy factors which complicate decisions about how to educate the early years workforce in Germany may help you to notice similar, but different, factors closer to home.

In Chapter 15, 'Children's well-being in the Majority World: developing sustainable life patterns', Valerie Huggins invites readers to adopt an even wider perspective. Recognising the very different kinds of challenges which face policy makers, practitioners and families in countries which do not share our relative wealth and stability can help us to recalibrate our assumptions about what is really important in children's lives. This chapter explores some of the consequences of the very uneven distribution of natural, physical, human, financial and social capital both between and within countries and identifies some of the consequences for children's economic well-being, their access to health care, education and adequate nutrition and their exposure to exploitation, armed conflict and other destabilising social and cultural situations. The efforts of non-governmental organisations to offer aid and support in areas where local governments are unable to meet people's needs raise some very difficult questions about how 'better off' nations can support the 'developing world' without imposing inappropriate cultural, social and political frameworks. The inhabitants of Majority World countries certainly do not appreciate being treated like children by paternalistic or proselytising 'do-gooders', but by investigating these issues students of early childhood can develop a heightened critical sensitivity to the workings of power relations – an intercultural sensitivity which will inform their work in settings and in families.

In Chapter 16, 'The research, policy and practice triangle in early childhood education and care', Verity Campbell-Barr examines how policies are developed, how they are sometimes informed and often challenged by research and how they are interpreted and adapted in practice, often in a variety of different ways. Research can help to stir the waters and reveal aspects of policy and practice which deserve closer critical scrutiny. Policies which are presented as being in the interests of children may also affect families and the wider economy. On the other hand, policies developed in other areas may turn out to have dramatic effects on children's lives. Particularly in the early stages of our career we may crave some clear guidelines and fixed points of reference and the intricacies of relationships within the research, policy and practice triangle may make it difficult to feel sure about anything. One of the responsibilities which come with a professional role, however, is that we have to be willing to question what we are asked to do and to examine issues from different perspectives; simply following instructions and 'delivering' policies is not an option. There will always be some 'play' in any policy, some room for creative interpretation and adjustment to meet the particular needs of individual settings, families and children.

Part 5 – Researching practice: developing critical engagement

One of the aims of any degree programme should be to leave students with a greater awareness of how much more there is still to learn. We have to be careful not to allow ECS degrees to be reduced to training courses, aimed at enabling students to accumulate competences until, when they have enough, they can be considered 'done' and safe to enter a particular area of work. One risk of a training model is that it can leave students feeling that no further study is needed once they have achieved the necessary levels of competence, unless, perhaps, they wish to proceed to the next rung on their career ladder. It is particularly important that people who will be working with young children and their families should actively promote a positive attitude to continuing learning and personal development because their example will inform children's learning dispositions at a time when these are especially sensitive to social influences.

In Chapter 17, 'In praise of reflective practice', Caroline Leeson and Victoria Bamsey show how an inquisitive, investigative attitude to all aspects of your own practice can help you to make the continuing development of your skills, knowledge and understanding an integral part of your professional development. While it may be tempting to settle into doing what has always been done and what has worked well enough in the past, professional practice requires a more engaged, active commitment to challenging and extending what we already know. As a professional you will need to keep up to date with research published by others but you will also be expected to maintain and develop a critical perspective on your own actions and decisions. Reflection always has a strongly personal component, drawing on soft intuitions as well as hard facts, but it can also be supported by interaction with other people; talking (and arguing) with trusted colleagues can be a particularly effective way of testing and clarifying your own thinking. Most importantly, by explicitly questioning, challenging and discussing aspects of your practice you will be providing a powerful example of positive learning dispositions, for the children you work with as well as parents and colleagues.

In Chapter 18, 'Research projects in Early Childhood Studies', Ulrike Hohmann and Christoforos Mamas explain what is involved in planning, conducting and writing up a small-scale research project. The research project or dissertation can provide opportunities for you to explore an area of personal interest at a depth which will often result in you knowing more about it than most of your peers and, in many cases, your tutors too. Developing an area of personal expertise can enable you to make the transition from seeing yourself as a knowledge consumer, dependent on work done by others, to also thinking of yourself as a knowledge producer, able to make a contribution to what is known about the lives and worlds of young children. The process of devising, developing, analysing and presenting your own empirical study can also give you valuable experience of a range of strategies for exploring, testing and refining your understanding of work with young children. While you may not regularly conduct similar studies in your working life, these strategies will inform your reflection on your own practice and will enable you to adopt a more critical perspective when you read research published by others.

Finally, in Chapter 19, 'Action research', Ulrike Hohmann and Karen Wickett show how practitioners in settings can establish systematic enquiry as a central feature of everyone's involvement in a setting's learning community. While undergraduate students have to work around the ethical and practical issues of negotiating access to settings, families and children as part of their research projects, practitioners enjoy daily access to rich opportunities to examine and reflect on how they go about supporting young children and their families. The chapter includes an account of Karen's work in the children's centre where she worked as a teacher. Her work with her colleagues to explore and develop their use of documentation provides a real-life example of how shared enquiry can contribute to the development of a 'buzz' within a setting as everyone is swept along by enthusiasm and interest in a common focus. Ulrike and Karen acknowledge that just 'talking about what we do' can sometimes leave more sensitive or difficult issues untouched which is why it may be important to look outside our own setting, to engage with theory and research findings which can drive us to challenge aspects of our own practice.

We all have much to learn from the study of early childhood. David Kennedy (2000: 516) has argued that 'the adult who understands children and the conditions of childhood better understands him- or herself' but also that 'adults who learn to identify and serve the needs of children with more sensitivity and precision learn to do so for each other as well'. Early Childhood Studies can certainly help us to develop a better understanding of the children we will work with but it also has the potential to inform wider social and cultural understandings, contributing to the development of communities in which people are more attuned to each other's needs and interests.

REFERENCES

Buber, M. (2004) *I and Thou*. London: Continuum.

Kennedy, D. (2000) The roots of child study: philosophy, history and religion. *Teachers College Record*, 102(3): 514–38.

Part 1

What can children do? Sociocultural factors in development

1   An introduction to child development

Rebecca McKenzie

What is development?

The study of development explores how we change from conception across our whole life span. In order to understand development we need to think about maturation, learning and the influence of the world we are born into. Maturation is the way that our genetic recipe unfolds as we get older. Genes make up the hereditary material we receive from our parents, which partly influences how we grow and change. Learning results from experiences situated in a social and cultural context and what we learn also encourages changes, particularly in how we act, think and make decisions.

In this chapter we will focus on child development. Early childhood is a period of very rapid growth and change and for this reason development is more apparent. We all change throughout our lives, but early development can be especially powerful in shaping the person we will become. Child development is a complex subject and one that crosses professional boundaries. For example, psychologists, sociologists, biologists and anthropologists all contribute to what is known about early development. The complexity of this area of study stems from the multilayered nature of development, which includes biological, cognitive and socioemotional and sociocultural change.

The study of child development often focuses on the changes experienced by an average child. In reality, of course, development is an individual journey which is different for each one of us. For some children their developmental experience may differ substantially from that experienced by a typical or average child. This is often the case for children who have conditions such as autism or Down's syndrome. It is, therefore, important not to make generalisations about the nature of child development without acknowledging that we do not all develop in the same way or at the same rate.

REVIEW QUESTIONS

What is 'maturation'?

What kinds of professions contribute to the study of child development?

Piaget's maturational theory of development

Piaget (1936) was the first person to develop a systematic theory of how children develop and learn. Piaget's theory was based on detailed observations of how children solve problems at different points in their development. Piaget's work has been highly influential in the field of child development. He believed that all children have an intrinsic drive to learn and all pass through the same stages of development. Piaget proposed four stages of development, which reflected the child's movement from a state of ego-centred, concrete thinking towards de-centred, abstract thought. Children move through these stages of development as they biologically mature and gain new insights from interaction with the environment. (For a detailed account of Piaget's stages see Smith *et al.*, 2011.) According to Piaget's theory, children actively construct their own understanding by solving problems within their environment. In engaging with the world around them, children internalise their actions through the creation of cognitive frameworks or schemas (Piaget, 1977). Schemas are mental representations, which provide a way of organising knowledge. Schemas are subject to change as the child matures and gains new experiences through their actions in the world. As they get older and explore the world further, children assimilate and accommodate knowledge into existing schemas. Assimilation is the process of fitting new knowledge into existing schemas, in order to make sense of experiences. Where new knowledge is in conflict with existing schemas, a state of disequilibrium occurs and provides the impetus for schemas to be adapted. Accommodation is the process of changing a schema, or creating new schemas in order to deal with new knowledge, which does not fit, or questions the validity of existing schemas. Accommodation allows the child to move towards a state of equilibrium where mental representations match the child's experience of their environment.

Piaget's work remains influential, but his theory has been criticised, most notably by Margaret Donaldson (1978). Donaldson and colleagues repeated many of Piaget's experiments, but gave the tasks a context or explanation that made sense to the child. As a result she was able to demonstrate that where the task is meaningful for the child, very young children can operate at higher stages than Piaget's theory would predict. Donaldson's work suggests that Piaget underestimated the competence of young children and failed to take account of social and cultural influences on development.

Biological development

As infants get older some of the most apparent aspects of development are that they grow, attain more control over their bodies, enjoy sensory experiences and begin to communicate and express their thoughts. Biology has an important role to play in these changes. Development begins with conception and the genetic material we receive from our parents provides a blueprint for aspects of our development such as the colour of our hair and the height to which we grow. This blueprint can be altered or realised in different ways depending on environmental, social and emotional factors encountered by the individual. In this way both nature and nurture contribute to the way we grow and change throughout our lives.

Fundamental biological anomalies at the very earliest stages of life can affect the development of a person throughout their life span. For example, chromosomal errors can lead to conditions such as Klinefelter's syndrome or Down's syndrome which result in distinctive physical features, medical problems such as heart defects and learning difficulties. Other factors during pregnancy can also have far reaching implications for the person we become. Maternal illness and toxins passed to the developing foetus via the mother, such as alcohol, nicotine and other drugs, can affect the course of development. For example, children whose mothers drink heavily during pregnancy may develop foetal alcohol syndrome, resulting in atypical physical development and lifelong problems with processing information (Olsen *et al.*, 1992).

Even before birth the foetus is able to recognise familiar stimuli, in particular the sound of the mother's voice (and sometimes the father's), the mother's heartbeat and other sounds they are regularly exposed to, such as pieces of music. Newborns carry these memories with them and familiar stimuli support ongoing primary relationships and interactions with the environment after birth (Kisilevsky *et al.*, 2003). Our senses, awareness and movement within our environment are important tools for interacting and learning about the social and physical world (Robinson, 2008). Most babies are born with basic reflexes such as sucking and grasping, but these rapidly give way to effortful and purposeful movement within the first few months of life.

Babies appear hardwired to attend to their primary caregivers' faces and newborns appear to imitate facial movements such as the parent sticking out their tongue. The biological basis of imitation has been attributed to mirror neurons within the brain, which become activated when an individual observes the actions of another person. The pattern of activation when we observe action is the same as the activation resulting from us carrying out the action ourselves (Rizzolatti *et al.*, 2002). It seems, therefore, that we are biologically programmed to make connections between our own actions and those of others. Interestingly, at around two months of age, babies no longer exhibit the ability to imitate faces, but this may simply be that they are now able to look more purposefully and their focus has moved towards social interaction through smiling and vocalisation. Imitation is of course a skill that we retain throughout our lives and it plays a role in learning and understanding others. Imitation acts as a social tool, not only between infants and their carers but also between any two people who have a close bond. This can be observed in interactions between individuals who are close, or like each other, as they tend to unconsciously mirror each other's actions. This unconscious mirroring appears to help cement and maintain friendships (see Chapter 3).

As children become able to coordinate their bodies, movement involves posture: sitting, reaching, turning, crawling and eventually walking. We can see the outward changes in children's ability to explore their world, but there are also changes occurring within their bodies including the development of the sensory system and changes to the brain. The infant's brain is relatively unspecialised and is remarkably flexible in how it can develop and adjust to trauma (Karmiloff-Smith, 1998). Our brains are made up of specialised cells called neurons. The adult brain has distinct regions which deal with different types of information, but when we are engaged in any kind of task, connections between the neurons that make up these brain regions are active. It takes time for the regions of our brain to become specialised and for connections between neurons to develop. The first four years of life are a time of rapid change, as the brain wires itself up (e.g. Knickmeyer *et al.*, 2008). The experiences we have support the development of connections between neurons and in this way biological changes are initiated and maintained by the external world. Networks are constantly being established, strengthened and pruned back, depending on how often those networks are activated. In this way the networks across our brain reflect the dynamic nature of our experience of the world. The brain is consequently a dynamic organ, which changes throughout our lives.

We may accept that many of the changes we see during early development are biologically programmed, but our physical and social environment have a large role to play in realising, shaping or changing the path that our genetic recipe provides. Experiences and associated stimulation influence our development including the way in which networks develop across the brain. This has far reaching implications for children who unfortunately have very limited or negative stimulation. For example, children who have spent their early lives in orphanages where they receive little opportunity to interact with their environment and restricted opportunities to form relationships exhibit a number of difficulties including atypical or delayed physical capabilities and restricted patterns of brain development compared to other children of the same age (Kumsta *et al.*, 2014). Similarly, neglected and abused children whose early environments may be characterised by a lack of positive stimulation and nurturing relationships tend to experience developmental delays, emotional and social difficulties and atypical brain patterns (Hart and Rubia, 2012).

REVIEW QUESTIONS

What features do you think you have inherited from your biological parents?

What aspects of your personality and behaviour have you learnt from your parents?

The English and Romanian Adoptee (ERA) study

Michael Rutter and colleagues (Kumsta *et al.*, 2014) carried out a longitudinal study of 165 children adopted into the UK from Romania before they were three and a half years old. Most of the children had spent their early years in Romanian orphanages where conditions ranged from poor to abysmal. In the orphanages children were often confined to cots with minimal social interaction and extremely limited care. The purpose of the study was to explore whether children could recover from extreme deprivation once they had been adopted into safe, nurturing families.

This study showed that the Romanian children who were successfully adopted made rapid developmental leaps in their psychological functioning, but many of them continued to experience significant problems into their teenage years.

The children were assessed at ages 4, 6, 11 and 15 years. Once the children were established with their new families, developmental improvements appeared rapidly and continued through their childhood. By the age of 11 years some of the children were behaving and learning in a similar way to their peers. However, a substantial minority displayed poor social understanding, emotional problems, poor attachments, atypical attention, over activity and learning difficulties, into their teenage years.

Cognitive development

Cognition is the act of knowing. The development of cognition is characterised by change in the processes involved in gaining knowledge, such as: attention, thinking, remembering, judging and solving problems. Infants are born with a sense of curiosity about the world and an amazing capacity to learn (Gopnik *et al.*, 1999). Infants are driven to achieve their own goals, for example, a two-month-old child will kick their legs to make a hanging toy move and at around five months they will reach for the toy they want. Typically by around nine months infants also begin to recognise the intentions of others around them (Behne *et al.*, 2005). Goal-orientated infants solve problems and develop and remember strategies that help them to interact with their environment.

As we have seen, the explosion in children's knowledge about their world is supported by biological changes. Children can move around their world, make choices, and pursue interests and goals. Stimulating experiences facilitate the rapid development of connections throughout the brain, which provide the capacity for more complex thinking, problem solving and remembering. Infants are, however, born into a social world. Communicative skills and social understanding necessarily involve learning through relationships with others. Infants are very focused on their caregivers and for many children these ongoing close relationships form the basis of cognitive development by supporting the child to attend, observe, imitate, remember and share interests and goals. Very early on caregivers and infants engage in a reciprocal dance of sounds, movements, pauses and outbursts, which is typically supported by the song-like use of high pitched, expressive baby talk, known as 'motherese'; an innate feature of primary caregivers' communication with babies (Robinson, 2011 and Chapter 3). This communicative dance helps to integrate the sensory experiences of the infant and develops later into 'peek a boo' games which encourage shared attention, turn taking, memory skills and understanding about the permanence of objects in the environment. In the first three years of life children also demonstrate and develop their abilities to use symbols and learn that one thing can represent another. This is of course particularly apparent in the development of language and imaginary play (Westby, 2000).

As children get older their knowledge increases and their ability to recall information improves. Children can integrate what they know with what might be, in order to reason about the world, solve problems and consider a range of possibilities (Harris, 2000). As Donaldson (1978) suggested, very young children often need the support of meaningful contexts such as stories to help them solve problems but older children begin to be able to think in a more abstract way and can manipulate less concrete information. This kind of thinking forms the basis of the study of science and mathematics and is described by Piaget as formal operational thought. Changes in cognition involve interplay between biological and social influences; our ability to remember, recall and manipulate information develops within the context of what we learn from the social and physical world around us.

REVIEW QUESTIONS

Think of a time when you had to solve a problem. What kinds of cognitive skills did you need in order to solve it?

Do you think children are born with these skills, or do they develop over time?

Vygotsky's social-constructivist theory of development

Vygotsky (1978a) saw development as fundamentally dependent on the social and cultural environment that a child was part of. He acknowledged that children were born with biological functions such as reflexes, but believed that it was through interaction with more capable others in a particular sociocultural context that a child was able to learn and acquire higher level functions such as memory, logic and focused attention. Development was played out initially in a sociocultural context and subsequently through individual psychological transformations. The child is an active partner in co-constructing new meanings within the zone of proximal development.

Development was therefore critically dependent on the social context and the growth of the child within it. In Vygotsky's theory the sociocultural world is internalised by the child. Internalisation determines the meanings children attribute to their world, but also the cognitive processes involved in thinking and learning. Vygotsky felt that language was the ultimate cultural tool and the dominant vehicle for the transmission of abilities needed to function within a specific culture such as categorisation and problem solving.

The zone of proximal development

Vygotsky (1978) believed that children's development was facilitated by interaction with adults or more competent peers. Such interaction bridged a gap between the child's developmental level and their potential. Vygotsky called this space the 'zone of proximal development'. Emergent psychological functions could be realised through the guidance and support of a more capable other, allowing development to progress. According to this model, new skills are initially shared ventures and the child is an active partner in co-constructing new meanings within the zone of proximal development. Parents and teachers may begin by supporting ways of thinking and remembering, such as prompting a child to think back to where they last saw a lost item. Later the child will be able to use similar prompts to encourage their own recall. In this way, shared ways of viewing the world and solving problems become internalised over time, allowing the child to reproduce them independently.

Socioemotional development

Human infants are especially vulnerable compared to the young of other species and rely upon their caregivers for survival. All infants are born with a drive to attach to other human beings and these early relationships have far reaching implications for social and emotional development. We should also recognise that a relationship has two sides and the child is an individual with their own temperament and personality to bring to social interaction with others.

Infants are born with a drive to be social and are especially focused on those that regularly care for them and interact with them. John Bowlby (1969) was the first person to develop ideas about these primary relationships into attachment theory. Bowlby and his student Mary Ainsworth explored the deep bond that develops between infants and their primary carers. The infant was perceived to use a variety of strategies to elicit care from their parent figure and avoid danger. Bowlby believed that these strategies were realised in a working model, which provided a pattern for future relationships. Where a parent was consistently available and nurturing the child developed a secure attachment. Ainsworth *et al.* (1978) also explored the implications of inconsistent care, neglect and significant separation from the primary carer. In such cases the child may develop an avoidant, ambivalent or disorganised attachment model. It is important to recognise that all attachment strategies are adaptive and function as a response to the potential danger of separation from caregivers experienced by vulnerable infants. For example, children with avoidant strategies may have learnt that protest such as crying elicits rejection rather than care and the best strategy is to remain placid and not make a fuss in order to remain close to the caregiver. On the other hand, a child with ambivalent strategies may have learnt that proximity and care can only be elicited by making exaggerated demands, or being 'clingy' towards the caregiver. Although all attachment strategies are adaptive, insecure patterns of attachment involve heightened anxiety and preoccupation coupled with a low sense of self worth. Consequently, insecure attachment has an impact on children's social, emotional and cognitive development. These patterns of emotional behaviour are long lasting and can form a model for relationships with other individuals outside the family. The child's working model tends to be carried into adulthood and is likely to inform the relationships they have as adults with their own children (Fonagy *et al.*, 1993).

Attachment theory provides a framework for understanding how children regulate their emotions. Infants are born with the ability to express emotions and it is apparent that small babies exhibit states of pleasure and distress. Toddlers can express a broader range of emotions through facial expressions, sounds and body language. The onset of spoken language allows children to describe how they are feeling and older children begin to be able to control or regulate their own emotions.

A key factor in regulating emotions is the development of the ability to understand the emotional states of others. It is our 'Theory of Mind' which allows us to understand the beliefs and feelings of others as being distinct from our own. Theory of Mind appears to take time to develop and very young children may not have a clear sense of themselves as separate from others. Theory of Mind is often assessed through false belief tasks such as the Sally-Anne task (Baron-Cohen *et al.*, 1985). In this task the child is told a story about Sally leaving her marble in a basket then going out to play. While Sally is away Anne comes in and moves the marble to a box. The child is asked where they think Sally will look for her marble on her return. Very young children tend to 'fail' this task and claim that Sally will look for her marble in the box, despite the fact that Sally did not see Anne place it there. False belief tasks of this type have been used to show that children below the age of three or four do not have a fully developed Theory of Mind. These kinds of tasks rely heavily on language, however, and simpler tasks which are enacted within everyday events such as snack-time have shown that children as young as 18 months have some appreciation of the beliefs and desires of others (Repacholi and Gopnik, 1997).

Theory of Mind is important for both social and emotional development. Schaffer (2006) describes the movement towards 'emotional competence' as being bound up with developing understandings of self and others and the nature of social relationships. The concept of emotional regulation is also vital to emotional competence. Young children rely on carers to organise and respond to emotional states on their behalf, for example being soothed by mother when distressed. As children get older they become more able to manage their own emotional states and discern emotional states in others. Relationships, therefore, play a central and ongoing role in developing models for social and emotional competence.

REVIEW QUESTIONS

How do you think attachment models are played out in adult life?

Think about your own close relationships. How do you respond to separation from those you are close to?

Marvin's Circle of Security

Marvin's circle of security (Powell *et al.*, 2013) is based on Bowlby's concept of the 'secure base'. It was initially developed as a tool to help parents understand the needs of their child. The model takes very complex ideas around attachment and emotional development, and represents them in a simple graphic format. Children need relationships with their caregivers, characterised by a sense of safety and security. From this secure base they can feel confident to explore the world with their primary carer watching over them and sharing the enjoyment of their pursuits. The child also needs to feel that they can return regularly to the safe haven of the relationship with their carer, in times of distress and anxiety. Marvin suggested that repeated reconnection with the secure base allowed the child to 'recharge their batteries' and return to exploring the world once again. In this way the secure base and the child's own goals and needs form a circle of repeated action.

Marvin and his colleagues used the circle of security model very successfully to help parents identify the need for change where insecure patterns of attachment had formed. For example, an anxious relationship might result in the child staying very close to the parent and showing a constant need for comfort. In this case the child may forego opportunities to explore their environment, for fear that the parent would not watch over them or enjoy their explorations. Marvin's model allows parents to recognise this pattern and make changes to their behaviour. Changes in the actions of the parent can encourage the child to become more confident that they can play and learn from their environment, in the knowledge that they have a safe haven to return to.

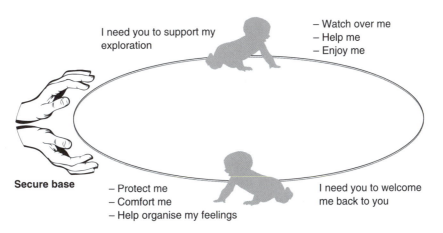

Figure 1.1 The circle of security (Powell et al., 2013)

Atypical development

The study of child development necessarily makes generalisations, which are not applicable to every child. All children are unique and their biological makeup, cultural context and socioemotional experiences differ. Some children may have atypical developmental trajectories, where they do not exhibit the same developmental milestones as most children or are slower in acquiring certain skills compared to their peers. For example, the development of children with Down's syndrome tends to proceed at a slower pace in comparison to children without the condition. Down's syndrome is caused by a chromosomal abnormality, which affects language and memory. Children with Down's syndrome often experience associated medical problems and may have motor and sensory difficulties. One reason for developmental delay stems from the fact that although their perception of the world around them is intact, children with Down's syndrome have difficulties using and interpreting what they experience. They also have a tendency to become fixated on one aspect of any given situation, hence they have a narrower focus than other children and often find it hard to interpret and build upon what they have experienced. Such problems affect the development of their ability to process complex information, understand and remember concepts, develop and maintain vocabulary and communicate with others (Turner *et al.*, 2008). Children with Down's syndrome vary in their biology and experience and early interventions and nurturing environments can help them to achieve their goals and learn about and understand the world, albeit at a slower rate than other children.

Children with Down's syndrome also show an uneven developmental profile in that they tend to have particular strengths which are unaffected by the condition. For example, they generally show the same early social behaviour as typical children and tend to be friendly individuals who build relationships, enjoy social communication and can bring happiness to those around them. Infants with Down's syndrome show a strong drive to be social and show engagement with their primary carers. They also tend not to show delays in early social behaviour such as smiling, babbling and the use of non-verbal communication and gesture.

Other children may show unusual developmental profiles, where they appear to experience and respond to the world very differently from typical children. Children with autism tend to have an uneven developmental profile but, in contrast to those with Down's syndrome, they appear to lack the drive to attend to other human beings, which is characteristic of other children. Autism is a spectrum condition and children vary in the degree to which their development is affected by the condition, but all children with autism have difficulties with communication, social interaction and flexible thinking. Autism is an intriguing condition and the causes are not fully understood, although it is widely accepted to have a genetic component (Abrahams and Geschwind, 2008). The unusual social behaviour of children with autism is characterised by a lack of interest in attending to faces, making eye contact and sharing attention. As the child gets older there is often a continued lack of interest in engagement with others and an inability to understand social situations including understanding the behaviour of other people. Children with autism tend, therefore, to fail false belief tasks and have everyday difficulties with Theory of Mind including identifying their own beliefs and the beliefs and intentions of others (Baron-Cohen, 2000).

Children with autism tend to have unusual obsessions and a restricted range of interests. Whilst they tend not to focus on the social world, they may be fixated on small details within their environment, which other children would fail to notice or to find meaningful (Happé and Frith, 2006). Children with autism also show delays in developing spoken language and around half of all children with autism develop no speech or very limited speech. Their communicative difficulties also extend to non-verbal communication such as facial expressions and body language. The lack of early attention to the social world appears to have far reaching implications for the development of children with autism and highlights the crucial role that early interactions play in helping us to understand the world around us.

REVIEW QUESTIONS

Look back at the findings of the ERA study. What symptoms do the Romanian adoptees have in common with children with autism? Why might they display some similar symptoms?

Autism and the enactive mind

Ami Klin *et al.* (2003) became interested in why individuals with autism can solve problems with social content in a similar way to their peers, but fail to understand social situations in everyday contexts. He used eye-tracking techniques to find out what individuals with autism attend to when watching social situations. For typical children and adults attention is focused on faces and particularly eyes during social encounters. Klin discovered that this was not the case for adults and children with autism, who tended to focus on the mouths of the social actors or objects in the background. In addition, where a person points to a particular object or scene, to invite the viewer to follow his/her gaze, the individuals with autism fail to look in the indicated direction. This finding suggests that even adults with autism have difficulties with joint attention, a basic early example of social behaviour. Klin found that toddlers with autism displayed similar atypical attention to social scenes when watching children's television programmes. The toddlers tended to become fixated on peripheral objects rather than the faces of the primary characters.

Klin concludes that the fundamental drive to attend to social stimuli is absent in children with autism. In typical children, there is an innate drive to attend to social phenomena and to regard social situations as intrinsically relevant. The continuous process of attending to social stimuli and striving to give meaning to them comes very easily to typical children and results in rapid contextualised social development. For children with autism the story is very different because social situations have no more relevance than a display of inanimate objects. Consequently children with autism tend not to pay particular attention to social scenes and to learn from, or give meaning to, social experiences. Their social understanding is consequently derailed by a lack of the fundamental building blocks such as facial recognition and joint attention, which facilitate social development. Klin provides a theory, therefore, which explains the social and communicative difficulties associated with autism, which stem from early inattention to social stimuli.

Conclusion

Child development is a vast and interesting topic, which involves psychological, social, biological and cultural elements. Children's genetic make up and their early experiences will influence the course of their life. Early childhood is a time of rapid and extraordinary change, which is the subject of innumerable research studies and yet there is still a lot to learn. Children are active agents in their own development and we should not underestimate the capabilities of young children. On balance it is fair to say that development reflects a complex interplay between nature and nurture. Studies of child development necessarily rely upon what is known about typical developmental trajectories, based on average rates of change. It is important to bear in mind that all children are unique and each child will have a different developmental experience. In some cases this experience may be very different from what we expect in the 'average' course of development. Societies are, however, enriched by the diversity of human experience and the distinctive journeys we all take as we grow and change.

ACTIVITY

Obtain permission to observe children and parents in a setting. Using Marvin's Circle of Security (Figure 1.1) as a model of parent–child interaction, observe children and parents. Do the children move away from the parents to explore their world? Do they regularly return to seek comfort and encouragement? How do the parents respond to the children's periods of rest and activity? Reflect on how parents encourage, comfort and support children. Do all parent–child dyads interact in the same way?

FURTHER READING

MacRae, C. (2008) Representing Space: Katie's horse and the recalcitrant object. *Contemporary issues in Early Childhood*, 9(5): 275–86.

This article offers an interesting critique of Piaget's stages based on a child's drawing.

Howlin, P. (2010) Evaluating psychological treatments for children with autism-spectrum disorders. *Advances in Psychiatric Treatment*, 16: 133–40.

An overview of interventions for children with autism which emphasises the importance of parent–child interaction.

Crittenden, P.M.K. and Dallos, R. (2009) All in the Family: Integrating Attachment and Family Systems Theories. *Clinical Child Psychology and Psychiatry*, 14(3): 389–409.

This article outlines a dynamic model of attachment relationships within families.

REFERENCES

Abrahams, B.S. and Geschwind, D.H. (2008) Advances in autism genetics: on the threshold of a new neurobiology. *National Review of Genetics*, 9(5): 341–55.

Ainsworth, M.D.S., Blehar, M., Waters, E. and Wall, S. (1978) *Patterns of Attachment: A Psychological Study of the Strange Situation*. Hillsdale, NJ: Erlbaum.

Baron-Cohen, S. (2000) Theory of mind and autism: a fifteen year review. In S. Baron-Cohen, H. Tager-Flusberg and D.J. Cohen (eds), *Understanding Other Minds: Perspectives from Developmental Cognitive Neuroscience*. Oxford: Oxford University Press.

Baron-Cohen, S., Leslie, A.M. and Frith, U. (1985) Does the autistic child have a Theory of Mind? *Cognition*, 21(1): 37–46.

Behne, T., Carpenter, M., Call, J. and Tomasello, M. (2005) Unwilling versus unable: infants' understanding of intentional action. *Developmental Psychology*, 41(2): 328–37.

Bowlby, J. (1969/1982) *Attachment and Loss, Vol. 1: Attachment*. New York: Basic Books.

Donaldson, M. (1978) *Children's Minds*. London: Fontana.

Fonagy, P., Steele, M., Moran, G.S., Steele, H. and Higgitt, A.C. (1993) Measuring the ghost in the nursery: an empirical study of the relations between parents' mental representations of childhood experiences and their infants' security attachment. *Journal of the American Psychoanalytic Association*, 41(4): 957–89.

Gopnik, A., Meltzoff, A. and Kuhl, P. (1999) *How Babies Think: The Science of Childhood*. New York: Harper Collins.

Happé, F. and Frith, U. (2006) The weak coherence account: detail-focused cognitive style in Autism Spectrum Disorders. *Journal of Autism and Developmental Disorders*, 36(1): 5–25.

Harris, P. (2000) *The Work of the Imagination (Understanding Children's Worlds)*. Oxford: Wiley-Blackwell.

Hart, H. and Rubia, K. (2012) Neuroimaging of child abuse: A critical review. *Frontiers in Human Neuroscience*, 6(52): 1–24.

Karmiloff-Smith, A. (1998) Development itself is the key to understanding developmental disorders. *Trends in Cognitive Sciences*, 2(10): 389–98.

Kisilevsky, B.S., Hains, S.M.J., Lee, K., Xie, X., Huang, H., Ye, H. H., Zhang, K. and Wang. Z. (2003) Effects of experience on fetal voice recognition. *Psychological Science*, 14, 220–4.

Klin, A., Jones, W., Schultz, R. and Volkmar, F. (2003) The enactive mind, or from actions to cognition: lessons from autism. *Philosophical Transactions of the Royal Society of London*. Series B, Biological Sciences, 358(1430): 345–60.

Knickmeyer, R., Gouttard, S., Kang, C., Evans, D., Wilber, K., Smith, K., Hamer, R.M., Lin, W. and Gilmore J.H. (2008) A structural MRI study of human brain development from birth to 2 years. *Journal of Neuroscience*, 28: 12176–82.

Kumsta, R., Kreppner, J., Kennedy, M., Knights, N., Rutter, M. and Sonuga-Barke, E.J.S. (2014) Psychological consequences of early global deprivation: an overview of findings from the English and Romanian Adoptees Study. *European Psychologist* (In Press).

Olsen, H.C., Sampson, P.D., Barr, H., Streissguth, A.P. and Bookstein, F.L. (1992) Prenatal exposure to alcohol and school problems in late childhood: a longitudinal prospective study. *Development and Psychopathology*, 4: 341–59.

Piaget, J. (1936) *Origins of Intelligence in the Child*. London: Routledge & Kegan Paul.

Piaget, J. (1977) *The Essential Piaget* (ed. Howard Gruber). New York: Basic Books.

Powell, B., Cooper, G., Hoffman, K. and Marvin, B. (2013) *The Circle of Security Intervention: Enhancing Attachment in Early Parent–Child Relationships*. New York: Guilford Press.

Repacholi, M. and Gopnik, A. (1997) Early reasoning about desires: evidence from 14 and 18 month olds. *Developmental Psychology*, 33(1): 12–21.

Rizzolatti, G., Fadiga, I., Fogassi, I. and Gallese, V. (2002) From mirror neurons to imitation: facts and speculation. In A.N. Meltzoff and W. Prinz (eds), *The Imitative Mind: Development, Evolution and Brain Bases*, New York: Cambridge University Press.

Robinson, M. (2008) *Development from Birth to Eight*. Maidenhead: Open University Press.

Robinson, M. (2011) *Understanding Behaviour and Development in Early Childhood: A Guide to Theory and Practice*. London: Routledge.

Schaffer, H.R. (2006) *Key Concepts in Developmental Psychology*. London: SAGE.

Smith, P.K., Cowie, H. and Blades, M. (2011) *Understanding Children's Development* (5th edn). Oxford, Blackwell Publishing.

Turner, S., Alborz, A. and Vernon, G. (2008) Predictors of academic attainments of young people with Down's syndrome. *Journal of Intellectual Disability Research*, 52(5): 380–92.

Vygotsky, L.S. (1978) *Mind in Society: The Development of Higher Psychological Processes*. Cambridge, MA: Harvard University Press.

Westby, C.E. (2000) *Play Diagnosis and Assessment*. New York: John Wiley and Sons.

2 Children at play: evolution, playfulness and creativity

Mandy Andrews

Introduction

'Play' is a word that is widely used, but poorly defined. It is a topic that most people consider they know something about, perhaps through remembering their own experiences of play as a child. If you look at any early years magazine you will see the word 'play' peppered throughout the articles. We read that 'taking risks in play is invaluable for leading children's learning' (Martin, 2010: 107). Many early years settings claim to have a 'play-based curriculum' and the Early Years Foundation Stage (DfE, 2014) offers guidance on how learning in the early years should be supported by child-initiated play as well as adult-led learning activities. The word is used so much that it seems to need no explanation but actually has many different interpretations. Play, as a broad concept, can be viewed through different lenses, from developmental psychology and evolutionary biology to historical and socio-cultural perspectives. Each viewpoint can help us to understand what might be going on when children are 'at play'.

What is play?

Children, like the young of many mammals, have a biological drive to 'play' (Fagen, 1981; Else, 2009; Pellis and Pellis, 2009; Burghardt, 2011; IPA, 2014). Play is a complex concept that includes many types of behaviour, feelings and attitudes. It should therefore be no surprise that it is difficult to define. Janet Moyles (1994: 5) likened the attempt to define play to 'trying to seize bubbles, for every time there appears to be something to hold on to its ephemeral nature disallows it being grasped'. Many people have a cultural understanding of play that draws on their own childhood experiences, perhaps supported by idyllic representations of childhood found in literature, films and media advertisements. Others have embedded understandings from formal schooling that highlight the distinction between 'play times' and 'work times'.

Susan Isaacs (1930: 9) is often cited for her controversial claim that 'play is a child's work'. Those supporting Isaacs consider that she was trying to secure recognition for something that was considered trivial, but others are critical of play being aligned with what they regard as its antithesis, 'work'. In the playwork field, play is usually identified by ownership of the activity, and was often defined as 'freely chosen, personally directed behaviour' (JNCTP, 2002). The emphasis of this definition is on children selecting their own play response to situations, incidents and their environments in order to creatively explore a range of possibilities and solutions. In the Western world play has increasingly been given a developmental function, harnessed to the demands of early schooling. Different modes of play might thus be identified with a range of related cognitive and social skills, and fantasy and role play might be linked to children exploring identities within their relationships with others. Broadhead and Burt (2012) identified the educational benefits of the intellectual challenge afforded by 'open ended play' in planned learning environments such as schools.

Roopnarine (2011: 33) reminds us that in other communities play has a different and often overlooked role in 'the reproduction of cultural practices and skills' as children learn subsistence skills and domestic tasks through early participation and imitation. They explore their culture in fantasy play, and whilst there may be free choice in this play there is more emphasis on imitation than creativity. Vygotsky (1966: 16) also valued play as 'a leading activity that determines the child's development' in a sociocultural context.

Play can therefore be freely chosen, personally directed behaviour offering opportunity for creativity and adaptation, allowing the child to explore, imitate and assimilate sociocultural skills and rituals. Play does not just happen between child and child, or in a child's interaction with their environment: adults around the child may also feel compelled to participate in their social play activity. What we call play can have its origins in very early playful social relationships (Lewis, 1979). Parents and carers may instigate play with very young children as a form of relationship building, offering a playful cue to elicit a social response (Trevarthen, 2005). We can see the give and take of conversational patterns when a parent blows on a child's toes to prompt a playful squeal or throws a two-year-old into the air, offering the security of a safe catch after the child's brief moment of fear, followed by eye contact and laughter. Humans thrive because of our ability to work in groups, and to adapt to our environment. This 'evolutionary' perspective recognises play as a 'tool' to support the social bonding that offers security in relationships with others.

If we adopt a standpoint as an external observer of play it can be divided into a range of 'types'. Hughes (2012) identified 16 play types ranging from communicative, physical and fantasy play to 'deep' play and mastery play. These can be useful in acknowledging the range of behaviours, but seem to focus on what we think children will gain. Play is much more affective (or emotional) and spontaneous than adult categorisation would imply and a playful nod can bring children together in a play episode that could go in many different directions. A three- to four-year-old child does not usually say 'I am going to role play today', but they will somehow 'fall into' play with a friend; and perhaps explore physical prowess and rough and tumble at one moment and the role and powers of Superman the next. The children may then get distracted by the need to make a castle, or the superhero's lair and shift again into constructive play. Whilst 'types of play' may help us to reflect on what might have been going on, children's regular 'shifting' means any classification by type cannot be used to predict outcomes.

The unpredictable nature of play is sometimes a problem for educators who wish to use it as a vehicle for delivering measurable achievements. In recent years more writers are indicating that play without adult involvement is not sufficient for children to learn and achieve (Brooker, 2010; Edwards *et al.*, 2010; Wood, 2010). Could the problem be our failure to acknowledge and value the play learning that we have not planned? The child-led nature of play requires that adults who wish to support the activity, or perhaps to play alongside the child, should be prepared to adopt a reflective analytical stance in order to offer the best support.

Perspectives on play

Ethology

In recent years there has been renewed interest in the ethologist Fagen's (1981) evolutionary work on play. Ethology is a broad field of biology that draws on other disciplines and recognises that animals and humans are influenced by and influence the environments in which they exist. Recognising that all mammals play, Fagen drew on observations of both animal and human behaviours in an attempt to identify defining features of play. He asked key questions along the lines of: what causes this behaviour; how does it develop as the mammal grows; and what is the useful consequence of this behaviour? Whilst play was extremely risky for young mammals, the exercise of play in youth led to greater potential for long-term survival. Play appeared to have a purpose in biological adaptation to the specific environments in which animals found themselves. This was not simple, immediate adaptation, but one that had an 'evolutionary' role, changing over time and impacting on future generations. Fagen recognised that play was therefore 'a mechanism by which animals can influence their development … and improve the flexibility of their behaviour and learning' (1981: 476). A rabbit 'plays' at exploring its burrow so that it knows how to escape from an intruder; young foxes or weasels 'play' at fighting so they are able to twist and turn, leap and bite with skill; a monkey plays with sticks and stones developing skills it will need to hold its young.

Although Fagen's research dates back to the 1980s his book, *Animal Play Behaviour*, is considered to be a seminal text on play. Burghardt (2011) refined Fagen's work and listed five clear criteria for recognising play:

a) it is not merely functional and focused on immediate survival;

b) it is 'autotelic' or freely chosen and done for its own sake;

c) it is an action that is incomplete, awkward or has unusual patterns and behaviours;

d) it is repetitive;

e) it is only initiated when the player is healthy, has essential needs met, and is not under stress.

Burghardt identified that all five criteria must be met, in at least some respect, for an activity to be considered as play. In addition Bateson and Martin (2013) emphasise that the unusual patterns and behaviours seen in play are creative. They offer a sixth feature which focuses on the 'feeling' of play as, 'playful play ... is accompanied by a particular positive mood state in which the individual is more inclined to behave (and, in the case of humans, think) in a spontaneous and flexible way' (Bateson and Martin, 2013: 13).

This positive state can be compared with Csikszentmihalyi's (2002) concept of 'flow'. He wrote that when a child chooses to play, this leads to:

- levels of concentration or involvement in which the child is not thinking about something, but is immersed in doing it, becoming unaware of expectation, end products, or even the surrounding environment;

- a 'filtering out' of other influences or stimuli;

- memory becoming very short-term as the player is concerned only with the enjoyable, intrinsically rewarding activity of the moment; sense of time becomes warped, either seeming very compressed as the child is jolted out of their exploration or reverie, or expanded, as their involvement has led to fast complex thinking in this heightened state.

'While *in flow* you feel in control as no one else is reaching you to direct you' (Csikszentmihalyi, 2002: 59).

Bateson and Martin (2013) also argue that for a child's action to be 'play' it must be 'intrinsically motivated'. The motivation to play should come from within the person who is playing. Play has no immediate survival purpose, though it may have a longer term survival implication. It is not an activity directed by essential needs for food or shelter, nor is it controlled by others indicating a need to achieve an end product or measurable achievement. A child chooses to play, or not to play, in any given moment and context, prompted by people, resources and environment. When a child is 'told' to do something it may cease to be play because the child's internal drive and engagement with the environment are interrupted. The spontaneity of free choice leads to a lack of foreseeable product or outcome, making play difficult for adults to define (and manage); it is this indeterminacy that offers the greatest scope for creativity and adaptation.

From this ethological perspective, play, whether it be physical, social or emotional, has a key role in stimulating cognitive and physical adaptation to the environment in which children find themselves as they grow and develop. The intrinsic motivation, the autotelic choice, the 'bubbling up' of play (Frost, 2010: 267) is a response to the specific development needs of the child at that particular time and in that particular context (Pellegrini, 2011). Imagine children in the nursery playing with blocks. Children with different experiences and heritages will play differently with the same blocks, according to their background and their experiences up to that point. Ethologists recognise that individuals both shape and are shaped by their environment. As the environment is adjusted, so that influences the child's response.

Linked to these ideas of a form of 'ecology' of play in which environment and child interact is the concept of 'affordances' (Gibson, 1996). The term 'affordances' recognises that objects or aspects of the environment invite us to use them in certain ways. It implies a complementarity of the person and the environment. Something in the environment triggers a response that leads to a new, adapted behaviour. Well-designed objects may afford obviously consistent responses from different users, (a chair affords sitting, for example, or a button, pushing). In other cases different people may have very different responses according to their own experiences. A large cardboard box can 'afford' putting things inside it, or becoming a house. Wooden blocks have many affordances, including stacking, lining up, balancing, building and so on. Landscapes also have 'affordances'. In the built environment a sculptured sphere used as a bollard in the street may 'say' to an onlooker 'balance on me', in the natural environment a fallen tree may make a similar call: 'climb on me'. The architect Nicholson (1971: 30) recognised that the degree of inventiveness and creativity in an environment was directly related to the number and range of variables or 'loose parts' in it.

Through 'intrinsic motivation' children select and respond to affordances according to their need. A child experiencing a domestic break up at home may choose role play to explore contexts and responses in a safe environment and to learn how to handle things in future. A child who has just learnt to walk may see new affordances in a landscape and 'play' at repetitive behaviours, such as walking up and down slopes, to better embed the cognitive and physical coding involved in shifting balance when toddling up or down. There is a potential element of anarchy in this intrinsic motivation to play. Urban landscapes may be designed in such a way as to encourage sitting, but a child's playful response may transform seats into steps, or an opportunity to practise balancing.

Developmental psychology

Developmental psychology also considers children in relation to their environment. However, whilst ethologists will understand the child's relationships with others and the environment in terms of prior knowledge and understanding, a developmental psychologist may consider each 'episode' and each child individually. 'Episodes' of play can therefore be captured and measured in terms of the nature of response and what they 'do' for the child. Piaget (Piaget and Inhelder, 1969) observed his own children to identify the value of play. He was interested in how play could actively support children's ability to take on new information offered by their environment and how they would adjust their existing understandings as a result, leading to intellectual development. Piaget called the taking on of new information 'assimilation'. He termed the subsequent adaptation of existing groups of ideas, or 'schemas', 'accommodation' (see Chapter 1).

An important aspect of Piaget's theories is his argument that we are driven to seek a state of balance or 'equilibrium', in which our ideas match our experiences. This recognises the 'affect' or emotional aspect of play, exploration and knowledge creation. Piaget observed that children use practical action and play to organise their world into schema or clusters of related experiences. An example of a schema might be a child's repetitive interest in water, exploring concepts of form and volume by showing an interest in pouring in and out of a range of containers. If the water behaves as expected the child is operating in a state of equilibrium, with their actual experience matching their cognitive understanding. However, if the water behaves unusually (perhaps because it is frozen), the child's understanding is challenged and they may feel 'disequilibrium' or an emotional reaction. This drives the child to adapt what they already know, creating new understanding as new ideas are assimilated or prior knowledge frameworks are accommodated to achieve equilibrium. Through such play processes and the adjustment of existing understanding, Piaget argued, children gradually acquire new knowledge, and experience cognitive development (Piaget and Inhelder, 1969).

The early childhood pioneer, Susan Isaacs, was influenced by the work of Piaget and recognised the value of play as 'nature's means of individual education' (Isaacs, 1930: 9). She highlighted that play, as 'a child's work' should be recognised as important but should retain its freedom as 'non work' unconstrained by expected output or product. Isaacs believed that this 'open-ended' freedom in an environment full of objects that offer multiple 'affordances' for learning was essential for the development of children's cognitive understanding. Her detailed records of children at play describe their responses to a range of environmental stimuli and are still worth revisiting today.

Social and emotional implications for play and playfulness

We briefly considered above how the emotions are involved in the struggle to 'understand'. The desire to achieve emotional and cognitive 'equilibrium' is a driver and motivator. Young children may have a tantrum when the struggle to know something becomes too demanding and equilibrium cannot be reached. Teachers on the other hand may encourage children to attempt an activity in a playful way, so that a learning activity 'feels' like play and children may more readily engage and remain motivated. Playfulness is an attitude of mind, or 'way of being' that affords enjoyment, 'flow' and creativity. It encourages a particular high mood state which 'allows thinking in a particularly spontaneous and flexible way' (Bateson and Martin, 2013: 13). Intrinsically motivated play, defined by the child's ownership of the process, leads to empowerment, freedom and a focus on the process rather than an end product. Such open-ended play can go in any direction chosen by the child, in response to holistic needs which go beyond mere cognition.

There is both a tension and synergy in relation to the terms 'play' and 'playfulness'. Drawing on social and ethological perspectives I have a desire to disentangle the two terms 'playfulness' and 'play' in an act of advocacy for the child's freely chosen instinctive play. Classroom-based 'playful learning', perhaps directed to an outcome identified by an adult, is not the same process, nor does it offer the same scope, as child-initiated play activity instinctively chosen to address individual need. In a situation with no boundaries, a tree stump spontaneously becomes a castle, for example, and peers can play at being the knights in some physical and social game with rules that can twist and turn, relatively unlimited by time constraints. Dens can be built and social rules or children's cultures created. Instinctive or 'pure' play can lead who knows where. A 'playful activity' organised by an adult may in contrast be loaded with intention, given direction and a time limit, and perhaps a limited spatial range.

Rautio and Winston (2013: 16), on the other hand, propose that we should aim to 're-entangle' the concepts of play and playfulness, arguing that the adult concern to differentiate between them does not serve the interests of children. Choosing play and being playful should remain entangled in the light of individual children's contextual responses to people, places and things. Rautio and Winston's desire to recombine the two terms, play and playfulness, highlights the relational function of play as a complex but transient response that involves both emotion or 'affect' *and* control by the player (or negotiation of shared control with other players).

Sociocultural

Sociocultural perspectives on play consider the nature of the activity and the gains for the child in relation to other people and groups of people. Many researchers have identified that in play the player is somehow protected from the consequences of normal 'serious' behaviour (Fagen, 1981; Burghardt, 2011; Bateson and Martin, 2013). As play is a particular social activity, children (and adults too) will signal to others that they are playing and not serious. Parents and carers can also offer those play signals to young children with smiles and exaggerated actions. Smith *et al.* (2011: 231) remind us that one key example of a behaviour that only occurs in play and which signals that the child is playing is the 'play face'. Usually in children this takes the form of an open mouth, broad smile and wide eyes which signal 'playfulness'. It is a subtle signal, but one that most people respond to. Look carefully at the children in your setting and consider how they signal playfulness to each other. A 'play face' to an adult will give a 'cue' or invitation to join in the play (Else, 2009). A 'play face' by an adult to a child may signal that normal constraints are temporarily removed and during physical play a play face will signal to other children that no malice is intended, protecting the child from a harsh response to initiation of rough and tumble play. Through such social symbols play is identified as something other than 'work', duty or conforming to rules. These signals can also create a 'play frame' or safe area between players within which norms can be challenged. Else writes of the play cue, and play return, which create a 'play frame' between child and other players or environmental stimuli. This is a relational activity in which both player and responder create a shared social understanding, in part as an evolutionary response, in part as a culturally identified signal. Children can use a ball to give each other play cues, catching and returning it to indicate their willingness to join in a game. Such play cues and play responses involve an element of trust, building further social understanding if all goes well.

Creativity as a social and cognitively playful process

Bateson and Martin (2013: 12) argue that play consists of 'actions or, in the case of humans, thoughts expressed in novel combinations'. Unconstrained by productivity, play can overturn the expected, offer different ways of doing things and create new insights through social interactions. Creative activity has always been one of the lynchpins of the early years, and is often considered as synonymous with the arts (Education Scotland, 2014). In the Early Years Foundation Stage creativity is included within the 'Expressive Arts' (DfE, 2014: 8) in which we are advised that children should 'explore and play with a wide range of media and materials', however it also recognises that creating and thinking critically is a characteristic of effective learning (DfE, 2014: 9). Creativity *in* play, however, is about seeking out and exploring novel approaches and new solutions to issues and problems rather than just constructing artworks, though these also have their place. Children playing creatively will make links between ideas and explore new ways to use the physical environment, for example climb *up* a slide, or walk *backwards* down some steps, using objects in a different way from the original affordance they were designed to offer. In a social context, children will be creative by changing the rules at short notice in a team game, or creating new situations in a role play.

Bob Hughes (2001: 138) referred to this technique of putting ideas together in a special way in response to a contextual stimulus, incident or problem as 'combinatorial flexibility':

> *What the term combinatorial flexibility describes to me, is a process of looking at a problem and then scanning one's memory bank for the tiny pieces of information that have been learnt, to see if any of those pieces, or any combination of those pieces of information, might contribute to a solution of the problem.*

Hughes' concept of cognitive flexibility for survival was challenged by Frazer Brown (2003) who recognised this connection between the child's thinking and the flexibility of the environment. He proposed the notion of 'compound flexibility'. This describes the interactive relationship between the flexibility and adaptability of the child and a flexible/adaptable environment:

> *given ideal conditions, the growing child makes use of whatever flexibility there is in the environment, and so becomes more flexible, and able to make even better use of elements of flexibility in the environment – and so on. This process may be characterized as 'compound flexibility'. (Brown, 2003: 53)*

Play as culture creating

Huizinga argued that the creativity of play has a role in creating new ways of being and acting, or new cultures (Huizinga, 1938/2014). He wrote in Holland just before the start of the Second World War, in a context of emerging sociopolitical theories and practices of oppression and constraint. Huizinga considered that play was a 'culture-creating force', led by creative freedom and inspiration not political intention or propaganda. He was aware that social civilisation requires self-limitation: an understanding of one's own needs in relation to others which he believed was developed through play. He also thought that play contributed to the evolution of social order: 'Play is older than culture for culture ... always presupposes human society' (2014: 1). Play is more than a physiological phenomenon or psychological reflex, 'it is a significant function – that is to say there is some sense to it. In play there is something which transcends the immediate needs of life and imparts meaning to the action' (2014: 2). Huizinga refers to the spirit 'sparking' between matter and mind in play, and how cultural ritual arises in play, as he states: 'We play and we know that we play, so we must be more than merely rational beings, for play is irrational' (2014: 4). He goes on to highlight that poetry was born in play with words, the rules of warfare arose from play rules in group games, the physical arts and music and dancing are play for adults. In fact, Huizinga states, 'civilisation in its earliest phases … arises in and as play and never leaves it' (2014: 173). Children develop tolerance when they have the freedom to create, frame and explore social tensions without interference, a process which 'recreates order and fairness but also creates new cultures' (2014: 173) as rules are played out and become part of the child's social mind. As a result, he argues, a new, fairer, society emerges.

If we consider Huizinga's words in a modern context we may consider how play with (or without) rules 'feels' chaotic to adult practitioners who may feel driven to step in and restrict boisterousness and argument to 'keep the peace'. In so doing they may actually restrict children's ability to learn to negotiate, imitate and invent rules relevant to their social and cultural context, limiting the development of their sociocultural awareness.

Bringing this cultural understanding up to date we might draw on the work of Barbara Rogoff (2003) or Bert van Oers (2010). Rogoff (2003) points out that Piaget's influence and scientific approaches often lead us to see a child at play as a lone explorer, dissociating them from their cultural and environmental situation. Rogoff understands that children's playful participation in role play with others, in narrative storytelling, in practising physical dexterity and in specific cultural skills (fishing for example) enables children to practise and become familiar with local cultural practices and traditions. She cites, for example, children in Taiwan playing at 'schools' and exactly echoing the attitudes and routines of the teacher they see daily.

Van Oers draws on cultural-historical activity theory (Leont'ev, 1981) and argues that play should not be seen merely as another activity to be compared with 'learning' or working. 'Unlike learning and working', he claims, 'play' has no object of its own, but always 'borrows' from other cultural activities or practices' (van Oers, 2010: 200). Play is therefore a cultural invention that makes adult practices accessible to young children but also a cultural adapter as rules and norms are turned in the light of the creative processes of role play and imitation.

Play thus becomes something that occurs at the boundaries of what is currently socially accepted and what is unacceptable, or what is known, or not yet fully known, or what can be done, but is not yet mastered. An example of spontaneous creativity and cultural awareness in a social and physical development context is how if children fall down whilst running they may create explanations for why they fell rather than face humiliation from others, for example saying, 'I meant to do that, I am a superhero, this is how they collect their powers'. This strategy may then be adopted by others.

Repetition for mastery and therapy

A further defining feature of play, given by the biological ethologists, is repetition. There may be several reasons for this repetition, some of which align with concepts of play as therapy. Repetition of physical activity in play, such as jumping, hopping or even spinning around and around, have a role in bodily awareness, balance and developing physical capability through practice. Caillois (2001: 12) acknowledges the rapid whirling or falling nature of some physical play which links the physical to the emotional in an exciting disorder he describes as 'ilinx' or 'dizzy play'. In animals such physical play with emotional reward may have a role in developing agility needed for future survival (Pellis and Pellis, 2009). Athey (2003), however, noticed that play happens at the border of what is known and mastered and what is not yet 'accommodated' or taken fully on board either cognitively or physically. Athey refers to children 'playing' at Ring-a-ring-a-roses and how this game is most popular at the time that children are building their ability to get up again when they fall down. This game play offers emotional reward and excitement when children have not fully mastered these skills. But when they have mastered the skills they become bored by their own competence in getting to their feet and the game holds less interest. Some types of play may have only a temporary, developmental relevance and children will move on as their competences change.

Another form of playful repetition may be therapeutic: that feeling of satisfaction that things are as they should be, or that capabilities have not changed. Think of some of those skilled activities which we call playing: the yoyo, bat and ball, juggling and so on are repetitive activities continued in play beyond the mere mastery of skills. Children will revisit tasks that are well within their capabilities when they need some therapeutic reassurance.

David Sobel (2002) draws on Jungian theory to explore the importance of play as a protected space that is used by children to support the development of their emerging selves. He highlights how we bond with parents or carers through play in infancy and early childhood, within an enclosed, secure space created by cues between parent or carer and child, and how this significant secure world expands outwards as children grow. The world of security becomes the house, then the neighbourhood, the community and so on, and 'each bonding moment must occur in sequence' (Sobel, 2002: 160). Developing this sense of spatial security also depends on the bonding of the child to the nearby natural world in play. The acknowledgement and creation of bonds with the environment, and with special places, is a part of what Jung refers to as the individuation of self. This recognises the growing identification of self as an individual emerging from the confusion of family identity and undifferentiated unconscious drives. Children's play at creation of, or finding, 'special places' is, Sobel argues, an aspect of 'roughing in' of self (2002: 71). Think here of how children will make links with the environment around them, identifying 'special places' in raised land, areas under a tree, dens and sheds. They find places where they can be themselves. The creation of such spaces is also a 'concretisation of the individuation process' (2002: 71). The special place serves to support the emergence of the child; a transition into the next stage of individual identity. Recollections of such special places are often found in poetry and art, such as in Dylan Thomas's (1943) account of his emergent play space:

> *And that park grew up with me, that small world widened as I learned its secret boundaries, as I discovered new refuges in the wood and jungles; hidden homes and lairs for the multitudes of imagination, for cowboys and Indians and the tall terrible half-people who rode on nightmares…*

Conclusion

Play offers opportunities for freely chosen, personally directed behaviour, creativity and therapeutic response. It can be solitary or social, responding to environment, things or people. If social, it uses particular signals to show others that it is safe to take risks, such as in play fighting, and it is perhaps accompanied by an attitude of mind, a playfulness, that allows the player to become engaged in an unbounded 'flow' (Csikszentmihalyi, 2002). Play may offer benefits to physical or social development, therapeutic comfort through transitions, mastery, creativity or some other aspect of development as yet unidentified. In fact the benefits of play are so broad it may be that the word 'play' itself is insufficient for all that it covers, and that there is a need for refinement of the term (Edwards and Cutter McKenzie, 2013). It will be important that however we refine and develop the term, as practitioners and facilitators of play we should continue to place the child at the centre, not focusing merely on a classification of play types reflecting adult concerns and control of children's lives and experiences.

You may consider that this kind of child-led play may be possible outdoors but not in the classroom. Broadhead and Burt (2012: 144), however, created child-led play environments or 'whatever you want it to be' places in the classroom and identified these 'play spaces' as:

> *shared sites of enterprise where children 'find themselves' and ... in playing together they learn over time which other children have interests that parallel and reflect their own and from these mutual engagements come levels of play complexity and depth that could only come from momentum building and familiarity with peers and with the environment.*

Perhaps these play spaces offer a way in which intrinsically motivated play can be experienced in early years classrooms and settings, not only in the adult-free context of Dylan Thomas's 'park over the road'.

ACTIVITY

When working with children in an early years setting, select an appropriate time to arrange the environment with 'loose parts' (Nicholson, 1971: 30) which offer children multiple affordances: planks, crates or blocks, fabric, pegs, poles, ropes, large cardboard boxes or virtually anything that you think a child could use in play alone or with others. Allow the children to start playing and step back and watch, trying not to interfere with the children's play unless invited. Reflect on whether the children's play echoes any of the theoretical understandings offered in this chapter. Are children honing their physical or cognitive and social skills? How much are children's actions influenced by culture? Is there any negotiation about rules? Do some children actively create 'secret spaces'?

FURTHER READING

I would always recommend trying to read some of the original writings of key past theorists and pioneers. Other reading:

Broadhead, P. and Burt, A. (2012) *Understanding Young Children's Learning Through Play: Building Playful Pedagogies.* London: Routledge.

A thoughtful and illustrative account of a longitudinal study of indoor and outdoor play environments in an early years unit which includes a discussion of the 'whatever you want it to be place' and how children's themes emerged in play.

Brock, A., Dodds, S., Jarvis, P. and Olusaga, Y. (2009) *Perspectives on Play: Learning for Life.* London: Routledge.

An accessible text which explores and debates theories of play.

REFERENCES

Athey, C (2007) *Extending Thought in Young Children.* London: Paul Chapman Publishing.

Bateson, P. and Martin, P. (2013) *Play, Playfulness, Creativity and Innovation.* Cambridge: Cambridge University Press.

Broadhead, P. and Burt, A. (2012) *Understanding Young Children's Learning Through Play: Building Playful Pedagogies.* London: Routledge.

Brooker, L. (2010) Learning to play or playing to learn: children's participation in the cultures of homes and settings. In L. Brooker, and S. Edwards (2010), *Engaging Play.* Maidenhead: Open University Press.

Brown, F. (2003) *Playwork: Theory and Practice.* Buckingham: Open University Press.

Burghardt, G.M. (2011) Defining and recognising play. In A.D. Pellegrini (ed.), *The Oxford Handbook of the Development of Play.* Oxford: Oxford University Press.

Caillois, R. (2001) *Man, Play and Games* (trans. Meyer Barash). Urbana: University of Illinois Press.

Csikszentmihalyi, M. (2002) *Flow: The Psychology of Happiness* (2nd ed). London: Random House/ Harper Row.

DfE (Department for Education) (2014) *Statutory Framework for the Early Years Foundation Stage: Setting the Standards for Learning, Development and Care for Children from Birth to Five.* London: DfE Publications.

Education Scotland (2014) Creativity, plans, portals, practitioners and children. *Early Years Matters*, 1(2). Available at: http://www.educationscotland.gov.uk/earlyyearsmatters/c/genericcontent_tcm4720627. asp (accessed 13 April 2015).

Edwards, S. and Cutter-Mackenzie, A. (2013) Pedagogical play types: what do they suggest for learning about sustainability in early childhood education? *International Journal of Early Childhood*, 28(7): 922–36.

Edwards, S., Cutter-MacKenzie, A. and Hunt, E. (2010) Framing Play for Learning: Professional Reflections on the Role of Open-Ended Play in *Early Childhood Education*. In L. Brooker and S. Edwards (eds), *Engaging Play.* Maidenhead: Open University Press.

Else, P. (2009) *The Value of Play.* London: Continuum.

Fagen, R. (1981) *Animal Play Behaviour.* Oxford: Oxford University Press.

Frost, J. (2010) *A History of Children's Play and Play Environments: Toward a Contemporary Child-Saving Movement.* London: Routledge.

Gibson, J.J. (1996) *The Ecological Approach to Visual Perception.* New Jersey: Lawrence Earlbaum.

Hughes, B. (2001) *Evolutionary Playwork and Reflective Analytic Practice.* London: Routledge.

Hughes, B. (2012) *Evolutionary Playwork and Reflective Analytic Practice* (2nd edn). London: Routledge.

Huizinga, J. (2014) *Homo Ludens: A Study of the Play Element in Culture* (1950 edn, reprinted 2014). Mansfield Centre, CT: Martino Publishing.

IPA (International Play Association) (2014) *Children's Right to Play: An Examination of the Importance of Play in the Lives of Children Worldwide.* Available at: http://ipaworld.org/ipa-working-paper-on-childs-right-to-play (accessed 25 February 2015).

Isaacs, S. (1930) *Intellectual Growth in Young Children: with an Appendix on Children's 'Why' Questions by Nathan Isaacs.* London: Routledge.

JNCTP (Joint National Consultancy on Training for Playwork) (2002) *Making the Case for Play: Building Policies and Strategies for School-aged Children.* London: National Children's Bureau.

Lewis, M. (1979) The social determination of play. In B. Sutton-Smith (1979) *Play and Learning: The Johnson and Johnson Pediatric Round Table III.* New York: Gardner Press.

Leont'ev, A.N. (1981) *Activity, Consciousness, and Personality.* Englewood Cliffs, NJ: Prentice-Hall.

Martin, E. (2010) Play as an emotional process. In J. Moyles (2010) *Thinking About Play: Developing a Reflective Approach.* Maidenhead: Open University Press.

Moyles, J. (1994) *The Excellence of Play.* Buckingham: Open University Press.

Nicholson, S. (1971) The theory of loose parts – how not to cheat children. *Landscape Architecture Quarterly*, 62(1) October: 30–5.

Pellegrini, A. (ed.) (2011) *The Oxford Handbook of the Development of Play.* Oxford: Oxford University Press.

Pellis, S. and Pellis, V. (2009) *The Playful Brain: Venturing to the Limits of Neuroscience.* London: Oneworld Publications.

Piaget, J. and Inhelder, B. (1969) *The Psychology of the Child* (trans. Helen Weaver). New York: Basic Books.

Rautio, P. and Winston, J. (2015) Things and children in play – improvisation with language and matter. *Discourse: Studies in the Cultural Politics of Education*, 36(1): 15–26.

Rogoff, B. (2003) *The Cultural Nature of Human Development.* Oxford: Oxford University Press.

Roopnarine, J.L. (2011) Cultural variations in beliefs about play, parent-child play, and children's play: meaning for childhood development. In A.D. Pellegrini (ed.), *The Oxford Handbook of the Development of Play.* Oxford: Oxford University Press.

Smith, P. K., Cowie, H. and Blades, M. (2011) *Understanding Children's Development (5th edn).* Oxford, Blackwell Publishing.

Sobel, D. (2002) *Children's Special Places.* Detroit: Wayne State University Press.

Thomas, D. (1943) *Reminiscences of Childhood.* BBC Wales. Available at: https://www.youtube.com/watch?v=Ce_qzuBPQpc (accessed 11 April 2015).

Trevarthen, C. (2005) First things first: infants make good use of the sympathetic rhythm of imitation, without reason or language. *Journal of Child Psychotherapy*, 31(1): 91–113.

van Oers, B. (2010) Children's enculturation through play. In L. Brooker and S. Edwards, *Engaging Play.* Maidenhead: Open University Press.

Vygotsky, L. (1966) Play and its role in the mental development of the child. *Soviet Psychology*, 5(3): 6–18.

Wood, E. (2010) Developing integrated pedagogical approaches to play and learning. In P. Broadhead, J. Howard and Wood, E. (eds), *Play and Learning in the Early Years.* London: SAGE.

3 Developing communication: getting to know each other

Rod Parker-Rees

Introduction

'Communication and language development' is one of the three prime areas in the revised Early Years Foundation Stage (DfE, 2014: 7) but it is sometimes difficult to see where communication other than language development is acknowledged under this heading. The 'guiding principle' that 'children learn to be strong and independent through positive relationships' (2014: 6) and the requirement to identify a 'key person' for each child (2014: 10) acknowledge the wider importance of communication but these aspects of early learning are addressed more in another prime area: 'personal, social and emotional development'. In this chapter I will argue that we should give greater recognition to the development of forms of communication which underpin, frame and enrich language development, recognising the full extent of what is included in 'Communication *and* language development'.

One of the great benefits of studying early childhood is that an understanding of the beginnings of particular areas of learning can help us to recognise aspects of development which might otherwise be overlooked or undervalued. Studying the earliest stages of the development of communication obliges us to look beyond language, to notice how babies and infants participate in communicative interactions well before they begin to speak. Once we have become more aware of these non-verbal aspects of communication we are more likely to notice the important part they continue to play in later childhood and in adulthood.

In a world in which so much of our interaction is conducted at a distance, by means of emails, texts, social messaging and other written media, it is easy to forget how much we still communicate with each other *around* the words we use, especially when we are able to interact 'face to face'. John Shotter (2010: 20, my emphasis) notes that 'words *in their speaking*' communicate much more meaning than can be carried by '*already spoken* [or written] words'. Even when we have mastered the use of language we still learn about people, and get to know them, by paying attention not only to *what* they say but also *how* they say things and, most importantly, how it *feels* when we interact with them:

> *What is that person doing in saying that? How are they using that word, in this situation, here and now? What are we feeling as we experience them speaking? And so on.'* (Shotter, 2014: 6)

If our understanding of communication is too narrowly focused on what is being said, we risk losing sight of a more primary function of interactions, which is to allow us to get to know who we are meeting: the person behind the words.

Mapping communication

We all regularly communicate in a wide range of ways beyond speaking, listening, reading and writing but we are not often aware of these non-verbal channels. Try going through a typical day in your mind, identifying all the different forms of communication which you might experience: choices you make and choices you notice other people making, from when you get up and what you choose to wear to all forms of touch, gesture and movement as well as signs and labels, messages, web pages or TV programmes which bring you information about your environment. You can develop your first list further by exploring the modes of communication which you have identified, for example 'drawing' could branch into doodling, diagrams, maps and plans and 'music' could include *what* you (and others) listen to, *how* you listen, *when* you sing along and when you don't. When you have built up and developed this list, adding other, less everyday forms as they occur to you, you can try arranging all these different kinds of communication in a spatial array, with the most intuitive, natural forms (like touch, facial expressions and body language) at the bottom and the most formally structured, rule-bound forms (like academic writing, musical notation, mathematical formulae, and other symbol systems which have to be learned) at the top. Working on this with one or two friends should generate some useful discussions about where particular forms should/could be placed and you may find that you need to unpick some of your categories further; how, for example, does dancing relate to other forms of body language and where does it blend into something like 'style'; the way people habitually carry themselves (rather stiff and controlled or lolloping!) which allows you to recognise different friends just by the way they walk.

When communication is mapped in this way you may begin to notice shifts in the qualities or 'feel' of communication as you work up the list: from intimate to public; from 'warmer' to 'cooler'; from involuntary and uncontrollable to deliberate and purposeful; even from natural and 'honest' to contrived and manipulative! You may also notice that the lower part of your map of communication is rather crowded and that more of your communication is represented here than in the higher reaches. However, we are so used to thinking only about the more public, shareable forms of communication that you may not have identified the full range of less conscious, less deliberate ways of communicating.

Every choice we make, in how we act and react, what we enjoy, what we avoid and who we spend time with, and even how we choose to smell, tells other people something about who we are or who we would like to be. Adults, who have developed awareness of how their choices are likely to be interpreted by others, may be consciously aware of many of their communicative decisions and use these to project an image of themselves to others, constructing a protective 'front' which is only set aside in relaxed, intimate interactions with close friends. Young children are usually much less self-conscious and therefore 'easier to read', but, like adults, they will communicate much more in playful interactions with familiar, known and trusted people.

Communication and concepts of development

Our understanding of how children develop is closely bound up with our concepts of childhood (Chapter 13). If we think of childhood as a pre-adult, primitive stage, closer to the animal origins from which civilisation has elevated us, we will understand development in terms of progressive mastery of ordered, shared systems such as good manners, reading and writing, logic, music and mathematics. If, on the other hand, like many who choose to work with young children, we share Rousseau's romantic view of childhood, we are more likely to value the directness and intensity of more 'primary' forms of communication (Parker-Rees, 2007b), such as touch, eye contact and gesture. We may then understand development in terms of allowing time for these skills to 'unfold' and we may feel we should protect children from undue pressure to 'move on' too quickly.

The beginnings of communication – before birth

If we extend our understanding of communication to encompass everything we can do to share information about ourselves, our affective state, our interests and our concerns, it is clear that we begin to communicate well before we are born. From conception we are immersed in an intimate, but by no means simple or straightforward, relationship with our mother. Foetal development involves social processes from the outset, including chemical and immunological conflicts as well as opportunities for the growing foetus to tune in to a wide range of patterns in the mother's behaviour: her eating and sleeping patterns, the structure and rhythms of her speech and even her favourite music, including the signature tunes of TV programmes which she watches regularly (Hepper, 2003). As we grow inside our mother's womb, we have plenty of time to absorb these patterns in her life, so that we are born already attuned to her and able to 'sing along' in early forms of communicative interaction (Trevarthen, 2003).

Melvin Konner (2010) has suggested that human babies, like kangaroos, are born before gestation is complete. Our upright gait has compromised the shape of the human pelvis so that the birth canal is too narrow to accommodate a 'fully developed' infant's head and our babies must be born after just nine months. While the kangaroo joey completes the later stages of gestation in its mother's pouch, human babies have traditionally undergone their 'fourth trimester' in their mother's arms or in a fabricated sling or carrying device. Because newborn babies' motor development lags considerably behind their sensory capabilities, they are ideally equipped to use this intermediate stage, between womb and world, to refine and tune their early feel for patterns in the structure of their social environment. Imagine how different the relationship between mother and child would be if the baby's development was fully precocial, like a foal or a lamb. If, within moments of being born, babies were already on their feet, gambolling and frisking around the delivery room, there would be much less opportunity for mother and baby to continue to develop their expertise in the details of each other's movements, expressions, responses and rhythms.

Imitation

When Meltzoff and Moore (1977) recorded evidence of very young babies imitating facial expressions they were intrigued by this evidence of what looked like an innate ability to connect perceptual information with corresponding patterns of motor control. How could the newborn baby relate the still very blurry and indistinct visual image of a protruding tongue to the combinations of muscle actions required to make his/her own tongue stick out? And how might mother and baby benefit from this seemingly precocious ability to imitate?

Imitation is much more than a simple, automatic process of 'monkey see, monkey do' (Hurley and Chater, 2005; Parker-Rees, 2007a). Our ability to connect with other people by responding to their actions suggests that we may not be as separate, distinct and 'individual' as we have come to believe. Research by Rizzolati and colleagues (1996) suggests that babies are equipped, from birth, with 'mirror neurons', particular links in the fantastically complex web of brain connections which link motor control with sensory perception so that seeing someone else performing an action can stimulate the equivalent premotor activity in our 'own' brain. This means that we are intricately interconnected with other people. You may have noticed that your hands sometimes get 'twitchy' as you watch someone struggling with a tricky manipulation, such as a child trying to fit a piece into an inset puzzle or someone having difficulty opening a packet or container. When we notice another person's facial expressions, the premotor response triggered in us by our mirror neurons, also produces the emotional state that we associate with these facial movements (Kugiumutzakis *et al.*, 2005). When you see someone frown, the neurons associated with the earliest stages of producing a frown are stimulated in your own brain and this mirror response triggers in you a *feeling* of puzzlement or distress. Seeing someone else smile or hearing other people laughing can also be enough to lift your spirits – smile and the world smiles with you!

This 'built in' ability to connect directly with other people's mental states by responding to their physical expressions, combined with plentiful opportunities to pay 'close up' attention to a caregiver's actions, expressions and interactions, means that the human baby is particularly well placed to practise and refine *intersubjectivity* – the ability to make one's own intentions known and to recognise the interests and concerns of other people (Trevarthen, 1979).

After a couple of months of 'peripheral participation' (Lave and Wenger, 1991), literally 'getting a *feel* for interaction' while recovering from the trauma of delivery (and allowing their mothers to recover), babies show clear signs of primary intersubjectivity (Trevarthen, 1979) when they begin to participate actively and *intentionally* in communicative exchanges. This is a very special time, not only in the development of the baby but also in the development of the bond between baby and primary caregiver (usually, but not necessarily, the mother).

Communication and socialisation

On the map of forms of communication mentioned earlier, primary intersubjectivity is clearly well down in the intuitive depths where communication is not so much about 'taking turns' to exchange specific items of information as a form of *communing* which serves to establish and maintain relationships and which is enjoyed for its own sake. Robin Dunbar (1998) argued that language developed out of the social interaction (picking nits out of each other's hair) used by other apes to allow members of groups to 'keep in touch' with each other and maintain complex webs of relationships. As group sizes increased, to provide greater protection from large predators, keeping in touch by means of physical contact would have become increasingly impractical and an early form of vocalisation may have emerged as a more efficient alternative, as it allows us to commune with several others at the same time. An added benefit of group conversations is that, like focus groups in research studies, they allow participants to learn about each other by noticing interactions between others as well as with themselves. Gossip or 'idle chat' preserves this social function and most people would agree that the pleasure to be derived from this kind of interaction has very little to do with the topic of conversation. As in the intimate exchanges characteristic of primary intersubjectivity, the interaction is enjoyed for its own sake, as a way of maintaining and celebrating social contact and trust among a group of friends. The more familiar we are with people we know, the more relaxed and playful we can be in our interactions, allowing us to reveal more of ourselves to each other, which is one of the reasons why relaxed social chat is such a powerful way for people to get to know each other (Parker-Rees, 2014).

From very early on, babies are aware of a *felt* difference between what it is like to interact with people, who respond socially to the baby's actions, adjusting their own behaviour to 'find a fit', and with objects, which generally do not respond in this contingent way. In a study of babies' memory, Carolyn Rovee-Collier (Rovee-Collier and Hayne, 1987) tied a ribbon to babies' ankles, connecting them to a mobile which was hung above their cot so that their kicking would cause the mobile to move. The babies were quick to notice the relationship between their movements and the movements of the mobile and appeared to be delighted by the feeling that the movements of the mobile were an extension of their own actions. These babies experienced their connection to the mobile not in terms of a physical link but in terms of an observable 'fit' between what they did and what the mobile did. What I find particularly interesting, however, is that the babies would often smile and coo at the mobile as they played, responding to its contingent response to their movements much as they would respond to an interested human playmate. It may be that babies are more aware of the *feel* of this fit between what they do and what they see happening around them than they are aware of other participants as separate individuals.

This sensitivity to contingency has also been demonstrated in a series of studies by Cohn and Tronick (1987) in which babies' reactions to 'live', responsive feedback from their mothers was compared with their behaviour when their mothers adopted a 'still face', deliberately avoiding giving their babies any facial feedback. Three-month-old babies would often turn away from their mother's still face or show signs of distress. Murray and Trevarthen (1985) extended Cohn and Tronick's study, observing two-month-old babies' reactions to a live video link with their mothers. This meant that the babies and mothers could see each other on TV screens allowing the real-time contingency of the interaction to be maintained. Murray and Trevarthen then repeated the observations but this time they delayed the video signal which meant that the babies saw their mothers reacting to what they had been doing 30 seconds previously. Even this short delay was enough to disrupt the babies' ability to sustain interaction and again some babies (and mothers) were clearly disturbed by their partner's failure to respond properly to their efforts at communication. Further evidence of babies' sensitivity to the contingency of their communication partner's responses comes from studies of mothers who suffer from post-natal depression (Field, 2005). Depressed mothers are less likely to engage fully with their babies and, as a result, their babies adjust to this familiar level of engagement and may become less interested in initiating interaction with their mothers and less comfortable with high levels of contingency in interactions with other people.

We are not usually consciously aware of how we respond to other people when we communicate with them, indeed we may feel uncomfortable when talking with people who seem to be managing their responses to us a bit too deliberately – we don't always like it when we notice that we are being manipulated, 'treated' or taught. Nevertheless, even when we communicate with young babies, our interactions are co-regulated (Fogel, 1997) or jointly and simultaneously 'steered' by *everyone* involved. In the early stages this co-regulation is not symmetrical. Adults work quite hard to give babies what they want and babies have limited scope for returning the favour. Most babies are, however, equipped with a very effective tool for rewarding adults who take the trouble to engage with them in co-regulated, contingent interaction. The intentional smile, when skilfully deployed along with the contrasting furrowed brow and quivering lip, can entrap adults into devoting huge amounts of time to entertaining babies, willingly exploring ways of giving them what they want.

The emotionally intense, highly empathetic 'gooiness' of these early exchanges provides the ideal environment for advancing a baby's awareness of the social patterns and rules which shape interactions within a particular culture.

> *Metaphorically speaking, the adult caretaker orients a mirror that is magnifying back to the infant an image of emotional expressions that are greatly exaggerated.*
> *(Rochat, 2004: 267)*

Rochat argues that this exaggeration of the baby's expressions in the adult's responses helps to differentiate between the adult's 'ordinary' actions and those which *intentionally* reflect the baby's communicative acts, much as the heightened pitch of 'motherese' or Infant Directed Speech (IDS) serves to differentiate between talk specifically for the baby and (less interestingly modulated) speech for other people. But what the adult offers is much more than a mirror, even a magnifying one. By tidying up the baby's actions, gestures, expressions and sounds before returning them in a form which follows the rules of social and cultural conventions, the adult is acting as the baby's *social editor*. A baby's 'first draft' of a smile comes back in the form of the adult's much more fluent (and exaggerated) social smile. The 'accidental' sounds of early babbling are returned in the form of a tidy sequence of phonemes, the common, public sounds of the parent's language. Parents' brains are adapted (by years of experience as speakers of particular languages) to pay special attention to these sounds so we are predisposed to hear linguistic meanings 'into' the sounds produced by babies. It is no accident that the sounds which babies are most likely to produce first, *ma, pa, da* and their reduplications, *mama, papa, dada*, have been adopted in almost every language as identifiers for their eager parents. Anything vaguely resembling an /m/ sound is likely to be responded to with enthusiastic and partisan editing, transforming it into 'mama', 'mum' or 'mummy', and babies are as responsive to the *enthusiasm* as to the language sounds which come back to them.

Babies are extraordinarily good at discovering patterns and variations in the relationships between their own actions and the changes in perceptual information which result from these actions. This intuitive gift for learning from experience allows the baby to extract information not only from what other people do and say but also from how others edit the baby's own actions when they respond to them: what is kept, what is left out and what is changed. As adults we still get to know our friends and calibrate our awareness of social rules by unconsciously noticing the ways in which stories, anecdotes and accounts of our own and other people's behaviour are subtly transformed and edited as they are retold by different others.

In a fascinating study of jazz, improvisational theatre, conversation and children's play, Keith Sawyer (2001) argued that one of the fundamental rules of improvisation, the 'yes, and ...' rule, informs effective social interaction in all of these different kinds of cultural activity. The 'yes, and ...' rule requires that any contribution should be both acknowledged (yes) and built on by the respondent (... and ...), so that each contributes to both a supportive feeling of community and a satisfyingly new and interesting shared performance. You can probably think of conversations in which this rule was *not* followed; when someone is so preoccupied with what *they* want to say that they neglect to acknowledge *your* contributions (not enough 'yes') or when someone is so busy 'hearing' you that they have nothing to offer themselves (not enough 'and'). In interactions between babies and their caregivers, social editing operates in just this way, showing that the baby's contribution has been acknowledged but also adding something to it by returning it in a more culturally 'ruly' form.

First-hand exploration

After several months of wallowing in this pure form of primary communication, at about the age of four months, babies begin to turn away from their adult partners, seeming to prefer active exploration of the physical world of manipulable objects.

By this age, babies are developing the muscle control and strength that will enable them to sit up, freeing their hands for exploration of the stuff around them and allowing a shift of focus, from a 'Vygotskian' participation in social exchanges to a more 'Piagetian' dedication to exploration and investigation. While social editing may be hugely beneficial for learning to join in with cultural practices, it is less welcome when one's focus is on empirical examination of one's physical environment, where what is needed is, quite literally, first-hand, unmediated experience. In some cultures this transition is marked by turning the baby around to face out towards the world from its mother's lap (Martini and Kirkpatrick, 1981). In Western cultures, however, parents may experience a slight sense of loss as their cooing, gurgling partner starts to push them aside to embark on 'single-handed' voyages of discovery. But if children are to take their place in the social processes of conversation they must begin to acquire their own experiences so that they too can contribute (yes, and ...) as well as simply listening and observing.

In the course of this exploratory period, infants begin to realise that they can influence other people's behaviour merely by indicating their own intentions, allowing them to 'outsource' some of the work involved in dealing with the world. To begin with, gestures such as reaching and pointing may be features of the child's relationship with an object but, as children notice that these actions sometimes influence the behaviour of other people, the focus of their attention shifts to the person whose behaviour they are able to control. Reaching for an object, especially if accompanied by appropriately plaintive noises, turns out to be enough, sometimes, to cause someone else to bring the object within one's reach. Simply holding up one's arms (again with optional accompanying noises) may be enough to get one picked up and one's carrier can then even be steered by a subtle combination of gaze direction, reaching and vocalising. Another person's body can thus be recruited as an extension of one's own physical capabilities, like a human-powered exoskeleton.

Garcia (2002) and Acredolo *et al.* (2002) have explored ways of extending this natural, emergent vocabulary of infant gestural communication by developing it into a form of hand-signing. When parents use 'baby sign' to support their interaction, preverbal babies, as young as six months old, can begin to develop a vocabulary of signs which they can use both to let other people know what they want and to understand what people want from them. Many of the gestures used in baby signing resemble the actions they represent, like miming drinking from a cup to indicate that you want a drink. In terms of Bruner's (1966) taxonomy of modes of representation they bridge the gap between enactive and iconic modes and prepare the ground for the later emergence of the symbolic representation on which language depends, where the connection between sounds and the ideas they represent is almost entirely arbitrary. Merlin Donald (1991) has argued that the evolution of the human mind involved a transition period, which he calls 'mimetic culture', when early humans were able to communicate deliberately through action, signing or mime. Donald argues that mimesis would have allowed early people to develop a shared culture of rituals: formalised patterns of movement which would enable communities to share knowledge and, most importantly, to pass knowledge from one generation to the next. What seems to be important, both in baby signing and in this concept of a mimetic culture, is that certain kinds of action are marked as signs, giving them a special status, outside the ordinary processes involved in dealing with the physical world of objects.

Noticing what others notice

From about the age of nine months, infants show signs of what Trevarthen and Hubley (1978) describe as secondary intersubjectivity. Where primary intersubjectivity was entirely contained within the interaction between the people involved (usually the baby and a parent), secondary intersubjectivity involves three-way relationships between the child, another person and an object or event to which *both* are paying attention. What seems to be particularly important about this 'relatedness triangle' (Hobson, 2002) is that the child can now pay attention to the *meanings* which adults attach to objects and events, including intentional communicative gestures such as signs and speech.

When children under the age of nine months are confronted by a surprising situation they will usually stare intently at whatever caused this surprise but children over nine months are more likely to look at a familiar adult, to read their reaction for clues about how this situation should be understood (Gauvain, 2001). This 'social referencing' provides immensely valuable access to the cultural worlds of other people, outsourcing interpretation of unfamiliar situations much as gestures allowed the infant to outsource physical activity. By communicating with others about objects and events, infants can learn not only about their environment, but also about the *meaning* other people attach to aspects of their world: what is considered important, dangerous, disgusting, funny, rude, kind or cute. Towards the end of their first year, children are particularly interested in how adults react to what *they* do, and they actively explore ways of using this knowledge. Once a child knows, for example, that approaching something dangerous or disgusting will provoke a strong response in a caregiver, they are able to use this knowledge very effectively to manage an adult's attention. If your mother is preoccupied, browsing the internet perhaps, and not offering as much attention as you need, all you have to do is toddle over to the nearest bin and begin to rummage. The attention you get may not be exactly what you would like but it may be much better than no attention at all (and a well-timed smile may turn it around). What this example highlights is that what you *do* (rummaging in the bin) may be pretty insignificant in terms of your communicative intentions – poking at a plug socket or pulling the cat's tail would probably do just as well. When children begin to use words and later phrases, sentences and stories, to communicate, it is as well to remember that what they are *saying* may be much less important than the levels of communicative intention which lie beneath the surface of their words. When a parent cuddles up with a child to share a book the communication which they both enjoy is much richer than the words and pictures in the book could ever convey. The book provides a useful tool for sharing attention but what it contains is less important than the communicative experiences which come to be associated with it.

Enjoying the company of other people

When we think about communication in the special context of education it is easy to overlook its fundamentally social functions: to focus on language development rather than on personal, social and emotional development. Paying close attention to the early stages of communication reminds us that what people say and do is no more than the tip of the communication iceberg. When people have got to know each other well they become able to read meaning into the subtlest variations in a familiar gesture or comment. A hug or a handshake can tell us immediately about how another person is feeling, a particular look can tell us what a friend thinks about what someone else has just said. I think of this in terms of the relationship between the 'already spoken words' of a script or a musical score and the unique significance of the 'words in their speaking' each time that play or that piece of music is performed. For an audience who know the score it becomes possible to detect tiny variations in its performance which allow a connection to be made, a felt experience of what the music means to the performer.

For a young child (but also for adults) it is much easier to notice the significance of variations in another person's behaviour when both the other person and the environment are familiar. Judy Dunn's (1988) wonderful observational study of two-year-olds joining in with all aspects of life at home with their families clearly shows how their social abilities are inseparable from the familiar contexts and familiar relationships. When they are 'at home' they, and their families, are able to relax and 'be themselves', enabling them to function well beyond what is possible in situations where they constantly need to be alert, struggling to make sense of unfamiliar people doing unfamiliar things.

As soon as children move into the culture of the primary school, from the 'free-flow' of life at home or in a nursery setting, they learn to call some parts of the day 'play time' and some parts of the space 'play grounds', learning at the same time that other times and other spaces are 'not for play'. After many more years of formal education in school environments, where 'acceptable' forms of communication often centre on displays of knowledge, we learn to differentiate between 'work communication' and 'play communication' or 'social chat'. Purposeful, business-like talk or writing, to convey a message as efficiently as possible, is separated off from 'just' talking, where the focus is on getting to know people or enjoying the pleasure of their company.

Nell Noddings has challenged this dissociation between work/learning and play/ socialising orientations in school settings, arguing that we should focus much more on the social environments which we provide for children and less on crude measures of how much knowledge they have managed to accumulate:

> *Schools should become places in which teachers and students live together, talk to each other, reason together, take delight in each others' company. Like good parents, teachers should be concerned first and foremost with the kind of people their charges are becoming. My guess is that when schools focus on what really matters in life, the cognitive ends we are now striving toward in such painful and artificial ways will be met as natural culminations of the means we have wisely chosen. (Noddings, 1991: 161)*

We should remember that all forms of communication, even the driest and most formal, are social processes, grounded in the negotiation and sharing of *common* understandings. Even when we communicate with strangers we have to make assumptions about how we can expect them to respond. What will be too obvious to be worth mentioning? What will be familiar, interesting, challenging, confusing or irritating? Arriving at a common understanding is much easier in situations which can be co-regulated by all participants; where responses can be monitored and misunderstandings can be repaired almost before they happen. When this is not possible, when communicating with a child's family by means of an entry in a diary, a newsletter or notices and signs, for example, or when writing a report for a practitioner from a different background or for a child's next teacher, it is all the more important to draw on available knowledge about how a particular form of words might be (mis)construed. Time invested in 'idle' chat with children, colleagues and parents can allow us to get to know them (and let them get to know us), adding to the store of intuitive awareness which will inform our communication with them in the future. If we have taken time to get to know people we will be more able to tap into implicit, intuitive 'action guiding anticipations' (Shotter, 2010: viii) about how we would expect them to respond, allowing us to role-play a conversation with them in our heads.

We do not feel the need to keep checklists of what we have learned about people in the course of friendly chat because we trust the automatic processes which allow us to sift out information about their personality, likes, dislikes and interests from the kinds of contributions they make (and don't make). Getting to know people is therefore importantly different from getting to know *about* people and getting to know the children in an early years setting is very different from assessing or profiling them. Studying the earliest stages of communication may help us to think carefully about how our cool, professional discourses and practices might be warmed up if we were prepared to pay more attention to the human aspects of how we live and work in social communities:

> the main function of conversation is not to get things done but to improve the quality of experience (Csikszentmihalyi, 1992: 129)

ACTIVITY 1

How much can video capture?

Make a short video recording of interaction between children under three years old (preferably under two) or between one child and an adult or older child. Make sure you obtain the parents' permission both to make the recording and to share it with a colleague. Two or three minutes will be enough but you will probably need to record much more in order to be able to pick out a short sample which is reasonably 'natural' (an adult encouraging a child to 'perform' will be much less interesting). Watch the video carefully and

(Continued)

try to record what is happening: a) as a transcript of what is said and b) with explanatory notes about gestures, body language, mood, etc. to try to capture as much as possible of what was going on. Of course you cannot hope to capture exactly how the participants understood their interaction but you can try to explain what you felt (the difference between being there and just seeing the video). You may find it helpful to present both transcripts in parallel columns, one for each participant, so that you can show how their actions and speech overlap.

Share your observations with a colleague, as follows:

1. *First let them read just the bare transcript (no scene setting or explanations). How much sense can they make of what is going on? Are they willing or able to comment on how the participants may have felt?*
2. *Now play just the soundtrack of the video (minimise the window or blank the screen). What additional information does this provide?*
3. *Now reveal all! Play the video again, this time with sound and pictures. How much is added to what your colleague was able to make of the soundtrack alone?*
4. *You could go on to give your colleague your full transcript (with explanatory notes) and talk about how you 'read' the interaction before playing the video one last time. Note how our understanding of social interactions is changed when we are able to tune in to contextual information.*
5. *Now switch roles and see what you can make of your colleague's piece of video.*

This should help you to appreciate how much we rely on non-verbal channels of communication of which, in everyday life, we are scarcely aware. Be prepared to have your interpretation challenged and to challenge your colleague's interpretation of his/her piece of video.

Looking below the surface

Develop the habit of standing back from different kinds of social interaction (lectures, discussions, gossip, arguments) to monitor what is being communicated. What do people express through the way they speak, what they emphasise, what they ignore, facial expressions, posture, etc. and how much of this is picked up by others? You may find that it is easier to note what you feel about what is going on and then try to work out what may have informed that feeling (this is a valuable skill to develop, and catching your reaction to things you read, in the form of responsive annotations, can be a good way to practise). Be warned that if your friends notice that you are analysing their interaction, they may object!

FURTHER READING

Carpendale, J. I. M. and Lewis, C. (2006) *How Children Develop Social Understanding*. Oxford: Blackwell.

This is an excellent review of research in child development, with a strong focus on children as social agents.

Corke, M. (2012) *Using Playful Practice to Communicate with Special Children*. Abingdon: Routledge.

Margaret Corke provides practical advice on playful activities which can help practitioners to 'break through' barriers to communication with children with severe learning difficulties.

Dunn, J. (1988) *The Beginnings of Social Understanding*. Cambridge, MA: Harvard University Press.

This is a very readable account of Dunn's ground-breaking study, observing two-year-olds playing and joining in with family life in their familiar home environment – showing how much more they are able to do when they know (and are known by) the people with whom they are interacting.

Murray, L. (2014) *The Psychology of Babies: How Relationships Support Development from Birth to Two Years*. London: Constable and Robinson.

Lynne Murray provides a very accessible account of early social development, with excellent series of colour images from video recordings to illustrate early interactions. Chapter 1 'Social Understanding and Cooperation' is particularly relevant.

Nelson, K. (2007) *Young Minds in Social Worlds: Experience, Meaning and Memory*. Cambridge, MA: Harvard University Press.

Katherine Nelson has been researching young children's entry into a 'community of minds for more than 40 years and in this book she explains how the ability to share meanings with others develops.' Chapter 3, 'Being an Infant, Becoming a Child' details the early stages of communication, in the first year.

Saxton, M. (2010) *Child Language: Acquisition and Development*. London: SAGE.

This is a useful review of research in language development, written in an engaging and accessible style with anecdotes from the author's own experience.

Tortora, S. (2005) *The Dancing Dialogue: Using the Communicative Power of Movement with Young Children*. Baltimore, MD: Brookes Publishers.

Tortora explains her use of sympathetic movement to engage with children who cannot be reached through language. This book contains excellent examples of rich, detailed accounts of non-verbal communication.

REFERENCES

Acredolo, L., Goodwyn, S. and Abrams, D. (2002) *Baby Signs: How to Talk with Your Baby Before Your Baby Can Talk*. London: Contemporary Books/McGraw Hill.

Bruner, J.S. (1966) *Toward a Theory of Instruction*. Cambridge, MA: Harvard University Press.

Cohn, J.F. and Tronick, E.Z. (1987) Mother–infant face-to-face interaction; the sequence of dyadic states at 3, 6, and 9 months. *Developmental Psychology*, 23(1): 68–77.

Csikszentmihalyi, M. (1992) *Flow: The Psychology of Happiness*. London: Rider Books.

DfE (Department for Education) (2014) *Statutory Framework for the Early Years Foundation Stage: Setting the Standards for Learning, Development and Care for Children from Birth to Five*. London: DfE Publications.

Donald, M. (1991) *Origins of the Modern Mind: Three Stages in the Evolution of Culture and Cognition*. Cambridge, MA: Harvard University Press.

Dunbar, R. (1998) *Grooming, Gossip and the Evolution of Language*. Cambridge, MA: Harvard University Press.

Dunn, J. (1988) *The Beginnings of Social Understanding*. Cambridge, MA: Harvard University Press.

Field, T. (2005) Prenatal depression effects on the foetus and neonate. In J. Nadel and D. Muir (eds), *Emotional Development*. Oxford: Oxford University Press.

Fogel, A. (1997) *Developing Through Relationships: Origins of Communication, Self and Culture*. Chicago: University of Chicago Press.

Garcia, J. (2002) *Sign With Your Baby: How to Communicate with Infants Before They Can Speak*. Seattle: Northlight Communications.

Gauvain, M. (2001) *The Social Context of Cognitive Development*. New York: Guilford Publications.

Hepper, P. (2003) Prenatal psychological and behavioral development. In J. Valsiner and K.J. Connolly (eds), *Handbook of Developmental Psychology*. London: SAGE.

Hobson, P. (2002) *The Cradle of Thought: Exploring the Origins of Thinking*. London: Macmillan.

Hurley, S. and Chater, N. (2005) *Perspectives on Imitation: From Neuroscience to Social Science* (Vols. 1 and 2). Cambridge, MA: MIT Press.

Konner, M. (2010) *The Evolution of Childhood: Relationships, Emotion, Mind*. Cambridge, MA: Harvard University Press.

Kugiumutzakis, G., Kokkinaki, T., Makrodimitraki, M. and Vitalaki, E. (2005) Emotions in early mimesis. In J. Nadel and D. Muir (eds), *Emotional Development*. Oxford: Oxford University Press.

Lave, J. and Wenger, E. (1991) *Situated Learning: Legitimate Peripheral Participation*. Cambridge: University of Cambridge Press.

Martini, M. and Kirkpatrick, J. (1981) Early interactions in the Marquesas Islands. In T.M. Field, A.M. Sostek, P. Vietze and P.H. Leiderman (eds), *Culture and Early Interactions*. Hillsdale, NJ: Erlbaum.

Meltzoff, A.N. and Moore, M.K. (1977) Imitation of facial and manual gestures by human neonates. *Science*, 198: 75–8. (Also in A. Slater and D. Muir (eds) (1999) *The Blackwell Reader in Developmental Psychology*. Oxford: Blackwell.)

Murray, L. and Trevarthen, C. (1985) Emotional regulation of interactions between two-month-olds and their mothers. In T. Field and N. Fox (eds), *Social Perception in Infants*. Norwood, NJ: Ablex.

Noddings, N. (1991) Stories in dialogue: caring and interpersonal reasoning. In C. Witherell and N. Noddings (eds), *Stories Lives Tell: Narrative and Dialogue in Education*. New York: Teachers' College Press.

Parker-Rees, R. (2007a) Liking to be liked: imitation, familiarity and pedagogy in the first years of life. *Early Years*, 27(1): 3–17.

Parker-Rees, R. (2007b) Primary communication – what can adults learn from babies? In J. Moyles (ed.), *Early Years Foundations: Meeting the Challenge*. Maidenhead: Open University Press/McGraw Hill.

Parker-Rees, R. (2014) Playfulness and the co-construction of identity in the first years. In L. Brooker, S. Edwards and M. Blaise (eds), *SAGE Handbook of Play and Learning in Early Childhood*. London: SAGE.

Rizzolatti, G., Fadiga, L., Gallese, V. and Fogassi, L. (1996) Premotor cortex and the recognition of motor actions. *Cognitive Brain Research*, 3: 131–41.

Rochat, P. (2004) Emerging co-awareness. In G. Bremner and A. Slater (eds), *Theories of Infant Development*. Oxford: Blackwell.

Rovee-Collier, C. and Hayne, H. (1987) Reactivation of infant memory: implications for cognitive development. In H. Reese (ed.) *Advances in Child Development and Behavior*. New York: Academic Press.

Sawyer, R.K. (2001) *Creating Conversations: Improvisation in Everyday Discourse.* Cresskill, NJ: Hampton Press.

Shotter, J. (2010) *Social Construction on the Edge: 'Withness'-thinking and embodiment.* Chagrin Falls, Ohio: Taos Institute.

Shotter, J. (2014) Agential realism, social constructionism, and our living relations to our surroundings: sensing similarities rather than seeing patterns. *Theory & Psychology*, 24(3): 305–25.

Trevarthen, C. (1979) Communication and cooperation in early infancy: a description of primary intersubjectivity. In M.M. Bullowa (ed.), *Before Speech: The Beginning of Interpersonal Communication.* New York: Cambridge University Press.

Trevarthen, C. (2003) Making sense of infants making sense. *Intellectica (Revue de l'Association pour la Recherche Cognitive)*, 34: 161–88. Available at: http://intellectica.org/SiteArchives/archives/n34/34_8_Trevarthen.pdf (accessed 24 February 2015).

Trevarthen, C. and Hubley P. (1978) Secondary intersubjectivity: confidence, confiding and acts of meaning in the first year. In A. Lock (ed.) *Action, Gesture and Symbol: The Emergence of Language.* London: Academic Press.

4 Spirituality and young children's well-being

Philip Selbie

Introduction

This chapter is about young children's spirituality and well-being and how the two contribute to healthy personal development in early childhood. More specifically, it is about valuing and nurturing the spiritual dimension in young children's lives as a basis for establishing and maintaining positive relationships within young children's worlds. What is meant by spirituality and the notion of spiritual development in the lives of young children? How does spirituality in early childhood relate to well-being and why should we consider the spiritual dimension to life as significant when working with young children today? The chapter highlights the recognition given to young children's spirituality within Te Whāriki (New Zealand Ministry of Education, 1996) and asks why, despite the numerous references to children's spiritual development in policy documents, it appears to be relatively neglected within English early years provision today.

The notion of well-being should need little introduction. Achieving a state of well-being has been the concern of philosophers since Aristotle (384–322 BC) and lies at the heart of human existence to the point where some would consider it as the ulti-mate goal of human endeavour. In recent years there has been a growing body of research in the UK into what contributes to the quality of people's lives and how this affects their well-being. National public interest in this field has grown significantly since the publication in 2005 of the first edition of *Happiness: Lessons from a New Science* (Layard, 2011) and the *National Accounts of Well-being* report by the New Economics Foundation (NEF) in 2009. The NEF report proposed that 'national govern-ments should directly measure people's subjective well-being … [and the] measures should be collected on a regular, systematic basis and published as National Accounts of Well-being' (2009: 8). Following the launch of a national debate on well-being in November 2010 the Office for National Statistics (ONS) has been publishing data on the nation's subjective well-being for the last three years (ONS, 2012).

This interest was preceded by a great deal of national concern surrounding the well-being of children and young people, generated by the publication of *Child poverty in perspective: An overview of child well-being in rich countries* (UNICEF, 2007) and the Children's Society's inquiry into what constitutes a 'good' childhood (Layard and Dunn, 2009). These reports draw on research findings to argue that threats to a child's physical, emotional or mental well-being will compromise healthy per-sonal development, may result in persistent negative perceptions of life and possibly endanger the cohesion and stability of society.

A decade ago this was acknowledged at a policy level in the Labour government's Every Child Matters (ECM) agenda (DfES, 2004). High profile cases in the media such as the deaths of Victoria Climbié and Peter Connolly added strength to the argument that too many children and families were receiving poor services, caused by professionals failing to work together in a multidisciplinary manner (see Chapter 10). Well-being then featured prominently in the subsequent Children Act 2004 which sought to make the UK a better and safer place for all children and, specifically, to improve the overall well-being of children and young people. Three years later the launch of the Children's Plan (DCSF, 2007: 5) set out a vast array of measures to achieve a set of goals by 2020 and boldly declared its aim to 'make England the best place in the world for children and young people to grow up'.

More detailed attention to the well-being of young children appeared in the 1997–2010 Labour government's non-statutory guidance to the Early Years Foundation Stage (EYFS) (DCSF, 2008a), introduced into schools and early years settings from September 2008. Echoing the ECM aims for children and young people to 'stay safe' and 'be healthy', the theme of 'The Unique Child' stated that young children 'develop resilience when their physical and psychological well-being is protected by adults' and they 'have emotional well-being when their needs are met and their feelings are accepted' (DCSF, 2008c: cards 1.3 and 1.4).

The importance of quality early education and care for young children's well-being has continued to be emphasised since the formation of the coalition government in May 2010. Provision of funded part-time nursery places has been maintained together with the recent extension of the Pupil Premium to the early years and the beginning of funded part-time entitlement for some two-year-olds (ONS, 2014). Changes in policy have been accompanied and informed by an increase in attention being paid to well-being as a prerequisite for a healthy childhood and high quality early years provision (Collins and Foley, 2008; Roberts, 2010; Waters, 2014).

Spirituality, education and legislation

Acceptance of the contribution well-being makes to children's early development has been in marked contrast to attitudes towards promoting the spiritual in children's lives and especially in any educational context. There continues to be much debate about the difference between 'spiritual development' and 'spirituality'. Meehan (2002) suggests that 'spiritual development' refers to a universal educational intention whereas 'spirituality' is a more religious term and may therefore be less widely accessible.

Fears about spirituality being synonymous with religious indoctrination run deep and are not difficult to understand given the lessons from history and the potential threat to human well-being posed by culturally irrelevant or ill-intended expressions of religious practice. For many the notion of spirituality is also likely to encroach upon personal or sensitive issues which ought not to be discussed in public let alone in relation to young children. This fear of addressing taboo subjects can result in unintended consequences as recent cases surrounding the risks posed to children and young people have shown. Those with extreme views or inappropriate behaviours who exploit the cover of silence and denial to operate under the guise of care and concern need to be challenged in order to protect vulnerable children and young people. Whilst reasonable caution should naturally be exercised, the potential for the spiritual dimension to enhance young children's well-being and personal development must not be neglected due to irrational fears or prejudice.

A willingness among professionals to improve understanding of the spiritual dimension is an important first step in protecting the positive contribution this can make to the lives of children and young people. It is worth noting that despite adult uneasiness, mention of children's spiritual development has featured in legislation concerned with the education of children for almost 70 years. The Education Act 1944 stated that education authorities had a duty 'to contribute towards the spiritual, moral, mental and physical development of the community' (1944, section 7). The equally significant changes introduced by the Education Reform Act 1988 linked the responsibility for spiritual development to the newly introduced National Curriculum, stating that it should 'promote the spiritual, moral, cultural, mental and physical development of pupils and of society' (1988, section 1.2a).

Specific reference to the spiritual development of very young children then appeared in the School Standards and Framework Act 1998. Under this statute Her Majesty's Chief Inspector of Schools in England was charged with 'keeping the Secretary of State informed about the spiritual, moral, social and cultural development of children for whom relevant nursery education is provided' (1998, section 122.3a).

In addition the non-statutory guidance accompanying the introduction of the EYFS (DCSF, 2008a) makes clear reference to the spiritual dimension of young children's lives. Not only is 'spiritual well-being' identified as contributing to children's health but practitioners are encouraged to plan activities that 'promote emotional, moral, spiritual and social development together with intellectual development' (DCSF, 2008c: card 4.4). Furthermore, spiritual development and physical, cognitive, linguistic, social and emotional areas of early development are all 'equally important' (DCSF, 2008c: card 1.1).

Wider recognition of children's spirituality is set out in the UN Convention on the Rights of the Child (UNICEF, 1989) where children's spiritual rights are referred to in four of the articles. Whilst recognising the role played by the mass media in children's lives, Article 17 seeks to ensure that children have access to a wide diversity 'of national and international sources, especially those aimed at the promotion of his or her social, spiritual and moral well-being and physical and mental health'. Article 27.1 acknowledges that spirituality needs to be nurtured and recognises the need to secure the right of every child to a standard of living 'adequate for the child's physical, mental, spiritual, moral and social development'.

Despite the numerous references in legislation there remains an absence of an agreed description of what young children's spirituality might look like or guidance about how to promote spiritual development. At the time of the Education Act 1944 the agreed syllabuses indicate that Christianity was the religion taught in schools and therefore it was considered logical that pupils' spiritual development would take place within a Christian context. However, today British society is no longer predominantly Christian and so any definition of spirituality, and how to develop it, needs to take into account a wider range of faith perspectives (including none at all) which means the task has changed significantly over the past 70 years. This presents not just policy makers but also practitioners with some difficulty in knowing where to look for the spiritual dimension and how to nurture it in young children's lives.

Spirituality and the whole child

One of the traditional hallmarks of early years education and care has been an emphasis on developing the whole child and the fundamental importance of personal, social and emotional development. This holistic view of the child can be traced back over the last two and a half millennia to the time of Plato (428–347BC) who stressed the necessity of children developing socially, morally and emotionally as well as cognitively. Aristotle favoured education for children under the age of six and also concluded that humans were social beings and that supreme goodness was happiness. He was concerned with the search for personal well-being and insisted that education had a role to play in this quest, believing education should develop habits which encouraged cognitive ability but also moral and rational virtues.

The influential 17th-century educational reformer Comenius (1592–1670) wrote *The School of Infancy*, published in 1631 (Comenius, 1956), in which he highlighted the importance of educating young children under the age of six and stressed the significant role of parents and particularly mothers in this task. Comenius wrote of the power of education to transform individuals as well as society (Spinka, 1943) and ultimately to lead humanity to achieve its fullest potential and to enjoy harmony with the created world.

Personal, social and emotional development were central to the educational philosophy of Locke (1632–1704) who also advocated children's moral development and promoted the importance of a holistic model of early education in order to advance the human condition. Rousseau (1712–1778) also considered that the spiritual dimension to life made an important contribution to a holistic view of the child and was an essential part of equipping young learners for life in a civil society, bringing them into harmony with the natural order (see Chapter 13).

Fröbel (1782–1852) was perhaps the most influential pioneer of early education to hold the spiritual dimension in high regard when working with young children. He respected the inherent nature of the child, which he believed was deeply spiritual. According to Fröbel, education should not be about the search for reason, but instead the unfolding of the divine within the child. Fröbel urged respect for the spontaneous and creative nature of this process and he had a deep reverence for the natural world, believing that early education should not be hurried but rather should bring the child naturally to a clear understanding of himself.

Amongst these and other historical pioneers of early education there was general acceptance of the existence of a spiritual dimension to life and its relationship to a common value system that at the time found its roots within the Christian tradition. This in turn gave rise to a common consensus about the importance of moral goodness and the role it played in a young child's personal, social and emotional development. Spirituality was naturally associated with religion, which had a powerful although sometimes negative influence upon young children's early development.

Today, the link between a spiritual dimension to human development and the concept of the whole child finds a clear expression in the New Zealand early childhood curriculum. The title Te Whāriki refers to a woven ceremonial mat used by the indigenous Māori people and is based on a model of learning that 'weaves together intricate patterns of linked experience and meaning rather than emphasising the acquisition of discrete skills' (New Zealand Ministry of Education, 1996: 41). This bicultural curriculum framework was developed nearly 20 years ago, giving a central place to the voice of the Māori people and explicitly encourages adults to recognise the important place of spirituality in the development of the whole child (Lee *et al.*, 2013).

What are we searching for?

In cultures where the spiritual dimension to life is not so readily accepted, contemporary debates about the notion of spirituality often seem to falter at the point of finding an agreed definition. Without a shared understanding of what it is we hope to develop, it is likely to be difficult to agree on what we should be doing. Rose (2001: 1) comments that spirituality 'seems to be a neat catch-all, intimating a certain something without necessarily revealing much about what it entails' and Best (2000: 10) reminds us that 'of all experiences, it is the spiritual which, it seems, is most resistant to operational definition. At its worst, attempts to pin it down lead only to a greater awareness of its intangibility and pervasiveness.'

On the other hand, eluding formal definition need not be entirely negative as language has its limitations and may be too reductive in the search for a common dialogue about spirituality. Priestley (1997: 29) proposes that the search for a definition is 'akin to asking a child on a stormy day to go out into the playground and to collect a jar of wind and to bring it back into the classroom for analysis'. King (2013) suggests that there may be no common definition to be found and that instead we should be content with describing the spiritual in terms of our own observations rather than searching vainly for a definition. King (2013: 4) instead recommends an open-ended description whereby 'spiritualities' signify or suggest 'those ideas, practices and commitments that nurture, sustain and shape the fabric of human lives'.

Hay (2007: 2) takes the view that our difficulty in arriving at a definition of spirituality may be no more than the result of 'the default assumption about human nature ... that we are born atheists who come to subscribe to a specific faith through socialisation into a religious culture'. In addition, despite the various expressions of

Christianity that have characterised Europe for centuries, the Enlightenment period, when logic and rationality were highly prized, still casts a long shadow and has led to a repression of what Hay (2007: 3) argues is 'our natural spirituality'. The idea that children have a natural affinity with the spiritual realm was celebrated by Romantic poets of the early 19th century such as Wordsworth (1770–1850) and Keats (1795–1821).

King (2013) develops this further by suggesting that there is a biological basis for spiritual awareness in children and that spirituality is a natural part of human evolution rather than an element implanted through culture and education. King (2013: 5) states 'there exists a pre-linguistic experiential foundation of spiritual sensibility in human beings' which is something to be cherished and celebrated. This is a view shared by Hay and Nye (2006) who also argue that spirituality is an innate human quality and so is not necessarily dependent upon association with a religious faith.

Prentice (1996: 325) echoes the 'self-actualisation' at the peak of Maslow's hierarchy of needs, when he asserts

> that to be human is to be spiritual, that is to say, there is within each of us, unless we are brutalised, a desire to manifest a range of qualities and capabilities more fully. This desire to become our fullest selves is there just as much as the constancy of the mountain, or the 'desire' of the rose to bloom in perfection or of the horse to run and express its 'horseness'.

Charged with the duty of reporting on the ability to promote children's spiritual, moral, social and cultural (SMSC) development, Ofsted has required schools to address the issue of human spirituality and its development. Previous guidance material for Inspectors has recognised a 'non-material element of a human being which animates and sustains us' and also refers to 'the development of a sense of identity, self-worth, personal insight, meaning and purpose' (Ofsted, 2004: 12).

The search for meaning

Young children begin their search for meaning in their very early experiences. From the moment of birth infants seek attachment with a 'significant other' and there is an urge to meet physical needs. As time progresses these physical needs become more varied and complex; social and emotional dimensions begin to play a part in a young child's attempts at satisfying these needs and patterns and routines then form part of experience. This in turn leads to a certain amount of physical and emotional security based upon some sense of order in a world that can initially seem unpredictable and insecure. Although, these experiences are unfortunately not part of every childhood, the early development of many young children is supported by safe and reliable relationships which provide the self-confidence to be outgoing and independent from that same secure base (see Chapter 1).

This healthy state of affairs continues into adulthood for many of us and our lives are filled with human relationships of varying depths, from fleeting encounters to long-term partnerships and we exist in a matrix of connections that link us to those around us. Relationships are characterised by spiritual qualities such as love, trust and forgiveness which are an integral part of living in a communal or social domain. We also exist in relationship to a personal domain as we have the capacity not only to inter-relate with others but also to intra-relate with ourselves. The search for purpose and meaning in our own lives is closely related to self-awareness, self-fulfilment and personal identity and this is very much part of spiritual development for young children too (Adams *et al.*, 2008).

Elkind (2001) suggests that laying the foundation for interpersonal relationships depends on adults helping young children to develop an understanding that the world is a safe place and people are well meaning and caring. If this sense of trust is lost or damaged 'so too is the child's sense of self and his or her trust in interpersonal relations' (Elkind: 205). The EYFS theme of Positive Relationships refers to the Key Person as someone who 'develops a genuine bond with children and offers a settled, close relationship' (DCSF, 2008c: card 2.1). Close relationships form a secure base from which young children develop a sense of belonging which is fundamental to their emotional well-being and a strong indicator of quality provision. The EYFS also states that 'children must be provided with experiences and support which will help them to develop a positive sense of themselves and of others ... [and]... providers must ensure support for children's emotional well-being to help them to know themselves and what they can do' (DCSF, 2008b: 12).

An emphasis on relationships is also a feature of Te Whāriki which puts Relationships alongside the other broad principles of Empowerment, Holistic Development and Family and Community. Early childhood settings in New Zealand are able to create their own curriculum by weaving common themes, including the four principles, into their own patterns of experience and in this way they have flexibility to be responsive to the needs of young learners.

Where Te Whāriki differs from the EYFS, though, is that children are believed to learn through responsive and reciprocal relationships not just with people but also with places and objects. Te Whāriki acknowledges young children's ability to establish such relationships and encourages an understanding of the physical nature of an area such as a river or a mountain, alongside the spiritual significance it holds for the local community.

Connectedness – the heart of children's spirituality

In their research into children's spirituality, working with 38 children between the ages of 6 and 11, Hay and Nye (2006) highlighted two significant themes. Firstly, the children viewed themselves as connected to others through relationships but not just with friends and family. They also felt a 'connectedness' to the wider community, the environment and also some transcendent Other. Secondly, the research discovered amongst the children 'a distinctly reflective consciousness' (2006: 109) somewhat similar to the term 'meta-cognition' used within developmental psychology. However, in this context reflective consciousness is described as something different. Rather, the children exhibited the ability to be objectively aware of themselves as 'subjects' when examining and understanding their worlds, especially in relational terms.

Hay and Nye (2006: 109) observed that the features of the relationships described by the children often 'added value to their ordinary or everyday perspective'. The children sometimes expressed this special sense as one of having a particular form of 'awareness' and the term 'relational consciousness' is used to describe this. Indeed Hay and Nye (2006: 109) suggest that out of this central core of a relationship arise 'meaningful aesthetic experience, religious experience, personal and traditional responses to mystery and being, and mystical and moral insight'.

De Souza (2009) develops this further when aligning the various 'directions' in which relationships develop with the spiritual journey she suggests we all undertake. When in a secure place, adults and children move 'outwards' from themselves towards those who are familiar and then onwards to connect to others who are different and unknown. However, the journey also necessitates 'going within' as we discover new parts of ourselves that resonate with what we have learnt of others. Personal qualities such as empathy and compassion begin to be manifested at the outer boundaries of our character and lead to our greater self-knowledge within. This connectedness both to others and ourselves promotes a sense of self and of our place in the community to which we belong which then gives a sense of meaning and purpose to life (Hyde, 2008).

Developing young children's spirituality

This chapter has highlighted the possibility for spiritual development in children's lives and located it within the relational domain of young children's experiences. In addition, it has suggested that acknowledgement of spirituality provides a deeper dimension to our common understanding of the 'whole child' and that nourishing children's early development from this perspective contributes to a child's sense of personal well-being. How then might practitioners, carers and parents foster this dimension in young children's lives and is it particularly significant when there appears to be little consensus about traditional and formal expressions of spirituality?

Goodliff (2013) highlights creative and imaginative activity as having great potential for drawing out and developing young children's spirituality. In an ethnographic study of children as young as two- and three-years-old, she found that young children's spirituality became evident when they were encouraged to think, reflect and express their feelings.

Traditional views about how children evidence their spirituality tend to focus on their expressions of 'awe and wonder' at the mysterious and incomprehensible such as a spider's web, a rainbow or stars in the night sky. These are undoubtedly important signs of spiritual awareness and young children are capable of both asking and discussing such questions within the relational space shared with sensitive and caring adults. Adams *et al.* (2008: 45) suggest that practitioners need to search for the spiritual within their own everyday experiences as, 'if one cannot marvel at the intricacies of the natural world, how can one learn to find one's voice to express concerns about the destruction of the planet, care for its resources, appreciate its beauty or its complexities?' Freedom to express ideas of a spiritual nature can contribute to increased self-confidence and self-esteem which contribute to young children's personal and emotional development and play an important part in shaping their identity.

Despite the many opportunities for practitioners to support children's spiritual development, it is notable that only the Welsh Foundation Phase Framework for children aged 3–7 (DCELLS, 2008) retains any explicit mention of this. In contrast there is no specific reference to spirituality in the current version of the EYFS (DfE, 2014) or in the latest version of the accompanying non-statutory guidance published as Early Years Outcomes (DfE, 2013). However, Goouch (2010: 51) argues that 'we must provide spaces and places for children to experience their childhood rather than serve a curriculum'. We should therefore seek out opportunities for young children to develop a sense of themselves as creators and managers of their space rather than being controlled by the environment around them (see Chapter 6).

Children will continue to use 'cultural tools' in their natural everyday relationships with others in order to make sense of the world around them as well as to develop their own spiritual lives and a sense of identity within relationships. Communication and Language features alongside Personal, Social and Emotional Development in the EYFS (DfE, 2014) as a Prime Area of learning and so early communication in all its forms is vitally important for developing the deepest levels of thinking for children. Drawing upon the work of Vygotsky (1978), Nye (1996) suggests that the use of language especially in imaginative and creative play is the basis for human reflective consciousness which allows creativity and spirituality to be expressed and allows us to reflect on our spiritual experiences.

Explicit attention to children's entitlement to spiritual, moral, social and cultural (SMSC) development under section 78 of the Education Act 2002 is also important for developing a space for children to talk and express themselves in relation to issues of a spiritual nature. Young children respond very well to activities which help them to develop an understanding of their place in the world, to exercise a set of values and to experience ways of resolving relational differences.

As an early years teacher, my own observations often centred upon what young children were saying and doing in relationships with their peers. In playful and imaginative scenarios children developed important vocabulary and the skills of language but they also established and nourished relationships through which they gained an understanding of the world and their place in it. Notions of fairness were tested, trust was extended, bonds were broken and restored and above all young children learned skills of negotiation and cooperation. In addition they grew in confidence and self-awareness and began to develop a sense of meaning and purpose in their lives. Such opportunities to develop their consciousness give children the ability to reflect not only on their relationship with others but also on their relationship with themselves.

Greater opportunities for this have arisen as children have been introduced to Philosophy for Children (P4C) which provides them with opportunities to join a 'community of enquiry'. Young children have the capacity to engage in 'thinking about thinking' (Haynes, 2008) and can enjoy discussing questions such as 'How do I know I am alive?' In my experience, children's natural curiosity takes them into the realms of spiritual as well as philosophical ideas and illuminates their ability to intra-relate with themselves as well as to interrelate with those around them.

Spirituality, well-being and young children today

To conclude this chapter it is worth considering possible reasons for identifying and nurturing young children's spirituality. Are we doing any more than using just another word to describe the experiences of young children as they begin to negotiate their way through life? Does recognition of children's spirituality offer something extra to our understanding of the multidimensional nature of early childhood? Most importantly, is a willingness to support and nurture the spiritual dimension likely to make a difference to young children and support them in valuing their journey through life?

The chapter has attempted to establish that spirituality is part of human experience and that, despite the controversy and misunderstanding often associated with it, there is a place for spirituality in the study of young children's lives. In addition, while spirituality is closely allied to well-being and has much in common with it, there is a distinctiveness to it that makes an important contribution to personal, social and emotional development. Young children develop in a holistic and integrated way and they require meaningful relationships with others to help them make sense of the world around them. The unique contribution that spirituality can make to the relational dimension of children's lives is that it can deepen their awareness not only of themselves but also of their relationships to the physical, social and mysterious elements of their environment.

Coming to terms with uncertainty and the inability to put into words certain life experiences is something that is part of being human and so, like children, adults also try to bring meaning to their lives within relationships. Daly (2004: 215) laments that too many of us 'live at surface level, not belonging to any group at any real depth. People are unable to be intimate with themselves or with others and a spiritual vacuum exists which needs to be filled.' Daly also contends that human spirituality is in danger of becoming extinguished due to our modern day preoccupation with economics, technology and consumer culture. On the other hand being in relationship with another at the deepest of levels brings a sense of fulfilment and growth which she concludes has a spiritual dimension and 'has to do with living life to the full and is about discovering how to become more fully human' (2004: 240).

King (2013: 5) suggests that our understanding of how we first become aware of our own spirituality and then embark upon a spiritually active approach to life is still very underdeveloped and 'we need to give far more attention to the education of the human spirit, both in children and adults'. King (2013: 14) further suggests this can be done 'through significant encounters with teachers, friends, or family members … [and] … intergenerational links between the young and the old are also an important resource for inspiring a spiritual awareness in children' (see Chapter 13).

Perhaps the biggest contribution we can make in this respect is by being more pre-pared to listen to young children as they ask questions. It is relatively easy to respond to the straightforward everyday questions that characterise the curious and enquiring mind of a young child. On the other hand, some questions have a special significance and need adults to pay particular attention to the whole child and not just the words they use. Big questions such as 'Who am I?' and 'Why am I here?' require an honesty of response that may not come so easily to adults and often reveal glimpses of a realm we don't always understand. Daly (2004: 224) writes that 'children are spiritual beings and have naturally what adults spend years trying to reclaim'.

In a predominantly secular Western society, we should welcome greater awareness of the spiritual element in life, especially as we have reached a point in history where many young children's lives are shaped by material certainty but may lack relational stability and a sense of value. We can enrich young children's well-being by acknowl-edging and nurturing their spirituality but the challenge is to provide genuine spaces for that to happen while at the same time acknowledging young children's valuable contribution to the development of our own sense of the spiritual.

ACTIVITY

Try writing a definition for what you consider to be your own understanding of spirituality. You might like to begin by talking with a close friend about what you most value in life as that might be a good starting point for your definition. What do you do to remind your-self of your values and how might being more explicit about them support your work with young children?

FURTHER READING

1. For an insight into how an understanding of spirituality informs practice within the health professions consider reading the following:

    Wright, S. (2005) *Reflections on Spirituality and Health.* Chichester: Wiley-Blackwell.

    What can you learn about spirituality from the perspective of health professionals and how might it inform your work with children in the early years?

2. This chapter makes reference to the widespread concern generated by the publication of **UNICEF**'s *Innocenti Report Card 7* in 2007 which presented a very bleak picture of child well-being in the UK. UNICEF published Innocenti Report Card 11 in 2013 which updated the earlier comparison of Child Well-Being in Rich Countries: http://www.unicef-irc.org/publications/pdf/rc11_eng.pdf

    Where have there been improvements and why do you think this is the case?

3. Read a copy of the summary of the latest Good Childhood Report from the **Children's Society** website: http://www.childrenssociety.org.uk/

    Consider the research findings exploring the relationships between children's well-being and a number of factors in their lives. *In what respects do the findings reflect your childhood experiences and what does the report suggest are the biggest influences on children's well-being today?*

WEBSITES

Action for Happiness: http://www.actionforhappiness.org/

Action for Happiness is a movement of people committed to building a happier and more caring society where people care less about what they can get just for themselves and more about the happiness of others. Richard Layard, the author of *Happiness: Lessons from a New Science* (mentioned above in the chapter), is one of the founders of the movement.

British Association for the Study of Spirituality (BASS): http://www.basspirituality.org.uk/

The British Association for the Study of Spirituality aims to facilitate increasing awareness, understanding, respect for and support of people's spirituality, both in professional contexts and the wider community.

International Association for Children's Spirituality (IACS): http://www.childrenspirituality.org/

The International Association for Children's Spirituality seeks to promote and support research and practice in relation to children's spirituality within education and wider contexts of children's care and well-being.

REFERENCES

Adams, K., Hyde, B. and Wooley, R. (2008) *The Spiritual Dimension of Childhood*. London: Jessica Kingsley Publishing.

Best, R. (2000) Introduction: Where are we going with SMSC? *Education for Spiritual, Moral, Social and Cultural Development*. London: Continuum.

Children Act 2004 c.31. London: The Stationery Office. Available at: http://www.legislation.gov.uk/ukpga/2004/31/contents (accessed 21 February 2015).

Collins, J. and Foley, P. (eds) (2008) *Promoting Young Children's Wellbeing: Policy and Practice*. Bristol: The Policy Press.

Comenius, J. (1631/1956) *The School of Infancy* (ed. Ernest M. Eller). Chapel Hill: UNC Press.

Daly, M. (2004) *Developing the Whole Child: The Importance of the Emotional, Social, Moral and Spiritual in Early Years Education and Care*. New York: Edwin Mellin Press.

DCELLS (Department for Children, Education, Lifelong Learning and Skills) (2008) *Framework for Children's Learning for 3–7 Year Olds in Wales*. Cardiff: Welsh Assembly Government.

DCSF (Department for Children, Schools and Families) (2007) *The Children's Plan: Building Brighter Futures*. Norwich: The Stationery Office.

DCSF (Department for Children, Schools and Families) (2008a) *Statutory Framework for the Early Years Foundation Stage: Setting the Standards for Learning, Development and Care for Children from Birth to Five*. Nottingham: DCSF Publications.

DCSF (Department for Children, Schools and Families) (2008b) *Practice Guidance for the Early Years Foundation Stage*. Nottingham: DCSF Publications.

DCSF (Department for Children, Schools and Families) (2008c) *Principles into Practice: Cards for the Early Years Foundation Stage*. Nottingham: DCSF Publications.

De Souza, M. (2009) Spirituality and well being. *International Journal of Children's Spirituality*, 14(3): 181–4.

DfE (Department for Education) (2013) *Early Years Outcomes: A Non-statutory Guide for Practitioners and Inspectors to Help Inform Understanding of Child Development through the Early Years*. London: DfE.

DfE (Department for Education) (2014) *Statutory Framework for the Early Years Foundation Stage: Setting the Standards for Learning, Development and Care for Children from Birth to Five.* London: DfE Publications.

DfES (Department for Education and Skills) (2004) *Every Child Matters: Change for Children.* Nottingham: DfES Publications.

Education Act 1944 c.31 (7 and 8, Geo 6). London: HMSO. Available at: http://www.legislation.gov.uk/ukpga/Geo6/7-8/31/contents (accessed 21 February 2015).

Education Act 2002 c.32. London: The Stationery Office. Available at: http://www.legislation.gov.uk/ukpga/2002/32/contents (accessed 21 February 2015).

Education Reform Act 1988 c.40. London: HMSO. Available at: http://www.legislation.gov.uk/ukpga/1988/40/contents (accessed 21 February 2015).

Elkind, D. (2001) *The Hurried Child: Growing Up Too Fast Too Soon* (3rd edn). Cambridge, MA: Da Capo Press.

Goodliff, G. (2013) Spirituality expressed in creative learning: young children's imaginative play as space for mediating their spirituality. *Early Child Development and Care*, 183(8): 1054–71.

Goouch, K. (2010) Playful teachers, playful pedagogies: intuition, relationships and ideologies. In K. Goouch, *Towards Excellence in Early Years Education: Exploring Narratives of Experience.* London: Routledge.

Hay, D. (2007) *Why Spirituality Is Difficult for Westerners.* Exeter: Societas.

Hay, D. and Nye, R. (2006) *The Spirit of the Child* (2nd edn). London: Jessica Kingsley.

Haynes, J. (2008) *Children as Philosophers: Learning through Enquiry and Dialogue in the Primary Classroom* (2nd edn). Abingdon: Routledge.

Hyde, B. (2008) *Children and Spirituality: Searching for Meaning and Connectedness.* London: Jessica Kingsley.

King, U. (2013) The spiritual potential of childhood: awakening to the fullness of life. *International Journal of Children's Spirituality*, 18(1): 4–17.

Layard, R. (2011) *Happiness: Lessons from a New Science* (2nd edn). London: Penguin.

Layard, R. and Dunn, J. (2009) *A Good Childhood: Searching for Values in a Competitive Age. The Landmark Report for the Children's Society.* London: The Children's Society.

Lee, W., Carr, M., Soutar, B. and Mitchell, L. (2013) *Understanding the Te Whāriki Approach: Early Years Education in Practice.* Abingdon: Routledge.

Meehan, C. (2002) Resolving the confusion in the spiritual development debate. *International Journal of Children's Spirituality*, 7(3): 291–308.

NEF (New Economics Foundation) (2009) *National Accounts of Well-being: Bringing Real Wealth onto the Balance Sheet.* London: NEF.

New Zealand Ministry of Education (1996) *Te Whāriki: He Whāriki Matauranga m ng Mokopuna o Aotearoa: Early Childhood Curriculum.* Wellington: Learning Media.

Nye, R. (1996) Childhood spirituality and contemporary developmental psychology. In R. Best (ed.) *Education, Spirituality and the Whole Child.* London: Cassell.

Ofsted (2004) *Promoting and Evaluating Pupils' Spiritual, Moral, Social and Cultural Development.* London: Ofsted.

ONS (Office for National Statistics) (2012) *Analysis of Experimental Subjective Wellbeing Data from the Annual Population Survey, April to September 2011.* Available at: http://www.ons.gov.uk/ons/dcp171776_257882.pdf (accessed 22 February 2015).

ONS (Office for National Statistics) (2014) *Measuring National Well-being: Children's Well-being, 2014.* Available at: http://www.ons.gov.uk/ons/dcp171776_355140.pdf (accessed 22 February 2015).

Priestley, J. (1997) Spirituality, curriculum and education. *International Journal of Children's Spirituality*, 2(1): 23–34.

Prentice, R. (1996) The spirit of education: a model for the twenty-first century. In R. Best (ed.), *Education, Spirituality and the Whole Child.* London: Cassell.

Roberts, R. (2010) *Wellbeing from Birth.* London: SAGE.

Rose, S. (2001) Is the term 'Spirituality' a word that everyone uses, but nobody knows what anyone means by it? *Journal of Contemporary Religion*, 16(2): 193–207.

School Standards and Framework Act 1998 c.31 London: The Stationery Office. Available at: http://www.legislation.gov.uk/ukpga/1998/31/contents (accessed 21 February 2015).

Spinka, M. (1943) *John Amos Comenius: That Incomparable Moravian.* Chicago, IL: University of Chicago Press.

UNICEF (United Nations Children's Fund) (1989) *UN Convention on the Rights of the Child.* Available at: http://www.unicef.org/crc/ (accessed 28 February 2015).

UNICEF (United Nations Children's Fund) (2007) *Child poverty in perspective: an overview of child well-being in rich countries*, Innocenti Report Card 7. Florence: UNICEF Office of Research.

Vygotsky, L. (1978) *Thought and Language.* London: MIT Press.

Waters, J. (2014) Wellbeing. In T. Waller and G. Davis (eds) *An Introduction to Early Childhood* (3rd edn). London: SAGE.

Part 2

Working with children: extending opportunities for participation

5 Observing children: the importance of personal insight and reflective action

Mandy Andrews and Karen Wickett

Introduction

Children are now widely recognised as having agency and self-reliance in creating their own life journeys. To gain a sense of these experiences and understandings it is necessary for those working with children to closely observe the activity, interests, capability and growth of the children in their care. However, our experiences indicate that many practitioners are still not clear what to observe or why. In fact, in so many cases observation in the nursery becomes a mere jotting down of a few words on a sticky note with a date indicating that the child has met the next adult intended milestone in a form of race towards achievement of the early learning goals (DfE, 2014). Such an approach fails to capture the essence of the individual child. Yet human beings are skilled observers and most practitioners will have observed much about each child they are working with that is not necessarily written down, but will nonetheless inform their practice. What is captured through such observations will have been shaped by our own experiences and understandings. In other words, we bring to the practice of observation our cultural expectations and biases, which will lead us to spot some things, and not others. However, we can extend our own observational understanding by fully engaging in collaborative reflection with others, seeking alternative and wider perspectives to complement our own. This chapter aims to explore a range of understandings about the purpose and processes of observation, including processes of personal awareness, engagement and collaborative reflection.

Above we used the term 'observation', a term which can have different meanings for different people. Other terms, such as 'pedagogical documentation' and 'assessment', can be used interchangeably and form part of the process of 'tuning into the child' (Stern, 2000: 223). We are also aware that there are interpretations and practices that can reduce the activity of observation to a simplistic assessment checklist. Our position in this chapter is that seeing the child, pedagogical documentation (Dahlberg, 2013: 88) and the action of reflection on what we have seen, can all be encompassed by the term 'observation'. Together we recognise that a range of processes of seeing and understanding form a relational developmental journey for child and adult. We recognise that although young children may not always articulate their needs, feelings and understandings verbally they are still effective communicators. A baby a few days old can tell us if they are hungry, tired, uncomfortable or in need of a hug. As we look more closely we can also see and hear their patterns of communication, the effort of movement as they seek muscle control, and their personal emotional responses. Such detailed understanding of the baby requires more than merely 'seeing'.

There has been a long history of observing young children. Perhaps the earliest developmental records of children's development were those noted by Charles Darwin who compiled daily observations of his eldest son's development (Darwin, 1878/2010). Margaret McMillan (1919: 322) advocated that trainee teachers needed observation practice and opportunities to work alongside the skilled observers engaged in implementing what she termed 'The New Scientific Pedagogy' in order to promote children's health, development and education. Montessori, in Italy in the early decades of the 20th century, also promoted observation as a primary activity of the practitioner (Lilliard, 1982). Montessori encouraged us to 'listen to the child' and considered that good practice required humility in the practitioner:

> *Adults must aim to diminish their egocentric and authoritarian attitude towards the child and adopt a passive attitude in order to aid his (or her) development. They must approach children with humility, recognising their role as a secondary one, listening, and responding. (Lilliard, 1982: 79)*

Observation is really about listening as well as looking and involves multisensory engagement and reflection. The practitioner must step back, 'listen' and observe young children as the starting point to understanding them and supporting their development.

A few years later Susan Isaacs, at The Malting House School (1924–1927), advocated close and detailed observation in order to gain an understanding of children and their learning. The value of her detailed and thoughtful observations of children is evidenced by the fact that they are still analysed today (Arnold, 2003). The legacy of Susan Isaacs' work has encouraged us to look 'with attention, at everything that children do (and think and feel) as they live and learn' (Drummond, 2000: n.p.). Isaacs and McMillan recognised that children's learning and development is in part a response to their environment and experiences and therefore is a process that should be seen as individual and unique. Such individuality was also recognised by Steiner (1924) who suggested that a teacher's relationship to children was similar to reading. It is not enough when reading merely to know how to describe individual letters; we bring so much more than that to a story. The relationship of teacher to child 'must constitute a reading of the human being', seeking their essence rather than that 'the letter B is shaped like this, the letter C like that and so on' (Steiner, 1924: 35). Steiner asserted that focusing only on the separate parts 'is similar to an illiterate person who can only describe the forms of letters, but not the book's meaning' (1924: 35).

Isaacs knew of the scientific work of the new developmental psychologists including Piaget, and worked to integrate this increasing theoretical knowledge of child psychology with practical methods of working with children, leading her to advocate for narrative observation and analysis. Whilst some early advocates of observation such as Gesell (1941) emphasised observation as a tool to be used in experimental study of children's development to identify and classify stages of growth, this scientific approach has subsequently been questioned with the rise of a sociocultural understanding. Today we understand that development and learning are a dynamic response to social and environmental factors (Smith and Thelen, 2003; Goswami and Bryant, 2007).

In New Zealand at the turn of the 21st century Margaret Carr (2001) questioned what she called the 'folklore' approach to observations. She realised they were more about checking whether 'nearly school-aged children' had acquired 'the requisite skills for school' (2001: 1) than truly seeing each child as unique. As a young early years teacher she recognises that she had 'looked out for the gaps in a school-readiness repertoire, keeping a checklist, and used some direct teaching strategies to do something about them in the months before school' (2001: 1). Subsequently she had reached a realisation that such an approach was more about her need to prove her own expertise and achievement as a teacher than an appreciative focus on the child. Expressing her discomfort with the checklist approach she moved on to explore the appreciative purposes of observation to identify children's prior knowledge, dispositions and attitudes for learning through richly detailed observations of learning episodes (Carr, 2001; Carr *et al.*, 2009). Carr and her colleagues had found a new way of working with an openness and awareness of their own bias. She came to recognise observation could provide broader recognition of children's existing understandings and cultural experiences beyond the setting. She offered a method of assessment practice which promotes looking carefully to 'describe' what the child is doing, then discussing with others before documenting in order to keep a record that can be shared, and then finally 'deciding' what to do. She offered the concept of 'Learning Stories' (2001), drawing on a range of methods of observation, capturing what children could do, rather than what they could not, including the unexpected and previously not considered. Learning stories were captured in a range of ways and might contain short narrative observations, annotated photographs and comments from the child, parents and colleagues to offer insight into what is seen. This advocacy for observations which 'capture' the child in the moment is in direct opposition to the approach which looks for gaps and deficits in relation to a perceived school readiness (a 'readiness' agenda that we can still see emphasised in Early Childhood Education and Care settings in England today despite widespread awareness of Margaret Carr's work).

Another sociocultural approach with a particular focus on observation is one which sees a positive future arising from children shaping their own worlds. In Italy, after World War II, a new approach to early childhood education was emerging that aimed to enable the child to grow in a way that supported a new future for a community that had been 'pulled apart' by their wartime experiences. The practitioners of Reggio Emilia recognised the value in seeing what children can do, and what they may wish to explore, leaving openings for development of a new society, rather than offering a pre-planned curriculum based on adult understandings of their childhood learning. Again the importance of observation was promoted and this led to systems of documentation designed to gain insights into children's understandings of the world. In Reggio Emilia practitioner and child discussion, arising from observation of interests and achievements, is a mediating tool for understanding the child and for future planning, drawing on both child and adult perspectives. Detailed observations inform discussions with the child about next steps which can be planned and constructed by the adult and child together. Loris Malaguzzi, the principal of Reggio Emilia schools and a recognised Early Childhood pioneer himself, also recognised that the traditional emphasis on early years provision as preparation for school leads to a model that 'ends up as a funnel', the purpose of which is to '...narrow down what is too big into what is small' (cited in Edwards *et al.*, 2011: 63). He wanted to reverse that funnel effect of education, recognising the 'hundred languages' in which children can express themselves: 'a hundred ways of thinking, of playing, of speaking' (cited in Edwards *et al.*, 2011: 3). Malaguzzi recognised the contribution children make to their culture and that they are 'rich in potential, strong, powerful, competent' and connected to others. It was important, he said, to 'leave room for learning'. Just as Montessori had argued for humility and stepping back, so Malaguzzi prompted practitioners to observe, reflect and question their assumptions about what the children were doing. This openness to children's thinking and learning would, he argued, result in more effective teaching and support for children's unique paths of development, but required a commitment to 'seeing, talking and acting in a different way' (Rinaldi, 1994 cited in Scott, 2001: 23). Malaguzzi recognised the hundred languages of children and several 'voices' of teachers, of which one is that of researcher, 'trained to be attentive to what children say and do ... what they are doing in effect is gathering evidence ... It is important to note that this recording and documentation has little or nothing to do with ticking boxes, meeting predetermined goals or passing tests. It is a very human way of gathering evidence about everyday events in the lives of the children and their teachers' (Smidt, 2013: 72).

With greater global awareness of differences across cultures and contexts, the focus of observation shifted to encompass a more sociocultural approach to understanding the child and her/his context. Konner (1991) had observed children at play in a range of communities around the world and Rogoff (2003) recognised that children observe intently as they participate in daily activities in cultural contexts. This is central to the child's process of co-constructing their understanding of how the world works. Thompson and Hall (2008: 89) have suggested that children enter our settings with 'virtual school bags of knowledge, experiences and dispositions'. Another useful concept that captures children's and families' knowledge and experiences is 'funds of knowledge' (Moll *et al.*, 1992). This refers to 'the historically accumulated and culturally developed bodies of knowledge and skills' (Gonzalez *et al.*, 2005: 133) that are constructed by children and community members when participating in daily tasks. As observers we need to be open to these possibly unfamiliar and different ways of seeing the world, as close observation may reveal how children not only mimic but also adapt an activity and take it to a new level as they internalise their understanding.

Deleuze and Guattari's work (1987) argues for a more 'rhizomatic' approach to observation which recommends that we do not pick the technique first according to our expected needs, but should be prepared to 'let go' and allow the observation to follow the child's lead. A rhizome is a root that 'buds' outwards in different directions (think of a ginger root, for example). The rhizomatic approach aligns with process approaches to engagement, outlined above, and may begin with a narrative approach that merely intends to capture something, but then identifies from the first observation that there are many ways forward, and choices must be made as to which to follow first. 'The Rhizome operates by variation, expansion, conquest, capture, offshoot...' (Deleuze and Guattari, 1987: 21). It is the detailed seeing, combined with reflective practice, that gives the greatest depth of understanding. This and the process of reflecting with others has, over the course of time, made us aware of six guiding principles which inform our understanding of observation.

Our principles for observation

Principle 1: Awareness of our beliefs and how these shape what we notice

As observers, we have constructed unique understandings and beliefs about the world throughout our life course (Elder, 1988). Our experiences not only shape our understandings of the world but also inform our values, principles and beliefs. It will be these that will guide us during our personal and professional lives. Chapter 6 discusses how our beliefs and principles guide our practice when creating 'enabling environments' for young children's learning. However, these will also guide us when we observe children. These implicit theories will influence what we observe during children's learning and development and our 'judgements and interpretations' (Clark, 1988: 6). We should be aware of our long-held beliefs and understandings, but also sometimes be brave enough to challenge them, especially where they could limit children's learning by excluding awareness of their existing 'funds of knowledge'. Rogoff (2003) points out how we often view a child at play as a lone explorer, dissociating them from their cultural and environmental situation. We choose to foreground and background certain aspects of the things we see as if one is more important and the other is a secondary influence. These selections may not even be conscious but our focus on the individual could mean that we fail to acknowledge even the social and cultural relationships between two children playing next to each other.

Principle 2: Respect for the child

Our second principle is an ethical one of moral purpose and respect. We should not fool ourselves that we can observe children without having an impact on what they do; the very fact of our being there places an adult in a child's culture. Children will get used to seeing observers nearby, or cameras in the corner, but will be aware of their presence and may adjust their behaviour as a result. Else (2009: 57) writes of adults' impact on children's play as 'adulteration'. Our moral purpose is to observe with respect and to see the child as a being in their own right, not a specimen to be controlled. Moss (2013) indicates that, from birth, a 'rich child' has a strong drive and need to make sense of the world and is active in the process of constructing knowledge and social understandings with us. This is illustrated by the example below.

Karen noticed a child playing in the home corner. Before entering the home corner she knocked on the door (a bookcase). The child said, 'Come in! Do you want a cup of tea?' Karen replied, 'Yes please – green tea please'. The child said 'I don't have green tea but brown tea'. He pretended to fill the kettle with water from the sink tap, put the kettle on the cooker to boil, went to the cupboard to find a cup and teabag and continued to follow the rules of making and giving a cup of tea. By observing others he would have learnt how to make tea and that tea is brown. Therefore, we must appreciate that children's social, cultural and historical context influences and shapes their learning and development (Hedegaard and Fleer, 2008). A child who has had different experiences and consequently different understandings of making tea will construct a different narrative.

Principle 3: Observation is not a passive activity

'What we see depends on what we look for' (Devereux, 1996: 1). Our third principle is that, while many may consider that observing children is a neutral and passively objective role, even when observing children informally we are making conscious or unconscious decisions about how to watch and what to notice, thereby capturing different elements. The observer is active in both their selection of what to observe, and the nature of the analysis during and after the process, though they may not be aware of the choices they are making. Taguchi (2010), for example, warns against the use of 'habitual developmental thinking' that limits our perspective and prevents us from visiting the child's world.

Helen Bilton argues that it is important to appreciate the significance of non-verbal indicators through 'behaviour and gestures and not dialogue' (2010: 172). She was looking for children's ability to plan, monitor, control and evaluate their own work. She asserts that it is children's actions, not only their words, that reveal such evaluative activity. Think here perhaps of a child or group of children admiring a den they have built, standing quietly looking at it and then clapping their hands with pleasure. Here 'a job well done' is indicated through the children's physical actions, not by verbal communication (see Chapter 3).

Principle 4: 'Reflecting through different lenses'

We have already recognised that we see what we look for and that we should be self-aware when observing children, acknowledging our own stance or position. One strategy for such awareness is to actively engage in reflection with others, including parents, colleagues, children and other professionals. Through such reflective dialogue we can find other perspectives and interpretations than our own. Consideration of different perspectives from a few observers with appreciation of the different 'lenses' that colleagues may bring, can help us to gain further depth in our own understandings of both the child and ourselves (see Chapter 10).

Limiting children

Karen and her team did not encourage superhero play in the nursery as usually the boys would run around being very noisy and playing with guns. When discussing the play together the team realised that they did not approve of guns, they thought the running around was chaotic and pointless and that other children were being hurt. All agreed that planning for these opportunities was difficult and when the game was stopped the boys were angry and their behaviour became aggressive. It was easy for us to believe it was the gun play that made them aggressive. However, as a team we realised through reflecting upon action (Schön, 1991) that stopping the play was not a satisfactory outcome, as the children were then unhappy and not enjoying nursery. Together we reminded ourselves that children were competent and capable and that they were developing their understandings of the world they had constructed beyond the setting. We decided that several of us should observe the children and then discuss what was happening. We were all surprised when we observed the children constructing a story line, planning and negotiating rules. Each character had objects that had a different super power. The pencils could shoot fire, the hoops could catch baddies, the balls told time and were compasses. When we observed more closely we noticed that each superhero had these objects but they were the same colour, so the children had sorted the colours into groups and themes. We also found that the running around was in fact carefully planned and performed so no other child's play was disturbed and no one was hurt. It was then decided to document the stories in the boys' superhero play and share them with other children in the setting. It became apparent that each story had a strong sense of justice. Also on reflection the boys did not become angry with the practitioners. They were happier, wanted to come to nursery and were delighted that the stories were being shared and valued.

This seeking the other also includes being open to, and appreciating, the many and varied ways that children interpret the world, challenging our 'taken for granted' view of how things are.

Principle 5: Enjoy the process!

Observation of children should be enjoyable and will be enlightening. It is a means of engagement with and insight into the child's world. Increasingly there is an argument for a process-orientated approach to understanding the child, revisiting the child's world and attempting to identify, through detailed observation and careful reflection, what is really going on, who with, and in what context (Dahlberg *et al.*, 1999; Rogoff, 2003). Drawing on playwork theory we can look to Hughes (2001) who argues for a 'reflective analytic practice' in which practitioners reflectively immerse themselves in children's activities at a depth that enables new and important insights regarding the mechanisms and motivations behind it to emerge. He recognises that this immersion has 'the effect of opening up long-forgotten sensory and affective play memories' that allow the playworker 'not to be in the cockpit with the child, but certainly flying in parallel' (Hughes, 2001: 183).

Again we see this idea of humility, of stepping back and not being in the driving seat. Through experiencing with and alongside the child the practitioner can unlock an understanding of the child's experience and consequent meaning. In a new process approach to observation practitioners seek to capture something more of the essence of the child and their dispositions and interests in play than mere progress towards set goals. These are respectful educators, who are also active participants in the learning and listening process (Nutbrown, 1996).

In observing thoughtfully we may also find joy and remind ourselves of those phenomena which we experienced and learnt as a child and perhaps now take for granted. The process of consciously observing, with a level of immersion and appreciation of what the child can do rather than what they cannot, encourages us to slow down and notice in detail what is interesting and fascinating to young children. These are things we will often overlook. Consider how, for instance, children will stop and marvel at a spider's web on a dewy morning, or explore the shapes thrown by ice on a frozen puddle, or even puzzle over the construction of a den. Through the eyes of the child we are also reminded of such phenomena, and of fundamentally satisfying and challenging activities, and dispositions of eager curiosity which we may forget and overlook in our busy lives. This insight brings us closer to the child's world.

Principle 6: Seeing and challenging policy expectations

Our final principle is the maintenance of a questioning approach to policy and guidance. It is not only our own life experiences, values and beliefs that can limit children's learning and marginalise their funds of knowledge, but also adherence to a narrow interpretation of government policy expectations. Currently children at the end of the Early Years Foundation Stage (EYFS) are expected to reach the 17 Early Learning Goal (ELG) descriptors (STA, 2013). Practitioners are expected to make judgements through 'ongoing observation and assessment in the three prime and four specific areas of learning, and the three characteristics of effective learning' (STA, 2013: 4). In the EYFSP Handbook the purpose of this political guidance is stated as:

- To inform parents about their child's development against the ELGs and the characteristics of their learning.

- To support a smooth transition to key stage 1 by informing the professional discussion between EYFS and key stage 1 teachers.

- To help year 1 teachers plan an effective, responsive and appropriate curriculum that will meet the needs of all children. (STA, 2013: 7)

Unfortunately this can again reduce practitioners' observations to 'hunting' (Parker-Rees, 2014) for certain skills and knowledge to check if children are 'conforming to a set of standards' (Dahlberg *et al.*, 1999: 146). In consciously making choices the observer is politically active. Mac Naughton (2005) reminds her readers that even within Early Childhood services there are common understandings, normalised 'regimes of truth', which are presented by researchers, local authorities, or government bodies and become understandings to which practitioners may adhere without thinking. Such 'regimes of truth', she argues, are practices of power and control that, rather than being brought into the nursery and perpetuated, can be questioned. The practitioner does not need to be the powerful judge as shown in the following example.

> Sally was sharing an observation she had written about Simon with Karen. She read from her observation, 'Simon can stand momentarily on one foot when shown'. When Karen replied, 'Okay, we can tick that you have seen the child stand on one foot in the area of Physical Development (30–50 months) [looking at Early Education, 2012: 24], but what does this tell us about the child's interests and learning?' The practitioner replied, 'We need to plan for him to stand on the other foot'!
>
> We can be prevented from noticing what children can do by our individual understandings and beliefs, led by technical adherence to policy. These can prevent us from listening to children. The limited view arising from the practitioner's observation of the child above did not in fact allow for insight into the child's understanding of the world or recognition that learning and development is culturally situated. The observation merely demonstrated an aspect of physical development and that the child could carry out an instruction.

Dahlberg (2013) reminds us that the formal skills and knowledge that practitioners are expected to observe are in fact evident through children's play and learning:

Of course, maths, language and science are important. But if we only looked and listened … children were using maths all the time. We prefer to test and diagnose at a distance rather than participate to better understand what children are doing, for example through pedagogical documentation. (2013: 88)

'Hunting' for certain skills and knowledge (Parker-Rees, 2014) can position a child in deficit and does not allow for acknowledgement of the family cultures and the child's funds of knowledge. 'Gathering' appreciative narrative observations gives greater detail and enables deconstruction and reconstruction of meaning (Mac Naughton, 2005). The narrative or annotated observation is a 'text' recording an experience, and we can revisit these as 'fragments' of a child's life and way of being for greater understanding. We can ask how these data fragments can connect to each other, who was present in the observations, how the context influences the action, how the narrative fragments fit together and how they connect with the observer (Mac Naughton, 2005).

It has been noted that a further challenge for adults when they are with children is that the systems of our Western society are dominated by speaking and not listening (Back, 2007) and it is generally those with the appropriate authority and knowledge who are listened to (Belenky *et al.*, 1986). Children in some situations may be expected to be silent and listen to adults. In his famous poem, *The Hundred Languages of Children*, Malaguzzi claims 'The school and the culture (prompts children) … To listen and not to speak' (Edwards *et al.*, 1998: 3). In the earlier examples of practice the practitioners were uncomfortable as the boys' movements seemed out of control until they took time to look, listen and question. In the second example where the boy stood on one leg he had to listen to the instruction of the adult, who in turn was being prevented from listening and seeing by her awareness of policy expectations.

Considering methods of observation

There are many different ways to approach observation of children. You will have noticed that we have had little to say about observation methods in this chapter. We believe that the openness and reflective awareness of a practitioner to 'tune into' the child is of paramount importance. The selection of the methods is secondary to this principle and follows from the aim and intention of child and practitioner in context. We support a narrative style of recording, together with use of other forms of documentary evidence: photographs, artefacts, notes from parents and carers, and communication with the child in a form of scrapbook selection. However, awareness of a range of methods aligned to perspectives can form part of a principled, ethical approach to observation. At the end of this chapter we offer some reading that may support you in further exploration of a range of observation methods.

Conclusion

In our discussion on observation we have identified six key principles:

1. Act with self-awareness
2. Respect the child and act with moral purpose
3. Observation is not a passive activity
4. Reflection is important to interpret and assess what we have seen
5. Enjoy the process
6. Feel confident to challenge policy expectations

ACTIVITY

Now that you have read the chapter take a moment to consider how it has affected the way you think about observation.

- *Consider how you draw on observations in your work*
- *Do you tend to use observation as a developmental checklist or as an appreciative seeking of children's lead, their interests and capabilities?*
- *What do you do with your observations?*
- *Is there opportunity to discuss these with your friends and colleagues?*
- *What are your and your colleagues' definitions of the practices and processes of observation?*

Podmore, V. and Luff, P. (2012) *Observation: Origins and Approaches in Early Childhood.* Maidenhead: Open University Press.

In this book Valerie Podmore and Paulette Luff discuss observation practices in both the New Zealand and English context. The comparison offers interesting insights into the practices of observation that are often taken for granted. The authors also discuss different observational techniques and approaches.

Willan, J. (2009) Revisiting Susan Isaacs – a modern educator for the twenty-first century. *International Journal of Early Years Education*, 17(2): 151–65.

Jenny Willan discusses the life and work of Susan Isaacs and her contribution to the practices of ECEC practitioners in her day. This article develops our discussion by also providing examples of Isaacs' observations and also considering what we can learn today from Isaacs' practice.

Arnold, C. (2003) *Observing Harry.* Maidenhead: McGraw-Hill.

Back, L. (2007) *The Art of Listening.* Oxford: Berg Publishers.

Belenky, M.F., Clinchy, B.M., Goldberg, N.R. and Tarule, J.M. (1986) *Women's Ways of Knowing: The Development of Self, Voice, and Mind.* New York: Basic Books.

Bilton, H. (2010) *Outdoor Learning in the Early Years: Management and Innovation* (3rd edn). London: David Fulton.

Carr, M. (2001) *Assessment in Early Childhood Settings: Learning Stories.* London: Paul Chapman Publishing.

Carr, M., Smith, A. and Duncan, J. (2009) *Learning in the Making: Disposition and Design in Early Education.* Rotterdam: Sense.

Clark, C.M. (1988) Asking the right questions about teacher preparation: contributions of research on teacher thinking. *Educational Researcher*, 17(2): 5–12.

Dahlberg, G. (2013) A dialogue with the co-author of 'the vision of a meeting place'. In P. Moss (ed.) *Early Childhood and Compulsory Education: Reconceptualising the Relationship.* Abingdon: Routledge.

Dahlberg, G., Moss, P. and Pence, A. (1999) *Beyond Quality in Early Childhood Education and Care: Postmodern Perspectives.* London: Routledge Falmer.

Darwin, C. (1878/2010) Biographical sketch of an infant. *Annals of Neurosciences*, 17(4): 187–90.

Deleuze, G. and Guattari, F. (1987) *A Thousand Plateaus: Capitalism and Schizophrenia.* London: Athlone Press/Continuum.

Devereux, J. (1996) What we see is what we look for: observation as part of teaching and learning in the Early Years. In S. Robson and S. Smedley (eds), *Education in Early Childhood.* London: David Fulton.

DfE (Department for Education) (2014) *Statutory Framework for the Early Years Foundation Stage: Setting the Standards for Learning, Development and Care for Children from Birth to Five.* London: DfE Publications.

Drummond, M.J. (2000) Comparisons in early years education: history, fact and fiction. *Early Childhood Research and Practice*, 2(1): n.p. Available at: http://ecrp.uiuc.edu/v2n1/drummond.html (accessed 28 February 2015).

Early Education (2012) *Development Matters in the Early Years Foundation Stage (EYFS).* London: Early Education.

Edwards, C., Gandini, L. and Foreman, G. (1998) *The Hundred Languages of Children: The Reggio Emilia Experience in Transformation.* London: Ablex.

Elder, G. (1998) The life course as development theory. *Child Development*, 69(1): 1–12.

Else, P. (2009) *The Value of Play*. London: Continuum.

Gesell, A. (1941) *The First Five Years of Life: A Guide to the Study of the Pre-School Child*. London: Methuen.

Gonzalez, N., Moll, L.C. and Amanti, C. (2005) *Funds of Knowledge: Theorizing Practices in Households, Communities, and Classrooms*. Abingdon: Taylor & Francis.

Goswami, U. and Bryant, P. (2007) *Children's Cognitive Development and Learning*. Cambridge: University of Cambridge Faculty of Education. Available at: http://www.cne.psychol.cam.ac.uk/pdfs/publication-pdfs/PrimaryReview_Goswami_Bryant_2007.pdf (accessed 23 January 2015).

Hedegaard, M. and Fleer, M. (2008) *Studying Children: A Cultural-Historical Approach*. Maidenhead: Open University Press.

Hughes, B. (2001) *Evolutionary Playwork and Reflective Analytic Practice*. London: Routledge.

Konner, M. (1991) *Childhood: A Multicultural View*. London: Little, Brown and Company.

Lilliard, P.P. (1982) *Montessori: A Modern Approach*. London: Arrow.

McMillan, M. (1919) *The Nursery School*. London: J. M. Dent & Sons, Limited.

Mac Naughton, G. (2005) *Doing Foucault in Early Childhood Studies: Applying Poststructural Ideas*. Abingdon: Routledge.

Moll, L.C., Amanti, C., Neff, D. and Gonzalez, N. (1992) Funds of knowledge for teaching: using a qualitative approach to connect homes and classrooms. *Theory into Practice*, 31(2): 132–41.

Moss, P. (ed.) (2013) *Early Childhood and Compulsory Education: Reconceptualising the Relationship*. Abingdon: Routledge.

Nutbrown, C. (ed.) (1996) *Respectful Educators – Capable Learners: Children's Rights and Early Education*. London: SAGE.

Parker-Rees, R. (2014) Hunting and gathering: two distinct forms of learning from play. In J. Moyles (ed.), *The Excellence of Play* (4th edn). Maidenhead: Open University Press/McGraw Hill.

Rogoff, B. (2003) *The Cultural Nature of Human Development*. Oxford: Oxford University Press.

Schön, D. (1991) *The Reflective Practitioner: How Professionals Think in Action*. Surrey: Ashgate Publishing Limited.

Scott, W. (2001) Listening and learning. In L. Abbott and C. Nutbrown (eds), *Experiencing Reggio Emilia: Implications for Pre-School Provision*. London: Routledge.

Smidt, S. (2013) *Introducing Malaguzzi: Exploring the Life and Work of Reggio Emilia's Founding Father*. London: Routledge.

Smith, L.B. and Thelen, E. (2003) Development as a dynamic system. *Trends in Cognitive Sciences*. 7(8): 343–8.

STA (2013) *The Early Years Foundation Stage Profile Handbook*. London: Department for Education.

Steiner, R. (1924) Lecture Three, Stuttgart, Morning, 10 April. In R. Steiner (1997) *The Essentials of Education*. New York: Anthroposophic Press.

Stern, D. (2000) *The Interpersonal World of the Infant: A View from Psychoanalysis and Developmental Psychology*. New York: Basic Books.

Taguchi, H.L. (2010) *Going Beyond the Theory Practice Divide in Early Childhood Education: Introducing an Intra-active Pedagogy*. London: Routledge.

Thomson, P. and Hall, C. (2008) Opportunities missed and/or thwarted? 'Funds of knowledge' meet the English National Curriculum. *Curriculum Journal*, 19(2): 87–103.

6 Providing an enabling environment

Karen Wickett and Philip Selbie

Introduction

One of the fascinating and unique aspects of working with babies and young children is that learning 'happens' and as it happens the learners become more engaged with their environment. At the same time they become more aware of themselves and their potential to discover and explore their surroundings. Learning appears to be a cyclical process; when observing very young children their natural curiosity to discover seems to indicate that learning is already 'energised', it feeds off itself and has the potential to continue indefinitely. The environment makes a significant contribution to this process and when the conditions are less than supportive, the quality of the process, if not the process itself, is threatened.

This chapter is partly about learning but more importantly it is about the 'places and spaces' in which this process takes place. Some of them are visible to us in the sense that we can see them, plan them and arrange them. However, we believe that some are not so clearly identifiable. We aim to highlight the significance and value of these places and spaces in supporting the learning process while encouraging practitioners to develop professionally at the same time.

The Early Years Foundation Stage (EYFS) identifies 'Enabling Environments' as one of its themes and suggests that practitioners are guided by the principle that 'children learn and develop well in *enabling environments*' (DfE, 2014: 5). Within these environments there should be opportunities for children and adults to foster relationships, to develop their thinking and ideas, to grow emotionally and spiritually, to contribute to the culture of the learning community and, of course, to develop physically.

The learning environments that practitioners encounter are as multifaceted, dynamic and evolving as the young children who inhabit them on their developing learning journeys. The Cambridge Primary Review (Alexander, 2010: 90) highlights the greater recognition that now exists 'of the inter-relatedness of the biological, social, emotional and intellectual aspects of children's psychological make-up and their dependence on the socio-cultural environment'. Children are very competent, capable and active learners. As the process of learning in the early years supports a child's growth, the environments where this learning happens play a considerable role in 'enabling' the learner.

Enabling environments also influence and contribute to young learners' developing awareness of themselves as competent individuals. Allied to this view of the competent child is the recognition that learning begins first and foremost with the child. Learning is not something that can ever be done 'to the child' or 'for the child'. It is surely something that must be carefully revealed from within the child, as they participate in activities with us.

Starting with the child

Over 40 years ago the Plowden report (CACE, 1967: 9) boldly declared that 'at the heart of the educational process lies the child' and championed the cause of play as a way of enabling the learning process for all children. Although there have been significant influences that have shaped early years practice in recent years, the principle of 'starting with the child' remains as powerful in guiding practice today as it did over 40 years ago. All high quality learning begins by putting the learners at the centre and appreciating that the child is a partner in the process of constructing the environment based on their interests and their fascinations. Echoing some of the spirit of the Plowden era, the EYFS (DfE, 2014) has remained committed to keeping the child at the centre of the learning process. It also acknowledges the uniqueness of every young child, and most significantly, it recognises the status of babies as active learners.

The EYFS emphasises once more the importance of a play-based approach when planning learning and it is important to note here the contribution that play makes to the environment in which powerful learning occurs. Play makes a significant contribution to early learning and as Moyles (2005: 35) states, 'play is a means by which babies and young children explore their environment and the people that are special to them'. This idea is also a feature of the EYFS: 'Play is essential for children's development, building their confidence as they learn to explore, to think about problems, and relate to others' (DfE, 2014: 9).

Whenever and wherever play is encouraged, babies and young children will be learning through exploration both at a practical level but also in self discovery. Learners will be discovering more about themselves and their own capabilities; as Friedrich Fröbel (1782–1852) stated long ago, 'Play is the highest expression of human development in childhood for it alone is the free expression of what is in a child's soul' (Fletcher and Welton, 1912: 50).

The legacy of the early pioneers and the more recent introduction of government legislation that puts children and play at the heart of early learning is one thing but how do such aspirations become realised for young learners? In addition, what relationship is there between policies on the one hand and the places and spaces in which practitioners can provide high quality, transformative learning experiences for children?

A principled approach

Most early years practitioners who work with or study babies and young children welcome the recognition by policy makers of the importance of the earliest years of a child's life and of the need to provide an enabling environment for them. However, there are challenges to overcome as the constant advice, intervention and expectations from government can be overwhelming at times. In order not to succumb to these external pressures practitioners should consider what they believe our youngest children might need in their earliest experiences in order to lead full and satisfying lives, not only in the future but also at the present time. As Nutbrown asks:

> *'What sort of things might be good for them to do? What kinds of adults might be best suited to their needs and the ways in which they spend their time? These are important questions whatever our working context, culture or country.'* (Nutbrown, 2001: 112)

When making decisions which affect the learning environment, such as the type of resources to be provided or the role of the adult in children's learning, practitioners must be guided by their own principles. It is essential that practitioners understand and are able to articulate their principles for as Edgington (2004: 16) states 'teachers whose work is not underpinned by principles which they can back up with research evidence are less likely to be able to see a clear direction for the development of their practice'. Practitioners should be provided with opportunities to reflect on the decisions they make and to consider the principles that underpin their work.

Such a process will also support them in articulating their beliefs and their understanding of children as learners and their role in the process, so they will be able to enter into dialogue with others and confidently explain their actions in a clear and informed manner. This is particularly important in times when increasing attention from policymakers can cause confusion for practitioners and result in them losing sight of their vision. The Cambridge Primary Review draws attention to this by stating early in its report that 'it is the principles by which productive teaching is underpinned which should first command teachers' attention' (Alexander, 2010: 7).

Competent learners

History has given us different images of the child as a learner, from Locke (1632–1704) who declared that adults played a crucial role in the learning process, to Rousseau (1712–1778) who claimed that children would develop naturally and that there should be minimal intervention by adults (see Chapter 13). Locke viewed the child's mind as blank or empty and in need of being filled, stating that 'The senses at first let in particular ideas, and furnish the yet empty cabinet...' (Locke, 1689/1824: para 146). On the other hand, Rousseau professed that children learn through experiences and exhorted adults to 'Give nature time to work before you take over her business, lest you interfere with her dealings' (Rousseau, 1762/1911: 71).

After the Second World War and as the new preschools of Reggio Emilia were beginning to develop, Loris Malaguzzi (1920–1994) stated that children are 'rich in potential, strong, powerful, competent and, most of all, connected to adults and other children' (in Penn, 1997: 117). Those who let their principles guide their image of the child as a competent learner found a new opportunity to consider the interests of the children. One of the principles that guided Malaguzzi and his colleagues was that 'things about children and for children are only learned from children' (1998: 51). As the preschool buildings arose out of the desolation and empty destruction of the past, the future for the next generation was being built upon the needs of the present one.

Most recently, our view of babies and young children as competent learners has been influenced by technology that has introduced us to new ways of examining the marvels of the brain. Babies' lifelong, developmental journey commences in the womb and at birth a baby is born with a brain that contains most of the neurons or nerve cells it will ever have. This number will remain almost the same until around the age of 65, although a considerable amount of 'rewiring' of connections takes place after birth and especially in the early years. Babies have already been active in the process of making sense of their experiences in the womb, and are ready to continue learning in their new world from the moment they are born. As Gopnik *et al.* (1999: 142) state, 'babies are born with powerful programs already booted up and ready to run'.

The theme of the 'Unique Child' states that 'every child is a unique child, who is constantly learning and can be resilient, capable, confident and self-assured (DfE, 2014: 6). We might even ask whether babies, young children and, for that matter, adults are ever not inclined to learn. Indeed, Gerhardt (2004: 18) states:

> Each little human organism is born a vibrating, pulsating symphony of different body rhythms and functions, which co-ordinate themselves through chemical and electrical messages.

More recently, neuroscientists have suggested that babies and adults have very similar mechanisms for learning. Adults and young children are not receivers of knowledge, but instead active participants in the learning process. Through participating in activities with other children and/or adults, children will learn about themselves, others and the world. Therefore, when children arrive at an Early Childhood Education and Care (ECEC) setting they will bring with them 'virtual school bags of knowledge, experiences and dispositions' (Thomson and Hall, 2008: 89).

Recognising the journey

When planning the learning environment, practitioners need to take into account each child's unique journey and the virtual school bag they bring with them. Within the EYFS it is an expectation that practitioners use their and parents' observations of children to 'shape learning experiences for each child reflecting those observations' (DfE, 2014: 13).

Margaret Carr developed 'Learning Stories' (2001) as a framework to document children's learning. Practitioners record in writing what they see and photographs are used to support the writing. After the learning story is written it is analysed using five domains of learning dispositions: 'Taking an Interest', 'Being Involved', 'Persisting with Difficulty', 'Expressing an Idea or a Feeling' and 'Taking Responsibility'. Carr claims that this process 'sharpens the focus on important features of children's learning' (2001: 137) which then enables practitioners to listen to the children, have open minds and plan environments informed by the children's interests, development and learning. Therefore, 'they help practitioners to construct a learning community with shared values, and they extend that community out to the families' (2001: 141). Including parents in this process of planning and assessing learning through discussion gives value to the culture of the home and the community as partners in the learning process. Not only does this approach recognise and value learning as a process but it also helps us 'to bring learning into view, so that it can be seen, reflected upon and discussed' (Luff, 2007: 192).

Having considered the centrality of the unique child, a principled approach and an informed view of the learner, we now turn our attention to asking where it is that these 'spaces for learning' exist and what are the different ways they support learning for babies and young children?

Enabling environments inside and outside

Whether it is in the womb before birth, in the home or in the garden, in the role-play area or in the sandpit, a physical place is where we can naturally observe learning taking place. First-hand sensory experiences, which involve young children doing practical things such as sitting or standing, looking or listening, talking or touching, provide opportunities for learning to take place. In a literal sense learning happens in a physical space; it is located in a place *somewhere*.

Places such as these support the process of learning, sometimes with the involvement of an adult who may plan the resourcing, but on many occasions these places enable learning by virtue of their very nature. They are 'cradles for learning': places which foster the natural curiosity of young children to explore and discover the potential of the environment as well as the potential within themselves.

Maria Montessori (1870–1952) quickly recognised the powerful potential for learning that could be realised by matching a supportive environment to a strong disposition to learn. In her work with young children in her 'Casa dei Bambini' in Rome at the beginning of the 20th century, Montessori recognised the power of the environment both to enable and to hamper the learning of young children. She was astounded to observe that many schools were poorly equipped and not suitable for young children and so quickly set about 'having school equipment made proportionate to the size of the children that satisfied the need they had of moving about intelligently' (Montessori, 1948/1967: 46).

Montessori believed in 'setting the child free' by removing obstacles to their natural desire for independence and mastery of their world both physically and intellectually. This was developed further as Montessori observed that the children she worked with were particularly attuned to a sense of order during the first two years of life. These early discoveries provided the foundation for the development of the Montessori Method which still continues to emphasise the physical environment and practical activities during the first six years of a child's life. Montessori referred to this as the period of the 'absorbent mind' which 'reflected her belief that children in this stage were engaged primarily in absorbing sensory perceptions and information from their environment' (Gutek, 2004: 50).

The importance of the outdoor space, and in particular the garden, was evident in the writings and practice of early pioneers such as Friedrich Fröbel in the 19th century and Margaret McMillan and Susan Isaacs in the 20th century. McMillan believed that a healthy body was necessary for a healthy mind (Bilton, 2002: 26) and set up her first open-air nursery in Deptford, London in 1914, arguing that 'the best classroom and the richest cupboard is roofed only by the sky' (in Ouvry, 2003: 5). As the 20th century came to a close the use of the outdoors for early learning on a widespread scale received relatively little attention from practitioners who, for a variety of reasons, ranging from poor funding to insufficient training, often failed to exploit the enormous potential of the nursery garden.

The use of the outdoors has regained recognition again following the introduction of the EYFS, as there is a clear recognition that 'outdoor play is central to young children's learning, possibly more to some children than others' (Bilton, 2002: xii). Not long before the introduction of the EYFS, the *Learning Outside the Classroom Manifesto* (DfES, 2006) set out the government's vision of enabling every young person to experience the world beyond the classroom as an essential part of their learning and personal development. One of the aims of the document was to support the potential for learning from direct experience coupled with the belief that *how* and *where* young children learn was as important as *what* they learn.

Within the EYFS, the outdoors is now valued as much as the indoors and therefore practitioners are encouraged to plan both outside and inside learning environments, so that children 'have the confidence to explore and learn in secure and safe, yet challenging, indoor and outdoor spaces' (DCSF, 2007: card 3.3). The outdoor learning environment is no longer seen purely as a place for children to release excess energy while practitioners take a step back. Instead it is now recognised as a valued learning environment in itself, where children should be able to spend considerable time learning, developing, playing and exploring alongside involved practitioners. Just as practitioners observe and plan for children's learning inside, there is now an expectation that this practice will continue outdoors too. For example, if a child is observed enjoying making marks inside then they should also be able to make marks outside through the provision of paint brushes and buckets of water or through encouragement to explore naturally occurring resources such as sticks and muddy puddles.

The outdoor environment adds a valuable dimension to the learning opportunities available to children and gives them direct first-hand opportunities to develop their learning independently as well as with others. Growing acknowledgement by practitioners of the potential for learning in the outdoor environment is helping to underline the notion that conceptual boundaries between learning inside and learning outside may exist in the minds of some adults, but only in a small minority of children.

Enabling environments in the community

The *Learning Outside the Classroom Manifesto* also stated that settings need to 'identify ways of encouraging parents, carers and the wider community in learning outside the classroom activities' (DfES, 2006: 20). For instance a piece of research undertaken by Karen explored how to extend children's learning using the resources of the community. Practitioners had observed that a group of three-year-old boys were interested in motorbikes so they arranged to take them to a motorbike shop.

During the visit the boys took pictures of the motorbikes, helmets and other pieces of motorbike paraphernalia. They returned to the nursery and developed the storyline of their play by including what they had learned during the visit to the shop. Not only were practitioners making links with the community but they were also enhancing the boys' experiences with their families, as one father had told a practitioner that he often took his son to the motorbike races. This child had instigated the motorbike theme with his friends. From these opportunities to make links between the setting, the community and home, the children gained some long-term, deep learning experiences about themselves as learners and about their world. Their new learning was embedded in a context which made sense and which built on their existing understanding and experiences (Wickett and Huggins, 2011).

The EYFS encourages practitioners to recognise the wider context of a child's learning and development, for instance in their local community and home life. Beyond the immediate boundaries of the setting there are many opportunities to extend children's learning and make connections between learning within the setting and in the community.

Environments as enabling places

We have identified some of the environments where learning happens and what those environments might look like and so it now remains to explore how different environments 'enable' young children's learning in different ways. Learning outdoors will, by its very nature, provide more space and greater sensory stimulation and practitioners may use these features in order to support the learning process. The womb is another rich learning environment for the developing foetus and is one that naturally supports the learning process even before a baby is born. However, to what extent can some learning environments be more consciously arranged by practitioners and contribute more deliberately to the learning process?

Loris Malaguzzi is well known for his belief in the environment as the 'third educator' (Forman and Fyfe, 2011: 266). This aptly describes the important role played by the environment in partnership with children and adults as they in turn co-discover learning in a way so crucial to the Reggio Emilia philosophy. Every Reggio preschool has a space known as the 'atelier' which might be described as a workshop or studio where children and adults discover and research their interests together. These studios are designed to engage children in skills and techniques; they are places where children master the skills needed to realise creative ideas and bring projects to life. Many individual classrooms also have an atelier, an environment which supports adults as they observe children investigating and expressing themselves as the learning process becomes visible and can be documented and shared with others. It is a feature of the Reggio Emilia philosophy that 'young children are encouraged to explore their environment and express themselves through all of their available expressive, communicative and cognitive languages' (Edwards *et al.*, 1988: 7).

Whether it is purpose built or a carefully used space within a refurbished building, every Reggio preschool is designed with attention to detail and a creative use of light and colour. Each preschool has a central piazza designed for children and adults to meet and perform together while the space for eating together is generally at the heart of the preschool and close to the open plan area where food is prepared. There is a deliberately planned relationship between the function and beauty of the architectural spaces and the potential for learning in the children and adults that inhabit them. Bishop (in Nutbrown, 2006: 73) expresses this relationship well when he states:

> *The unique qualities of each building come not from the formal arrangement of parts but from the pragmatic relationship between person and place, detail and material, building and building, building and site.*

The contribution of the environment to enabling young children's learning is also a feature of Steiner Waldorf Kindergartens where emphasis is given to ensuring that the space in which children play is carefully arranged by the practitioner to maximise the interaction with the environment and thereby the child's learning. Early learning experiences will develop in a space that is conducive to child-initiated activities and Steiner practitioners make sure that 'the physical environment is treated with a degree of care and reverence which goes beyond the concern for quality and aesthetics which marks good practice in any early years setting' (Parker-Rees and Rees, 2011: 41). Young children use all their senses to gain an understanding of their worlds and their worlds exist within environments where resources, furniture and toys are made of natural materials such as wool, wood and stone. As the beauty of the environment is highly valued 'very careful consideration is therefore given to the detail of the quality of all aspects of the kindergarten environment to ensure that it is gentle to the eye, ear and all the senses' (SWSF, 2008: 3). As the very youngest children make the transition from home to school, Steiner practitioners seek to make the learning spaces as 'homely' as possible in order to ease the child's transition from one environment to another.

'Rhythm and repetition are crucial' (SWSF, 2008: 3) within these environments and the rhythms of the daily routine ensure the children feel secure and confident, as they know what will happen next. The children themselves determine how long an activity will last and the repetition of activities and daily routines also supports a sense of security allowing the children to revisit, practise and deepen their developing skills and learning. The benefits of the rhythms and repetitions of the day and the importance attributed to the learning environment are evident in the words of a Steiner practitioner below:

> *It [the room] tells you when it's done ... It just shines when everything is in its place and it sounds ridiculous I know ... but ... the room speaks. If something is out of place it jars ... keeping the place clean and just the care of it, it speaks, it sings. (Drummond and Jenkinson, 2009: 8)*

Steiner learning environments offer young children infinite opportunities to imagine and consider possibilities. This contrasts with some learning environments that are characterised by a sense of 'visual busy-ness' and which reduce the learner to little more than a consumer of information rather than one who is curious and capable of contributing to the culture within the environment. Tarr (2004: 3) makes this point after encountering learning environments for young children filled with displays, mobiles and bright colours to the point where 'the mass of commercial stereotyped images silence the actual lived experiences of those individuals learning together'. Enabling learning environments should make a positive contribution to young children's learning although naturally it must be left to the informed and sensitive practitioner to determine how this is done.

Relationships as enabling environments

When young children feel safe and know that there is someone nearby on whom they can depend, they quickly develop the self-confidence to attempt new challenges. They are prepared to take risks in their learning, they explore and experiment, relate well to others and becoming increasingly independent. The EYFS promotes the use of the 'key person' approach (Elfer *et al.*, 2012) as good practice in the early years and it is the work of the skilled practitioner to identify an individual child's needs and organise routines and a pattern to the day that will help the child predict what is likely to happen and when. In such environments, practitioners use not only the physical space and resources to enable learning but also the relational space that exists between themselves and the child, taking careful account of the child's well-being and in particular their emotional needs.

The EYFS emphasises this feature of the learning environment through the theme of 'Positive Relationships' where there is a clear emphasis on the need to value the human above the material resources that are more typically associated with the learning process. The principle underpinning the theme is 'children learn to be strong and independent through *positive relationships*' (DfE, 2014: 6).

There is a sense too in which a supportive environment which places a strong emphasis on the quality of relationships between practitioners and young children requires the adult to be available to the child at an emotional level. In other words, in the same way the adult is learning about the child, the child needs to be able to learn about and interact at an emotional level with the adult. According to Gerhardt (2004: 18) 'the baby is an interactive project not a self powered one'. This can be demanding for a key person who is supporting several young children's learning at the same time and so requires careful monitoring by setting managers. However, when loving, trusting and respectful relationships are able to flourish this leads to a powerful and enabling environment for learning.

Such an emphasis on relationships is a feature of the New Zealand early childhood curriculum Te Whāriki (New Zealand Ministry of Education, 1996) which, like the EYFS, puts 'Relationships' alongside the other broad principles of 'Empowerment', 'Holistic Development' and 'Family and Community'. Where it differs from the EYFS though, is in the notion that 'children learn through responsive and reciprocal rela-tionships between people, places and things' (New Zealand Ministry of Education, 1996). One of the unique features of the country's first bicultural curriculum is the emphasis on relationships and holistic development that reflects the Maori culture from which so much of its design and philosophy is drawn. The title 'Te Whāriki' refers to 'a woven mat for all to stand on' and recognises that children learn in a holistic way, woven from many different views or 'themes'.

Such relationships need to be established but they also require nurture, development, enhancement and maintenance if babies and young children are to learn and develop to their fullest potential. Almost without question we value 'positive' relationships but how often do we stop to think about what such relationships create space *for* or, put another way, what might evolve or develop for *both* partners within a good relational environment? It might be a greater understanding of the other person and what they bring to the relationship, it might be a greater sense of 'unity' with the wider world or it might just be time to think and live together.

Anning and Edwards (2006: 60) note 'caring and reciprocal relationships are cen-tral to the co-construction of mind and this is markedly so throughout the early years of life'. Adults play a familiar role in the co-construction of meaning with young children; this might be conceived of as a collaborative journey towards the ultimate discovery of meaning. If we are truly respectful of young children as 'powerful' as well as strong and competent learners we should be prepared to stand alongside them and let them show us their power as well as their compe-tence. We must allow ourselves to be surprised by their abilities while at the same time we must let them lead us to meaning that exists in spaces with which we may not be familiar.

Conclusion

Within this chapter we have explored a variety of practices and learning environ-ments for young children's learning from within and beyond England and the UK. These enabling environments have been informed by practitioners who recognise the complexity of providing for young children's learning and believe that the child is a unique, competent learner. In addition, it is accepted that the practitioners are learning alongside the child; children are learning about their worlds and adults are learning about children as learners. Both are active in the process of constructing understandings. This is work which requires high levels of skill and dedication from those who work with young children and who care deeply about helping them to learn and develop as unique individuals.

There continues to be a vigorous debate about the necessity for a universal and standardised framework such as we now have in the EYFS: not least, whether certain aspects of it deny children the opportunity to learn at a pace that takes full account of their individual needs. However, there is much to celebrate, not least that within the EYFS the unique child is valued, play is promoted and practitioners are encouraged to put the child at the centre of planning for learning.

Developing a genuinely enabling environment in the early years is not an easy task. It requires recognition not just by practitioners, but also by external agencies and policy makers, of the multifaceted nature of the term 'environment', as well as an appreciation of the complexity of the different forms that environments can take. All those involved with the provision of enabling environments for babies and young children are therefore responsible for keeping themselves informed and up to date with current research and practice.

In addition, practitioners must have a reflective attitude towards their beliefs and principles in order to gain an insight into what guides decisions and develops their understanding of young learners. Policy and legislation must also be interpreted in a way that suits the needs of the children, families and communities with which practitioners work. Babies and young children now have a legal entitlement to be at the centre of the policies which guide those who care for and support their learning in the early years. Most important of all, they deserve rich and diverse learning environments which will enable them to be competent, motivated and powerful learners.

ACTIVITY 1

In 2007 the Department for Children, Schools and Families (DCSF, 2007) developed a set of cards which explored the principles and themes that underpinned the Early Years Foundation Stage. These have since been archived and can be found at http://webarchive. nationalarchives.gov.uk

Find these cards online and share them with your colleagues as a starting point to reflect on your practice.

ACTIVITY 2

Reflect upon your own personal learning journey to date. Which experiences did you learn most from? What did you learn? Where did this learning take place? Who was there? What was their role during the experience?

Consider how these learning experiences shaped your principles and beliefs.

CASE STUDY

In the early 1990s a practitioner managed a day nursery based upon her belief that children learn best through play. In 1996 the government introduced the Desirable Learning Outcomes and Ofsted Inspections. Gradually the practitioner realised the setting was not providing the learning environment she wished and the practice was being compromised. Instead of having long periods of play children were expected to do more formal activities.

(Continued)

CASE STUDY *continued*

The practitioner returned to university to explore young children's learning further. Her studies gave her the opportunity to reflect and gain a deeper insight into her beliefs and attitudes about children's learning which had informed her principles. She found that her studies not only supported her principles with evidence from reading and research, but also enabled her to articulate and share her principles and understanding of children's learning with others.

After completing her degree she felt more able to provide the learning environment for children and adults that reflected her principles.

Questions

1. *Having read the chapter, how has it developed your view of an enabling environment for young children's learning?*
2. *How would you begin to provide an enabling environment informed by your principles?*

FURTHER READING

Fisher, J. (2013) *Starting from the Child: Teaching and Learning from 4 to 8* (4th edn). Maidenhead: OUP.

This practical and inspirational book discusses how recent research continues to shape our understanding of early learning and would be a natural source of further reading to link theory and practice. The book contains many ideas for practitioners to consider when planning to build on children's competence as learners and to develop appropriate learning environments.

REFERENCES

Abbott, L. and Nutbrown, C. (eds) (2001) *Experiencing Reggio Emilia: Implications for Pre-school Provision*. Maidenhead: Open University Press.

Alexander, R. (ed.) (2010) *Children, Their World, Their Education: Final Report and Recommendations of the Cambridge Primary Review*. Oxford: Routledge.

Anning, A. and Edwards, A. (2006) *Promoting Children's Learning from Birth to Five: Developing the New Early Years Professional* (2nd edn). Maidenhead: Open University Press.

Bilton, H. (2002) *Outdoor Play in the Early Years Management and Innovation* (2nd edn). London: David Fulton Publishers.

Carr, M. (2001) *Assessment in Early Childhood Settings: Learning Stories*. London: Paul Chapman Publishing.

Central Advisory Council for Education (CACE) (1967) *Children and their Primary Schools*. London: HMSO.

DCSF (Department for Children, Schools and Families) (2007) *Principles into Practice: Cards for the Early Years Foundation Stage*. Nottingham: DCSF Publications.

DfE (Department for Education) (2014) *Statutory Framework for the Early Years Foundation Stage: Setting the Standards for Learning, Development and Care for Children from Birth to Five*. London: DfE Publications.

DfES (Department for Education and Skills) (2006) *Learning Outside the Classroom MANIFESTO*. Nottingham: DfES Publications.

Drummond, M. and Jenkinson, S. (2009) *Meeting the Child: Approaches to Observation and Assessment in Steiner Kindergartens.* Plymouth: University of Plymouth.

Edgington, M. (2004) *The Nursery Teacher in Action: Teaching 3, 4 and 5 Year Olds* (3rd edn). London: Paul Chapman Publishing.

Edwards, C., Gandini, L. and Foreman, G. (1998) (eds) *The Hundred Languages of Children* (2nd edn). Norwood, NJ: Ablex.

Elfer, P., Goldschmied, E. and Selleck, D. (2012) *Key Persons in the Early Years: Building Relationships for Quality Provision in Early Years Settings and Primary Schools.* London: David Fulton.

Fletcher, S. and Welton, J. (eds) (1912) *Fröbel's Chief Writings on Education.* London: Edward Arnold & Co.

Forman, G. and Fyfe, B. (2011) Negotiated learning through design, documentation and discourse. In C. Edwards, L. Gandini and G. Forman (eds), *The Hundred Languages of Children: The Reggio Emilia Experience in Transformation.* Oxford: Praeger.

Gerhardt, S. (2004) *Why Love Matters: How Affection Shapes a Baby's Brain.* Hove: Brunner Routledge.

Gopnik, A., Meltzoff, A. and Kuhl, P. (1999) *How Babies Think: The Science of Childhood.* New York: Harper Collins.

Gutek, G. (2004) *The Montessori Method: The Origins of an Educational Innovation.* Lanham, MD: Rowman & Littlefield Inc.

Locke, J. (1689/1824) No Innate Principles in the Mind. In *The Works of John Locke in Nine Volumes* (12 edn), vol. 1, chap. II. London: Rivington. Available at: http://oll.libertyfund.org/title/761/80711/1923121 (accessed 24 February 2010).

Luff, P. (2007) Written observations or walks in the park? Documenting children's experiences. In J. Moyles (ed.), *Early Years Foundations: Meeting the Challenge.* Berkshire: Open University Press.

Malaguzzi, L. (1998) History, ideas and basic philosophy: an interview with Lella Gandini. In C. Edwards, L. Gandini and G. Foreman (eds), *The Hundred Languages of Children: The Reggio Emilia Approach – Advanced Reflections* (2nd edn). London: Ablex.

Montessori, M. (1948/1967) *The Discovery of the Child* (6th edn) (trans. M. Costelloe). New York: Random House.

Moyles, J. (2005) *The Excellence of Play* (2nd edn). Maidenhead: Open University Press.

New Zealand Ministry of Education (1996) *Te Whāriki: He Whāriki Mātauranga mō ngā Mokopuna o Aotearoa: Early Childhood Curriculum.* Wellington: Learning Media.

Nutbrown, C. (2001) Creating a palette of opportunities: situations for learning in the early years. In L. Abbott and C. Nutbrown (eds), *Experiencing Reggio Emilia: Implications for Pre-school Provision.* Maidenhead: Open University Press.

Nutbrown, C. (2006) *Threads of Thinking: Young Children Learning and the Role of Early Education* (3rd edn). London: SAGE.

Ouvry, M (2003) *Exercising Muscles and Minds: Outdoor Play and the Early Years Curriculum.* London: NCB.

Parker-Rees, R. and Rees, S. (2011) How the Steiner Kindergarten environment helps adults and children to get to know each other. In R. Parker-Rees (ed.), *Meeting the Child in Steiner Kindergartens: An Exploration of Beliefs, Values and Practices.* Abingdon: Routledge.

Penn, H. (1997) *Comparing Nurseries: Staff and Children in Italy, Spain and the UK.* London: Paul Chapman Publishing.

Rousseau, J.J. (1762/1911) *Émile* (trans. B. Foxley). London: Dent.

SWSF (Steiner Waldorf Schools Fellowship) (2008) The Kindergarten Day. Available at: http://www.steinerwaldorf.org/downloads/earlyyears/More_details_about_Steiner_EY.pdf (accessed 24 February 2010).

Tarr, P. (2004) Consider the walls. *Beyond the Journal: Young Children on the Web*. Available at: http://www.naeyc.org/files/yc/file/200405/ConsidertheWalls.pdf (accessed 24 February 2010).

Thomson, P. and Hall, C. (2008) Opportunities missed and/or thwarted? 'Funds of knowledge' meet the English National Curriculum. *Curriculum Journal*, 19(2): 87–103.

Wickett, K. and Huggins, V. (2011) Using the local community as part of the early years learning environment. In S. Waite (ed.) *Children Learning Outside the Classroom*. London: SAGE.

7 Children, inequality and risk

Caroline Leeson and Julia Morgan

Introduction

This chapter will address the anxiety relating to the concepts of risk and inequality and their impact on social policy as well as on the relationships between adults and children in both personal and professional scenarios. The chapter will start by defining what we mean by the terms 'risk' and 'inequality' before exploring the critical connections between them. Using three examples, we will highlight aspects of risk and inequality that are part of the lived experience of many children and seek to understand and challenge the underlying beliefs and lack of action.

Risk

Risk is actually a very difficult term to define as it has been used in a number of both negative and positive contexts; is it about threat and possibility of loss or about challenge and the possibility of gain? What we know is that a concept of risk has been part of society for centuries. McElwee (2007) talks about the existence of risk assessors in 3200 BC who were called upon to use their skills of divination and assessment to give advice regarding a wide number of circumstances such as a purchase of land or a marriage contract. So, we see that a balancing of existing risk factors leading to a determination of the actual risk has been a pervasive way of viewing and engaging with the concept of risk. Many situations have involved a mathematical construction of risk, giving various risk factors numerical values and coming to a conclusion as to likelihood and level that will aid decision making as to whether a risk is worth taking. For example, we see an engagement with statistics which show how likely it is that we will contract diabetes or experience a plane crash. This is a positivistic approach to risk that looks at predictability and encourages us to take a simplistic and reductionist attitude – if A + B then C is likely to happen (and a statistical figure is attributed such as 25 per cent probability).

Many social policy and social welfare systems such as health, education and social work are based on positivistic models of understanding risk. For example, when looking at safeguarding children a number of risk factors are identified in any given situation, resulting in a prediction as to which children are vulnerable to abuse and what actions should be taken to avoid that circumstance occurring. One great attraction of a positivistic view of risk is the ability to deal with the world around us with a degree of certainty and to do so by objective mathematical mechanisms that do not invoke emotional reactions. The obvious criticism of this stance is the failure to take into account the impact upon individuals or their relationship with the identified risk. Sheppard (2003) writes of the different perceptions that exist in safeguarding situations where a social worker may regard a mother as being engaged in high risk childrearing practices which indicate the need for serious intervention whereas that mother sees herself as coping very well, given a complex and difficult set of circumstances. Thus, we would argue that risk has to be subjective – everyone has something to win or lose and the impact will be felt more or less by different people involved in the situation. Another criticism is the inappropriateness of the use of positivistic risk theories, intended for use with large populations, to predict what will happen in specific situations, leading Munro (2010: 128) to state unequivocally:

> what should be abandoned is any claim to be able to foretell the future with sufficient accuracy to warrant singling out one child as 'a future menace to society' or any parent as 'a future abuser'.

It may be that complexity theory is helpful, as it acknowledges and seeks to make explicit the highly complex set of circumstances that lead to risk being experienced and thus enables us to make better judgements as to our own calculation of risk for ourselves and our families. Complexity theory looks at the interplay of a number of social and individual systems to understand why events happen and how very minor differences in initial conditions can lead to very major differences in outcomes. For example, two street children may have very different experiences of risk depending on what other resources are available both internally (their own resilience and personality) and externally (informal and formal support mechanisms, schools, health facilities). A child with no access to support mechanisms and with poor self-esteem will be more vulnerable to manipulation than one who knows where to run to or feels that she is an individual worth protecting.

Beck (1992) argues that we live in a 'risk society' where risks are inevitable and we are driven to control and neutralise their threats. We can certainly see this in official government health advice regarding healthy eating to avoid the risk of diabetes or cancer. Beck feels that there has been a rise in experts to help us seek control but the problem is that what is true of large populations cannot simply be scaled down to create a statistical likelihood for small groups or individuals and thus we have seen many of these experts fail. Consequently, we fear their fallibility, which in its turn creates further anxieties about the present circumstances we live in and the future. Modernisation, technology and globalisation have all contributed to increasing our fears as they have created a whole set of circumstances which we do not understand or are unable to predict, along with the knowledge that any compensatory mechanisms are inadequate to the vast tasks they may be asked to perform. As a consequence, we are further driven to control our world, to find certainty and predictability. Hence the rise of the oft stated but erroneous phrase 'we will learn lessons, this will never happen again'. The subjective perception of risk has therefore changed in this global world and we have become more risk averse, obsessed with risk avoidance which may have the effect of immobilising us. Furthermore, Beck talks about a new dialogue that has emerged about the redistribution of risk – who or what should experience the least or most risk. Certainly when we consider national and international social policy in respect to children's lives we can see the inbuilt divisiveness of this development. We assert that every child matters, but closer interrogation shows that our systems and structures imply that some children matter more and some matter less. A risk-averse mentality can give rise to a 'hear no evil see no evil' approach where we refuse to acknowledge the presence of risk until the weight of evidence is overwhelming and demands for change are too loud to be ignored. This has certainly been the case in recent cases of child sexual exploitation and in the current situation in Africa with regards to Ebola, where attracting funding to support victims is proving very difficult.

There are, however, criticisms of over emphasis of the negative aspects of risk in Beck's account of a risk society. Austen (2009) explores the meaning of risk with young people and highlights the positive aspects of risk – the challenge and excitement that taking risks and engaging in risky behaviour can elicit in an individual. She found that young people rejected the negative labels attached to these behaviours – some of which were socially constructed as undesirable and therefore very risky – and that they did not display uncertainty about their behaviour or that of their peers. It would seem that a wide view of what risk means to the individuals concerned continues to be important for any policies or strategies that seek to keep children and young people safe and able to realise their potential.

Inequality

Inequality refers to the systematic differences between individuals, groups and countries that tend to be 'socially' or 'structurally' produced and hence are unfair and inequitable. An understanding of the concept of social justice is important in understanding the notion of inequalities. Rawls (1999: 4) defines 'social' justice as 'a proper distribution of the benefits and burdens of social cooperation'. According to this definition, a fair society would be one in which there was equality of opportunity and equal access to freedom and rights for all citizens. Moreover, for Rawls, a just society would ensure that those who are vulnerable are protected and taken care of. Although Rawls puts emphasis on equality in his definition of social justice this does not mean that he thinks that everyone has to be the same and in fact he states that inequality can be an acceptable factor in life as long as everyone has a fair chance or opportunity to succeed in life – equality of opportunity as opposed to equality of outcome. In other words outcomes may be different and that is acceptable as long as opportunities were equally open to all. Structural and systematic inequalities in society, however, can impede social justice because certain groups and individuals do not have a fair chance in life or fair access to opportunities and this can impact on their well-being and their ability to lead a fulfilling life. The range of different types of inequalities includes social inequality, which relates to unequal opportunities according to social class or caste, as well as inequalities associated with gender, ethnicity, disability, age and geographical region.

Health inequalities also exist between groups and countries, and are defined as 'health differences between groups linked to broader social inequalities and unequal societal structures' (Graham, 2007: 4). If we focus on the global infant mortality rate we can see how there are huge differences in the mortality rates between countries in the global South and those in the global North. For example, a child born in Sierra Leone is nearly 55 times more likely to die before the age of five than a child born in Iceland (World Bank, 2014). As Whitehead and Dahlgren (2006: 2) have stated, 'no Law of Nature, for instance, decrees that the children of poor families should die' at this rate. Tackling health inequalities is, therefore, a top priority for practitioners and policy makers and much policy is focused on narrowing the health gap between disadvantaged groups, communities and the rest of the population as well as between countries.

Poverty

Poverty – definitions

Absolute poverty

Absolute poverty is a universal poverty indicator and is understood as not having the minimum needed to sustain a good standard of living or basic needs such as access to safe drinking water, food, sanitation, shelter, health and education. It is normally expressed as living on less than X dollars per day – this is the amount needed for basic survival. The Millennium Development Goals refer to poverty in this way with their aim to 'reduce by half the proportion of people living on less than a dollar a day'. Please see the Millennium Development Goals at http://www.undp.org/content/undp/en/home/mdgoverview.html

Some theorists and commentators have also argued that the concept of absolute poverty is relevant to the UK but that the definition of less than a dollar a day is problematic. Thus, in relation to the UK they will talk about 'minimum income standards' and what is the minimum that is needed to buy an agreed basket of goods and services which are seen as necessities. Those families, for example, who fall below this agreed threshold will be seen to be in absolute poverty.

Relative poverty

Relative poverty is different from absolute poverty. Relative poverty is not about basic needs but instead is about being poor in relation to a society's standards. It is, therefore, context-specific. An income-related example used in the UK defines people as living in poverty if their income is less than X per cent of median UK income. Relative poverty is about inequality; it is about not being able to participate in what is customary within a civilized society. Relative poverty is sometimes seen as a cause of social exclusion. Wilkinson and Pickett (2010) have argued convincingly that countries, such as the UK, which have high levels of inequality, measured as the gap between rich and poor, are more likely to have lower levels of child well-being and health. Inequality, therefore, can impact on well-being.

Chronic or persistent poverty

This refers to a situation where individuals or groups are in poverty over an extended period of time. In relation to children, those who are in persistent poverty are defined as those children who have lived in poverty for three out of the last four years. It is not short-term poverty.

Poverty is another form of inequality and can be defined in a number of ways. In the UK when we talk about poverty we are normally referring to relative poverty as defined above. Relative poverty, however, does not necessarily just refer to income poverty but can also include other non-income aspects of deprivation and disadvantage which can in turn lead to social exclusion:

Individuals, families and groups in the population can be said to be in poverty when they lack the resources to obtain the types of diet, participate in the activities, and have the living conditions and amenities which are customary, or at least widely encouraged or approved, in the societies to which they belong. Their resources are so seriously below those commanded by the average individual or family that they are, in effect, excluded from the ordinary living patterns, customs and activities. (Townsend, 1979: 31)

One in four children in the UK lives in relative poverty and surprisingly two-thirds of these children are living in a household where at least one person is in paid employment (Child Poverty Action Group, 2014; MacInnes, 2014). Because of poor wages, seasonal work and the part-time nature of many jobs, working is not necessarily a way out of poverty. Poverty, especially chronic or persistent poverty, has numerous impacts on children including:

- stigmatisation, marginalisation and bullying;
- reduced social activities;
- poor quality housing and homelessness;
- poorer educational outcomes;
- a decrease in health and well-being;
- living in poor neighbourhoods with less access to safe space;
- lack of household income;
- an increase in accidents (Ridge, 2002).

Child poverty in the UK, although it has decreased since the 1980s, is forecast to rise by the year 2020 from 2.9 million in 2015/2016 to 3.3 million by 2020/2021 (Brewer *et al.*, 2011). This rise in poverty levels is also a trend which is seen globally with the gap between the rich and poor widening and inequality becoming more entrenched at a global level (UNDP, 2014).

Children 'as risk' and children 'at risk'

Childhood is a social construction and, thus, how it is understood and made meaningful will vary at different times and in different places. However, although this is the case there are a number of common discourses in Western society about children and childhood. The romantic discourse positions children as innocent, pure and vulnerable, with the role of the adult being to protect and look after them. Children in this discourse can be seen as being 'at risk' from a number of threats to their inherent goodness and emphasis is, therefore, placed on providing an 'appropriate' childhood to mitigate these risks. In the UK, an 'appropriate' childhood would include schooling, opportunities for play, a loving family and protection from adult experiences such as work and sexual activity.

An alternative discourse, however, positions children 'as risk'. Here, the threat does not necessarily come from the outside world but is seen as emanating from the children themselves. Thus, children are viewed as potentially dangerous or a threat and in need of adult control and supervision until they become civilised individuals. Children who do not have an appropriate 'civilising' influence may be depicted as 'feral' or out of control and a risk to those around them or a risk to the well-being of society. This type of discourse is evident when we explore how groups of children and young people, who 'hang around' in public places together, are represented in the UK; their behaviour is often problematised as antisocial and they are sometimes seen as a threat which needs to be dealt with punitively (Hier, 2004). The Office of the Children's Commissioner in 2008 mounted a campaign to stop shopping centres using the 'Mosquito' – a device that emits a high pitched noise audible only to young people – to prevent children and young people from simply 'hanging around'. Moral panics about the behaviour of children and young people, the declining standards of parenting and changes in childhood, normally for the worse, are often evident in both the media and social policy and those children who transgress the expected norms of childhood are often vilified. They (and their families) may also be held to account for any difficulties they encounter as a consequence of their behaviour, problems that for other children would evoke sympathy and support.

However, when we look in more detail at which children are 'at risk' and which are viewed 'as risk' we can see that poverty and social class are often implicated. Also, we may see decisions being made (or not) that have the effect of redistributing risk, giving more to those who might be seen as less worthy or more culpable. Risk, therefore, in the context of childhood, can often be a proxy for inequality and poverty remains one of the key factors implicated in children being looked after by the local authority (Davies, 2008). Children who live in poverty in the UK, therefore, may be seen as more likely to be 'at risk' of poorer childhoods which don't match up to the ideal of childhood as a time of innocence. This risk is also disproportionate given the widening gulf between the rich and poor in the UK. Policies and structures are put in place that seek to minimise any risks and in so doing extol middle-class values, positioning working-class childhoods and parenting as deficient. Gillies (2005: 849) has shown, for example, that working-class parents are held accountable for 'failing to equip their children with the right skills for social improvement' and hence their children are more likely to be seen as 'at risk' of not fulfilling their potential. Furthermore, children who live in poverty have also been identified as more likely to live in families where parental supervision may be low and where parenting is more problematic, resulting in poorly socialised children who are more likely to exhibit behaviour which is seen as 'risky' to others. This can lead to an increase in interventions aimed at 'troubled' families to ensure that their children have the 'right' kind of childhood (based on middle-class ideals) and grow up to be the 'right' type of citizen.

Age is also a major determinant of inequality and how risk is viewed, as children below the age of eight (early childhood) tend to be more likely to be seen as innocent because young children are less likely to challenge adults' views or concepts of childhood. As these children grow older, whilst many of them are still seen in this way, they become more likely to be seen as a threat especially if their behaviour does not conform to what is expected of them in a given society (Hier *et al.*, 2011). Moreover, in many societies, the step from childhood to adulthood is seen as a liminal stage and those in between are seen as dangerous – they are neither child nor adult – they are anomalies in a binary system and hence initiation rites are utilised, in many societies, to mark this boundary between childhood and adulthood. Furthermore, we react disproportionately badly to evidence of young children engaging in risky behaviour, often with severely punitive measures, for either the child concerned or their families, which may deny them their right to justice. For example, the two ten-year-old boys who killed James Bulger were convicted through an adult court after a moral panic about the issue of young children being capable of committing serious crimes (Hay, 1995; Franklin and Petley, 2005).

The link between risk and inequality

As Olofsson *et al.* (2014: 420) identify, risk and inequality are created and developed through 'complex social processes that express power structures, different social values, conflict over knowledge and social differentiation'. They are combined and connected in various dimensions and provoke emotional reactions that are not always helpful to the children concerned. In the next section we identify and debate the issues of risk and inequality involved in three experiences that children may face. The first example focuses on children with a parent in prison, the second on children who live and work on the streets and the third on children who are exposed to sexual exploitation.

Children with a parent in prison

In 2009, it was estimated that approximately 200,000 children had a parent in prison in England and Wales (Williams *et al.*, 2012). Children who experience a parent spending time in prison are more likely than any other group of children to be seen as 'at risk' of experiencing severe disadvantages including increased poverty rates; an increase in caring responsibilities; an increase in being bullied; a decrease in school attendance and attainment; and increased mental health problems (Gill and Morgan, 2013). However, at the same time, this group of children are also viewed 'as risk' and there is a focus on the intergenerational transmission of antisocial and criminal behaviour from parent to child, with children of prisoners being identified as being at least three times more likely than their peers to develop antisocial behaviour (Murray and Farrington, 2008). This can lead to children of prisoners being labelled as potential criminals and this is especially the case when this group of children become teenagers. However, whilst Murray and Farrington found associations between parental criminality and child antisocial behaviour in the UK, this was not the case in Sweden and it has been suggested that this is because children who experienced parental imprisonment in Sweden were offered appropriate support which mitigated many of the risk factors which were present (SCIE, 2008). This is not the case in the UK and support for this group of 'hidden' children is minimal, resulting in children of prisoners who exhibit poor behaviour being more likely to be demonised and stigmatised and often seen as deserving a share of the social stigma 'earned' by their parent's transgression.

Furthermore, we should bear in mind that maintaining a narrow focus on the problems that may ensue for children with a parent in prison fails to take account of the many children who do cope and who may even be relieved that their parent is no longer present. These children are most likely to be causing the least concern to professionals such as teachers and social workers and thus may not be receiving any attention. However, their support needs may be just as great – many carry a significant burden of care, looking after their remaining parent and siblings and worrying about their parent in prison. Oversimplifying their relation with risk fails to acknowledge the many different scenarios that these children find themselves in and the different kinds of help they may require (Morgan and Leeson, 2015).

Children who live and work on the street

In many countries across the world, children live and work on the street and 'street children', as they are commonly known, are often positioned as both 'at risk' and 'as risk'. For example, they are represented by many as victims who are homeless, exploited and abandoned by parents and thus at risk of a number of poor outcomes. The street, in this type of discourse, is seen as a dangerous place that is not child-friendly and is viewed in opposition to the home where children 'belong' (Ennew, 1995). As a result, these children are 'out of place' and are in need of saving and protection and there are numerous charities worldwide which work with 'street children'. However, other discourses position 'street children' in opposition to 'normal' children and they are consequently viewed as a risk. This type of discourse may represent 'street children' as out-of-control, drug-taking delinquents who are sexually active, immoral, criminally inclined, aggressive and lacking in respect for the social order (Bleazley, 2003). Instead of behaving like children they are viewed as behaving like adults, and this transgression often results in them being dealt with punitively and brutally by some adults including those who are meant to protect them (Sondhi-Garg, 2004). Again, a narrow focus only on risk fails to acknowledge the incredible resilience that is often shown by the children and does not permit the development of structures to effectively harness, develop and protect that strength, thus leaving children who work or live on the street even more disadvantaged, neglected and rejected. Moreover, focusing on children who live on the street as risk or at risk overlooks how many street children use positive mechanisms to deal resourcefully with very difficult situations and hostile environments.

When we look at the position of 'street children' in more depth we can clearly see that inequality and poverty are at the heart of why many of the children end up on the street. Research has shown that many children who live on the street may have better nutrition, increased income from working and, if they get into a centre for street children, a better education than they would have had if they had stayed within 'slum' communities. So 'going to the street' may be an effective strategy used by some children to deal with poor living conditions at home (Ferguson and Heidemann, 2009). As a result, many interventions which aim at re-uniting 'street children' with their families often find that children once re-united return to the streets again. Although the children are returned to their 'rightful' place, at home with family, nothing has been done to change the poverty, inequality and risk within the home. This poverty, risk and inequality at home, because it is not generally visible to outsiders, is not normally given the same attention as the phenomenon of 'street children' who are highly visible and thus highly risky. Street children, therefore, are problematic for many in terms of risk because they are a visible reminder of gross inequalities in terms of poverty and wealth (Wells, 2009).

Children who are exposed to sexual exploitation

The recent high profile reports on the experience of children and young people in Rochdale (RBSCB, 2012) and Rotherham (Jay, 2014) demonstrate the ambivalence with which those who experience sexual exploitation are regarded. The reports are densely populated with accounts of children and young people actively seeking help for their situation and being ignored, often negatively characterised as promiscuous, out of control and beyond help – they were seen to constitute a threat and were therefore regarded as a risk with the consequence that their plight was ignored. Yet, any babies born in this situation are seen as innocent and therefore at risk and measures are taken to protect them ('Suzy' in RBSCB, 2012). Since the stories broke, the public breast beating of various stakeholders has been quite spectacular but continues to fail to address the needs of children and young people affected by sexual exploitation; the first priority is to prosecute the perpetrators rather than support the victims through effective therapeutic measures.

Many of the children and young people who were targeted for sexual exploitation came from backgrounds of poverty and lack of opportunity. Also, many were already in the care of the local authority having been removed from abusive or complex families to what was erroneously seen as a place of safety. Addressing the multitude of issues present in these circumstances does not require simple solutions. Further removal and stringent controls that further isolate and thus appear to blame the victims for the situation they find themselves in, is not desirable, yet that is often what happens. If the detection and investigation processes used by key agencies were clearer, that would help as would any work to challenge their institutional prejudices, but the main concern should be to change the lens through which these children and young people are regarded and consider the aspects of risk and inequality that continue to underpin their experiences.

Conclusion

A common thread that runs through the three examples examined above is the failure to embrace an understanding of risk as a complex concept that involves a substantial number of factors that inter-relate in complex ways and cannot be resolved by simple solutions. Furthermore, turning a critical lens on the manner in which we regard children and young people affected by poverty or other attributes of inequality will enable us to develop more effective policies and strategies that recognise the complexity of their lives and seek to properly address the inequalities they experience daily. Risk is not exclusively negative – many will experience the positive thrill of challenging themselves and even children in the situations we have highlighted draw many positives from surviving against the odds. These strategies for survival may involve both positive and negative ways of dealing with the situation including, for example, taking drugs to overcome feelings of unhappiness and hunger as well as to overcome experiences of abuse as happens with some 'street children'. Where these strategies for coping with hostile situations contribute to the perception of children as a threat it is all too easy to end up blaming children for the circumstances in which they find themselves. Circumstances, we would argue, that invariably have more to do with structural inequalities than with the individual behaviour or choices of the child or young person involved.

We conclude by stating that many children and young people can be seen simultaneously *as* risk and *at* risk and these children should be responded to with compassion and care, not with punitive measures because of assumptions or ways of thinking about what 'good' children or childhoods are like. Practitioners and policy makers therefore need to reflect upon their own attitudes to risk and inequality and how they may view some children and young people as more deserving than others.

ACTIVITY **1**

Reflect on the concept of inequality. What do you think causes inequality and why do you think it is so difficult to bring about change in terms of levels of inequality and disadvantage in the UK?

ACTIVITY **2**

Reflect upon your own attitudes and values in relation to disadvantaged families and children. What has informed your values and attitudes around disadvantage and poverty? How do you think that your attitudes and values may impact upon your working relationships with disadvantaged children, families and communities? Why is it important to be aware of this?

There are numerous quality resources online and for those interested in finding out more about the issues we recommend the following websites.

Children of prisoners

Social Care Institute for Excellence (SCIE) (2008) *Children's and Families Resource Guide 11: Children of Prisoners – Maintaining Family Ties.* London: SCIE.

This is an excellent booklet and can be downloaded along with a number of other e-resources from: http://www.scie.org.uk/publications/elearning/childrenofprisoners/index.asp

I-Hop is a resource funded by the Department of Education which focuses on supporting practitioners to support children of prisoners. The webpage has a number of high quality resources and can be accessed from: http://www.i-hop.org.uk/

Street children

The Consortium of Street Children is an NGO which advocates on behalf of street children and provides some high quality information on the issue. This can be accessed from: http://www.streetchildrenday.org/csc/

Child sexual exploitation

Barnardos' work on child sexual exploitation can be accessed from: http://www.barnardos.org.uk/what_we_do/our_projects/sexual_exploitation.htm

The report into child sexual exploitation in Rotherham can be accessed at: http://www.rotherham.gov.uk/info/200109/council_news/884/independent_inquiry_into_child_sexual_exploitation_in_rotherham_1997_%E2%80%93_2013

Austen, L. (2009) The social construction of risk by young people. *Health, Risk & Society*, 11(5): 451–70.

Beck, U. (1992) *Risk Society: Towards a New Modernity.* London: SAGE.

Bleazley, H. (2003) Voices from the margins: street children's subcultures in Indonesia. *Children's Geographies*, 1(2): 181–200.

Brewer, M., Browne, J. and Joyce, R. (2011) *Child and Working Age Poverty from 2010 to 2020.* London: Institute for Fiscal Studies with Joseph Rowntree Foundation.

Child Poverty Action Group (2014) Child Poverty Facts and Figures. Available at: http://www.cpag.org.uk/child-poverty-facts-and-figures (accessed 1 March 2015).

Davies, M. (2008) *Eradicating Child Poverty: The Role of Key Policy Areas. The Effects of Discrimination on Families in the Fight to End Child Poverty.* York: Joseph Rowntree Foundation. Available at: http://www.jrf.org.uk/sites/files/jrf/2271-poverty-exclusion-discrimination.pdf (accessed 1 March 2015).

Ennew, J. (1995) Outside childhood: street children's rights. In B. Franklin (ed.), *The Handbook of Children's Rights: Comparative Policy and Practice.* London: Routledge.

Ferguson, K.M. and Heidemann, G. (2009) Organizational strengths and challenges of Kenyan NGOs serving orphans and vulnerable children: a template analysis. *International Journal of Social Welfare*, 18(4): 354–64.

Franklin, B. and Petley, J. (2005) Killing the age of innocence: newspaper reporting of the death of James Bulger. In J. Pilcher and S. Wagg (eds), *Thatcher's Children? Politics, Childhood and Society in the 1980s and 1990s.* London: Routledge.

Gill, O. and Morgan, J. (eds) (2013) *Children Affected by the Imprisonment of a Family Member: A Handbook for Schools Developing Good Practice.* London: Barnardos. Available at: http://www.

barnardos.org.uk/what_we_do/policy_research_unit/research_and_publications.htm (accessed 1 March 2015).

Gillies, V. (2005) Raising the 'Meritocracy': parenting and the individualization of social class. *Sociology*, 39(5): 835–53. Available at: http://www.academia.edu/964719/Raising_the_Meritocracy (accessed 15 April 2015).

Graham, H. (2007) *Unequal Lives: Health and Socioeconomic Inequalities*. Maidenhead: Open University Press.

Hay, C. (1995) Mobilisation through interpellation: James Bulger, juvenile crime and the construction of a moral panic. *Social and Legal Studies*, 4(2): 197–223.

Hier, S.P. (2004) Risky spaces and dangerous faces: urban surveillance, social disorder and CCTV. *Social & Legal Studies*, 13(4): 541–54.

Hier, S.P., Lett, D., Walby, K. and Smith, A. (2011) Beyond folk devil resistance: linking moral panic and moral regulation. *Criminology and Criminal Justice*, 11(3): 259–76.

Jay, A. (2014) *Independent Inquiry into Child Sexual Exploitation in Rotherham 1997–2013*. Rotherham: Rotherham Metropolitan Borough Council.

McElwee, N. (2007) Riding the juggernaut in the risk society. *Child & Youth Services*, 29(1): 71–101.

MacInnes, T. (2014) In work poverty. *Poverty*. Available at: http://www.cpag.org.uk/sites/default/files/CPAG-in-work-poverty-Jul14.pdf (accessed 15 April 2015).

Morgan, J. and Leeson, C. (2015) How can schools support children who experience the imprisonment of a parent or close relative? *Every Child Journal*, 5(1): 20–6.

Munro, E. (2010) Conflating risks: implications for accurate risk prediction in child welfare services. *Health, Risk & Society*, 12(2): 119–30.

Murray, J. and Farrington, D.P. (2008) Parental imprisonment: long-lasting effects on boys' internalizing problems through the life course. *Developmental Psychopathology*, 20(1): 273–90.

Office of the Childrens' Commissioner (2008) Buzz off campaign. http://www.11MILLION.org.uk (accessed 15 April 2015).

Olofsson, A., Zinn, J., Griffin, G., Giritli Nygren, K., Cebulla, A. and Hannah-Moffat, K. (2014) The mutual constitution of risk and inequalities: intersectional risk theory. *Health, Risk & Society*, 16(5): 417–30.

Rawls, J. (1999) *A Theory of Justice*. Oxford: Oxford University Press.

Ridge, T. (2002) *Childhood Poverty and Social Exclusion: From a Child's Perspective*. Bristol: Policy Press.

Rochdale Borough Safeguarding Children Board (RBSCB) (2012) *Review of Multi-agency Responses to the Sexual Exploitation of Children*. Rochdale: Rochdale Borough.

Sheppard, M. (2003) *Prevention and Coping in Child and Family Care: Mothers in Adversity Coping with Child Care*. London: Jessica Kingsley Publishers.

Social Care Institute for Excellence (SCIE) (2008) *Children's and Families Resource Guide 11: Children of Prisoners – Maintaining Family Ties*. London: SCIE.

Sondhi-Garg, P. (2004) *Street Children: Lives of Valor and Vulnerability*. New Delhi: Reference Press.

Townsend, P. (1979) *Poverty in the United Kingdom: a survey of household resources and standards of living*. Harmondsworth: Penguin Books. Available at: http://poverty.ac.uk/free-resources-books/poverty-united-kingdom (accessed 15 April 2015).

UNDP (United Nations Development Programme) (2014) *Humanity Divided: Confronting Inequality in Developing Countries.* Available at: http://www.undp.org/content/undp/en/home/librarypage/poverty-reduction/humanity-divided--confronting-inequality-in-developing-countries/ (accessed 14 November 2014).

Wells, K. (2009) *Childhood in a Global Perspective.* Cambridge: Polity.

Whitehead, M. and Dahlgren, G. (2006) *Levelling up (part 1): a discussion paper on concepts and principles for tackling social inequities in health.* World Health Organisation. Available at: http://www.who.int/social_determinants/resources/leveling_up_part1.pdf (accessed 15 April 2015).

Wilkinson, R. and Pickett, R. (2010) *The Spirit Level: Why Equality Is Better for Everyone.* London: Penguin.

Williams, K., Papadopoulou, V. and Booth N. (2012) *Prisoners' Childhood and Family Backgrounds: Results from the Surveying Prisoner Crime Reduction (SPCR) Longitudinal Cohort Study of Prisoners.* London: Ministry of Justice.

World Bank (2014) Infant Mortality Rates. Available at: http://data.worldbank.org/indicator/SP.DYN.IMRT.IN (accessed 15 April 2015).

8 Tackling inequality in early years settings

Ulrike Hohmann

Introduction

Equality of opportunity, or the lack of it, has an impact on everybody's life. Children, parents and early years practitioners are affected by structures of inclusion and exclusion and play an active part in developing inclusive and anti-discriminatory practice. This chapter unravels some of the complex issues associated with the notion of equal opportunities and their implications for work with young children. Early years practitioners have to be aware of the political and social context within which the demands for tackling inequalities develop and of a variety of arguments that are used to support or criticise attempts to define equal opportunities for children and their families. The examples in this chapter are mainly drawn from the 'classical' areas of discrimination: class, ethnicity, gender and ability. This is not a comprehensive list but serves as a starting point. As some forms of undue discrimination are curtailed, new forms emerge. For example, many unaccompanied asylum-seeking children are falling through the gaps in equality legislation (Wirtz *et al.*, 2009) and there are disturbing reports about young children suffering mentally and physically when forced to live in immigration detention centres (Lorek *et al.*, 2009; Barnardos, 2014).

The general context

The Children Act 1989, *Every Child Matters* (DfES, 2003) and a number of Education Acts from 1944 onwards emphasise the rights of children in Britain to equal opportunities and protection from unfair discrimination. On an international level such concerns are addressed by the United Nations Convention on the Rights of the Child (UNCRC), (UN, 1989). As well as having to work within these legal frameworks, early years practitioners are expected to be active in promoting equality of opportunities and anti-discriminatory practice for all children. In 2008 the Department for Children, Schools and Families declared the overarching aim of the Early Years Foundation Stage as:

> *providing for equality of opportunity and anti-discriminatory practice and ensuring that every child is included and not disadvantaged because of ethnicity, culture or religion, home language, family background, learning difficulties or disabilities, gender or ability. (DCSF, 2008a: 7)*

Six years and a change of government later the aim was shortened to 'The EYFS seeks to provide … equality of opportunity and anti-discriminatory practice, ensuring that every child is included and supported' (DfE, 2014a: 5).

In addition to concerns about children and equal opportunities, there are concerns about equality of opportunities for adults. The Early Years Development and Care Partnerships (EYDCPs) are charged with the responsibility of providing equal opportunities for men, for people with disabilities and for older people who work in childcare settings and with actively encouraging their participation.

Equal opportunities and early years employees

Early years practitioners who become employers, for example as proprietors of a private nursery or manager in a Children's Centre, have a duty to implement equal opportunities and anti-discriminatory practice for staff, as established in the Equality Act 2010, which replaces a wide range of Acts dealing with equal pay, discrimination on the grounds of age, race relations and religious hatred, disability and special educational needs, work and family, and connects to the Human Rights Act 1998. Employers encounter the practicalities of equal opportunities when they employ new staff or when conflicts emerge between employees, or employer and employees. The Equality Act 2010 is also called upon when planning the environment of a nursery, including access to outdoor activities.

Equal opportunities – creating the ethos

Providing equal opportunities is not just a matter of legislation. It is unlikely that the legal framework can be brought to life without staff in early years settings having a cognitive and affective commitment to equal opportunities. Equal opportunities for young children are predicated on two main arguments. Firstly, there is a moral obligation to provide children, like everybody else, with equal opportunities. Because children are not in control of their own lives but are dependent on their parents for their social and economic position, it is incumbent upon society to protect their rights and treat them equally. For example, Child Benefit is a universal benefit for all children, rich and poor, and any increases to address poverty will be equally applicable to all children. In contrast, adults' eligibility for benefits may be connected to employment, training or actively seeking work because adults are perceived as being largely in control of their own social and economic destinies. Secondly, there is the argument that sees children as our future and as the makers of future societies. This argument is connected to a belief that we should aspire to provide children with the social competence to respect other groups and individuals (Lindon, 2012; Siraj-Blatchford, 2014). This approach looks towards the future in its desire for a particular version of a just world that has not yet been reached but that, with suitable nurturing, may be achievable in future generations.

Definitions

Equality of opportunities appeals to our sense of justice, but it is not an easy notion to work with. It lacks a clear definition and is used in different contexts and for a wide range of purposes. Equal opportunities can be based on 'minimalist' or on 'maximalist' principles. The 'minimalist' position aims to create 'level playing fields' for competition, to avoid unjust discrimination; it results in unequal but fair outcomes. For example, providing free nursery education for all four-year-olds could be interpreted as providing the necessary conditions for fair competition in school, leading to fair competition for university places in the future. The 'maximalist' position attempts to rectify both discrimination and disadvantage and aims to create equal outcomes (Alcock *et al.*, 2002; Blakemore and Griggs, 2013). An extreme way to accomplish this might be through a generous citizen's income, payable to all individuals, independent, for example, of age and of labour market participation. The New Labour government (1997–2010) had adopted some characteristics of the 'maximalist' principles in declaring its aim to abolish child poverty through a system of benefits available to all lower-income families with children.

In the field of early childhood studies, the definition of equal opportunities depends on how we see children and their role in society. Early years provision can fulfil a number of functions depending on how narrowly equal opportunities are defined. They may be defined as the duty to prepare children for future competition in the educational system and in the labour market. They may be defined in terms of eliminating the disadvantages experienced by certain groups of children, for example by those from ethnic minorities, by boys or by children with disabilities. Equal opportunities may focus on the provision of an environment free from discrimination, to be enjoyed by children here and now. Projects like Sure Start aim to combine all these aims by providing high-quality preschool education and play in high-quality buildings situated in areas of disadvantage. In addition it is hoped that elimination of disadvantage for preschool children may result in long-term benefits for society in terms of reduction in crime and unemployment. Tackling multiple disadvantages early in the lives of children may help break the cycle of social exclusion. The short-term costs will be more than offset by a reduction in the long-term need for social welfare and benefits, by reduced levels of crime, and by an increased level of income tax received by the Exchequer (Glass, 1999 and see Chapter 16). Lessons learnt from Sure Start inform the 3,500 new Centres of Excellence which the Labour government promised to establish by 2010. The coalition Government, which came to office in 2010, paid lip service to the over 3,500 Sure Start Children's Centres but felt no inhibitions about cutting funding. Consequently some centres shut their doors, others had to limit their services, engendering a sense of uncertainty, and further funding cuts threaten the remaining 3,300 centres (4Children, 2014; Nursery World, 2014).

Attempts to find an acceptable position between a 'minimalist' and a 'maximalist' definition do not adequately represent the complexity and interdependence of potential detriments. The capabilities approach (Sen, 1985; Nussbaum, 2003) avoids undue emphasis on disadvantages by focusing not simply on people's freedom from harm but on what they need to enjoy the freedom to flourish as human beings, ensuring they have genuine autonomy to shape a life worth living. In order to tackle inequality for children it may be helpful to map children's situations. For this purpose Burchardt *et al.* (2009) have drawn up a special capabilities list for children, building on three types of inequality: of outcome, process and autonomy. These are set out in ten domains: Life; Health; Physical Security; Legal Security; Education and Learning; Standard of Living; Productive and Valued Activities; Individual, Family and Social Life; Identity, Expression and Self-respect; and Participation, Influence and Voice.

Challenging discrimination

The legal framework and the various standards pertaining to children and early years provision provide some indication of the kinds of disadvantage and discrimination at work in Britain, for example gender, ethnicity, physical and mental ability, and perhaps overlapping these, language and religion. They enshrine the belief that we all have an obligation to challenge sexism, racism and 'ableism' (a term linked to discrimination on the grounds of disability). Gaine (1995: 27) defined racism as:

> *a pattern of social relations and structures, and a discourse (a linguistic and conceptual process of defining and positioning) which has specific outcomes operating against less powerful groups defined 'racially'.*

This definition may be adapted to each of the different forms of discrimination by replacing racially with, 'by sex', 'by ability' and so on. This exercise can help us to distinguish between children who are more likely to start from a disadvantaged position and those who suffer unfair discrimination. The distinction between disadvantage and discrimination also helps us to keep in mind that patterns and relationships change over time and can be demonstrated through example – for instance, through the idea of 'sexism'. Children in Britain grow up in a society where women and men have equal rights. However, women do not have financial equality with men. In spite of the fact that women have equal voting rights, equal pension rights and equal employment rights, that they are present in large numbers in the labour market, and that fathers are spending more time with their children (Hatten *et al.*, 2003; McVeigh and Finch, 2014), women still earn on average 19.7 per cent less than men (Equal Pay Portal, 2014). The gap between men's and women's earnings in full-time employment is continuing to narrow but is increasing for those in part-time work. In addition, despite their equal rights, women are far less likely to be in powerful positions such as company managers, civil servants and politicians.

A good example of the importance of distinguishing between disadvantage and discrimination is the academic achievement of boys and girls. Recently girls' examination results at all levels have been better than boys'. What does this mean? Does it mean that boys are disadvantaged by the present system of schooling? Do we need to redress the balance with some gender-specific strategies (Arnot *et al.*, 1998; Skelton and Hall, 2001; Francis and Skelton, 2005)? Or does it mean that educational settings are now discriminating against boys? What does it mean for the future? Does it mean that once this generation of pupils has reached the labour market, women will progress faster up career ladders and earn more money than their male contemporaries? Or will gender-specific power relationships continue to cancel out educational achievements?

Working with ambiguous concepts of equal opportunities

An example of ambiguity in interpretation of equality of opportunity is the approach towards children whose first language is not English. Some would argue that these children are disadvantaged in relation to their English peers and, in order to create a 'level playing field', they would benefit from additional English language support. Once these young people have achieved an approximately equal command of the English language they are in a better position to compete in school, later on in the labour market and in further and higher education. This perspective led, not so long ago, to a demand in some quarters for parents to speak English at home to 'overcome the schizophrenia which bedevils generational relationships' (Blunkett, 2002: 77). On the other hand, research has shown that bilingual children who are supported in the development of their home language go on to achieve higher standards in English (Cummins, 1984; Cummins, 2000; Smidt, 2008). Children growing up with more than one language and receiving support in developing language skills also achieve more highly in other areas of the curriculum (Brown, 1998). Early years practitioners ought to be aware of these issues when they are devising programmes for children whose first language is not English.

What are the wider implications of equal opportunities for early years settings? Providers of care and education for young children are required to comply with equality legislation. However, discrimination can take place in quite subtle ways. It can be difficult to translate theories of equality into actual practice. Siraj-Blatchford (2014) observed that some children are disadvantaged because some early years staff have a poor understanding of children from diverse backgrounds.

For example, the two concepts 'race' and 'ethnicity' are often confused – not only by early years practitioners. The term 'race' rests upon beliefs about the importance of supposed biological differences; these differences are then linked to differences in intelligence and social behaviour. Genetic differences determining skin colour are minimal and do not support 'race' as a scientific argument. Individual differences within a group are much greater than between groups. Some people argue that race is a purely social construct based on observed physical and cultural characteristics of individuals (Banton, 1987) and bound in the historical and political context of the time when it emerged (Baldock, 2010). The concept 'ethnicity' moves away from biological explanations and includes the historical, social and cultural context in which people live. An ethnic group is seen as a group of people who hold a sense of identity which may arise from a distinct history, nationality, language, norms, beliefs and traditions. This is expressed in many different ways and is often quite striking at the level of detail. For example, the food we eat, how we prepare it and what counts as good table manners vary enormously. Norms and traditions can be accepted as just 'doing things differently'. Ethnicity as a concept becomes problematic when these traditions are perceived as being too tight, an unchangeable state of affairs which ignores the agency of people and that people can be members of a number of different communities. Not all emerging conflicts can be avoided by working on becoming more and more flexible and accepting of differences (Anning and Edwards, 2006). Also, when children need protection, care pathways may be counter to the belief systems of their parents, for example regarding mental health services and social care and welfare interventions, and in the interest of the child, parental wishes and feelings may be overridden (EHRC, 2008). Examples can be found in relation to role expectations for girls and boys and approaches to corporal punishment. At times norms and traditions come into conflict with the law of the host country. For example, the practice of taking child brides is illegal in Britain although it may be condoned among certain ethnic groups who live here.

Chris Gaine, a former teacher in a predominantly white school, was interested in how teachers continue to claim that racism is not a problem in their school. He identified a number of reasons why teachers and other professionals do not see racism. They may ignore racism because they are unwilling to challenge their own prejudices; they may not have been confronted directly with racism themselves; or they may believe that dealing with racism is not their business. They may feel reluctant to approach such a sensitive and potentially explosive issue (Gaine, 1995, 2005). This reluctance to confront discrimination may be a problem for practitioners in early years, too.

Creating equality of opportunity in early years settings

One starting point for creating equality of opportunity in early years settings is for practitioners to look more closely at how children relate to each other. Literature on children and equal opportunities provides many examples of children using other children's gender, race, religion, language and the sexual orientation or the economic position of their parents to call children names or to exclude them from their activities (Claire *et al.*, 1993; Brown, 1998; DCSF, 2008b; DfE, 2014b). Accidental eavesdropping on children and anecdotal evidence suggests that not much has changed. Why do children do this? Some illumination is provided by research into gender. Broadly there are two schools of thought. One explains gender differences in biological terms ('nature'); the other explains it with reference to socialisation ('nurture'). Practitioners who are more convinced by biological explanations, such as different hormone levels or gender-specific brain functions, may be more inclined to accept and accommodate the view that boys do not behave like girls and vice versa. Those who lean towards explanations linked to the socialisation process are interested in how gender roles are constructed and how they change over time and across different contexts and may be inclined to resist the idea that certain activities may be more suitable for boys or for girls. However, others argue that 'nature' and 'nurture' are so interdependent that attempting to disentangle them is unhelpful (Head, 1999). Biological explanations may lead straight into gender dualism, but *learning* to be male or female may also result in very similar generalisations with a focus on differences between boys and girls. From a very early age, children learn what boys and men do and what girls and women do. It has been suggested that when children display 'gender appropriate' behaviour they are rewarded by adults, who may not be aware that they treat boys and girls differently. At the same time others argue that children are active in constructing their own gender roles, forming their gender identity by acting out behaviour that they perceive to be opposite to that displayed by the opposite sex. This explanation emphasises the fluidity of the concept of gender and of children's attempts to 'try out' roles (Skelton and Hall, 2001; Martin, 2011).

Children's developing understanding of self and others

In the same way that children identify with and construct gender roles, they also learn and construct attitudes towards ethnic groups. Milner (1983) found that by the age of two children notice differences in skin colour and between three and five they come to learn, regardless of their own skin colour, that in Britain it is 'better' to be white than black. What is known about children's development of gender identities may be adapted to other areas of their identity. Children develop an understanding of themselves and of others from a number of key sources: their parents and wider family, their peers, their early childhood settings, their neighbourhoods and the media. The implication for work with young children is that we have to find ways of supporting children's growing sense of self in an atmosphere where difference itself is valued and not perceived as a threat. The task of early childhood settings is to foster positive attitudes and behaviour by engaging in anti-discriminatory practice and including all children and families. Writing about the effects of racism on young children, Derman-Sparks (1989) states that early childhood educators have a responsibility to prevent and oppose any damage from racism before it becomes established. Many textbooks on early years practice refer to, or have sections on, equal opportunities. They appeal to practitioners' duty to implement anti-discriminatory practice (Bruce *et al.*, 2010; Lindon, 2012) or provide lists of recommendations for becoming an inclusive setting. However, what do we mean by 'inclusive'? Striving towards multiculturalism in settings has come under attack for ignoring power relationships and being uncritical (Baldock, 2010). What exactly does a multicultural setting look like? Is there a danger, for example, in introducing children to other cultures through studying what might be termed 'exotic' (romanticised, tokenistic and perhaps even incorrect) versions of different cultures (Houlton, 1986)? Practitioners planning to use persona dolls as a tool to introduce young children to people from cultural minorities have experienced some difficulties in challenging their own stereotypes (Farmer, 2002). Is it possible that in our endeavour to include as many different ways of living together as possible, we are distracted from thinking more deeply about the stereotypes we may actually be promoting (Woods, 1998) and that we are avoiding consideration of issues of power and structure? A shift towards a focus on how people relate to each other and the potential of supporting intercultural competence or cultural capability (Baldock, 2010; Andreotti, 2011; Trahar, 2011) may help to develop good practice.

Challenging adult stereotypes

To unravel the question of how to develop cultural capability we have to recognise that we all operate with stereotypes. At one level people have to operate with simplifications in order to think with concepts and to make quick decisions. All adults hold deep-seated ideas about gender, ethnicity, age and so on, and about what constitutes appropriate behaviour within their cultural and/or religious framework. Children pick up both positive and negative attitudes and behaviours. In order to help children to unlearn misconceptions and stereotypical thinking that they may have absorbed (Brown, 1998), early years practitioners have to become aware of their own stereotypical assumptions. Stereotypes are oversimplified generalisations and, if based on misleading information or mistakenly applied, can have negative implications. Take for example the stereotypical assumption that black people are good at sport. For the athletic black child it can be a great source of reassurance and identity. But stereotypes like this can undermine the confidence and feelings of self-worth of black children who are not good at sport. Additionally, they can have negative implications for black children who are steered towards sporting achievement but get less support for academic attainment. The effect on white children could be negative, too.

Inclusion and exclusion

How do we know whether our beliefs, values and practices are based on ill-informed stereotypes preventing us from acknowledging complex situations? Asking this question is itself a good starting point. The question forces us to think more widely about the concepts and debates around, for example, sex and gender, race and ethnicity and integration and inclusion. An understanding of the theoretical models which explain differences can be useful. These theoretical frameworks can help us to explore issues of inclusion and exclusion, discrimination and anti-discriminatory work and to examine areas of equal opportunities in relation to our own life.

As important as it is to look at the stereotypes individuals hold, it does not mean that the context within which they are formed, accepted and spread is less significant. More effective anti-discriminatory practice can be supported by using the PCS analysis (Thompson, 2006). The 'P' stands for the personal, including prejudice and practice, which is embedded in the cultural, reflected in commonalities, consensus and conformity (the 'C'). 'C' also includes the 'comic' or humour. Jokes are powerful in passing on stereotypes and can be very hurtful but humour is also a potent strategy against oppression. The personal and the cultural are embedded in 'S', the structural, for example existing social divisions and the struggle over these, and 'S' is reflected in legal frameworks. None of these perspectives by itself can explain existing discrimination or show ways to move towards more acceptable practice.

A good example of how theory informs practice and supports reflexivity is provided by two models of disability which have held sway over the past century. For much of the 20th century, the cause of a disability was seen as physical and residing within the individual person. This perspective is referred to as the 'medical model'.

The medical model understands disability as the outcome of disease, trauma or health condition. Disability is the outcome of a 'tragic event' and there is no cure. Disabled people cannot participate fully in society and are dependent on others. Until the 1970s many children with any form of disability were seen as 'ineducable' and removed from their parental homes to spend their lives in institutions. After the Education Act of 1970 made local education authorities responsible for the education of all children, children with impairments most frequently found themselves in special schools, segregated from mainstream education (Wall, 2011).

In contrast to a focus on the individual, the 'social model' of disability looks at the context within which impairments become disabilities. Disability is seen as a socially created problem. Features in specific physical environments and in the culture and prevalent attitudes can present barriers to full participation for individuals. For example, it is not the inability to walk but the lack of an affordable wheelchair, and the lack of ramps or lifts that prevent a partially paralysed child from gaining easy access to a school built on different levels. Another barrier can be bullying (DfE, 2014b). Within the social model the problem of disability demands a political response. This perspective requires the development of social welfare strategies that support autonomy and promote independence.

Segregating children with impairments into institutions was widely criticised. The first move to end this segregation was to 'integrate' children with disabilities into mainstream schools. Integration sometimes takes the form of a special school and a mainstream school sharing premises; sometimes schools offer separate lessons for children with special educational needs but allow for shared break times; sometimes schools offer some shared lessons. These forms of integration of children in mainstream services are all informed by the medical model. The focus is on the individual child: he or she will be assessed by a specialist; the diagnosis will specify expected outcomes and recommend an individually tailored programme. Ainscow (1995) suggested that this definition of integration merely means making a few additional arrangements for individual children with disabilities and has little overall effect on their opportunities for becoming full members of the group (for more on interpretations of integration see Chapter 9).

Since the late 1980s, 'inclusion' has superseded 'integration'. 'Inclusion', based on the social model, focuses on the classroom, looks at teaching and learning factors and aims to create an adaptive, supportive regular classroom which will benefit all children. In the context of school education, inclusion is a 'process of increasing the participation of students in, and reducing their exclusion from, the cultures, curricula and communities in local schools' (Centre for Studies on Inclusive Education, 2010 in Wall, 2011). This definition does not emphasise the active part children with disabilities can play. Farrell (2001: 7) argues that 'for inclusion to be effective pupils must actively belong to, be welcomed by and participate in a school and community – that is they should be fully included'. So, inclusive education is the outcome of a collaborative approach by the whole school community. This should include a more critical examination of the use of teaching assistants. They are often used to substitute for teacher's time resulting in children with SEN having less access to support from more highly qualified teachers (Lamb, 2009).

In the past, the government has shown a strong commitment to inclusion (DfES, 2004; Cabinet Office, 2005; DfES, 2006; DCSF, 2008a; DCSF, 2009). Cuts and changes in funding can be confusing for parents and service providers alike. The Children and Families Act 2014 does not use the term inclusion, despite setting out the duties in respect of vulnerable children. From the perspective of children with disabilities and their families there is plenty of room for improvement. A review of service provision for children with disabilities and their families showed that they face a lottery of provision and access, often depending on how hard parents can push; they have to rely on a patchwork of services, which sometimes offer too little, too late (Audit Commission, 2003; Lamb, 2009). An inclusive approach may meet resistance from specialists in special schools because they feel their expertise is overlooked. There may also be resistance from teachers and practitioners from mainstream services because they feel ill-equipped to implement inclusive practice (DfES, 2004). It appears that tensions between the medical model and the social model of disability continue to impact on service provision and on the attitudes of all involved.

Conclusion

In terms of 'natural justice', equality of opportunity is like apple pie and motherhood – it appeals to all of us. But equality of opportunity is not an easy concept to work with. It requires a lot of hard thinking on the part of practitioners and that requires us to abandon common-sense beliefs based on uncritical stereotyping. Critical reflection offers an opportunity to think more widely and to examine our vision of the future for our children. This chapter has traced some of the ways in which we can think critically about equality of opportunity. Reflecting on our own values and ways of thinking about equality of opportunities and the engagement with the context within which they emerge also strengthens our ability to develop a critical stance. If we do this, the children we are working with may also develop an appreciation for the benefits of differences, which will contribute to children's wider learning and development.

Debates around equal opportunities involve arguments about 'nature' and 'nurture'. Although it has been pointed out that 'nature' and 'nurture' are intertwined and that to some extent this relationship cannot be undone, it is still valuable to examine the arguments and decide what is and is not acceptable. To use the minimal genetic differences between people of different skin colour as justification for discrimination is not acceptable, nor is it acceptable, for example, to prescribe medicines which may have been tested only on a limited sample of the population (one size fits all). However, exploring the medical needs and differences of children with disabilities can positively inform the process of becoming an inclusive day centre or school. Inclusion and exclusion, discrimination and anti-discriminatory practice are processes which take place on a number of interlinked levels. Equal opportunities cannot be achieved by stopping short at the individual level, by blaming cultural differences or by declaring that social structures are fixed (Thompson, 2006).

This chapter has used a number of examples of discrimination to draw out common patterns. It can only provide a brief introduction. Focusing on areas of conflict and difficulty can give the impression that a mass of interdependent problems must be tackled before we can develop truly inclusive practices. However, benefits achieved by thinking through and practising ways of letting positive relationships grow, where children, practitioners, parents and friends gain, cannot be highlighted strongly enough. Early years practitioners play an important role in supporting discussions and practices that allow everyone to be part of creating an inclusive setting: colleagues, children, parents and the community. Equality of opportunity cannot be prescribed through legislation alone and, as early years practitioners, we have a duty to involve ourselves in the long process of developing satisfactory anti-discriminatory practices. This is a particularly clear example of the fact that attitudes are not changed by policies or practices but by the processes by which policies and practices are explored, negotiated, agreed and reviewed. The theoretical and practical engagement with inclusion has a huge potential for developing satisfactory relationships within and between communities.

ACTIVITY 1

Tackling inequality in your nursery

Imagine that you are a member of staff who has recently been given responsibility for equal opportunities in a Children's Centre in a predominantly white rural community. What elements would you include in a policy document supporting equal opportunities for the children and parents? What obstacles do you foresee in changing attitudes and incorporating the policy into practice? How might you work with others to tackle these obstacles?

ACTIVITY 2

Getting in the picture

Select a range of media intended to entertain and educate children, like picture books, television programmes, DVDs and children's songs. How are gender, ethnicity and class relationships represented? Do they pick up issues like disability, migration and different family forms? If yes, how are children and adults represented? You will find some ideas on how to analyse these representations in Saunders' (2000) book Happy Ever Afters: A Storybook Guide to Teaching Children about Disability. *What would you change?*

FURTHER READING

Dickins, M. (2014) *A – Z of Inclusion in Early Childhood.* Maidenhead: Open University Press.

Dickins provides an easy to read introduction to key terms and major themes of exclusion and inclusion. Key points, case studies and activities help the reader to engage with the themes of disability, gender and race and show how to tackle inequalities in early years settings. She also tackles some of the more difficult theoretical issues.

Martin, B. (2011) *Children at Play: Learning Gender in the Early Years.* Stoke on Trent: Trentham Books.

This book is the result of a two-year observation of young children as they develop and practise gender identity. The discussion contributes to critically exploring gender dualism and makes a strong case that practitioners have to intervene so children can cross gender borders successfully.

Nutbrown, C. and Clough, P. (2013) *Inclusion in the Early Years.* London: SAGE.

This book offers a readable account of inclusive practice in the early years, making links to relevant theories. The strength of the book is the wider focus on talking about exclusion of children, their families and communities, including staff working in early childhood settings.

Channel Four (2003–2013) *Born to be Different,* Series 1–7.

The series follows six children born with a disability from birth in Britain. This documentary presents an empathetic but unsentimental account of the experiences of the children and their families.

REFERENCES

4Children (2014) *Sure Start Children's Centres Census 2014: A National Overview of Sure Start Children's Centres in 2014.* London: 4Children.

Ainscow, M. (1995) Education For All: Making it Happen. *Support for Learning,* 10(4): 147–54.

Alcock, P., Erskine, A. and May, M. (eds). (2002) *The Blackwell Dictionary of Social Policy.* Oxford: Blackwell.

Andreotti, V. (2011) *Actionable Postcolonial Theory in Education.* New York: Palgrave MacMillan.

Anning, A. and Edwards, A. (2006) *Promoting Children's Learning from Birth to Five: Developing the New Early Years Professional* (2nd edn). Maidenhead: Open University Press.

Arnot, M., Gray, J., James, M. and Rudduck, J. (1998) *Recent Research on Gender and Educational Performance.* London: HMSO.

Audit Commission (2003) *Services for Disabled Children: A Review of Services for Disabled Children and their Families.* London: Audit Commission.

Baldock, P. (2010) *Understanding Cultural Diversity in the Early Years.* London: SAGE.

Banton, M. (1987) *Racial Theories.* Cambridge: Cambridge University Press.

Barnardos (2014) *Cedars: Two Years On.* London: Barnardos.

Blakemore, K. and Griggs, E. (2013) *Social Policy: An Introduction* (4th edn). Buckingham: Open University Press.

Blunkett, D. (2002) Integration with diversity: globalisation and the renewal of democracy and civil society. In P. Griffith and M. Leonard (eds), *Reclaiming Britishness.* London: The Foreign Policy Centre.

Brown, B. (1998) *Unlearning Discrimination in the Early Years.* Stoke on Trent: Trentham.

Bruce, T., Meggitt, C. and Grenier, J. (2010) *Child Care and Education* (5th edn). London: Hodder Education.

Burchardt, T., Tsang, T. and Vizard, P. (2009) *Specialist Consultation on the List of Central and Valuable Capabilities for Children.* Manchester: Equality and Human Rights Commission.

Cabinet Office (2005) *Improving the Life Chances of Disabled People.* London: Strategy Unit.

Claire, H., Maybin, J. and Swann, J. (eds) (1993) *Equality Matters: Case Studies from the Primary School.* Clevedon, PA: Multilingual Matters.

Cummins, J. (1984) *Bilingualism and Special Education: Issues in Assessment and Pedagogy.* Bristol: Multilingual Matters.

Cummins, J. (2000) *Language, Power and Pedagogy: Bilingual Children in the Crossfire.* Bristol: Multilingual Matters.

DCSF (Department for Children, Schools and Families) (2008a) *Statutory Framework for the Early Years Foundation Stage: Setting the Standards for Learning, Development and Care for Children from Birth to Five.* Nottingham: DCSF Publications.

DCSF (Department for Children, Schools and Families) (2008b) *Bullying Involving Children with Special Educational Needs and Disabilities. Safe to Learn: Embedding Anti-bullying Work in Schools.* London: DCSF Publications.

DCSF (Department for Children, Schools and Families) (2009) *Special Educational Needs (SEN) – A Guide for Parents and Carers.* London: DCSF Publications.

Derman-Sparks, L. (1989) *Anti-bias Curriculum: Tools for Empowering Young Children.* Washington, DC: NAEYC.

DfE (Department for Education) (2014a) *Statutory Framework for the Early Years Foundation Stage: Setting the Standards for Learning, Development and Care for Children from Birth to Five.* London: DfE Publications.

DfE (Department for Education) (2014b) *Preventing and Tackling Bullying: Advice for Headteachers, Staff and Governing Bodies.* London: DfE.

DfES (Department for Education and Skills) (2003) *Every Child Matters: Green Paper.* London: The Stationery Office.

DfES (Department for Education and Skills) (2004) *Removing Barriers to Achievement: The Government's Strategy for SEN.* Nottingham: DfES Publications.

DfES (Department for Education and Skills) (2006) *Implementing the Disability Discrimination Act (DDA) in Schools and Early Years Settings.* London: DfES Publications.

EHRC (Equality and Human Rights Commission) (2008) *Response of the EHRC to the Consultation on a National Framework for Assessing Children and Young People's Continuing Care.* London: Department of Health.

Equal Pay Portal (2014) Statistics. Available at: http://www.equalpayportal.co.uk/statistics/ (accessed 17 October 2014).

Farmer, G. (2002) Dolls with stories to tell. In C. Nutbrown (ed.), *Research Studies in Early Childhood Education.* Stoke-on-Trent: Trentham.

Farrell, P. (2001) Special education in the last 20 years: have things really got better? *British Journal of Special Education*, 28(1): 3–9.

Francis, B. and Skelton, C. (2005) *Reassessing Gender and Achievement: Questioning Contemporary Key Debates.* London: Routledge.

Gaine, C. (1995) *Still No Problem Here.* Stoke-on-Trent: Trentham Books.

Gaine, C. (2005) *We're All White Thanks: The Persisting Myth About 'White' Schools.* Stoke-on-Trent: Trentham Books.

Glass, N. (1999) Sure Start: the development of an early intervention programme for young children in the United Kingdom. *Children & Society*, 13(4): 257–64.

Hatten, W., Vinter, L. and Williams, R. (2003) *Dads on Dads: Needs and Expectations at Home and at Work.* London: MORI.

Head, J. (1999) *Understanding the Boys.* London: Falmer.

Houlton, D. (1986) *Cultural Diversity in the Primary School*. London: B.T. Batsford Ltd.

Lamb, B. (2009) *Lamb Inquiry: Special Educational Needs and Parental Confidence*. London: DCFS.

Lindon, J. (2012) *Equality in Early Childhood: Linking Theory and Practice* (2nd edn). London: Hodder Education.

Lorek, A., Sheridan, M., Ehntholt, K., Nesbitt, A., Wey, E., Githinji, C., Rossor, E. and Wickramasinghe, R. (2009) The mental and physical health difficulties of children held within a British immigration detention centre: A pilot study. *Child Abuse and Neglect*, 33(9): 573–85.

McVeigh, T. and Finch, I. (2014) Fathers spend seven times more with their children than in the 1970s. *Guardian*, 15 June.

Martin, B. (2011) *Children at Play: Learning Gender in the Early Years*. Stoke on Trent: Trentham Books.

Milner, D. (1983) *Children and Race – Ten Years On*. London: Ward Lock Educational.

Nursery World (2014) 120 Children's Centres to close or under threat. Available at: http://www.nursery-world.co.uk/nursery-world/news/1148721/120-childrens-centres-close-threat (accessed 16 December 2014).

Nussbaum, M. (2003) Capabilities as fundamental entitlements: Sen and social justice. *Feminist Economics*, 9(2–3): 33–59.

Saunders, K. (2000) *Happy Ever Afters: A Storybook Code to Teaching Children about Disability*. Stoke-on-Trent: Trentham.

Sen, A. (1985) *Commodities and Capabilities*. Oxford: Elsevier Science Publishers.

Siraj-Blatchford, I. (2014) Diversity, inclusion and learning in the early years. In G. Pugh and B. Duffy (eds), *Contemporary Issues in the Early Years* (6th edn). London: SAGE.

Skelton, C. and Hall, E. (2001) *The Development of Gender Roles in Young Children: A Review of Policy and Literature*. Manchester: Research and Resources Unit, Equal Opportunities Commission.

Smidt, S. (2008) *Supporting Multilingual Learners in the Early Years: Many Languages – Many Children*. Abingdon: Routledge.

Thompson, N. (2006) *Anti-Discriminatory Practice: Challenging Discrimination and Oppression* (4th edn). Baskingstoke, New York: Palgrave.

Trahar, S. (2011) *Developing Cultural Capability in International Higher Education: A Narrative Enquiry*. Abingdon: Routledge.

UN (United Nations) (1989) UN Convention on the Rights of the Child. Available at: http//www.unesco.org/education/pdf/CHILD_E.PDF (accessed 7 January 2010).

Wall, K. (2011) *Special Needs and Early Years: A Practitioner's Guide* (3rd edn). London: SAGE.

Wirtz, L., Franks, M., Johnson, F. and Nandy, L. (2009) *Hidden Children – Separated Children at Risk*. London: The Children's Society.

Woods, M. (1998) Early childhood education in preschool settings. In J. Taylor and M. Woods (eds), *Early Childhood Studies: An Holistic Introduction*. London: Arnold.

Part 3

Multiprofessional practice: developing empowering communities

Language, cultural identity and belonging

Sofia Chanda-Gool and Mandy Andrews

Introduction

Young children are particularly open to social and cultural influences. Working with young children and families presents special opportunities for enhancing equality across families and communities. Yet there are also challenges in delivering inclusive practices within a diverse society.

This chapter arose from a conversation we had as colleagues discussing language in relation to our teaching around the subject of equality. We realised that we both had different interpretations of one word: integration. We had a common purpose in the promotion of multicultural awareness yet we momentarily did not understand each other and each felt a little disequilibrated. The word was insufficient to enable transfer of the concepts we wished to express. Our different understandings separated us. In time we considered that if we were confused, others might be too and that the language of inclusion, identity and feelings around ownership of language and meaning were worth exploring further and sharing. This chapter arose from these discussions. We recognise that language can liberate or alternatively constrain; it can include or exclude us. It can convey our beliefs and values, our shared meanings, or conversely it can be ambiguous revealing difference, prejudices and power struggles. We will consider the importance of language and the power that resides in the naming of identity, culture and belonging, and how ownership and complexity arise from relational activity between people.

Language conferred upon us

At the beginning of our lives, language is conferred upon us through the specific language or languages that our carers introduce us to. Chomsky (2006) argues that we all have an innate language acquisition device enabling any child to 'pick up' languages. However, Vygotsky's (1978) social constructivist perspective highlights that learning and language are embedded in a social context. He recognised that children learn in communities that have already accommodated understandings and which subtly engage young children in acquiring shared meanings. As neonates our capacity to communicate how we feel, think and what we want is crucial to our survival but we do not yet use conventional language; carers are intimately involved in interpreting what we want, giving us a name, helping us to become part of the world we have arrived into and in turn guiding us into shared meanings. Rogoff (1990) expands this notion and offers illustrations of the processes of 'guided participation' through which parents and carers convey sociocultural meanings to their children. Young children are open to learning a particular perspective and understanding of the world from adults. The way carers choose to respond to us, and what they draw our attention to, is interwoven with cultural beliefs, practices, assumptions and experiences that in turn influence our own perceptions and understandings. There is also a personal dimension: 'our name' and the way our carers communicate with us give us a sense of identity.

Language defines who we are, how others see us and how we see ourselves

It is through language that we discover how we are to be called and who we belong to: our community. Beliefs and experiences are communicated and absorbed through language. The way we 'see' or perceive our world often relates to a range of particular concepts conveyed through language and embedded in our culture. Suzanne Romaine (2014) recently expressed her concern that the present global loss of languages perpetuates not only the loss of culture but also, for some societies, loss of access to a future. Writing for the *New Internationalist*, Romaine identifies how in many rural areas of developing countries languages are becoming extinct as a few dominant languages such as English take over. Castells (2006) analyses how, challenged by globalisation and the potential homogenisation of cultures, different identities may also struggle to survive. Romaine (2014: 26) argues that: 'The issue of language loss cannot be separated from people, their identities, their cultural heritage, their wellbeing and their rights…'. Without preservation of language some groups face a psychic extinction, because language conveys not just material needs and tangible realities but also more mysterious and transient hopes and feelings. The struggle to retain and communicate particular experiences, feelings and cultural beliefs has been realised in the revival of an Australian Aboriginal language: 'Kaurna' which has in turn helped to revive the identity, artistic expression and culture of the Kaurna People (Emery, 2012).

We use words and language to define ourselves daily, to express how we feel and experience different contexts. At one moment a person can be 'a mother', and in the next perhaps an 'Asian woman', 'a lecturer' or 'a Christian'. These words all convey concepts in symbolic form and we choose which concepts to present depending on the context and our desire to merge with others or assert a powerful identity. However, these identities convey meanings to others and children will in time learn the symbolic messages offered by the adult's choice.

Language embedded in cultures and conveying meanings

The mental images children and adults hold may merely offer symbolic shorthand for complex concepts and understandings. This can be illustrated by thinking of a job role such as 'fireman' or 'doctor'. We would expect others to be able to visualise these roles, in part by uniform perhaps, and in part by cultural understandings introduced and absorbed in childhood. We may even ascribe a typical gender to this job role. If asked to draw people with these job roles, we would expect there to be some similarity within the Western world. Words and phrases enable us to own and share such symbolic understandings, though not always entirely accurately as stereotypes may have created dominant assumptions and associations. West and Hewstone (2011) identify how we absorb associations with certain words and concepts, such as 'good' and 'bad', very early on in life; for example we are likely to see insects or 'black people' as less attractive than 'white people' or flowers – we have formed judgments early on in life. These judgments have consequences for those who are thus labelled. In their seminal study, Kenneth and Mamie Clark (1947) identified that black children were sometimes identifying themselves as white to avoid lowering their self-esteem. Similarly Oliver (1990) identifies how people with disability are perceived as dependent, inferior or helpless and this has implications for how they are treated and feel about themselves. Thus one word can evoke powerful feelings and meanings.

One of the key messages from the disability movement is that people should not make assumptions about what a person may be experiencing, nor who they are, on the basis of medical classifications of impairment. Their needs are not determined by what 'people like them' can or cannot do. Experiences are individual and we need to check with people how they see themselves and what requirements *they* consider they have. The point being that use of language and 'shorthand' terminology such as 'autism', or 'wheelchair-user' prompts certain expectations around disability and can lose the distinctiveness of the person in the shared conceptual understanding. Meanings associated with certain words or terms therefore can affect our capacity to recognise someone as another human being or even to understand them. These assumptions also shape our attitudes.

Attitudes embedded within language can lead to simplified symbolism. 'Muslim' is a term that has recently acquired negative connotations as a result of the actions of certain groups who claim to be Muslim. Our views or attitudes about Islam may be simplified symbolic prejudices attached to the word 'Muslim' that do not encapsulate the complex and diverse range of beliefs and practices included within this term (Armstrong, 2000). Said (1993) highlighted that 'the West' can use a stereotyped view of Islam as a means of asserting its own self-importance or superiority. As noted above, such emerging connotations can have a profound effect on how confident or valued children and people from other cultures feel about themselves. Muslims living in the UK may feel inferior, undermined or threatened when they realise that some people in the UK see their religion as aggressive, dangerous, obsessive or even old-fashioned (Yildiz and Verkuyten, 2013). They may even want to pretend they do not adhere to the Muslim faith and use silence rather than voice their beliefs. Parpart and Kabeer (2010) highlighted how the non-use of language, silence, is also a powerful act, contradicting the normal understanding of 'giving voice' to express oppressions. The non-expression of suffering by women may play a role in the preservation of self and family. Remaining silent, not using language, can therefore be a form of passive power.

Language therefore becomes a site of conflict as different groups of understanding struggle to assert power in relational activity, but relational activity is complex, and language use is sometimes the outward acknowledgement of that struggle. Research has identified that people may have multiple social identities, but that having too many may have a negative mental impact on a human being. Is this perhaps because of the complexity of choices made? Shih and Sanchez (2005) describe 'marginal man' caught between two cultures but in reality not a member of either world. He can assume the mantle of accepted language, but this may hide a complex self-structure which has psychological implications about what he wants to portray about himself. In part it is a human desire to be a part of a social grouping that may encourage some to acquiesce, conform and thereby endorse the beliefs and values of the dominant majority within the wider society. It is sometimes hard to stand out from the crowd, or even to see alternative perspectives. Questioning dominant values may also shake our supportive social groupings, and we may lose some of our anonymity and interdependence if we do so. For example Pakistani children may feel compelled to deny their Muslim identity if they sense they will become vilified if they assert their beliefs and 'admit' to being Muslim (see Chanda-Gool, 2006).

Such identity and self-esteem issues are not just limited to race considerations. Shakespeare (2002) notes that disabled children are often unwilling to identify themselves as disabled. In part this is due to a fear that their abilities will be marginalised by the priority given to classification of their impairments. Their individuality can be dissolved into a symbolic concept. So paradoxically whilst a classification or diagnosis of someone's ability or disability has the potential to offer access to resources and support, it can also reduce that individual's self-concept to a homogenised stereotype. Therefore identities and identity concepts are not static, but reflect dynamic and evolving processes of self-structure and external labelling and definition. 'You are disabled' can be challenged by a self-construct that asserts 'I have different capabilities'. Therefore language is a site of power.

Language as a site of power

Much as language can be adopted to empower an individual, so it can be commandeered by social groups and by power relationships among people. As Romaine (2014: 26) asserts:

> *The poorest tend to have least access to the languages preferred in school ... children can more easily learn to read in a language they know, which provides a secure foundation for learning others later on. This then enables them to access wider opportunities and participate in life beyond their communities.*

Languages used within schools can be empowering for those who are familiar with the preferred language but disempowering for those who are less familiar with it. Bourdieu (1992) in his discussions on the concept of cultural capital used the term 'symbolic violence' to identify how the education system exerts power, specifically symbolic power, over its more subordinate members such as pupils or parents, through the use of language. He argues that when a system selects particular language, arbitrary knowledge and symbols and claims they are irrefutable and finite it thereby undermines other cultural knowledge, language and symbols. Even Bourdieu's choice of language – 'symbolic' and 'violence' – conveys something of a war waged through language. The educational system can paradoxically both enhance and develop knowledge and understanding and yet inhibit certain views and experience by reifying a specific language: it has its own bias (see Chanda-Gool, 2006).

Reclaiming language

Bourdieu (1992) argues that this symbolic power is only effective if people subordinate their other values, beliefs and languages to the dominant system: they have to be complicit. People can also defy the dominant power. Blackledge (2000) identifies how, for example, when members of a Bangladeshi community realised their languages and beliefs were ignored by the school, they defied the school's construction of knowledge by turning in on their community and rejecting the system. They then avoided attending parent and teacher meetings and engaging with the school. The school had rendered the Bangladeshi parents 'voiceless' by failing to offer bilingual support in the form of interpreters or bilingual teachers. The consequence of this was that the Bangladeshi children from these communities lived in divided worlds; they had to 'mind the gap' between their communities and their schools. It is interesting to reflect on who we feel holds the 'symbolic power' in relation to childcare. Is it parents and carers, governments with their power to influence funding of certain programmes, social scientists who articulate what may be going on, social services that make decisions about families' futures, or the schools and settings with their capacity to nurture or ignore?

Kreiner and Sheep (2009: 24) remind us that the only constant is change and that there is a permanent struggle between self-identity and social cohesion, whether in the workplace, in social contexts, or with wider social implications. A 'teacher' may self-identify as such, but relies in part on the confirmation of others who experience their teaching and reflect back that they are 'a teacher'. A teacher who is not reaffirmed in such relational activity may be deluded! They can passively accept the judgment of others, or reclaim the word 'teacher' by applying and promoting new conceptual meanings. Generally accepted concepts of teacherliness can be further reinforced or undermined by government legislation, guidance and understandings of what it is to be and behave like a teacher. The concept of teacherliness may be differently held by each group despite the term 'teacher' being universally used in the dominant language. This illustrates that there is an inherent and ongoing struggle centred on whose values and beliefs are to dominate in any particular setting, and a minority setting may be overwhelmed by particular cultural understandings endorsed by a wider society. When we are rendered 'voiceless' through lack of language, or control of the symbolism of the language, as Blackledge (2000) suggests, we lose our capacity to assert who we are and how we think. However, there may come a 'tipping point' when enough people who are rendered voiceless wish to reclaim the language that was once theirs (and perhaps also to reclaim the related concepts).

Assertions and struggles to own how we are perceived

Freire (1996) recognised that sharing ownership of language was a balancing and equalising process; dialogue and discussion are empowering in this arena of equality. Freire reminds us that words are more than just instruments for communication and dialogue; they have power and are subject to interpretation. For Freire, writing for equality, words have the potential to 'transform the world' (1996: 68) through our processes of reflection and action. He argued that if we did not reflect on the language and meaning of words, and take action as appropriate, the use of words degenerated into 'idle chatter' or 'verbalism' which he describes as 'a mere 'blah' (1996: 68). On the other hand, Freire argued, if the word was merely seized upon as powerful, but contained no subtlety in our reflective awareness and true ownership of its meaning, it was converted to 'activism' without substance, a stance which was equally pointless and which prevented true dialogue. True dialogue is not the act of one person 'depositing' ideas on another, nor is it a theoretical argument without action; for Freire, true dialogue, which contributes to equality, is about an 'encounter' between people with different perceptions and a resultant 'act of creation' as new understanding is born.

Once we realise that language is a living expression of social and relational concepts we can achieve an element of liberation in the ways we use it and the challenges we can explore and present. Rather than being 'tied' to 'correct' language, and fearful of being 'wrong', we can be aware that concepts such as 'integration' or 'disability' may change or be refined over time, possibly being displaced by other words with more subtle meaning. For example 'black' began as a derogatory term for people who were 'not white' and therefore without power. Over time it became owned by those people who were oppressed. Malcolm X (1925–1965) and others leading the civil rights movement in America transformed the word 'black' to become a powerful descriptor of positive identity and defiance. So that to say 'I am black' became an empowering statement rather than an acknowledgement of submission. Thus the 'black' movement became a strong statement, claiming a place in discussions about equality. Older members of the white community who had tried not to align with the language of black slavery had begun, in the UK of the 1950s and 1960s, to use the word 'coloured', thinking it was less contrasting and derogatory than the stark 'black'. However, once the term 'black' was owned by the community, seeking freedom from oppression the word 'coloured' was also considered as dated, and representative of underlying values of segregation. Use of the word 'coloured' showed a lack of understanding of the black community. The term 'white' or 'not coloured' assumes that white is a 'natural' condition and therefore another shift from 'coloured' was to 'people of colour'. So we can see how language became 'owned' by the oppressed group and had moved on. The language of dialogue in relation to race continues with the refining of 'Black', to 'Black Asian', 'Black Muslim' or 'BAME' (Black And Minority Ethnic) and so on. These terms symbolise both a commitment to racial identity within a larger equality movement between black and non-black people and identification of specific cultural heritages.

'Disabled' is another term with meanings which have changed subtly over time as a result of critical reflection, dialogue and action. 'Disabled' was a term that also emerged in the 1950s and 1960s and was used to signify the disadvantage experienced by someone with a particular impairment. The placing of the term 'disabled' either before or after the person in a sentence structure has been an area for dialogue and creation of new understanding. People with specific impairments advocated collectively for changes in the law to enable access to premises, services and support. Whilst equality laws were being drafted, 'the Disabled movement' was an appropriate term. However, the term then began to be owned by those implementing policy and so people with impairments in a local authority area became 'the disabled'. Such a term was then seen as derogatory to those experiencing disadvantage as a result of their impairments, as it seemed to lack respect for individuality, and indeed for the human aspect. Disabled people felt dehumanised, identified primarily by their impairment, particularly when terms such as 'the blind' or 'the mobility impaired' omitted the word 'people' altogether. Growing awareness of the impact of this labelling led to a phase of putting the person before the acknowledgement of disability so local authority equality training days emphasised the importance of using the term in this order 'people with a disability'. However, dialogue continued as power was reclaimed by people with impairments who felt oppressed by their lack of access to services and of a 'voice' in decisions that affected them and who sought an equal dialogue. A growing awareness of the oppression of the medical model, in which impairments should be 'fixed' or ameliorated until they could be managed by the person with a disability, led to a rejection of this model and to recognition that people were 'disabled' by society and by attitudes toward them. A person with a disability became again 'a disabled person': it was not so much that they had a disability but that they were disabled by the way they were seen and treated by others. It was the social construct that held the disabling attitudes.

The term that began our discussion about concepts and terminology was the word 'integration'. To those engaged in promoting disability awareness the concept of 'integrated' education (in which disabled children were included in mainstream classes for some of their school day) was more positive than 'segregated' education (in which children with impairments were educated in an entirely separate school) but the term 'integration' still highlighted the impairments in an individual and the need for support or adaptations to meet the individual's special needs, rather than addressing broader social and environmental barriers. The term gives children with specific needs an identity of difference when they are 'integrated' into other provision, perhaps for fixed periods of time. The word preferred by the disability movement, recognising the human identity of all, despite outward appearances or specific impairments, is 'inclusion'. This is a term which respects that all people have differences and needs and implies belonging together, despite differences.

However, if you apply the word 'inclusion' to the Indigenous Peoples of Australia it becomes paradoxical: Indigenous people were by their very name the 'first people' so it is not for the white population to let them in! Within the context of Australia, these indigenous people's languages and cultures are no longer part of the mainstream society. When they attend mainstream schools, and are included, their experience is that their cultures are excluded or denied and in some cases denigrated (Morgan, 1988; Gool and Patton, 1998). Moreover the reclaiming of a language here transcended the mere word 'inclusion'. As we have discussed, the struggle for words to describe who we are and what we experience exists within a world of assumptions, beliefs, cultures and historically bound contexts.

Mac Naughton (2005: 27) draws on the writings of the philosopher Foucault to remind us that truths conveyed through language do not 'just happen, they are *produced* in our struggle to decide the meanings of our actions, thoughts and feelings'. She argues that our perspective on early childhood in the Western world privileges Western views of the 'normal' child and marginalises alternative interpretations and explanations. We in the Western world, she states, seem obsessed with 'developmental normality' which may have in part arisen from research techniques. Children from other cultures, those experiencing disadvantage from impairments, and children living with violence do not readily fit into our norms, but may offer us insights into other worlds and experiences. Yet their views can be marginalised. So it is that we have 'normalised views' of what children are like, how they develop, and how they should be supported in readiness for school, for example. These expectations limit the opportunities for understanding and engagement when they deny the different paths and paces of children's development.

Seeking the 'other'

Our views of what is 'normal' or what we expect can evoke a sense of fear if we see someone as different. Triandafyllidou (2012: 6) recognises that 'prejudice [has] more to do with our own fears rather than the differences of others'. Difference can be difficult to accept; it can be seen as a threat. Furthermore we may fear using the wrong term and being perceived as politically incorrect. Our fear of making mistakes and of our perceived difference can inhibit us.

Mac Naughton (2005) reminds us that we need to explore, question and address our own prejudices and actions and to seek other perceptions, experiences and concepts which will challenge our long-held beliefs. We can ask people what *they* want to be called and examine our response to difference. This is a deeply reflective process reliant on 'actively seeking the other'. Thoughts can awaken our desire to find out about contrasts and to reflect upon our own world, igniting a sense that we are enriched by knowledge of 'others'. Pareka (a former commissioner for racial equality) quoted in Jaggi (2000: 6) says 'If the dominant Western culture has no interlocutor it lives in a hall of mirrors'. This search for the 'other' can be manifest in a classroom 'package tour' around Indian culture through food and saris, through Muslim culture by fasting and Eid celebrations, and through Jewish culture in the form of a Passover feast, but this activity merely makes the classroom members into cultural tourists. To truly engage with difference and confront our fears and prejudices we need to step out to discover how different communities experience their lives, to explore different meanings and to ask them what language reflects their worlds.

The ethnographic approach to research offers a model for this production and discovery of others' words and worlds in relation to the researcher's own world, providing opportunities to ask questions and to create a platform for less powerful voices to be heard. Within its paradigms it also questions who the researcher is and interrogates the interpretation that the researcher gives. As Freire (1996: 71) asked, 'How can I dialogue if I always project ignorance onto others and never perceive my own?' He reminds us that in order to address issues of equality we must take time to be aware of our own prejudices and barriers, for we all have some, at some level. To seek equality and inclusion is a process of asking, questioning, seeking clarity, making mistakes. Social templates may not always work, and there is an element of courage in this search for a new understanding of difference. In the search we can also uncover debates about the changing nature of a word and its meanings. For example, a once liberating term like 'multiculturalism' is now controversial and this has implications for policy.

Multiculturalism and its meanings

A central tension in working with difference is between the use of language and the need for policy implementation. The concept of multiculturalism delivered policies to promote integration of differences. However, more recently the word has been criticised for being too static and state bound. Triandafyllidou (2012) has pointed out that there is a new and emerging term, 'interculturalism', which reflects an interplay of cultures: a process of dialogue and interaction or engagement between different cultures within a society. 'The intercultural perspective acknowledges that a multitude of cultures may co-exist within a society' (2012: 36). Any setting may include children from a wide range of cultures. An 'intercultural' approach would promote a creative dialogue between parents, carers and communities to share skills, knowledge and understanding. For Triandafyllidou 'multiculturalism' now has powerful politicised connotations of control, being a 'normative' term that refers to how and under what conditions different communities (different cultural groups) should be integrated into a society. Multiculturalism implies that it is the state that 'has the duty to assure that all citizens – regardless of religious faith, ethnic descent or cultural tradition – are able to enjoy their rights without being obliged to assimilate and adopt the majority culture or religion' (2012: 36). So for Triandafyllidou 'multiculturalism' wrests control from the community and is therefore perhaps less powerful than interculturalism which places difference back in communities. Baldock (2010) notes how in Spain the word '*interculturalidad*' is preferred to multiculturalism as it conveys the ideas of exchange, reciprocity and interaction – a sense of being creative and of cooperative contact. Yet, Meer and Modood (2012) argue that interculturalism as a discourse is insufficient as it does not yet offer a distinct perspective that addresses the matters of equality and complex identities at a political level.

These changing views on multiculturalism or interculturalism have become relevant in relation to current ideas about immigration and immigrants. There is currently a criticism of immigration policy in Britain which argues that multiculturalism results in residential ghettoisation and the social isolation of immigrants (Banting and Kymlicka, 2013). Banting and Kymlicka highlight how complex the situation is in Europe, with some countries rejecting multiculturalism in favour of policies of civic integration and an insistence on a new type of assimilation which is incompatible with multicultural support for diversity. In this period of 'demonising' multiculturalism, stereotypes are perpetuated which present immigrants as alien and threatening, giving rise to far-right populist policies.

A reflective practitioner may consider that both perspectives have value, that both state legislation and creative engagement are needed. Both concepts have to be evaluated in relation to the contexts in which they are used and the complexities they explain and support. Debate between academics helps to expose the implications of these concepts, both of which require reflective praxis (Freire, 1996) or taking action based on our understandings.

Language as a dialectical and creative process

Language is not entirely fixed by a commonly accepted definition given to us by others (as in a dictionary). It is organic and fluid because the meanings of words become part of a dialectical process in which they are assimilated, challenged and adjusted. Our brief excursion into the power of language has highlighted the struggles that occur as less dominant groups and communities in society search for a platform from which to voice their beliefs and identities – to assert their particular qualities and to claim their place in a wider society.

We have now identified that discrimination, integration and inclusion are concepts related to issues of power and control, and that it is our role to reflect on the meaning and use of these terms in different contexts. We have also identified that the control of language by the powerful to influence ideas is often counteracted by the adoption of different meanings by the powerless as they fight against this control, re-asserting their ownership of their identity. We have recognised that this shifting of meaning and control of language can make us feel vulnerable, without a clear template of response. We have also explored how we can engage with difference to discover how people want to be named and we have considered how our own sense of identity and belonging relates to how we are 'named' and how we define others and are defined by them.

This engagement with language allows us to be creative as language is a form of communication. Words represent thoughts and can be interpreted in different ways. In reality definitions of words subtly grow and change as our understanding changes. Language can be a site of power struggles, anarchy and desire to control yet, as Freire (1996) has articulated, language has the capacity to transform our understanding. Words are bound to meanings but one word can have several meanings. This fluid, lively and playful quality of language is not just a product of society. It is an interaction of thoughts and feelings. It embodies our relationships and our engagement with others and through these channels it has the potential to include everyone.

A dialogic approach

But does language capture this inclusivity? There are imbalances in power across qualitatively different communities, so how can we find agreement? Tedlock and Mannheim (1995) argue that culture is dynamic and dialogic; it is a synthesis of voices and thoughts that create culture so to understand ourselves and others is to negotiate meanings. They assert that dialogues are not a string of monologues 'but are the very scene of production for shared language structures' (1995: 1) and that

> *the shared worlds that emerge from dialogues are in a continuous state of creation and recreation, negotiation and renegotiation ... culture is an emergent phenomenon, ultimately beyond the control of individuals ... (1995: 3)*

This process of dialogue is how we begin to belong in our world because, as Street (1993) reminds us, culture is a verb as well as a noun.

The Reggio Emilia approach to childhood wanted to 'embrace, not ignore the concept of difference' (Soncini, 2012: 189), based on the understanding that children have a multitude of languages with which to express their ideas (Malaguzzi, 2012) including emotional, physical, social and tactile experiences among many others. If we watch the communication between newborn babies and their carers we see the dyadic relationship in action as the site of emergent language and intersubjectivity (Trevarthen, 2010 and see Chapter 3). This communication, punctuated by silences, moved by facial expressions and evoked through sounds reminds us of the creative potential of shared experience that offers us a sense of belonging and identity. Words are just one part of a fluid interplay of feelings and thoughts expressed through various means – intonations, glances, pauses, sighs. Our relational experience of life is celebrated in the creative, dynamic potential of developing understanding, searching for shared meaning by listening as well as speaking.

The effervescent quality of language has the potential to connect and delight; it can enable us to celebrate our shared humanity, and offer opportunities to explore and negotiate our differences. However, we should remain alert to the power that just one word can wield.

ACTIVITY

To truly engage with difference and confront our fears and prejudices we need to step out to discover how different communities experience their lives, to explore different meanings and to ask what language reflects other people's worlds.

Gather several newspaper articles on a theme relating to groups of people – this could be about immigration, teachers, celebrations, wars, fundraising for people 'in need' and so on. Analyse the articles in terms of the language used. What symbolic language is evident? Are there indications of power and oppression, of 'them and us'? Does the

(Continued)

ACTIVITY *continued*

language prompt a particular way of viewing the people portrayed? If there are quotes from people how are they described? What do they say? How are disabled people portrayed (feisty and brave are quite common epithets here)? Perhaps discuss these articles with others – what do they see in them? Were there any words or phrases that you struggled with when explaining to others? Is there anything you are uncomfortable about?

Discomfort and unease is a part of the process of dialogue arising from complexity. It is fine to feel this disequilibrium. Keep a diary or jot down your reflections.

FURTHER READING

Richardson, R. (2009) *Holding Together – Equalities, Difference and Cohesion: Guidance for School Improvement Planning.* London: Trentham Books for Derbyshire Education Authority.

This book informs practitioners about the implementation of policy. Settings have legal responsibilities in relation to disability, race, culture and gender but the early years practitioner can also promote community cohesion.

Hoque, A. (2015) *British-Islamic Identity: 3rd Generation Bangladeshis from East London.* London: Trentham Books.

This book considers contemporary issues of identity: language, race, religion, nation and gender and frames them within the context of young people's self-narratives. It offers important new insight and understanding of their stories of identity and allows us to hear their voices.

Triandafyllidou, A. (2012) *Handbook on Diversity and Tolerance in Europe.* Italy: European University Institute/European Commission. Available from the EUI institutional repository CADMUS: http://cadmus.eui.eu

An accessible 'handbook' that leads the reader to further reflection and consider the meanings of words related to diversity – although remember this too is from a particular perspective.

REFERENCES

Armstrong, K. (2000) *The Battle for God. Fundamentalism in Judaism, Christianity and Islam.* London. Harper Collins.

Baldock, P. (2010) *Understanding Cultural Diversity in the Early Years.* London: SAGE.

Banting, K. and Kymlicka, W. (2013) Is there really a retreat from multiculturalism policies? New evidence from the Multiculturalism Policy Index. *Comparative European Politics*, 11(5): 577–98.

Blackledge, A. (2000) Power relations and the social construction of 'Literacy' and 'Illiteracy'. Experiences of Bangladeshi women in Birmingham. In J. Benjamins (ed.), *Reading and Writing Different Worlds.* Amsterdam: Multilingual Literacies.

Bourdieu, P. (1992) *Language and Symbolic Power.* Cambridge: Polity Press.

Castells, M. (2006) Globalization and identity: a comparative perspective. *Transfer Journal of Contemporary Culture*, 1: 56–68.

Chanda-Gool, S. (2006) *South Asian Communities: Catalysts for Educational Change.* London: Trentham Books.

Chomsky, N. (2006) *Language and Mind* (3rd edn). Cambridge: Cambridge University Press.

Clarke, K. and Clarke, M.P. (1947) Racial identification and preference in the Negro children. In T.M. Newcombe and E.L. Hartley (eds), *Readings in Social Psychology*. New York: Holt.

Emery, R. (2012) The history of Aboriginal languages and linguistics. In N. Harvey, J. Fornasiero, G. McCarthy, C. Macintyre and C. Crossin (eds), *A History of the Faculty of Arts at the University of Adelaide*. Adelaide: Adelaide University Press.

Freire, P. (1996) *Pedagogy of the Oppressed* (trans. Myra Bergman Ramos). London: Penguin.

Gool, S. and Patton, W. (1998) Voices still to be heard. *The Australian Journal of Indigenous Education*, 26(1): 1–7.

Jaggi, M. (2000) First Among the Equalisers. *Guardian Profile*, 21 October 2000, 02.18 BST.

Kreiner, G.E. and Sheep, M.L. (2009) Growing pains and gains: framing identity dynamics as opportunities for identity growth. In L. Morgan Roberts and J.E. Dutton (eds), *Exploring Positive Identities and Organisations*. London: Routledge.

Mac Naughton, G. (2005) *Doing Foucault in Early Childhood Studies: Applying Poststructural Ideas*. Abingdon: Routledge.

Malaguzzi, L. (2012) History, ideas, and basic philosophy: an interview with Lella Gandini. In C. Edwards, L. Gandini and G. Forman (eds), *The Hundred Languages of Children: The Reggio Experience in Transformation*. Oxford: Praeger.

Meer, N. and Modood, T. (2012) How does interculturalism contrast with multiculturalism? *Journal of Intercultural Studies*, 33(2): 175–96.

Morgan, S. (1988) *My Place*. London: Virago.

Oliver, M. (1990) *The Politics of Disablement*. London: Macmillan Education.

Parpart, J.L. and Kabeer, N. (2010) *Choosing Silence: Rethinking Voice, Agency, and Women's Empowerment*. Working Paper #297. Michigan State University: Center for Gender in Global Context.

Rogoff, B. (1990) *Apprenticeship in Thinking: Cognitive Development in Social Context*. New York, Oxford: Oxford University Press.

Romaine, S. (2014) Of speech and species. *New Internationalist*, June, 473: 25–7.

Said, E. (1993) *Culture and Imperialism*. London: Vintage.

Shakespeare, T. (2002) The social model of disability: an outdated ideology? *Journal of Research in Social Science and Disability*, 2: 9–28.

Shih, M. and Sanchez, D.T. (2005) Perspectives and research on the positive and negative implications of having multiple racial identities. *Psychological Bulletin*, 131(4): 569–91.

Soncini, I. (2012) The inclusive community. In C. Edwards, L. Gandini and G. Forman (eds), *The Hundred Languages of Children: the Reggio Emilia Experience in Transformation*. Oxford: Praeger.

Street, B. (1993) Culture is a verb: anthropological aspects of language and cultural process. In D. Graddol, L. Thompson and M. Byram (eds), *Language and Culture*. Clevedon, PA: BAAL and Multilingual Matters.

Tedlock, D. and Mannheim, B. (eds) (1995) *The Dialogic Emergence of Culture*. Chicago: University of Illinois.

Trevarthen, C. (2010) What is it like to be a person who knows nothing? Defining the active intersubjective mind of a newborn human being. *'The Intersubjective Newborn', Infant and Child Development*, Special Issue (ed. Emese Nagy). pp. 1–20. Available at: http://www.psychologia.pl/lasc/Trevarthen2.pdf (15 April 2015).

Triandafyllidou, A. (2012) *Handbook on Diversity and Tolerance in Europe.* Italy: European University Institute/ European Commission. Available at: http://cadmus.eui.eu (accessed 15 April 2015).

Vygotsky, L.S. (1978) *Mind in Society: The Development of Higher Psychological Processes.* Cambridge, MA: Harvard University Press.

West, K. and Hewstone, M. (2011) Relatively socially acceptable prejudice within and between societies. *Journal of Community & Applied Social Psychology*, 22(3): 269–82.

Yildiz, A.A. and Verkuyten, M. (2013) 'We are not terrorists': Turkish Muslim organizations and the construction of a moral identity. *Ethnicities*, 13(3): 359–81.

10 Working in partnership: encounters with colleagues in the third space

Valerie Huggins and Caroline Leeson

Introduction

Changes in welfare and education policy and practice in the UK over the past 20 years have encouraged early years practitioners to stop thinking of themselves as 'just a teacher', 'just a social worker' or 'just an early years worker'. To be an effective early years practitioner now requires both an ability to understand the theoretical constructs of collaborative practice and the possession of skills that facilitate working positively with others from different professions and perspectives, often in difficult or complex circumstances.

In this chapter, we will explore some of the key issues in engaging in effective collaboration with colleagues. We seek to demonstrate the inter-relatedness of the core skills of communication and team working. We are living and working in increasingly diverse communities, and need to create connections built on understanding, empathy and mutual respect. This requires us to value and view critically our own cultural perspectives and practices and those of others (Huggins, 2013) and to argue for the promotion of intercultural capabilities at the heart of working in partnership with others. Essential to this process is the need for a 'third space' (Bhabha, 1994: 218), a place for sharing ideas and creating new discourses for working together.

Crucially, we will also be arguing that the concept of colleagues should be taken in its widest sense, encompassing friends, clients and families as well as professional and work colleagues. We also believe it is particularly important that we do not exclude children's voices throughout this debate on working together. It is our position that young children are capable of participating in complex decision making and should be actively involved.

The current early years context

Early years practitioners can no longer confine their attention to their own setting; they are now expected to have a holistic concern with children in wider family and social contexts. For instance, in the course of a single day a young child may be cared for by their parents, by a childcare team, by after-school club play-workers and by a child minder. The statutory guidance underpinning the Early Years Foundation Stage (DfE, 2014) recommends that in such a situation there has to be an effective sharing of relevant information between all the practitioners involved and the parents in order to ensure continuity and to improve the outcomes for the child. Where a child and family are experiencing particular difficulties such interagency sharing is even more critical. All this necessitates collaborative working with colleagues and therefore depends on the development of sophisticated understandings and intercultural capabilities.

Under the Labour Government (1997–2010) collaborative, multi-agency working was made a requirement and given a structure nationally, regionally and locally. The Every Child Matters (DfES, 2004a) agenda, implemented through the Children Act 2004, Child Care Act 2006, Early Years Foundation Stage (DfES, 2008), Early Years Professional Status (CWDC, 2007), and the Children and Young People's Workforce Strategy (DCSF, 2009), emphasised the necessity for agencies to work together as fully integrated services, meeting the needs of children and families with a seamless service provision based on 'a shared perspective, effective communication systems and mutual understanding' (Jones and Pound, 2008: 142). Furthermore, *Every Child Matters: Change for Children* (DfES, 2004b) advocated an approach in which a single Lead Professional liaised with the family to simplify and strengthen the support, especially for families with particular need, to coordinate the work of other colleagues, and to ensure there was clear accountability. Early Years practitioners from health, social care, welfare, education and the criminal justice system were required to work within a legislative framework demanding a multi-agency approach (Dunhill *et al.*, 2009). In 2008 Children's Trusts were set up with the aim of enhancing the partnership working of all professionals engaged in service provision for children and their families. Another part of government policy was its commitment to establish a Sure Start Children's Centre for every community by 2010, to provide health and family support services at a single point of contact.

The economic downturn and the change of government in 2010 led to huge structural changes to children's services at national, regional and local level. Children's Trusts were abolished; the number of Children's Centres was significantly decreased and the core offer of many settings was seriously cut (4Children, 2013) with a real impact upon their ability to meet the demand from families in their communities. The landscape of early years care and education has shifted and we now see a mixed economy with a large number of private, for profit, providers, many of whom come from professional backgrounds (Campbell-Barr, 2012). Moreover, there has been a change in the balance between education and care, with an increased focus on educational standards and a reduction in the ring-fenced funding for services that supported the overall well-being of the children. Local authority funding for Children's Centres and extended schools programmes has been reduced by a third since 2010 and the language of ECM has been replaced with the vague aim of 'helping children achieve more'.

Such huge structural changes to Children's Services at national, regional and local level have not been easy, especially when featuring a period of strong motivation and commitment followed by a period of financial restraint and political change culminating in ideological caution. Nevertheless the coalition government was still influenced by reports such as *Early Intervention: The Next Steps* (Allen, 2011) and *The Marmot Review* (2010); which both argued that the early years are important for children and that their life opportunities are enhanced by the effective working together of the professionals involved in their lives.

Despite the financial cutbacks, those Children's Centres that still exist are striving to provide creative and effective services for the communities they serve. The Children's Centre Census for 2014 (4Children, 2014) reported that one million families were being supported, including two thirds of the most vulnerable families with a child aged 0–5, but that many Centres face closure. The move from universal to targeted services, the introduction of charging for services and a growing reliance on volunteers have kept many Children's Centres open, but opportunities to deliver the promised joined-up services are being lost.

Working together in partnership

The challenge is therefore to work in an integrated and effective way, within an environment of structural change and variations in policy, whilst valuing the contribution of all the participants. This requires a shared vision and compatible ways of working to enable a diverse range of people to work in partnership.

Partnership is not a new term; it has been a key word in the lexicon of early years policy makers since the late 1980s (Hornby, 2000) and has been used to mean the increased involvement of families, children and carers, and the sharing of power between these groups and early years practitioners. There are proven benefits of working in partnership though these have sometimes been assessed in terms of increased 'efficiency' rather than in terms of how this improves outcomes for children and families. Working in partnership can increase the creative facility of agencies to provide bespoke services to children and families, while improving understanding of local needs and pressures and supporting the sharing of skills, roles and services.

In the past it was possible for early years practitioners to pay lip service to the idea of working closely and collaboratively with colleagues, whilst in practice resisting fiercely at both conscious and unconscious levels. This is no longer a sustainable position. But government policies will not in themselves bring about harmonious and effective collaboration. It is still necessary for early years practitioners to be clear about who their colleagues are and how to work with them, to be aware of the considerable barriers to collaboration that exist and to know how to build and sustain positive partnerships. We argue that the intercultural capabilities of the practitioners have a key role to play in this process. Colleagues from different professional backgrounds working in diverse communities need to recognise that their way of doing things is not the only way. They must be willing to accept that other approaches may be equally valid, recognising how they have been shaped by sociohistorical contexts and how they can offer valid alternatives for practice (Huggins, 2013).

Who are our colleagues?

In the past we have been prone to define 'colleagues' very narrowly – often as those with very similar professional backgrounds or who work in the same setting. The integrated approach to work within the early years sector means we have to reconsider the term. For the purposes of this chapter we are taking colleagues to mean all the people who interact and work together towards a common, identified goal. This will therefore include practitioners of all kinds working within the setting and in the wider community, as well as the children and families who access services.

Professionals as colleagues

Within the early years sector, people work together in a variety of situations, teams and frameworks – multi-agency projects, care management teams and strategic decision-making groups (Atkinson *et al.*, 2002). The Children Act 2004 and the Children and Young People's Workforce Strategy (DCSF, 2009) were intended to promote multidisciplinary work in order to improve services to families identified as needing intervention and assistance. However, there is persistent evidence that professionals are still defending their specialisms for fear of becoming deskilled and are jockeying to maintain their own power bases (Barker, 2009). As a consequence, they may fail to see the potential of collaborative work, where all positions and perspectives are valued and service provision can be seamless and meaningful.

Looking at the social psychology of work enables us to identify the cultural positions people start from and we can begin to understand the complexities of working effectively with colleagues. We should be mindful of the sense of duty that is often attached to people's attitudes to their work as well as the issues of power and territory that affect decision-making processes and subsequent action. Any developments in terms of working together have to recognise that early years work is people-based and therefore highly dependent on interpersonal relationships as well as on understanding how people operate and how they think about their work.

Links between agencies and participants should be developed in such a way that everyone is valued and respected – this includes children and their families. We cannot assume that all stakeholders will share the same view, so the development of respect for all points of view is paramount (Fitzgerald, 2004). Building such respect requires significant consistency and continuity in the make-up of teams. There should be a requirement within multidisciplinary work, at all levels, for professionals to build stable relationships with partners within their own co-located team or professional group as well as with partners from other professional groups and in other teams within the community. In order for this to happen there has to be a consistency of personnel as this is vital to build trust and respect, to nurture shared understandings and to develop a multidisciplinary attachment that will assist with some of the complex conversations and decision-making processes that take place. Sometimes more than one person from each service team will need to be involved and to be informed about the work being undertaken so that they can be part of a pool of familiar faces and a network is developed that can be effective and appropriately responsive to any situation that occurs.

If we are to develop effective multi-agency teams, appropriate styles of leadership are critical (Jones and Pound, 2008; Purcell, 2009). There have been some tentative shifts in leadership approaches (see Chapter 12) from top-down managerial models towards distributive, transformational models that offer opportunities for leadership to be shared throughout the team (Duffy and Marshall, 2007). Such a shift has helped to develop environments for effective and meaningful partnerships, with shared language, vision and direction (NCSL, 2004), by empowering and valuing the contributions of all parties.

Children as colleagues

When considering working together we often overlook the children. Too often we see children as helpless and incapable of making decisions for themselves: 'A factor that sustains adult–child power relationships is a belief that adults have superior knowledge' (Robinson and Kellett, 2004: 84). Children can feel a sense of powerlessness when they are not party to major aspects of the important decisions that affect them and this may have serious repercussions throughout their lives (Leeson, 2006; 2009). It is reported that adults who find it difficult to make relationships often reveal that they were not involved in even the smallest decisions as children and the resultant self-doubt has left them unable to make choices for themselves (Leeson, 2006).

Decision making has implications for building resilience and the way a situation is dealt with, the impact of the situation and the degree to which the child is involved can all have lifelong implications (Welbourne and Leeson, 2012). Being able to practise and become competent in decision making is crucial to emotional well-being and the development of integrated persons (Clarke and Clarke, 2003). Research into school councils (John, 2003), children experiencing divorce (Neale, 2002) and children being involved in decisions about their health (Thurston and Church, 2001) has pointed to the ability of children to discuss objectively and appropriately the important decisions that have to be made about their environment and their lives (Lansdown, 2010).

Furthermore, we appear to have a culture that regards children as either 'victims' or 'threats' (Hendrick, 2003) which interferes with our ability to view children as colleagues. It is our contention that this pervasive cultural stance has to be addressed as no amount of policy or political encouragement will further the interests of children until our restrictive beliefs about their abilities and status are challenged.

Professionals may tend to believe that children are dependent on their parents who will act as responsible advocates for them but this may not always be the case. A series of enquiries into abuse of children, including Jasmine Beckford (London Borough of Brent, 1985), Victoria Climbié (DoH and Home Office, 2003), Child B (Samuel, 2007) and Peter Connolly (LSCB, 2009) all show how children can get lost in adult agendas, no longer seen as separate beings with their own story to tell. More recently the same story has been brought into sharp focus with the various sexual exploitation scandals including Rochdale (RBSCB, 2012) and Rotherham (Jay, 2014). The argument is often made that young children especially cannot be involved in discussions as they are not fully cognisant of all the facts. But how often do adults have all the necessary information? People make decisions, plan, and act according to their beliefs at the time. We would argue that all children, irrespective of age, should have the same opportunity. Sometimes our underlying attitudes towards children prevent us from viewing them as valued members of the community or as colleagues working with practitioners to enhance their environment and/or community. This may be due to anxiety about relinquishing our own power and control; it may be about pressure of time, or poor skills or limited resources. Certainly, regarding children as colleagues would require a shift of focus away from adults delivering care to children towards adults and children working together to provide a caring environment for the benefit of all.

Viewing children as colleagues and co-constructors of our world has significant implications for the way we work together as adults, the way we shape our work and the way we maintain relationships with one another. We therefore welcome the insistent calls for children to be regarded as colleagues, as active participants in decisions that affect them and the quality of their lives and experiences (Cairns, 2006; Lansdown, 2010). We note that this began to appear in government policies such as the Early Years Foundation Stage (DCSF, 2008; DfE, 2014), where children were encouraged to take a lead in the learning process and the Children's Plan (DCSF, 2007), which promoted the role of children in helping to shape the services available for them and their families.

Parents as colleagues

This topic is fully explored in Chapter 11 by our colleague Marie Lavelle, but is also clearly relevant for working in partnership. There is a danger that the purpose of working with parents is largely seen as compensating for their perceived inadequacies, both in terms of their parenting skills and their limitations in understanding and providing for their children's needs. In the past the practitioners had all the power and the parents' participation in the relationship was very much in the role of recipients. This inequality potentially reduced the impact of their involvement. However, there has been a significant shift in models of working with parents towards one of empowerment (Whalley, 2008: 132), where parents are seen as colleagues and 'professionals actively promote parents' sense of control over decisions affecting their child'. Moreover, Devereux and Miller (2003: 86) argue that:

> *Working in partnership is not just about the two very different spheres of home and setting. It is also about people from different cultures learning to work together for the good of the child.*

In order to do this, practitioners have to accept caregivers as having equal, though different, expertise – both in their child and in their family culture. Practitioners have to develop their intercultural capabilities and be prepared to create a 'third space' where parents and practitioners from different professional backgrounds can share their perspectives, listen to each other respectfully and come to new understandings about the child's learning and development. Only then can parents move from a compensatory involvement to a fully participatory one (Ward, 2013). Such full participation is crucial if we are to achieve the wider benefits of working with parents.

These benefits are considerable. Desforges and Abouchaar (2003) confirm that parental involvement in early years settings and schools has a positive effect on children's achievement. This is supported by the Effective Provision of Pre-school Education (EPPE) case studies which show how 'parents and staff can work together so that "learning environments" of home and pre-school are harmonized and stretched' (Pugh and Duffy, 2006: 176). The role of parents as partners is enshrined in the Early Years Foundation Stage framework (DfE, 2014), with a requirement for every child to be assigned a key worker, which Elfer *et al.* (2012) argue is the most effective way of achieving the best possible human relationships within an early years setting. The key worker approach enables close attachments between an individual child and a practitioner, giving the parents confidence that their child matters. Another of the key findings of the EPPE project is that the quality of the home learning environment is more significant in promoting children's intellectual and social development than parents' occupations or qualifications (Pugh and Duffy, 2006), a finding which has been confirmed by more recent research, for example Hunt *et al.* (2010) and Siraj-Blatchford *et al.* (2013) although Serafino and Tonkin (2014) argue that it is the father's level of education that has the largest impact on educational outcomes.

Ongoing research is challenging many professional assumptions about the limitations of less advantaged families and underlines the importance of working with *all* parents as full colleagues. But it is still a huge challenge to combine and balance the practitioner's expertise in child development and learning with the parents' expertise in their child and their family culture, in order to produce the best outcomes for the child. It is essential for practitioners to be interculturally capable and willing to learn about the sociocultural history of the family and community and the child's learning outside the setting (Bligh *et al.*, 2013).

The personal and cultural assumptions of some families may be very different from those of the practitioners due to diverse beliefs about child-rearing practices (Tomlinson, 2013) or different views of the purpose of early years education, that have developed in differing sociohistorical contexts. These differences are not always easy to resolve but the arguments, both from research and from current policy requirements, for establishing a genuine partnership with parents are overwhelming. Parents are our colleagues and we must find ways of respecting and making full use of their contribution. Bax (2001) suggests that practitioners should be sensitive to the parents' right to participate in the range of services on offer at any level that they choose. They also need to consider imaginative ways to empower parents in their local context to enable them to participate (Whalley, 2008).

Obstacles to effective partnership

The dangers of *not* working in partnership have been highlighted in many inquiries into child deaths. The child abuse inquiries mentioned above have all found evidence of professionals' significant and systematic failure to work together effectively through the meaningful sharing of information and successful interagency working. Research consistently shows a number of key factors that prevent or inhibit successful interagency collaboration (Atkinson *et al.*, 2002; Lumsden, 2005; Anning *et al.*, 2006; Harris and Allen, 2009). These include:

- territorialism and role identifications, discussed above, including unhelpful stereotyping of each other's roles and reactions, leading to mutually unfulfilled expectations and disrespect for the expertise of others;

- status and power – working together can incur a perceived loss of status for key personnel who see their opportunities to exert power and authority curtailed or questioned;

- failure to share responsibility – apparent in the child abuse enquiries mentioned above;

- competition for resources – inherent within a managerialist system;

- different professional and organisational priorities;

- different value systems and attitudes towards children and their families;

- the use of professional jargon that erects ideological barriers between professions;

- the lack of ability or willingness to reflect on personal practice.

The Early Years Foundation Stage (DfES, 2014) puts partnership with parents at the heart of effective practice. It advocates that all parents should be involved in their child's learning and outlines various strategies to encourage practitioners to develop an effective partnership by showing respect, understanding the role of the parents, listening, being flexible, giving time, valuing different perspectives and collaborating in a genuine way. These expectations can be difficult to achieve, especially if families have had bad experiences with other professionals. Lumby and Coleman (2007) found that some professionals were reluctant to engage in partnership with parents because of anxieties about their professional role and their reluctance to share governance and power, echoing observations about barriers to collaboration between professionals. Equally, parents may experience a lack of confidence in their ability to communicate with professionals who appear to know what they are doing and may feel overwhelmed by their status and training. Roberts (2009) points to the requirement for professionals to clearly demonstrate their belief that parents are experts, can cope and can make a difference in order for a respectful, trusting and effective partnership to develop. Practitioners should therefore carefully reflect on how their own attitudes and values may create barriers to working as colleagues with parents, as well as with other professionals.

Managing conflict by the facilitation of more collegiate ways of working should be one of the goals of effective partnership (Darlington *et al.*, 2005; Anning *et al.*, 2006; West-Burnham *et al.*, 2007). On the assumption that at root all parents want the best for their children, when we encounter difficulties, we should ask what is making the partnership so hard to maintain, instead of abandoning the idea as soon as it becomes difficult.

Making partnerships effective

Atkinson *et al.* (2005) identified a range of key factors for successful multi-agency working and argued that the most important is the commitment and willingness to work together. However, as Fitzgerald (2004: 21) argued: 'For partnership to be maintained it is vital that there are effective strategies in place to facilitate two-directional communication and support.' But what are these effective strategies? Let us start with something simple. How do we refer to our partners? As clients, service-users, patients, mums and dads, cases ... colleagues? All of these terms are value-laden; some have negative connotations, implying a weaker or inferior position in relationship with the 'professional'. So we need to think very carefully about the labels we use and how we can promote partnership and collegiality. 'To work together all parties need to have a shared sense of what partnership means to them all' (Fitzgerald, 2004: 7). Defining what partnership means to us will affect the way we work – and will inform our attitudes and our policies.

There are various theoretical frameworks for supporting the development of partnerships, such as Hart's (1992) ladder of empowerment and Thomas's (2000) list of recommendations for partnership working with children. Both frameworks measure how meaningful and genuine the partnership is for all involved. They demand that we look at any situation and ask whether the plan we are developing is one of genuine empowerment and autonomy or one of lip service to a required code of practice. For a partnership to be effective, everyone needs to see how they fit into the partnership and what they bring to it in terms of an agenda, motivation, emotion, information and ways of working. The five outcomes of the Every Child Matters agenda help to facilitate this process, in that they provide a shared vision for parents and practitioners from different agencies to work towards (Stacey, 2009). They all can then discuss their roles and responsibilities in the effective implementation of policies and approaches that will promote the health and well-being of each child (Jones and Pound, 2008).

Fostering good communication

In this context, more effective multidirectional communication is needed, not just between the families and the professionals but between the professionals themselves. By recognising the different perceptions of the child/family which stem from their particular professional background (Anning *et al.*, 2006), professionals working within a multi-agency team can enjoy the benefits of having a much richer knowledge base that enables the development of a clearer picture of the needs of the child, and improved identification of how best to support the family (Stacey, 2009). Therefore, each participant and organisation involved in the care of a particular child should work hard to understand each other's points of view, to respect and value the differences and the similarities between those views, and to share information effectively, always operating from the assumption that everyone is working together for the good of the child and their family.

We acknowledge the enormous challenges in trying to coordinate communication, identifying points of contact, negotiating meanings and assumptions and overcoming the constraints and demands on organisations and individuals (Brechin *et al.*, 2000). The Laming Reports, firstly into the death of Victoria Climbié (DoH and Home Office, 2003) and secondly following the death of Peter Connolly (LSCB, 2009), both highlighted the ongoing problem of how, in both instances differing jargon, cultures and motivations prevented agencies from working together in meaningful ways. It should be noted that, despite a plethora of policies and guidance notes, there is still substantial evidence of a sustained gulf between professionals, with jargon and acronyms forming a substantial barrier to working effectively together. For example, the importance of intercultural capabilities is evident in social work and health training and appears in their working standards but it is not mentioned in the standards for teachers, nor is it explicitly present in current training programmes. Leiba (2003) talks about the 'codification of communication' between professionals, where conditions and significances in one professional code can exclude others, and it would seem that this culture is extremely hard to shift in any substantial form.

Good communication skills are therefore crucial. Good communicators express their meaning in all sorts of ways – through body language, through 'paralanguage' (the way they say things and the way they listen), through appropriate choice of vocabulary, through the medium in which they choose to communicate and through using their own experience of encouraging and promoting dialogue. Good communicators also listen with attention and empathy, actively seeking to understand and appreciate the points of view of others (Ellis and Fisher, 1994). Co-location of services within Children's Centres and Extended Schools has supported this process, as personal relationships between professionals are built up through daily conversations and exchanges in a safe third space for dialogue, but it is a long and slow process that requires considerable support and sustenance.

Conclusion

Vocational training for health workers, social workers and teachers is increasingly concerned with effective communication and working in partnership in all its different forms and contexts. All professionals working in the early years field are expected to liaise closely with one another for the benefit of the children in their care. Team building between agencies and within early years settings depends on a willingness to listen and a willingness to change, rooted in intercultural awareness and respect.

As practitioners working with young children and their families we must challenge ourselves, our assumptions and our ways of working if we are to achieve effective working relationships, in particular by addressing how we interact and communicate with others. We should be promoting the importance of working together and actively seeking ways to improve our ability to do so, which may involve renegotiating the roles and relationships we have with our existing colleagues and thinking about how we can involve new people. We may well need to reconceptualise the way we regard young children and our place in supporting their learning and development. Most importantly of all, we must make the fullest use of both formal and informal mechanisms to develop trust between all who are working together for young children.

ACTIVITY **1**

Over the next month, look through newspapers, journals and periodicals for coverage on health, education, police and welfare issues. See if you can identify some of the following:

- *Political bias*
- *Examples of good and poor collaborative practice*
- *Involvement of family and child in decision making*
- *Quality of the working relationship between agencies*
- *Communication issues*

From this, begin to develop your own idea of what contributes to effective collaboration between early years practitioners and of how partnerships may be helped or hindered by government policies.

ACTIVITY **2**

Compile a portfolio of your own experiences of the following:

- *Communication*
- *Teamwork*
- *Partnership*
- *Emotional literacy*

Examples of your own practice could come from work situations, group living, leisure activities or study experiences. What do these experiences tell you about these topics and your own skills? How have your experiences shaped your attitude towards working with others? What will you now seek to change?

ACTIVITY **3**

Prepare a presentation on one of the early years service professions. We would suggest you look at a professional you might work with in the future rather than the profession you think you might like to join. Try to find out about:

- *The history of this profession; when it was first created and how it has developed. How has training changed and what historical developments might help to explain the identity and nature of the profession? Are there key people who have pioneered the creation or development of this service?*
- *The laws which underpin the expectations placed on this group of professionals.*

(Continued)

ACTIVITY 3 *continued*

- *The current situation with this profession in terms of training, numbers, working patterns and ideologies.*
- *The hierarchy or accountability structure for this profession.*
- *Any professional bodies which support, monitor or police the actions of their members within this profession.*
- *The role this profession has in helping care for young children and their families. How is this role manifested?*
- *The responsibilities of this profession, whom they report to and any specific duties they have to perform.*
- *Any developments in the pipeline for this profession.*
- *Any other information that you feel it would be useful to share with your audience.*

FURTHER READING

Floyd, A. and Morrison, M. (2013) Exploring identities and cultures in inter-professional education and collaborative professional practice. *Studies in Continuing Education,* 36(1): 38–53.

In this desk-based research project, Floyd and Morrison discuss developments in interprofessional practice in the education, health and social care sectors, considering the historical, social and cultural narratives shaping the formation of interprofessional identities.

Dunhill, A., Elliott, B. and Shaw, A. (2009) *Effective Communication and Engagement with Children and Young People, their Families and Carers.* Exeter: Learning Matters.

This book contains examples of strategies to help practitioners working in multi-agency, interdisciplinary teams develop their communication and engagement with children, young people, their families and carers.

Elfer, P., Goldschmied, E. and Selleck, D.Y. (2012) *Key Persons in the Early Years: Building Relationships for Quality Provision in Early Years Settings and Primary Schools.* London: Routledge.

This text provides a clear guide to the role of the Key Person in early years settings. The authors draw on examples from practitioners to illustrate the benefits of the Key Person approach and some of the potential challenges.

REFERENCES

4Children (2013) *Children Centre Census 2013.* Available at: http://www.4children.org.uk/Resources/Detail/Children-Centre-Census-2013 (accessed 13 April 2015).

4Children (2014) *Sure Start Children's Centres Census 2014: A National Overview of Sure Start Children's Centres in 2014.* London: 4Children.

Allen, G. (2011) *Early Intervention: The Next Steps. An Independent Report to HM Government.* London: Cabinet Office. Available at https://www.gov.uk/government/uploads/system/uploads/attachment_data/file/284086/early-intervention-next-steps2.pdf (accessed 13 April 2015).

Anning, A., Cottrell, D., Frost, N., Green, J. and Robinson, M. (2006) *Developing Multi-professional Teamwork for Integrated Children's Services: Research, Policy and Practice.* Maidenhead: Open University Press.

Atkinson, M., Wilkin, A., Stott, A., Doherty, P. and Kinder, K. (2002) *Multi-agency Working: A Detailed Study.* Slough: National Foundation for Educational Research.

Atkinson, M., Doherty, P. and Kinder, K. (2005) Multi-agency working: models, challenges and key factors for success. *Journal of Early Childhood Research*, 3(1): 7–17.

Barker, R. (2009) *Making Sense of Every Child Matters: Multi-professional Practice Guidance.* Bristol: Policy Press.

Bax, M. (2001) Endeavours of parents (Editorial). *Developmental Medicine and Child Neurology*, 43(5): 291.

Bligh, C., Chambers, S., Davison, C., Lloyd, I., Musgrave, J., O'Sullivan, J. and Waltham, S. (2013) *Well-Being in the Early Years.* London: Critical Publishing.

Bhabha, H.K. (1994) *The Location of Culture.* London: Routledge.

Brechin, A., Brown, H. and Eby, M.A. (2000) *Critical Practice in Health and Social Care.* London: SAGE.

Cairns, L. (2006) Participation with purpose. In K. Tisdall, J. Davis, A. Prout and M. Hill (eds), *Children, Young People and Social Inclusion: Participation for What?* Bristol: Policy Press.

Campbell-Barr, V. (2012) Early years education and the value for money folklore. *European Early Childhood Education Research Journal*, 20(3): 423–37.

Child Care Act 2006 c.21. London: The Stationery Office. Available at: http://www.legislation.gov.uk/ukpga/2006/21/contents (accessed 21 February 2015).

Children Act 2004 c.31. London: The Stationery Office. Available at: http://www.legislation.gov.uk/ukpga/2004/31/contents (accessed 21 February 2015).

Clarke, A. and Clarke, A. (2003) *Human Resilience: A Fifty Year Quest.* Gateshead: Jessica Kingsley Publishers.

CWDC (Children's Workforce Development Council) (2007) *Prospectus: Early Years Professional Status.* Leeds: CWDC.

Darlington, Y., Feeney, J.A. and Rixon, K. (2005) Interagency collaboration between child protection and mental health services: practices, attitudes, and barriers. *Child Abuse and Neglect*, 29(10): 1085–98.

DCSF (Department for Children, Schools and Families) (2007) *The Children's Plan: Building Brighter Futures.* Norwich: The Stationery Office.

DCSF (Department for Children, Schools and Families) (2008) *Practice Guidance for the Early Years Foundation Stage.* Nottingham: DCSF Publications.

DCSF (Department for Children, Schools and Families) (2009) *2020 Children and Young People's Workforce Strategy.* Nottingham: DCSF Publications.

Desforges, C. and Abouchaar, A. (2003) *The Impact of Parental Involvement, Parent Support and Family Education on Pupil Achievement and Adjustment: A Literature Review.* Research Report 433. London: DfES Publications.

Devereux, J. and Miller, L. (eds) (2003) *Working with Young Children in the Early Years.* London: David Fulton.

DfE (Department for Education) (2014) *Statutory Framework for the Early Years Foundation Stage: Setting the Standards for Learning, Development and Care for Children from Birth to Five.* London: DfE Publications.

DfES (Department for Education and Skills) (2004a) *Every Child Matters: Next Steps.* Nottingham: DfES Publications.

DfES (Department for Education and Skills) (2004b) *Every Child Matters: Change for Children.* Nottingham: DfES Publications.

DoH (Department of Health) and Home Office (2003) *The Victoria Climbié Inquiry: Report of an Inquiry by Lord Laming.* London: The Stationery Office.

Duffy, B. and Marshall, J. (2007) Leadership in multi-agency work. In I. Siraj-Blatchford, K. Clarke and M. Needham (eds), *The Team Around the Child: Multi-agency Working in the Early Years.* Stoke-on-Trent: Trentham Books.

Dunhill, A., Elliott, B. and Shaw, A. (eds) (2009) *Effective Communication and Engagement with Children and Young People, their Families and Carers.* Exeter: Learning Matters.

Elfer, P., Goldschmied, E. and Selleck, D.Y. (2012) *Key Persons in the Early Years: Building Relationships for Quality Provision in Early Years Settings and Primary Schools.* London: Routledge.

Ellis, D.G. and Fisher, B.A. (1994) *Small Group Decision-making: Communication and the Group Process* (4th edn.) New York: McGraw-Hill.

Fitzgerald, D. (2004) *Parent Partnership in the Early Years.* London: Continuum.

Harris, A. and Allen, T. (2009) Ensuring Every Child Matters: issues and implications for school leadership. *School Leadership and Management* 29(4): 1–10.

Hart, R. (1992) *Children's Participation from Tokenism to Citizenship.* Florence: Unicef International Child Development Centre.

Hendrick, H. (2003) *Child Welfare, Historical Dimensions, Contemporary Debate.* Bristol: Policy Press.

Hornby, G. (2000) *Improving Parental Involvement.* London: Cassel.

Huggins, V. (2013) Widening our awareness of international approaches to Early Childhood Education and Care: an imperative for 21st century Early Years practitioners? In J. Georgeson and J. Payler (eds) *International Perspectives on Early Childhood Education and Care.* Maidenhead: OUP.

Hunt, S., Virgo, S., Klett-Davies, M., Page, A. and Apps, J. (2010) *Provider Influence on the Early Home Learning Environment (EHLE).* London: DfE.

Jay, A. (2014) *Independent Inquiry into Child Sexual Exploitation in Rotherham 1997–2013.* Rotherham: Rotherham Metropolitan Borough Council.

John, M. (2003) *Children's Rights and Power: Gearing Up for a New Century.* Gateshead: Jessica Kingsley.

Jones, C. and Pound, L. (2008) *Leadership and Management in the Early Years: From Principles to Practice.* Maidenhead: Open University Press.

Lansdown, G. (2010) The realisation of children's participation rights: critical reflections. In B. Percy-Smith and N. Thomas (eds), *A Handbook of Children and Young People's Participation.* Abingdon: Routledge.

Leeson, C. (2006) My life in care: experiences of non-participation in decision-making processes. Paper delivered at Childhood and Youth: Choice and Participation Conference, Sheffield Hallam University, July.

Leeson, C. (2009) The Involvement of Looked After Children in Making Decisions about their Present and Future Care Needs. Unpublished PhD Thesis, University of Plymouth.

Leiba, T. (2003) A model of collaboration. In J. Weinstein, C. Whittington and T. Leiba, *Collaboration in Social Work Practice.* Gateshead: Jessica Kingsley.

London Borough of Brent (1985) *A Child in Trust: the report of the panel of inquiry into the circumstances surrounding the death of Jasmine Beckford.* London Borough of Brent.

LSCB (Local Safeguarding Children's Board, Haringey) (2009) *Serious Case Review: Baby Peter. Executive Summary*. Available at: http://www.haringeylscb.org/sites/haringeylscb/files/executive_summary_peter_final.pdf (accessed 13 April 2014).

Lumby, J. and Coleman, M. (2007) *Leadership and Diversity: Challenging Theory and Practice in Education*. London: SAGE.

Lumsden, E. (2005) Joined-up thinking in practice: an exploration of professional collaboration. In T. Waller (ed.), *An Introduction to Early Childhood: A Multidisciplinary Approach*. London: SAGE.

Marmot Review, The (2010) *Fair Society, Healthy Lives. The Marmot Review Executive Summary*. Available at: http://www.instituteofhealthequity.org/projects/fair-society-healthy-lives-the-marmot-review (accessed 13 April 2015).

NCSL (National College of School Leadership) (2014) *National Professional Qualification in Integrated Centre Leadership (NPQICL)*. Nottingham: NCSL.

Neale, B. (2002) Dialogues with children: children, divorce and citizenship. *Childhood*, 9(4): 455–75.

Pugh, G. and Duffy, B. (eds) (2006) *Contemporary Issues in the Early Years*. London: SAGE .

Purcell, M. (2009) *Leadership Development Programme for Current and Aspirant Directors of Children's Services*. Nottingham: National College.

RBSCB (Rochdale Borough Safeguarding Children Board) (2012) *Review of Multi-agency Responses to the Sexual Exploitation of Children*. Rochdale: Rochdale Borough.

Roberts, K. (2009) *Early Home Learning Matters*. London: Family and Parenting Institute.

Robinson, C. and Kellett, M. (2004) Power. In S. Fraser (ed.), *Doing Research with Children and Young People*, SAGE: London.

Samuel, M. (2007) Parents jailed for 'sustained cruelty' to disabled daughter. *Community Care*, 9 February.

Serafino, P. and Tonkin, R. (2014) *Intergenerational Transmission of Disadvantage in the UK & EU*. London: ONS. Available at: http://www.ons.gov.uk/ons/dcp171766_378097.pdf (accessed 6 January 2015).

Siraj-Blatchford, I., Taggart, B., Sammons, P., Melhuish, E. and Sylva, K. (2013) *Effective Teachers in Primary Schools: Key Research on Pedagogy and Children's Learning*. Stoke on Trent: Trentham Books.

Stacey, M. (2009) *Teamwork and Collaboration in Early Years Settings*. Exeter: Learning Matters.

Thomas, N. (2000) *Children, Family and the State. Decision-making and Child Participation*. Chippenham: MacMillan Press.

Thurston, C. and Church, J. (2001) Involving children and families in decision-making about health. In P. Foley, J. Roche and S. Tucker (eds), *Children in Society: Contemporary Theory, Policy and Practice*. Trowbridge: Open University.

Tomlinson, P. (2013) The politics of childhood. In P. Jones, D. Moss, P. Tomlinson and S. Welch (eds), *Childhood Services and Provision for Children*. London: Routledge.

Ward, S. (ed.) (2013) *A Student's Guide to Education Studies* (3rd edn). Abingdon: Routledge.

Welbourne, P. and Leeson, C. (2012) Debating the complexities of policy and practice: attempting to improve the educational attainment of children in care. *Journal of Children's Services*, 7(2): 128–43.

West-Burnham, J., Farrar, M. and Otero, G. (2007) *Schools and Communities: Working Together to Transform Children's Lives*. London: Network Continuum.

Whalley, M.E. (2008) *Leading Practice in Early Years Settings*. Exeter: Learning Matters.

11 Parenting in trouble?

Marie Lavelle

Introduction

Parents have long been regarded as being a child's first and most enduring educators (Desforges and Abouchaar, 2003). Since it was first coined, the phrase has been quoted in many policy documents and guides for practitioners, including the Early Years Foundation Stage (DCSF, 2007: card 2.2). It places the centrality of children's learning experiences not within institutions such as schools or early years settings but within the home and with those who are experts in their children's lives – parents. As a parent, I see this as an irrefutable starting point for the discussion in this chapter. Whilst I did not start out, as a first-time mother, understanding the needs of my young baby (despite being a qualified midwife), with time he taught me how to be a mother, and along with his dad, how to be a parent. Yet for some the idea that parents cannot parent successfully without 'expert' advice and support has grown in strength as a result of changing political ideologies over the last 30 years (Gillies, 2008a; 2014). This is in parallel to the neo-liberal construction of the child as future citizen (Hendrick, 1997). Here all invest in childhood to ensure the best possible outcomes for children but with an economic emphasis on future income generation and market participation – the production of the 'homo-economicus' (Moss, 2009). Given the complex cultural, societal and political demands of bringing up children in today's UK society this might come as no surprise. Parents have been continually positioned as both problematic, the vehicle through which generational problems are reproduced, and as redemptive agents in the lives of children.

Having worked with parents for most of my working life and being a parent myself, the one key message I have learnt from parents is the importance of trust and the need for reciprocal trusting relationships. Learning, in my experience, is a two-way process, whether between adult and adult, child and child or child and adult. Imbued in these relationships is power. Whilst much discussion has centred on encouraging parents to engage in their children's learning and schooling, this chapter will explore whether a more fundamental change in the way we work with parents is possible. The approach centres on the construction of a relational space with parents and professionals in which democratic professionals (Moss, 2014) can engage in what Dahlberg and Moss (2005: 121) describe as 'minor politics'. It is through critical thinking, questioning, challenging and political playfulness that practitioners are awakened to the possibility of different ways of thinking and doing relationships with parents.

To start this discussion I feel it is important to start 'at home', and by 'at home' I mean with ourselves and by looking at how caring for others is inextricably linked to our care of ourselves.

Beginning at home

'Working with parents' invariably means caring. Yet we rarely stop to consider what this means: does caring come naturally? Is it something that can be learned, a skill to be demonstrated and examined or is it an attribute, a disposition, with which we are born and which is related to gender? Noddings (2002: 1) sees caring as 'a moral orientation, which is neither domain nor gender specific' but for which the domain of home is important; for Noddings, caring 'starts at home'. Here it is the connection with parental love which can help us to understand caring, the central premise being that 'everyone has a desire to be cared for' (Noddings, 2002: 1) and that this is essential to human life, centred on the need to encounter and relate to others. However, Noddings takes issue with what others have called 'an ethic of care', arguing that we need to examine the precursor to this. That is, when caring is 'natural', it does not require 'ethical effort to motivate it'; instead of it being an obligatory one-way act, caring is 'two-way' where 'both contribute actively' (Noddings, 2002: 2). Thus caring is about building relationships in order to *meet* individuals rather than seeing people as categories or groups. Therefore it is important to recognise each person who is a parent, rather than homogenise parents into one group; all parents are different, they are unique.

If caring is a two-way process, being receptive to care is crucial. 'A soul (or self) empties itself, asks a question, or signals a readiness to receive but the state that develops is thoroughly relational' (Weil in Noddings, 2002: 15). Here care is a mutual process involving two, 'a duality'. However, in this duality both are potentially vulnerable. For the parent asking for support there is a risk that their request will not be taken seriously or its seriousness will be misinterpreted as very serious; 'making a mountain out of a mole hill' (Lavelle, 2011). They may have had requests for support rejected in the past, been placed on waiting lists or 'signposted' to other services, waiting with no response. Often people seek support firstly from their own families and friends (Edwards and Gillies, 2004), and when they do seek support in the public arena their first port of call is often GPs and health visitors (Broadhurst, 2007). Children's Centres still remain an area of concern for families in terms of seeking support. Here parenting practices are potentially exposed and made visible, assessed and judged, and as a result parents feel they cannot be themselves (Lavelle, 2014). For practitioners, caring can also involve making themselves vulnerable if the care offered is rejected. Difficult situations can sometimes provoke negative feelings making it hard, as Noddings says, to feel sympathy, a word she prefers over empathy (Noddings, 2002). Here then is a point of commonality.

So if caring is about 'learning to love and nurture each other' (Swick, 2007: 97), how prepared are we to love and nurture parents as well as children? And what are the difficulties that get in the way of developing relationships with those closest to children? If we want the best for children we must be prepared to want the best for parents and this can sometimes be challenged by our own attitudes and how we value these important people. This is a problem often associated with romantic concepts of childhood, which result in the mistrust or dislike of adults (see Chapter 13). Before we explore some of this challenging stuff it is important to firstly deconstruct and problematise what is meant by the term 'parent'.

The 'p' word: parent

Parent: noun – a person's father or mother

From late middle English, Old French the Latin verb 'parere' to 'bring forth' verb in use since the 17th century. (Oxford Dictionary, 2014)

The above dictionary definition offers a simplistic starting point to our exploration of this term. It might be claimed that the process of raising children is a biological one, natural and instinctive, driven by the need for survival of the species. Yet we do not raise children in isolation from society. It is difficult to pin-point when the term 'parent' became part of our everyday vocabulary. But its use has seen an ideological shift in the roles of fathers and mothers in raising children. In the past (and some would argue in the present) roles were constructed as discursively distinct and separate. However, with the changing demography of the family – the increase in mothers working outside the home, the rise in the number of lone parent families, increase in divorce, remarriage and same-sex partnerships – the terms 'mother' and 'father', it might be argued, became problematic. By using the term 'parent', tricky issues about how families are constituted become to some extent more manageable. However, recognition of the importance of both mothers and fathers in caring for young children is potentially in jeopardy, as fathers in particular are at risk of being concealed within the term. This has been a particular concern for the Fathers Institute (2007) who have campaigned for the use of the term 'father', claiming 'parent' potentially excludes fathers. If professionals want to talk to fathers, it is argued, they need to use father-inclusive language, including addressing 'fathers' directly (Kahn, 2012).

Hence it is 'parents' who were and continue to be positioned at the centre of the debate about outcomes for children. Under the last Labour government, parenting was constructed in universal terms. Here *all* parents were positioned as being in need of support at some time in their lives (Home Office, 1998; DCSF, 2010). The principle of 'progressive universalism', widely used within Labour rhetoric (Balls, 2007) to reduce the stigma associated with supporting parents who might be struggling, remains today. Yet this approach has the potential to legitimate the surveillance of all parents in order to target (or select) parents who are in danger of raising children who are at risk of poor outcomes (Lavelle, 2011). Targeting within universal services remains a key strategy within services that support parents.

With the concerns over the changing form of families diminishing somewhat, the focus has switched to anxieties about parenting and parenting practices (Dermott, 2012).

This changing emphasis does two things: firstly it neglects the impact of wider social influences and, secondly, it shifts the care of children within a 'family', in the widest sense, with all the extensions of that family (grandparents, aunties, uncles) to one which sees the role of bringing up children as one which falls on parents, mothers and fathers, only. To explore this positioning and the way that parents (and mothers in particular) have become the site of increased surveillance, it is useful to explore this through the theoretical lens of poststructuralism and the work of Michel Foucault.

Foucault and working with parents

So far, the discussion has highlighted some of the challenges of establishing authentic, mutual and reciprocal relationships, and the way this does not happen in isolation. The French philosopher Michel Foucault can help us to explore what might get in the way of 'mutuality' and how parenting and working with parents can be seen in terms of politics and power. Foucault (1926–1984) was interested in how power operates within society. He argued that power operates through 'the little things', the microprocesses and practices of everyday life, 'local and specific' rather than grand global processes (Smart, 2002). This is often described as a poststructuralist perspective, but Foucault would, I imagine, have resisted being categorised in this way.

It might be argued that, for parents and practitioners, power is concealed behind a veneer of social investment and neo-liberalist claims of 'empowering' users and 'enabling' parents to make choices (Moss, 2009). Both terms are imbued with the discourse of 'giving' power to those who it is assumed do not have it; the empowerer has the ability to give power to (*empower*) those who are *disempowered*; the enabler to *enable* those who are *disabled*. Therefore it can be seen that language too is not neutral but is also a way through which power operates.

From a Foucauldian perspective gathering information on populations, including statistics and personal information, builds knowledge of problems that essentially did not exist before these new technologies identified them as problems. This problematising is an activity of government; it is linked to the ideologies circulated by government to highlight the 'failures' in society which it wishes to tackle (Miller and Rose, 2008: 61). Accumulating evidence from a wide range of perspectives, political analysis, research institutes and charities, creates a body of unquestionable knowledge and leads to government programmes to tackle the said issue. This makes 'the objects of government thinkable in such a way that their ills appear susceptible to diagnosis, prescription and cure by calculating and normalizing intervention' (Miller and Rose, 2008: 63). Hence such programmes can be seen to be located firmly within a medical model of intervention (diagnosing and treating) and include the coalition government's 'Troubled Families Agenda' (Levitas, 2012) at one extreme and other interventions such as Webster-Stratton's 'Incredible Years' (2013) at the other. Implicated in this are practitioners and others who work with parents and who may be involved with the 'diagnosis' of those who appear to be 'in need' or 'at risk' of failing their children. Hence practitioners too are part of the way that government operates at a distance to police the family. These discourses and practices infiltrate the spaces where parents and professionals work; they often go unnoticed, unchecked and unchallenged. The democratic practitioner is one who is able to identify when these powers are at play.

Power and parental participation: questioning the benefits of working together

The Bernard van Leer Foundation (ICDI, 2012) highlighted five key benefits of working with parents:

1. As children's first educators, parents have a right and a responsibility to be involved.

2. There is clear evidence that what parents do matters; this includes the way parents parent, being sensitive to children's needs, taking an interest in their learning and the outcomes of this learning and in the sorts of stimulating environment they provide at home.

3. When parents and professionals work together this benefits children; this involves 'respectful listening', acknowledging the importance of both learning environments along with the responsibility of all.

4. For settings, involving parents has been shown to improve the quality of provision.

5. When parents are involved in their children's learning, opportunities are created to support parents (ICDI, 2012: 6).

Some of these points are worth a closer look: firstly the suggestion that with rights comes responsibility. Here the rights agenda is underpinned by moral obligation and the view that participating in children's learning is something that parents 'ought' to do. This could be seen as an extension of the 'participatory imperative' (Shucksmith *et al.*, 2005) which defines responsible, good parents as those who engage with institutions in a way that prepares their children for school and who participate when they are there. However, evidence that early interventions and parental involvement in school make a difference remains questionable (Needham and Jackson, 2014; Robinson and Harris, 2014).

Although there is much evidence to support the idea that what parents do matters (Melhuish *et al.*, 2008), there is as much evidence that what parents have (in terms of material resources) also matters. Even parental participation cannot override lack of material resources in predicting outcomes for children (Desforges and Abouchaar, 2003). Whilst Feinstein (2003) claimed that high achieving children from 'poor' homes start school on or above a level with their peers, they are soon overtaken by their lower achieving more affluent classmates. The methodology of this research has subsequently been challenged (Jerrim and Vignoles, 2011). However, the level of social mobility for children from poorer social backgrounds in the UK has been and remains worrying (Blanden and Machin, 2007). Claims that the quality of a child's home learning environment can ameliorate the impact of poverty (Melhuish *et al.*, 2008), which have been widely accepted within policy frameworks, need to be explored critically. Evidence from the Millennium Cohort Study (CLC, 2014) highlights how improving this environment in isolation from other policies for improving outcomes for children cannot eliminate the cognitive skills gap but may reduce it (Goodman and Gregg, 2010).

What is interesting here is that there is leakage into the home of the discourse of quality which normally inhabits settings. This potentially creates a borderless landscape between being a parent and being a 'teacher', which is somewhat troubling. Teachers, and all those involved in children's learning, offer children valuable and sometimes distinctive perspectives of the world. Indeed Dahlberg *et al.* (2007) argue that children should experience environments within settings which are different from home. Just as settings should not be a home-from-home, home should not be a school-from-school. Despite this there have been some who are calling for Children's Centres to work with parents to 'give them the tools to be teachers too' within the home (Bertram and Pascal *et al.*, 2014: 5).

Although there has been an increasing emphasis on working in partnership with parents, there is a relatively small body of literature dedicated to exploring the issues of power in the relationship between parents and practitioners. The positive language of partnership cloaks the issues of authenticity and genuineness in this sort of working. 'Respectful listening' can be a challenge on both sides of the school or setting gate. One of the challenges to overcome is current moral panics about 'poor parenting' which have positioned parents as in deficit and 'in need' of support to bring up children. Parents are blamed for not giving their children enough time, not reading to them, not playing with them and not being involved in their children's learning. News headlines highlight this: 'Poor parent–child bonding "hampers learning"' (BBC News, 21.03.14) and 'Poor parenting and family breakdown "fuels rise in violent behaviour"' (BBC News, 30.03.12). More recently in an interview with *The Times* newspaper, OFSTED head Michael Wilshaw suggested that parents should be fined for non-participation in their children's school learning. Under the headline 'Fine parents who don't read to their children', Wilshaw advocated that parents who do not attend parents' evenings, do not read to their children or encourage them to complete homework should be fined (*The Times*, 17.06.14). Here the responsibilities discourse is strongly evident. Not only is there an expectation but this is now imperative, an obligation to be 'involved'. Headlines such as these imply that parents are not already doing this, and neglect the diversity of what it means to be 'involved' in children's learning (Desforges and Abouchaar, 2003). Indeed poor parenting has become irrevocably linked with societal ills, and parents are seen as both the cause and the cure, not just at the level of the individual child but also at a societal level (Gillies, 2008b).

Expert knowledge and the rise of the professional

Against the backdrop of increasing public debate about the quality of parenting, parents have felt increasingly under scrutiny. Some have argued that parental concerns about strangers, the increased surveillance of parenting and the fear of being judged have made being a parent a lonely activity (Furedi, 2008). This might be regarded as a pessimistic view of society and community. However, changes to demographics, a growing number of households where both parents work and the increasing distance of families from their own support networks have made this a reality for many parents. Yet despite claims to the contrary, parents are spending more time with their children than previous generations (Gauthier *et al.*, 2004) and the nature of this time use has been shown to be more 'intensive' (Craig *et al.*, 2014).

The shift to universalising the expectation that all parents will need support stems from a devaluing of the instinctive nature of parenting. There has been a steady 'de-legitimisation of "folk" or "tacit" knowledge' in parenting. Until recently, Lee (2014: 53) argues, both expert and folk knowledge were able to work together, albeit with 'expert guiding instinct'. Instinct, however, was still thought to be 'as good as anything else'. However, in statements about today's parents there is a tendency to reposition 'instinct' as either mythical or problematic (Lee, 2014: 53) and, I would add, risky. It is no longer acceptable for parents to rely on this knowledge and therefore seeking out professional expert support has become normalised, an unchallenged assumption and one which constructs 'good parents' as those who seek out such support. The pedagogicalising of the parent–child relationship and concerns about knowledge of 'child development' have made the acquisition of new skills the central focus of professional intervention with parents (Wood, 2014). However, when it comes to parental involvement in children's schooling, parental knowledge is often seen as inadequate, supplementary and unimportant. Hughes and Mac Naughton (2000: 243) identified this in relation to working with parents, where parents' knowledge was seen as 'anecdotal, subjective, ad hoc, individualised and only applicable to specific children'. It is professional knowledge which takes precedence when it comes to understanding children. For practitioners the building of a knowledge base is a part of the professionalisation of the early years worker. This has the potential to further marginalise the voice of parents and the knowledge they have of their children.

Evidence that settings are making a difference to the lives of children and families can lead to formal ways of working that create unintentional barriers to genuine partnerships (Lavelle, 2014). The offering or withholding of a cup of tea in a drop-in session, for example, can create barriers and missed opportunities for engagement. In my study of parental participation in two Sure Start Children's Centres, I found that the offering of tea gave parents the space to be themselves, to connect with others and to enjoy their child. Yet for staff in the Centres, it represented something that got in the way of them evidencing the difference they were making. When parents were given tea, they socialised with each other rather than interacting with their children. For parents (mothers) this was key to survival, having a 'cuppa and a chat' was a means of escaping the intensity of parenting, often in isolation. However, this added to practitioners' fears that parents did not interact with their children and it was their job to facilitate and improve this interaction despite resistance from some of the parents. In these spaces of surveillance, parents felt watched and judged. Being aware of and acknowledging the potential distance created by these small, seemingly insignificant acts, is the first step to creating a relational space for democratic practice.

What is important to remember, however, is that those who work in early years settings are also observed and assessed. They need to evidence the difference that they make to the lives of children and families and, in order to do this, I argue, they feel they need to create a distance from the 'other', the untrained, the unskilled, the parent/carer. Osgood (2006: 191) argues that this engagement in a 'discourse of derision' is a 'powerful self-regulation mechanism', one that legitimates the role of the professional. As a result of the increasing pressure to meet targets and outcomes, early years practitioners themselves have become part of the project of advancement (Osgood, 2006). However, this distancing and 'othering' is not inevitable; where there are restraints there are also opportunities for practising differently and for resisting.

The next section will look at ways of doing practice differently, drawing on an example of experience in practice. Some have called this democratic practice, others have stressed that this is a way of practising politics and others have extended this with the idea of a meeting place and a 'third space'; all can help contribute to working more authentically with parents.

Working with parents: creating a space for democratic practice

Clearly it is important to find honest, authentic and genuine ways of working with parents that not only seek to acknowledge the challenges but also work towards the development of genuine partnerships. Instrumentalist approaches of 'how to' work with parents, often pay lip service to issues of power and how power is hidden within everyday micro-processes and practices (Foucault, 1977). Crowley and Wheeler (2010) rightly acknowledge how forming good relationships with parents may be challenging for both practitioners and parents. Some practitioners, seeing themselves as 'experts', might distance themselves from parents, and parents might then find engagement with professionals difficult and uncomfortable (Gillies, 2008b). Dahlberg and Taguchi's (1994) 'meeting place' is a useful starting point for exploring the creation of another way of working with parents which does not attempt to by-pass these tricky and challenging issues. Here instead of engaging in the sometimes empty discourse of 'empowerment', performing what they call minor politics switches the emphasis to one which is about 'contesting power relations, including resisting dominant discourses and forms of injustice' (Dahlberg and Moss, 2005: 165). Importantly, parents are regarded as competent and able and, as a result, participation in decision making is potentially increased and 'diversity can flourish' resulting in new and creative approaches (Moss, 2007: 7). Yet creating spaces where this is possible does not happen by chance. The following vignette is drawn from a conversation with Kay, an early years teacher within an integrated setting. Here Kay talks of how she consciously sought to 'do something different' in the setting where she worked.

> I think wanting to do things differently came from the manager, myself and others, because our own personal narratives were ones that positioned us as being inadequate, like not being good at school. But also we had a belief that everybody and anybody has many possibilities. We recognised that it's a political occupation, working with children and families, and we wanted to work with people's strengths. It was about creating learning environments in which we were all learners, practitioners and parents. We wanted to gain a deeper understanding of the child and their experiences to provide them with the right learning environment. So we had to listen to parents and together we constructed a deeper understanding of the child. Working in a different way, having a social justice agenda and challenging things like 'schooling of young children' was made easier by having a supportive job-share partner. We were on the same wavelength which gave me confidence to do things differently. Having a team too, that was committed to working in this way helped. It was also about getting the balance right; making theory accessible to those who have the power to make change.

Kay, along with her team, created a culture of mutual learning not just with parents but also with other practitioners from other settings by 'welcoming curiosity, uncertainty and subjectivity' (Moss, 2007: 13). 'Third space' extends this idea further, creating a space where relationships are able to mutually flourish, without privileging access to knowledge and where the claims to expertise are challenged (English, 2004). Similar to Moss and Dahlberg's democratic meeting place, third space appears to have been side-lined, perhaps because of its abstract nature which makes it difficult to grasp and make tangible. What is useful to draw from the literature of 'third space' is the idea of creating other ways of thinking, doing and relating. Within this space people are encouraged to challenge dominant deficit discourses about parenting and negative stereotypes, and ways of working which allow practices in which power continues to operate almost unnoticed. The offering or withholding of a cup of tea is questioned not just by practitioners but by parents too; dissent is welcomed.

The democratic or third space practitioner is a 'politically astute practitioner' and one 'who pushes the boundaries … and in so doing, resists polarization, binaries and labels' (English, 2005: 87). However, establishing what this space means should be embedded in 'democratic' practice and locally determined (Dahlberg *et al.*, 2007). Parents should also occupy this space; here they should be able to 'speak back to dominant discourses' which can position them as lacking and in need of professional input (William Timm, 2014: 308). This might be difficult for practitioners and parents but so is caring (Noddings, 2002).

Deliberately practising for liberty

When working with parents it is often the little things that matter and which help to build trusting and long-lasting relationships. The offering or withholding of a cup of tea within stay and play groups might be regarded as such a trivial matter that it is unworthy of consideration in the discussion. Yet it reflects the way that power operates in relationships between parents and practitioners (Lavelle, 2014). It is difficult for practitioners to side-step demands to engage in instrumental measures of connecting with parents: collecting data about the number of parents who attend for example, their backgrounds, whether advice was given. However, questioning how and why this is done is a way of 'deliberately practising for liberty' (Mac Naughton, 2005: 50). Examining and deconstructing the practices that you are asked to engage in is crucial to creating an environment for liberty (or freedom) and a defining feature of professional practice. Practitioners here take stock of the demands placed on them and question the necessity of these taken for granted interventions. Whilst direct challenge might not be possible, questioning, and asking difficult questions, is always possible. The results can, however, be unsettling and painful and can sometimes put practitioners in a place of vulnerability.

Evidencing the difference a service, an interaction, an activity might have on a child or parent is problematic. There is an assumption that change needs to happen and that any change will be visible in a relatively short period of time. Whilst it may not be possible to opt out of these mechanisms, as they are often closely tied to funding and evidencing success, where there are constraints, resistance is always possible. Questioning policies and playing (toying) with them to fit them to the demands of a particular context is a fundamental responsibility of professional practice.

Conclusion

Working with the most important people in children's lives is rewarding, valuable and under-rated. Parents and the cultural capital they pass on to their children through a rich home learning environment are positioned as being central to the improvement of children's outcomes. However, this positioning of parental input may be problematic. While the great majority of families do provide this rich environment, moral panics about a crisis in parenting (as in childhood) encourage us to assume otherwise. Whereas the 'new sociology of childhood' (James and Prout, 1997) has challenged the way that childhood continues to be constructed as vulnerable, passive and fragile, the construction of parenting also requires re-examination. Here, I call for a new sociology of parenting, one which positions parents not just as central to their children's lives but as strong, active and able. Although some might say this is clearly the case within a 'market model', where choosing and purchasing care is seen as the conduit for power, this is problematic and exclusionary (Penn, 2013). Theoretical perspectives can help to unpick and deconstruct issues around how meaningful relationships are made, not just with parents but with colleagues, with communities and of course with children. Like parents, practitioners have an important role in exploring different ways of doing work with parents. Creating a space for democratic practice offers the possibility of constructing new ways of working which liberate not just parents but practitioners too.

ACTIVITY

Consider the following:

- *What data is routinely collected about parents and children?*
- *How is that data used?*
- *In what ways does the collecting of data have the potential to classify people?*
- *How are those classifications used to construct parents as in some way needing support?*

This might seem obvious and elementary, but too often we engage in practices and processes that not only configure practitioners as part of the machinery of government but also contribute to the construction of 'normal' children, families and parents.

FURTHER READING

Furedi, F. (2008) *Paranoid Parenting: Why Ignoring the Experts May Be Best for Your Child.* London: Continuum.

This passionate examination covers most of the difficulties faced by today's parents. At times it feels negative and overwhelming but I believe it gives hope to parents who might be trying to do parenting differently.

Lee, E., Bristow, J., Fairclough, C. and MacVarish, J. (eds) (2014) *Parenting Culture Studies.* Basingstoke: Palgrave MacMillan.

This collection of works comes from academics, including Frank Furedi, who are part of the Parenting Cultures Studies Group at Kent University. The book covers a range of contemporary parenting issues including Attachment Parenting and Helicopter Parenting. Visiting their website is also recommended: http://blogs.kent.ac.uk/parentingculturestudies/

REFERENCES

Balls, E. (2007) Childcare and child poverty: delivering solutions. Paper presented at Daycare Trust Conference, 13 June, London.

Bertram, T. and Pascal, C. (2014) *Early Years Literature Review.* Available at: https://www.early-education.org.uk/sites/default/files/CREC%20Early%20Years%20Lit%20Review%202014%20for%20EE.pdf (accessed 15 April 2015).

Blanden, J. and Machin, S. (2007) *Recent Changes in Intergenerational Mobility in Britain.* London: Sutton Trust.

Broadhurst, K. (2007) Parental help-seeking and the moral order. Notes for policy-makers and parenting practitioners on 'the First Port of Call' and 'No One to Turn To'. *Sociological Research Online*, 12(6) 4: 1–14. Available at: http://www.socresonline.org.uk/12/6/4.html (accessed 15 April 2015).

CLC (Centre for Longitudinal Studies) (2014) *Home of the 1958 National Child Development Study, the 1970 British Cohort Study and the Millennium Cohort Study.* Available at: http://www.cls.ioe.ac.uk (accessed 15 April 2015).

Craig, L., Powell, A. and Smyth, C. (2014) Towards intensive parenting: changes in the composition and determinants of mothers' and fathers' time with children 1992–2006. *British Journal of Sociology*, 65(3): 555–79.

Crowley, M. and Wheeler, H. (2014) Working with parents. In G. Pugh and B. Duffy (eds), *Contemporary Issues in the Early Years* (6th edn). London: SAGE.

Dahlberg, G. and Lenz Taguchi, H. (1994) Förskola och skola – om två skilda traditioner och om visionen om en mötesplats [Preschool and School – Two Different Traditions and the Vision of a Meeting Place]. Stockholm: HLS Förlag.

Dahlberg, G. and Moss, P. (2005) *Ethics and Politics in Early Childhood Education*. Abingdon: Routledge.

Dahlberg, G., Moss, P. and Pence, A. (2007) *Beyond Quality in Early Childhood Education and Care: Languages of Evaluation* (2nd edn). Abingdon: Routledge.

DCSF (Department for Children, Schools and Families) (2007) *Principles into Practice: Cards for the Early Years Foundation Stage*. Nottingham: DCSF Publications.

DCSF (Department for Children, Schools and Families) (2010) *Support for All: The Families and Relationships Green Paper*. Norwich: The Stationery Office.

Dermott, E. (2012) 'Poverty' versus 'Parenting'. An emergent dichotomy. *Studies in the Maternal*, 4(2): n.p. Available at: http://www.mamsie.bbk.ac.uk/back_issues/4_2/Dermott_SiM_4_2_2012.html (accessed 16 April 2015).

Desforges, C. and Abouchaar, A. (2003) *The Impact of Parental Involvement, Parent Support and Family Education on Pupil Achievement and Adjustment: A Literature Review*. Research Report 433. London: DfES Publications.

Edwards, R. and Gillies, V. (2004) Support in parenting: values and consensus concerning who to turn to. *Journal of Social Policy*, 33(4): 627–47.

English, L. (2005) Third-space practitioners: women educating for justice in the Global South. *Adult Education Quarterly*, 55(2): 85–100.

Fathers Institute (2007) Ten top tips for father-inclusive practice. Available at: http://www.fatherhoodinstitute.org/2007/ten-top-tips-for-father-inclusive-practice/ (accessed 15 April 2015).

Feinstein, L. (2003) Not just the early years: The need for a developmental perspective for equality of opportunity. *New Economy*, 10(4): 213–18.

Foucault, M. (1977) *Discipline and Punish: The Birth of a Prison*. London: Penguin.

Furedi, F. (2008) *Paranoid Parenting: Why Ignoring the Experts May Be Best for Your Child*. London: Continuum.

Gauthier, T., Smeedeng, M. and Furstenberg, F. (2004) Are parents investing less time in children? Trends in selected industrialized countries. *Population and Development Review*, 30(4): 647–71.

Gillies, V. (2008a) Perspectives on parenting responsibility: Contextualising values and practices. *Journal of Law and Society*, 35(1): 95–112.

Gillies, V. (2008b) Childrearing, class and the new politics of parenting. *Sociology Compass*, 2/3: 1079–95.

Gillies, V. (2014) Troubling families: parenting and the politics of early intervention. In S. Wagg and J. Pitcher (eds), *Thatcher's Grandchildren*. London: Palgrave Macmillan.

Goodman, A. and Gregg, P. (2010) Poorer children's educational attainment: how important are attitudes and behaviours? York: Joseph Rowntree Foundation. Available at: http://www.jrf.org.uk/system/files/poorer-children-education-full.pdf (accessed 15 April 2015).

Hendrick, H. (1997) Constructions and reconstructions of British childhood: An interpretative survey, 1800 to the present. In A. James and A. Prout (eds), *Constructing and Reconstructing Childhood: Contemporary Issues in the Sociological Study of Childhood*. London: Routledge.

Home Office (1998) *Supporting Families: A Consultation Document.* London The Stationery Office. Available at: http://www.nationalarchives.gov.uk/ERORecords/HO/421/2/acu/sfpages.pdf (accessed 15 April 2015).

Hughes, P. and Mac Naughton, G. (2000) Consensus, dissensus or community: the politics of parent involvement in early childhood education. *Contemporary Issues in Early Childhood*, 1(3): 241–58.

ICDI (International Child Development Initiatives) (2012) *Parental Involvement in Early Learning*. The Hague: Bernard van Leer Foundation. Available at: http://www.bernardvanleer.org/files/Parental_involvement_in_early_learning.pdf (accessed 15 April 2015).

James, A. and Prout, A. (eds) (1997) *Constructing and Reconstructing Childhood: Contemporary Issues in the Sociological Study of Childhood* (2nd edn). London: Routledge.

Jerrim, J. and Vignoles, A. (2011) *The use (and misuse) of statistics in understanding social mobility: regression to the mean and the cognitive development of high ability children from disadvantaged homes.* DoQSS Working Paper No. 11-01, April. London: Institute of Education, University College London.

Kahn, T. (2012) Early years settings. In R. Olley and C. Potter (eds), *Engaging Fathers in Early Years: A Practitioners Guide.* London: Continuum.

Lavelle, M. (2011) A Sociological Investigation of Sure Start Children's Centres: Understanding Parental Participation. PhD thesis, University of Plymouth. Available at: http://pearl.plymouth.ac.uk/handle/10026.1/888 (accessed 15 April 2015).

Lavelle, M. (2014) A storm in a tea-cup? 'Making a difference' in two Sure Start Children's Centres. *Children & Society*. Available at: http://onlinelibrary.wiley.com/DOI:10.1111/chso.12091 (accessed 15 April 2015).

Lee, E. (2014) Experts and parenting culture. In E. Lee, J. Bristow, C. Fairclough, and J. MacVarish (eds), *Parenting Culture Studies*, Basingstoke: Palgrave MacMillan.

Levitas, R. (2012) *There may be 'trouble ahead': What we know about the 120,000 'troubled' families*, Policy Response Series, No. 3. Bristol: Policy and Social Exclusion in the UK.

Mac Naughton, G. (2005) *Doing Foucault in Early Childhood Studies: Applying Poststructural Ideas.* Abingdon: Routledge.

Melhuish, E.C., Phan, M.B., Sylva, K., Sammons, P., Siraj-Blatchford, I. and Taggart, B. (2008) Effects of the home learning environment and preschool center experience upon literacy and numeracy development in early primary school. *Journal of Social Issues*, 64(1): 95–114.

Miller, P. and Rose, N. (2008) *Governing the Present*. Cambridge: Polity Press.

Moss, P. (2007) Bringing politics into the nursery: early childhood education as a democratic practice. *European Early Childhood Education Research Journal*, 15(1): 5–20.

Moss, P. (2009) *There Are Alternatives: Markets and Democratic Experimentalism in Early Childhood Education and Care*. The Hague: Bernard van Leer Foundation.

Moss, P. (2014) *Transformative Change and Real Utopias: A Story of Democracy, Experimentation and Potentiality*. Abingdon: Routledge.

Needham, M. and Jackson, D. (2014) Parental involvement and partnerships with parents. In M. Reed and R. Walker (eds), *A Critical Companion to Early Childhood*. London: SAGE.

Noddings, N. (2002) *Starting at Home*. Berkeley: University of California Press.

Osgood, J. (2006) Professionalism and performativity: the feminist challenge facing early years practitioners. *Early Years*, 26(2): 187–99.

Oxford Dictionary (2014) Available at: http://www.oxforddictionaries.com/definition/english/parent (accessed 15 April 2015).

Penn, H. (2013) Childcare markets: do they work? In E. Lloyd and H. Penn (eds), *Childcare Markets: Can they Deliver an Equitable Service?* Bristol: Policy Press.

Robinson, K. and Harris, A. (2014) *Broken Compass: Parental Involvement with Children's Education*. Princeton: Harvard University Press.

Shucksmith, J., McKee, L. and Willmot, H. (2005) Families, education and the 'participatory imperative'. In L. McKee and S. Cunningham-Burley (eds), *Families in Society: Boundaries and Relationships*. Bristol: Polity Press.

Smart, B. (2002) *Michel Foucault: Revised Edition*. London: Routledge.

Swick, K.J. (2007) Insights on caring for early childhood professionals and families. *Early Childhood Education Journal*, 35(2): 97–102.

Webster-Stratton, C. (2013) *The Incredible Years: Parents, Teachers and Children Training Series*. Available at: http://incredibleyears.com/team-view/carolyn-webster-stratton/ (accessed 15 April 2015).

William Timm, C. (2014) The space between: building liberatory capital in a school–community partnership. *International Journal of Qualitative Studies in Education*, 27(3): 308–29.

Wood, E. (2014) Standards, performance and professionalisation in the early childhood workforce: challenges and opportunities. Presentation given to The Early Childhood Workforce Conference, 20 June, Plymouth University.

12 Leadership in early childhood settings

Caroline Leeson

Introduction

Leadership is an important issue for *all* early childhood professionals, not just for those who hold leadership or management positions (Sharp *et al.*, 2012). According to Earley and Weindling (2004), how leadership is carried out is crucial in terms of the ultimate effectiveness of the organisation. Therefore the development of leadership skills has become increasingly important for all early years practitioners no matter what stage they are at in their career. What has become apparent over recent years is that, in order to cope with the rapid rate of change and development, leadership is required at all levels of an organisation. This requirement has signalled a shift from models of positional leadership to those of distributed or opportunistic leadership. This chapter seeks to explore the significant steps which can be taken to facilitate effective leadership in early childhood settings and will offer a critical examination of current theoretical models.

Over the last few years, the early years, education and child welfare sectors have embarked on interesting journeys towards creative and innovative forms of leadership which have been influenced by several, diverse drivers for change. Firstly, some serious reflection has taken place leading to the recognition of the importance of effective leadership in welfare services for young children and their families. This acknowledgement has created a demand to take leadership seriously and improve the calibre of leaders. For example, Lord Laming's report into the death of Victoria Climbié (DoH, 2003) was the first enquiry into the death of a child to criticise the calibre and expertise of leaders and managers in all services for young children rather than placing the blame on frontline staff. The collective failure of leaders to lead with vision and to take responsibility for managing their staff was seen as a major contributory factor in the events leading to Victoria's death. The Audit Commission (2003) was equally critical of the failure of local government to grasp the nettle of corporate governance, suggesting that, even at the highest levels, leaders are poor at communicating their vision and promoting their services effectively.

As a consequence, the Every Child Matters agenda (DfES, 2003) and the Children Act 2004 sought to address these criticisms by developing an expectation that managers should manage more effectively, accept accountability and be more proactive in developing multidisciplinary training opportunities for all frontline staff and that all of this would take place in a multiprofessional context. However, this has not been easy. Laming revisited his original recommendations in 2009 and found that few had been fully implemented. Questions of how individual professions work together and how this collaborative practice can be effectively led had still not been adequately addressed. Laming (2009: 20) recommended:

> *The Department for Children, Schools and Families should organise regular training on safeguarding and child protection and on effective leadership for all senior political leaders and managers across frontline services.*

Nevertheless, development has continued to be slow – the DCSF leadership programme was only established in 2009 (DCSF, 2009) and recent reports have indicated that there are still substantial difficulties in successfully leading Children's Services both within and across professions (Ofsted, 2013), leading to questions as to the wisdom of investing in training. Nonetheless, there is compelling evidence that good leadership can make significant contributions to successful service delivery and outcomes for children and families (NCLSCS, 2011). Within the early years sector, the National Professional Qualification in Integrated Centre Leadership (NPQICL) (NCSL, 2004; 2006), Early Years Professional Status (EYPS) (CWDC, 2006; 2010) and the new Early Years Teacher qualification (EYT) (NCTL, 2013) have all become key components of the leadership education landscape. However, a criticism of all the training available, in all sectors, is that it tends to be targeted at specific settings/sectors and individuals and usually at those people who hold a leadership position already. There are not, as yet, universal courses accessible by all who may be considering taking a leadership role or who find themselves, unexpectedly, in a leadership position.

Secondly we have seen a substantial development of policy strategy and legislation at national level, highlighting and promoting the need for good quality and effective leadership in the childcare and education sector (DfE, 2013). Indeed, the context within which services for children and families currently operate might be characterised as one of constant change in a fast moving world with ever shifting goal posts. For example, several sections of the National Childcare Strategy (DfEE, 1998), including the setting up of Early Excellence Centres, Sure Start local programmes and Neighbourhood Nurseries, gave the impetus for settings to become multidisciplinary and multifunctional. In 2003, as part of the Every Child Matters agenda, it was proposed that Sure Start Children's Centres should be opened in each of the 20 per cent most deprived neighbourhoods in the country by 2006 (DfES, 2003). This development continued the push towards a landscape of integrated services that is still present today although current financial constraints have led to a much slower rate of growth and some closures. The intention was (and still is) that these centres would 'combine nursery education, family support, employment advice, childcare and health services on one site' to provide integrated care and education for young children (DfES, 2003: 7). However, the idea of flexible, integrated services was not a new one. For example, a number of Nursery Centres were set up in London and other cities in the late 1970s, which offered state nursery education with wrap-around daycare facilities and, often, a range of other services to meet the needs of their local communities. These centres did not become a widespread phenomenon and the staff were definitely challenged to find new ways of working in partnership across different services such as Education, Social Services and Health. The Child Care Act 2006 gave parents a voice in the planning and delivery of services that suited their needs, as well as the right to expect high quality provision. It also placed a responsibility upon local authorities, as strategic leaders, to enhance partnership working across all sectors. This steady move towards integrated services, with its concomitant complexities, precipitated a tremendous rate of expansion of the functions, roles and responsibilities of early childhood professionals, giving rise to considerable debate on the most appropriate leadership styles and tone for these new ways of leading, managing and developing services for all service users (Lawler and Bilson, 2010). Furthermore, the steady move towards integration of all public services saw early years services frequently at the forefront of development, not only leading the way, but often finding new paths. Helping everyone involved to 'think outside the box' (or developing a box big enough or flexible enough for everyone to think inside) is therefore a major challenge and it appears we may still be a long way from fully embracing the need for visionary leaders who will effectively promote the needs and aspirations of young children and their families.

As a consequence of the above drivers for change, there was a period of significant investment in the early years sector between 2003 and 2010 with many diverse environments and settings for children and families being established that require the development of different models of leadership. The recent budgetary cuts following the international recession have made leadership developments difficult and have resulted in a preference for entrepreneurial frameworks that promote the mantra of 'doing more with less'. For example, the government report *More Great Childcare* (DfE, 2013) made the controversial suggestion that the ratio of staff to children could be increased, making a seismic shift in the way services are perceived by adopting a business model based on profit margins rather than effective care and education of young children. However, this report and the Nutbrown (2012) report that precipitated it both emphasised the importance not just of leadership, but of graduate leadership to improve services and outcomes in the early years sector. The drive towards this has been maintained even in a context of poorer financial support. Furthermore, in the last few years we have seen leadership become a key aspect of the Ofsted inspection process so the strengths and weaknesses of the leader or the leadership pattern of a setting have become an issue for formal scrutiny as never before.

Thus, the debate on what constitutes effective leadership has intensified in response to the expectations of the policymakers and other stakeholders and has articulated the aims and ethics of those who lead services for children and families.

One of the key difficulties for the development and articulation of leadership in the early years is the lack of theory to assist with the understanding and practice of leadership. Rodd (1994; 1998; 2005) argued that, although there is 'an abundance of literature on leadership as it pertains to business, industry, human services and education in general, little has been written specifically for the early childhood profession' (1998: xi). Furthermore, leadership happens within a cultural context yet is most often written about as a culturally neutral, universal truth (Coleman and Campbell-Stephens, 2010). Thus, considerable work has had to be done to rethink some of the models of leadership and management that already exist within local authority bureaucracies and to establish new ones that reflect the issues raised in recent reports and recommendations and which facilitate working together with the child at the centre of practice.

A crucial question posed by the current debate on leadership and the development of services has to be: do we want leaders 'to fix things' ('child menders or rule benders' Parker-Rees, 2007b: 35) in early childhood settings or is there/ should there be a different way forward? Should there be more emphasis on a collegial approach that has, at its core, the opportunity for all practitioners to develop leadership skills whatever their job description or level, or are we focused on offering cheap, preferably for-profit daycare for working families?

Certainly, it appears that all practitioners should be enabled to develop theoretical and practical frameworks for leadership and management appropriate to contemporary early years provision, based on knowledge of relevant theory and research. A criticism of the EYPS (CWDC, 2006), which was designed to establish leadership skills and abilities throughout the children's workforce, may be that this important theoretical underpinning was not sufficiently developed to enable the role to be truly effective. The new Early Years Initial Teaching Training (EYITT) (DfE, 2014) does not seem to address this oversight, leaving only the NPQICL qualification to encourage the development of theoretical perspectives through engaging in dialogue about what leadership means to participants in their setting.

What is leadership?

We have had a fascination with leaders for centuries, attempting to establish and understand what differentiates leaders from those they lead and trying to encapsulate strong and weak characteristics in order to test/predict or identify those who may lead in whatever field we are engaged in. Leaders are seen as having a profound effect on whatever organisation they are in charge of, sometimes beneficial and sometimes detrimental. Leadership is often seen as influencing the behaviour of others, often to persuade them to follow a path defined by the leader. Thinking about 'best' leaders and 'worst' leaders in history is an absorbing occupation, often engaged in by those attempting to make sense of the role of the leader.

Leadership theories have come, predominantly, from the field of industry. Throughout the 20th century, studies have focused on contributing towards a body of knowledge in order to give the world of business an understanding of what to look for and what to enhance in the leaders they employ. These theories have increasingly been used in other fields, and during the last 20 years in particular, have been scrutinised and developed within the areas of education and social welfare.

Leadership theories can be broadly divided into the following categories: trait theories, behavioural or style theories and transformational theories. They are not necessarily exclusive, as van Maurik (2001: 3) explains:

> *Although it is true that the progression of thinking tends to follow a sequential path, it is quite possible for elements of one generation to crop up much later in the writings of someone who would not normally think of himself or herself as being of that school. Consequently, it is fair to say that each generation has added something to the overall debate on leadership and that debate continues.*

Trait theories

Trait theory formed the basis of most leadership research up until the 1940s. Attempts were made to identify various personality traits or personal characteristics, which, if present in an individual, would indicate his or her suitability as a leader. Key traits were usually identified by studying successful leaders in history, e.g. Julius Caesar, Alexander the Great, Elizabeth the first, Mahatma Gandhi, Martin Luther King. Workers in this field developed tests that could predict which of the people applying for a leadership position possessed the desired traits and, therefore, were the most employable.

Using tests to establish whether people have particular identified qualities proved attractive to the business world for two reasons. Firstly, the predictive quality was regarded as promising less risk of employing the wrong person. Secondly, the innate-ness of trait theory suggested that money need not be spent on training leaders to do their job as eventually their skills would shine through.

Although there have been many criticisms of trait theory, aspects are still incorporated in training to support leaders (for example, head teachers) in education today. McClelland's (1987) seminal work on human motivation has been widely used by the National College (NC) where traits are described as 'non-conscious drivers', i.e. they influence our behaviour throughout many aspects of our lives including our working lives.

The major criticism of trait theory is that it is too simplistic, that other factors also need to be taken into account. So researchers began to focus on leaders' actions rather than just their attributes, considering the situations that leaders find them-selves in and how the traits or qualities required to deal with that particular situation might be predicted.

In summary, trait theory is based on an assumption that traits are innate rather than learned; that leaders are born rather than made. Experience, however, shows us that this is not the case: not all leaders are born leaders. Studies of successful leaders show that they do not all have identical qualities. Most of the early research focused on male leaders in history. What does this say about women leaders, particularly pertinent in the early years field where the vast majority of leaders are women? We might argue that it is too simplistic to define masculine and feminine traits; certainly research has shown that both male and female leaders are able to demonstrate all of the traits defined in this manner. Nevertheless, a great deal of time and energy has been devoted to this type of study and the trait landscape is dominated by concepts of masculinity and fem-ininity which, it has been argued, inhibits the development of desired characteristics such as passionate zeal (Murray and McDowall Clark, 2013). What can be seen, his-torically, is a gradual shift of emphasis from thinking about the leaders themselves to issues of leadership and what styles of leadership could be identified and described.

Behavioural or style theories of leadership

Writers who had become dissatisfied with the limitations of trait theory began to identify a range of leadership styles which could be used to develop tests to measure people's ability to lead and manage. The focus was now on how leaders behaved.

Dozens of leadership styles were identified by many writers using different words to describe essentially similar behaviours. Influential writers such as Blake and Moulton (1964), for example, developed a Managerial Grid to assist in this identification process with the assumption that there is a best style of leadership. Likert (1967), another key writer in the field, suggested four different styles:

- exploitative/authoritarian – leaders manipulate their subordinates and are used to prescribing tasks in the expectation that they will be obeyed without question by their staff;

- benevolent/authoritarian – leaders are used to being in charge and have a paternalistic approach to their employees;

- consultative – employees are asked their opinion prior to leaders making decisions; and

- participative – employees are involved in the decision-making processes.

Likert's typology, however, was based on the assumption that individuals are fixed with a particular style, therefore unable to shift from one style to another when the task and/or personnel change.

In the 1930s, Lewin *et al.* identified three different leadership styles: autocratic, laissez-faire and democratic. Autocratically led teams were those where the physical presence of the leader was required in order to get the work done. 'Follow me, I am right behind you' summarises a laissez-faire approach to leadership. Democratically led teams were those which could be given autonomy and responsibility and could be trusted to do their work without being constantly overseen. In order to be successful, the leader would need to be able to adopt the most appropriate style. Style theories, therefore, did offer the opportunity to begin to understand what has happened when leadership has appeared to go wrong, i.e. when a particular style has been used that was inappropriate for the team or the task that was being carried out.

Tannenbaum and Schmidt (1958) were interested in the processes of decision making and continued to work on defining the autocratic–democratic continuum. They outlined a spectrum of situations and styles that could be used to identify the leadership requirements at any one time. Context was beginning to be recognised as important. This proved useful as it began to show that, over time, leaders might need to move from one style to another as teams developed in competence and that an autocratic leader would not be successful with a team of capable people who would wish to develop their own autonomy.

Neugebauer (1985 cited in Rodd, 1994; 1998) related styles of leadership specifically to early years contexts with typologies of the Task Master, the Comrade, the Motivator and the Unleader, suggesting that the third was the most effective in these contexts. Again this may be a useful category as we see a move towards an increasingly autonomous workforce in early years with higher expectations regarding qualifications/experience and calibre of personnel.

A serious criticism of style theory is that people rarely lead using just one style. This approach did not take into account the changing contexts and situations that leaders might find themselves in. Frequently leaders have a variety of styles available to them, hence the development of contingency or situational theories where leaders adapt their leadership style to be effective in different contexts, what Fiedler and Chemers (1974) term 'leader-match'. Thus, the idea of 'best fit' emerges where leaders are chosen by the organisation as being most effective in a particular situation given the structure of the task, the characteristics of all the people involved, both leaders and led, and the nature and quality of the relationship between them. Contingency theory gave the opportunity to look at the situation and its impact upon leaders rather than on the traits of leaders and their impact upon the situation (Northouse, 2009). Furthermore, contingency theory recognises, for the first time, that leaders do not have to be effective in all situations (Northouse, 2009), being all things to all people.

With regard to situational leadership, Hersey and Blanchard (1977) identify four styles that leaders might use to lead in different situations, taking account both of tasks to be done and the relationships between the leader and others in the organisation. These were:

- telling – a style often required in situations where the task is repetitive or needs doing quickly;

- selling – a style that encourages and motivates people to do the tasks required;

- participating – a style required when the competence of staff is high, but unacknowledged by them so tasks still need facilitation, supervision and support by the leader;

- delegating – a style used where high staff motivation and competence means they are able to get on with the task without supervision or direct support.

In order to be successful, according to contingency or situational leadership theory, leaders and their organisations need to be skilful at reading the requirements of the context in which they work (Telford, 1996). A key question, therefore, is what style and traits can be utilised so that the best will be achieved in given situations?

Transactional and transformational theories

Burns (1978) developed another set of ideas by distinguishing between transactional leadership (getting things done) and transformational (visionary) leadership. According to Burns, transactional leadership, coming primarily from management literature, can best be described as management techniques that are now recognised as effective, good and proper management. It is, therefore, about the use of negotiation with the led, an exchange of services for various kinds of rewards (both extrinsic and intrinsic) in order to reach a point of mutual satisfaction resulting in completion of the task.

Important aspects include setting up procedures, clear job descriptions, appraisal of performance, management through the clarification of objectives, etc. The effectiveness and the importance of praise, recognition and the delegation of responsibility are also acknowledged in this style of leadership.

Transactional leadership can still, however, be seen as a top-down rather than a bottom-up model of leadership. Transformational leadership is defined by Burns (1978) as moving beyond this. In transformational or visionary leadership, the leader and led work together on common objectives towards common aims.

Bass (1985), however, was critical of Burns's view that the two theories were oppositional. He preferred to see them as complementary and useful to each other and expanded and refined ideas about transformational leadership. Van Maurik (2001) suggests that the two should be looked upon as progression from one to the other as demands upon leaders were becoming increasingly complex towards the end of the 20th century. Working from transactional towards transformational leadership helps and enables both leaders and led to navigate around high levels of uncertainty in unstable and uncertain times. It is hardly surprising, with the constant and rapid change which were characteristic of life through the 1980s and 1990s, that interest in transformational leadership rose to the fore at that time.

Research on emotional intelligence has provided a further dimension to models of transformational leadership. Goleman *et al.* (2002) set out why it is imperative to have emotionally literate leaders. These are leaders who are aware of their own emotions, are committed to the professional development of themselves and others, are empowering, trusting, optimistic, have a life outside the working environment and look after their own physical and emotional well-being (McBride and Maitland, 2001: 198–9).

Key aspects of transformational leadership are that it is about hearts and minds, about empowering people to learn and to seek change and improvement, not about controlling them. It is a people-oriented approach rather than focused mainly on tasks or products. It places an emphasis on trusting those with whom you work, transforming feelings, attitudes and beliefs and having an impact on the culture of the organisation. Transformational leadership has a central belief that anyone should be able to lead (Owen, 2000) – a belief that is contested but nevertheless has had substantial influence on subsequent leadership theories such as distributed and authentic leadership.

Collaborative leadership

Now, in the 21st century, definitions of effective leadership refer to 'shared', 'distributive', 'collaborative', 'invitational' and 'collegiate' ways of working. All of these qualities build on aspects of transformational leadership. Rodd (1994), Owen (2000) and Telford (1996) all advocate that anyone can take on a leadership role, given the right context and opportunity: 'Leadership, at its best, is a shared venture engaged in by the many' (Telford, 1996: 9).

Nias *et al.* (1989) were among the first to develop ideas about collaborative leadership within the school context, where leaders and led have shared values, beliefs and attitudes which assist them in working towards the overt goals of the organisation. Continuing with the context of schools, Southworth (1998) argues that as there is much to manage and less time for any individual to lead, schools actually need many leaders, who take and share leadership roles. He argues that this has implications regarding shared headship, otherwise there will just be a redistribution of management tasks rather than shared leadership. This may well be pertinent to leadership in multidisciplinary and multifunctional integrated early years settings.

Owen (2000) takes the view that it is an important part of the human spirit to wish to lead and to be able to do so. She identifies leaders as only being successful if they have effective structures around them, a relevant point, when we consider the anxieties surrounding multidisciplinary working in child protection. Bolman and Deal (1991, in Telford, 1996) consider transformational leadership in four contexts or frames in order to help us understand the theoretical underpinning of all leadership theories:

- structural – the formal roles and relationships of the workplace;
- human resource – focuses on the needs of the individuals within the workplace;
- political – the internal politics and power struggles; and
- symbolic – the culture of the workplace.

Again, from within the world of education, Telford (1996) argues that 'collaborative' leadership takes from all four frames, using them to analyse the tasks and work towards achieving the vision of the school.

Ethical leadership

Espoused by Bottery (1992), ethical leadership looks at the responsibility of the leader to think about how their setting fulfils its purpose. He argues that the legislation that frames the setting and its task is highly relevant and needs to be taken into consideration when embarking on any leadership decision making. For Bottery, ethical leadership is action with moral purpose.

> *Leadership in general must maintain an ethical focus which is oriented towards democratic values within a community. This has to do with the meaning of ethics historically – as a search for the good life of the community... ethics here refers to a more comprehensive construct than just individual behaviour; rather it implicates us and how we as a moral community live our communal lives. (Foster, 1989: 55)*

How does ethical leadership manifest itself in action? The answer to this question is particularly relevant to early years services where success depends on the interrelatedness of working with people and for people. Rodd (1998) for example, identifies four key areas within ethical leadership. These include:

- the promotion and protection of children's rights;
- the provision of a high quality and economically viable service which does not compromise children's rights;

- administration of services in accordance with the profession's ethical principles;

- employment of an early childhood code of ethics to guide the resolution of ethical dilemmas.

Interestingly, we still do not have written codes of ethics in the UK to inform workers in all early years settings.

Distributed leadership

Distributed leadership has now been with us for some time and has become the UK government's model of choice for early years, education and welfare sectors. Distributed leadership is the sharing of the responsibility of leadership by several people often at different levels (Gronn, 2002; NCSL, 2006), taking account of the context and focusing on the interaction between leaders and followers in getting tasks done. A distributed leadership framework is based on the claim that tasks may be too complex for one person to complete successfully and implies that there should be respect for the different skills and attributes of others who may be better placed or equipped to fulfil certain leadership functions. Distributed leadership has become popular because it is flexible, negotiable and adaptable, moving away from a focus on the leader as an individual with particular skills and attributes towards the effective sharing of tasks that need to be done (Earley and Weindling, 2004). In the complex, multiprofessional world of early years, it is not hard to see why distributed leadership has been embraced by some of the key writers (Aubrey, 2007; Jones and Pound, 2008) and organisations (National College). According to Aubrey (2007), distributed leadership allows for collaboration, interaction and interdependence, thus enabling the development of powerful and sustainable learning communities. However, distributed leadership has come in for a great deal of criticism. Both Harris (2007) and Hartley (2007) suggest that there is a lack of conceptual clarity which is a serious handicap; it is too flexible to be taken seriously as a substantial model of leadership. Torrance (2013) argues that distributed leadership is not as flexible as is often suggested because the hierarchical leader has to endorse it and take active steps to ensure it takes place. The consequence of this is that others in the organisation regard distributed leadership as a 'gift' from the leader and therefore any action/decision is still context specific and hedged with the hierarchical power of more traditional leadership models.

Authentic leadership

Authentic leadership is also relatively new, with enthusiastic adherents. It has not been as influential as distributed leadership, yet it appears to fit the requirements much better. It may well be that its lack of endorsement is due to the perception that it is not as pliable or flexible as distributed leadership, yet it would appear that authentic leadership enables resilience and confidence and the ability to withstand pressure. Authentic leadership takes inspiration from the work of Goleman (1998), amongst others, as a leadership 'from within' which is reliant on self-awareness, relational transparency, balanced processing and an internalised moral perspective (Champy, 2009) which enables the leader to be relatively immune to the pressures of the role by giving them the facility of being true to themselves. Authentic leadership recognises the complexity of modern leadership and the demands that are made on individual leaders to reach even greater heights in managing complicated situations (Avolio and Gardner, 2005). Taking account of the sociological concept of emotional labour (Hochschild, 1983), where people are expected to act in certain ways according to the demands of the organisation, authentic leadership seeks to find a path that leaders might follow that protects them from exhaustion and burn out by encouraging them to lead as they see fit, being authentic and true to themselves. Authentic leaders are defined as:

> those who are deeply aware of how they think and behave and are perceived by others as being aware of their own and others values/moral perspectives, knowledge and strengths; aware of the context in which they operate and who are confident, hopeful, optimistic, resilient and of high moral character (Avolio, Luthans and Walumba, 2004, cited in Avolio and Gardner, 2005: 321)

Like distributed leadership, authentic leadership promotes followership by fostering the development of authenticity in others within the organisation. Through the use of conscious personal reflective dialogues, authentic leaders are able to develop skills of professional effectiveness while being ethically sound and value based in their decision making (Begley, 2001).

Entrepreneurial leadership

Most recently, there has been an increased interest in entrepreneurial leadership which promotes the concept of a hero who will address all the issues and make everything perfect. The attraction for governments is that entrepreneurs are seen as skilled at doing more for less in straitened economic circumstances, which fits with our current situation. Entrepreneurial leaders are characterised as charismatic, powerful and confident people with strong internal drives for achievement and control (Vecchio, 2003; Bolton and Thompson, 2004; Garvey and Lancaster, 2011) and there have been a number of high profile success stories in the early education sector for a number of years (see National College website for examples) that promote an entrepreneurial ideology. A key problem has to be their longevity; entrepreneurial leaders in education have often left soon after making substantial changes, creating a further set of problems for the setting (Bolden, 2004). Furthermore, they may be difficult to follow as role models, leading to their being seen as 'superheros' and thus unusual, exotic and rare. More recently the literature on entrepreneurialism has looked at the concept of an entrepreneurial team rather than an individual (Harper, 2008) which may well be a more attractive proposition for the early years sector.

Conclusion

Despite the contested arena of what theoretical model of leadership should be used in early years settings, there is a discernible consensus amongst the key writers in this area as to what constitutes effective leadership:

- That there should be a shared, articulated philosophy firmly based on values and principles of social justice (Siraj-Blatchford and Manni, 2006; Whalley, 2006; Jones and Pound, 2008).

- That leadership should be visionary, inspiring others and leading the way, finding innovative and creative paths (Earley and Weindling, 2004; Moyles, 2006; Siraj-Blatchford and Manni, 2006; West-Burnham *et al.*, 2007; Jones and Pound, 2008).

- That leaders should facilitate the co-construction of the environment with those who share it (Siraj-Blatchford and Manni, 2006; Jones and Pound, 2008).

- That leadership should promote the central importance of relationships (West-Burnham *et al.*, 2007; Curtis and Burton, 2009).

- Thus service provision must be underpinned by the development of an ethic of passionate care in order to promote collective ownership (Osgood, 2006; Curtis and Burton, 2009; Murray and McDowall Clark, 2013).

- That the cultural context is regarded as relevant and key to shaping the style of leadership and its manifestation (cultural relativism – Fleer, 2003; Tobin, 2005).

- That leaders are change agents involved in the identification, implementation and evaluation of change that benefit the community (Earley and Weindling, 2004; Sylva *et al.*, 2004; Moyles, 2006; Jones and Pound, 2008; Curtis and Burton, 2009).

- That effective leaders are reflective practitioners capable of critical thought and of promoting development of the same in others (Moyles, 2006; Jones and Pound, 2008; Urban, 2008; Curtis and Burton, 2009).

- That successful leaders demonstrate certain valued personal qualities, not least the ability to be authentic and encourage authenticity in others (Sylva *et al.*, 2004; Moyles, 2006; West-Burnham *et al.*, 2007; Jones and Pound, 2008; Curtis and Burton, 2009).

- That leaders have to be effective communicators (Sylva *et al.*, 2004; Siraj-Blatchford and Manni, 2006).

- That leaders need to be present (Goleman *et al.*, 2002; Sauer and Kohls, 2011).

There is a sense that leadership theory has moved from the 'hard' world of industry and business towards a more 'touchy/feely' world where people are valued for themselves, not just the work they do. This is perhaps vital and may be inevitable as we have developed complex working worlds, trained and developed staff to higher competencies and created more service-oriented businesses as opposed to ones dealing in inanimate products.

However, this paradigm shift does not seem to be articulated in practice and backward steps are being taken in times of austerity. For example, Aubrey (2007) talks about the difficulties of effective leadership where the culture is collaborative but the structure is hierarchical. Furthermore, the role of chief executive as opposed to the role of leading professional seems to be the leadership model promoted by many government reforms and policies (DfE, 2013). The requirement to balance the books is therefore taking precedence over the inspirational aspects of leadership. This can clearly be seen in policies that allow businesses to take over so called 'failing' schools, hospitals and other public services, where they have no intrinsic understanding of the setting, but know how to manage finances.

There should be a more meaningful debate about what early years settings are for. We are no further forward in answering the question from earlier in this chapter: are settings designed to allow today's workforce to go about their business knowing their children are being educated and cared for (DfE, 2013) or is it about enhancing children's experiences in the here and now? Moss and Petrie (2002: 101) present a cogent argument that 'childhood is an important stage of the life course in its own right, which leaves traces on later stages'. If we believe this then there are huge implications in terms of relationships between children, between adults and between children and adults. As the special nature of relationships with families is a key feature of early years leadership, clear statements about our philosophy should be central to the debate on what sorts of leaders we want.

I would argue that leadership in early years settings should, first and foremost, be inclusive for all participants: staff, children, parents and leaders. Leadership is about learning, becoming wiser and more knowledgeable. This does not necessarily mean knowing a lot of things, but is more to do with knowing about self and acting in the right way given particular situations, developing learning cultures for staff and parents as well as children. We do not need superhuman leaders as they cannot be emulated by the many:

> *Even the most talented leaders require the input and leadership of others,*
> *constructively solicited and creatively applied. It's time to celebrate the incomplete –*
> *that is, the human – leader. (Ancona et al., 2007: 101)*

ACTIVITY **1**

During the next few weeks read a variety of national and local newspapers and collect articles that demonstrate aspects of leadership. These could include references to politicians, football managers, celebrities, local initiatives, businesses, public services, etc. What can you discern about preferred leadership styles and what you might wish to challenge within that debate?

Try to identify components of successful leadership which you can discuss in a small group.

ACTIVITY 2

In a small group, plan an early years setting of your choice. Consider the following aspects:

1. *Outline the vision, purposes and aim of your particular setting.*
2. *Describe, in detail, the services you will offer, the market you seek to serve and the premises you will require.*
3. *Identify the staffing implications of your plan, in terms of numbers, roles, qualifications, terms and conditions.*
4. *Identify how your setting will meet your needs and those of your staff, the children, their families and the wider community.*
5. *Develop short-term and long-term plans of what steps should be taken to create your setting.*

This could form the context for an assignment discussing key leadership issues related to your particular setting.

FURTHER READING

Ancona D., Malone, T.W., Orlikowski, W.J. and Senge, P. (2007) In Praise of the Incomplete Leader. *Harvard Business Review*, February, pp. 92–102. Available at: https://hbr.org/2007/02/in-praise-of-the-incomplete-leader (accessed 15 April 2015).

This article is inspirational; it reminds us how important it is to be human and that leadership is not about having all the answers, but about enabling and promoting the development of communities.

Woodrow, C. and Busch, G. (2008) Repositioning early childhood leadership as action and activism. *European Early Childhood Education Research Journal*, 16(1): 83–93.

This paper discusses the tension between the preferred models of leadership espoused by early years leaders and the demands of corporate childcare and the commodification of services. Using feminist work in the areas of leadership and professionalism, the authors argue that there are new opportunities for further development of early years leadership.

Whalley M. (2006) Leadership in Integrated Centres and Services for Children and Families – A Community Development Approach: Engaging with the Struggle. *Childrenz Issues: Journal of the Children's Issues Centre*, 10(2): 8–13. Available at: http://search.informit.com.au/documentSummary;dn=366901244258381;res=IELFSC (accessed 15 April 2015).

Margy Whalley has been at the forefront of leadership development in early years settings and led the creation of the NPQICL. Her values and principles have facilitated discussion about new ways of leading that have taken the leadership of children's centres in new and meaningful directions involving whole communities.

REFERENCES

Ancona D., Malone, T.W., Orlikowski, W.J. and Senge, P. (2007) In Praise of the Incomplete Leader. *Harvard Business Review*, February: 92–102. Available at: https://hbr.org/2007/02/in-praise-of-the-incomplete-leader (accessed 15 April 2015).

Aubrey, C. (2007) *Leading and Managing in the Early Years*. London: SAGE.

Audit Commission (2003) *Corporate Governance: Improvement and Trust in Local Public Services*. London: The Audit Commission.

Avolio, B.J. and Gardner, W.L. (2005) Authentic leadership development: getting to the roots of positive forms of leadership. *The Leadership Quarterly*, 16(3): 315–38.

Bass, B. (1985) *Leadership and Performance Beyond Expectation*. New York: Free Press.

Begley, P. (2001) In pursuit of authentic school leadership practices. *International Journal of Leadership in Education*, 4(4): 353–65.

Blake, R. and Moulton, J. (1964) *The Managerial Grid*. London: Bloomsbury.

Bolden, R. (2004) *What is Leadership? Leadership South-west Research Report*. Exeter: University of Exeter and SW of England Regional Development Agency.

Bolton, B. and Thompson, J. (2004) *Entrepreneurs: Talent, Temperament, Technique* (2nd edn). Oxford: Butterworth-Heinemann.

Bottery, M. (1992) *The Ethics of Education Management*. London: Cassell Educational.

Burns, J. (1978) *Leadership*. New York: Harper and Row.

Champy, J. (2009) Authentic leadership. *Leader to Leader*, 54: 39–44.

Child Care Act 2006 c.21. London: The Stationery Office. Available at: http://www.legislation.gov.uk/ukpga/2006/21/contents (accessed 21 February 2015).

Children Act 2004 c.31. London: The Stationery Office. Available at: http://www.legislation.gov.uk/ukpga/2004/31/contents (accessed 21 February 2015).

Coleman, M. and Campbell-Stephens, R. (2010) Perceptions of career progress: the experience of Black and Minority Ethnic school leaders. *School Leadership and Management*, 30(1): 35–49.

Curtis, L. and Burton, D. (2009) Naïve change agent or canny political collaborator? The change in leadership role from nursery school to Children's Centre. *Education*, 37(3): 287–99.

CWDC (Children's Workforce Development Council) (2006) *Early Years Professional National Standards*. Leeds: CWDC.

CWDC (Children's Workforce Development Council) (2010) *On the Right Track: Guidance to the Standards for the Award of Early Years Professional Status*. Leeds: CWDC.

DCSF (Department for Children, Schools and Families) (2009) *Statutory Guidance: The Roles and Responsibilities of the Lead Member for Children's Services and the Director of Children's Services*. Nottingham: DCSF Publications.

DfE (Department for Education) (2013) *More Great Childcare: Raising Quality and Giving Parents More Choice*. London: The Stationery Office.

DfE (Department for Education) (2014) *Early Years Initial Teacher Training (EYITT)*. Available at: https://www.gov.uk/early-years-initial-teacher-training-a-guide-for-providers (accessed 20 October 2014).

DfEE (Department for Education and Employment) (1998) *National Childcare Strategy*. London: DfEE.

DfES (Department for Education and Skills) (2003) *Every Child Matters: Green Paper*. London: The Stationery Office.

DoH (Department of Health) and Home Office (2003) *The Victoria Climbié Inquiry: Report of an Inquiry by Lord Laming*. London: The Stationery Office.

Earley, P. and Weindling, D. (2004) *Understanding School Leadership*, London: SAGE.

Fiedler, F.E. and Chemers, M.M. (1974) *Leadership and Effective Management*. California: Scott Foresman.

Fleer, M. (2003) Early childhood education as an evolving 'community of practice' or as lived 'social reproduction': researching the 'taken-for-granted'. *Contemporary Issues in Early Childhood*, 4(1): 64–79.

Foster, W. (1989) Towards a critical practice of leadership. In J. Smyth (ed.), *Critical Perspectives of Educational Leadership*. London: Falmer Press.

Garvey, D. and Lancaster, A. (2011) *Leadership for Quality in Early Years and Playwork*. London: National Children's Bureau.

Goleman, D. (1998) *Working with Emotional Intelligence*. London: Bloomsbury.

Goleman, D., Boyatzis, R. and McKee, A. (2002) *The New Leaders*. London: Little Brown.

Gronn, P. (2002) Distributed leadership as a unit of analysis. *Leadership Quarterly*, 13(4): 423–51.

Harper, D. (2008) Towards a theory of entrepreneurial teams. *Journal of Business Venturing*, 23(6): 613–26.

Harris, A. (2007) Distributed leadership: conceptual confusion and empirical reticence. *International Journal Leadership in Education*, 10(3): 315–25.

Hartley, D. (2007) The emergence of distributed leadership in education: why now? *British Journal of Educational Studies*, 55(2): 202–14.

Hersey, P. and Blanchard, K.H. (1977) *Management of Organization Behavior: Utilizing Human Resources* (3rd edn). Englewood Cliffs, NJ: Prentice-Hall.

Hochschild, A.R. (1983) *The Managed Heart: Commercialisation of Human Feeling*. New Jersey: University of California Press.

Jones, C. and Pound, L. (2008) *Leadership and Management in the Early Years: From Principles to Practice*. Maidenhead: Open University Press.

Laming, Lord (2009) *The Protection of Children in England: A Progress Report*. London: The Stationery Office.

Lawler, J. and Bilson, A. (2010) *Social Work Management and Leadership*. London: Routledge.

Lewin, K., Lippit, R. and White, R.K. (1939) Patterns of aggressive behavior in experimentally created social climates. *Journal of Social Psychology*, 10: 271–301.

Likert, R. (1967) *The Human Organisation: Its Management and Value*. New York: McGraw Hill.

McBride, P. and Maitland, S. (2001) *Putting Emotional Intelligence into Practice*. London: McGraw-Hill.

McClelland, D.C. (1987) *Human Motivation*. Cambridge: Cambridge University Press.

Moss, P. and Petrie, P. (2002) *From Children Services to Children's Spaces, Public Policy and Childhood*. London: RoutledgeFalmer.

Moyles, J. (2006) *Effective Leadership and Management in the Early Years*. Maidenhead: Open University Press.

Murray, J. and McDowall Clark, R. (2013) Reframing leadership as a participative pedagogy: the working theories of early years professionals. *Early Years: An International Research Journal*, 33(3): 289–301.

NCLSCS (National College for Leadership of Schools and Children's Services) (2011) *Resourceful Leadership: How Directors of Children's Services Improve Outcomes for Children*. Nottingham: NCLSCS.

NCSL (National College of School Leadership) (2004) *National Professional Qualification in Integrated Centre Leadership (NPQICL)*. Nottingham: NCSL.

NCSL (National College of School Leadership) (2006) *National Professional Qualification in Integrated Centre Leadership (NPQICL)*. Nothingham: NCSL.

NCTL (National College of Teaching and Leadership (2013) *Teachers' Standards (Early Years)*. London: NCTL. Available at: https://www.gov.uk/government/uploads/system/uploads/attachment_data/file/211646/Early_Years_Teachers__Standards.pdf (accessed 15 April 2015).

Nias, J., Southworth, G. and Yeomans, R. (1989) *Staff Relationships in the Primary School*. London: Cassell Educational.

Northouse, P.G. (2009) *Leadership: Theory and Practice* (5th edn). London: SAGE.

Nutbrown, C. (2012) *Foundations for Quality: The Independent Review of Early Education and Childcare Qualifications. Final Report.* London: DfE. Available at: https://www.gov.uk/government/publications/nutbrown-review-foundations-for-quality (accessed 15 April 2015).

Ofsted (Office for Standards in Education, Children's Services and Skills) (2013) *Social Care Annual Report 2012/13.* Manchester: Ofsted.

Osgood, J. (2006) Deconstructing professionalism in early childhood education: resisting the regulatory gaze. *Contemporary Issues in Early Childhood,* 7(1): 5–14.

Owen, H. (2000) *In Search of Leaders.* Chichester: Wiley & Sons.

Parker-Rees, R. (2007) Primary communication – what can adults learn from babies? In J. Moyles (ed.), *Early Years Foundations: Meeting the Challenge.* Maidenhead: Open University Press/McGraw Hill.

Rodd, J. (1994) *Leadership in Early Childhood.* Buckingham: Open University Press.

Rodd, J. (1998) *Leadership in Early Childhood* (2nd edn). Buckingham: Open University Press.

Rodd, J. (2005) *Leadership in Early Childhood* (3rd edn). Buckingham: Open University Press.

Sauer, S. and Kohls, N. (2011) Mindfulness in leadership: does being mindful enhance leaders business success? In S. Han and E. Poppel (eds), *Culture and Neural Frames of Cognition and Communication,* Vol. 3. Heidelberg: Springer.

Sharp, C., Lord, P., Handscomb, G., Macleod, S., Southcott, C., George, N. and Jeffes, J. (2012) *Highly Effective Leadership in Children's Centres.* Nottingham: National College for School Leadership.

Siraj-Blatchford, I. and Manni, L. (2006) *Effective Leadership in the Early Years Sector.* London: The Institute of Education, University of London.

Southworth, G. (1998) *Leading Improving Primary Schools: The Work of Headteachers and Deputies.* London: Falmer Press.

Sylva, K., Melhuish, E.C., Sammons, P., Siraj-Blatchford, I. and Taggart, B. (2004) *The Effective Provision of Pre-school Education (EPPE) Project: Final Report,* London: DfES/Institute of Education, University of London.

Tannenbaum, R. and Schmidt, W. (1958) How to choose a leadership pattern. *Harvard Business Review,* 36(2): 95–101.

Telford, H. (1996) *Transforming Schools Through Collaborative Leadership.* London: Falmer Press.

Tobin, J. (2005) Quality in early childhood education: an anthropologist's perspective. *Early Education & Development,* 16(4): 421–34.

Torrance, D. (2013) Distributed leadership: challenging five generally held assumptions. *School Leadership & Management,* 33(4): 354–72.

Urban, M. (2008) Dealing with uncertainty: challenges and possibilities for the early childhood profession. *European Early Childhood Education Research Journal,* 16(2): 135–52.

Van Maurik, J. (2001) *Writers on Leadership.* London: Penguin.

Vecchio, R. (2003) Entrepreneurship and leadership: common trends and common threads. *Human Resource Management Review,* 13(2): 303–27.

West-Burnham, J., Farrar, M. and Otero, G. (2007) *Schools and Communities: Working Together to Transform Children's Lives.* London: Network Continuum.

Whalley, M. (2006) Leadership in integrated centres and services for children and families – a community development approach: engaging with the struggle. *Childrenz Issues: Journal of the Children's Issues Centre,* 10(2): 8–13. Available at: http://search.informit.com.au/documentSummary;dn=366901244258381;res=IELFSC (accessed 15 April 2015).

Part 4

Comparing children's worlds: making the familiar strange

13 Concepts of childhood: meeting with difference

Rod Parker-Rees

Introduction

Childhood is a concept which seems simple and straightforward but the more we examine it the more we understand not only about what it means to be a child but also what it means to be an adult and a member of a community. Individuals may tell themselves that they have 'put aside childish things', preferring the civilised order of adult behaviour, but communities do not have this option. Children are a necessary feature of any group which intends to survive beyond one generation and childhood, specifically the relationship between children and adults, is a defining feature of human society. We are made human by opportunities to find out how other people behave and think but also by our interest in introducing newcomers to our ways. Teaching and learning (and assessing other people's behaviour) are central to the cultural lives of human communities and human individuals.

Working with other people's children obliges us to be critically aware of our own attitudes. We are bound to meet parents and colleagues whose perspectives on childhood will be different from ours and we have to recognise how our assumptions affect our judgements and our responses to other people. This chapter will examine the complexities involved in the development of concepts of childhood and will consider how a deeper awareness of the nature of concepts can influence how we feel about meeting with people who do not see things quite as we do. I will argue that we should not be looking for a single, universally applicable, 'best' concept of childhood because children are better served by a continuing, critical discussion fuelled by a diverse range of voices and personal experiences. Indeed, we cannot understand childhood unless we recognise it as part of a dynamic process of interactions which allow both individuals and communities to adapt and adjust to changing environments.

If you are interested in working with young children it is likely that you are more than usually comfortable with meeting people who do not see the world quite as you do. One of the characteristics of children is that they have not yet learned how to 'fit in' with the rules and conventions of their society and this means that they have a tendency to confront us with embarrassing questions and fresh insights which help us to notice assumptions we might otherwise take for granted. For some people, particularly those who like things to be clearly organised and predictable, this is distinctly uncomfortable. The history of the concept of childhood can be mapped out in terms of a centuries-long argument between adults who want to educate children out of childhood as quickly as possible and those who value the special contribution which children can make to a family or community.

David Kennedy (Kennedy and Kohan, 2012) has characterised this argument as evidence of a tension between the child's direct interest in what is *different* and the adult's reliance on being able to count on other people seeing things in the *same* way. A degree of sameness in how people think and behave is a fundamental requirement for survival in closely packed groups. If we could not predict how others could be expected to behave we would have to be in a constant state of hypervigilance, unable to relax and always watching out for any sign of possible risk or threat. The social contract, which allows us to function in large groups with relatively infrequent explosions of violence, relies on shared concepts which have to be learned through participation in the social activity of a group. This need to 'learn the ropes', to gradually work out what is and is not OK in different social contexts, constructs a divide between those who know (adults) and those who don't yet know (children). It also constructs a divide between the unique phenomenology and difference of individual experience and the partially shareable epistemology of uniquely human 'higher mental functions' (Vygotsky, 1997: 106).

When we explore concepts of childhood we have to acknowledge differences in children's and adults' ways of engaging with the ideas which inform their culture. Our interactions with children remind us that the social conventions and habits of thought which frame our day-to-day interactions are inventions rather than given features of a natural order (James and Prout, 1997). Engaging in pedagogy, an inescapable feature of all human societies, regularly confronts us with the challenge of explaining and justifying everyday behaviours and practices which familiarity would otherwise render invisible. Spending time with children reminds us of the individual differences beneath the superficial sameness on which our social interactions depend.

We can also remind ourselves of difference by studying the history of concepts of childhood. History provides valuable opportunities for trying to see how other people at other times, with other concerns, fears, hopes and priorities may have thought and felt about their relationships with children (Brockliss and Montgomery, 2013) and can help us to develop critical attitudes and dispositions which can inform our meetings with other people in the present (Cunningham, 2006). Even now, when we have so much more in common with most of the people we meet, there are still important differences between us. How we function as professionals will depend on how willing we are to engage with these differences, to learn from them, and sometimes to challenge them. It is easy to assume that if someone treats children in ways which make us uncomfortable they must be wrong and our professional duty is to educate and correct them. Our duty to safeguard children will sometimes require us to challenge abusive or neglectful behaviours but in many cases, if we are able to recognise that people may have compelling reasons for their choices and decisions, these can offer us windows into their life, allowing us to get to know them as complicated, different people rather than as interchangeable representatives of a category or type.

'My' childhood and 'my' concept of childhood?

It is widely recognised that young children do not have concepts of childhood in the way that adults do (Alderson, 2013) because concepts have to be distilled out of experience. Whereas children live *in* their childhood, adults are able to think *about* childhood, to stand back from it and to consider it as an idea. To complicate matters further, we tend to imagine that our own concept of childhood is privileged because we have experienced it for ourselves, so we know what we are talking about (Kennedy, 2001). What we forget, when we remember our own childhood, is that remembering is a cognitive process which has to be learned. We do not have to learn how to *have* experiences but we do have to learn which aspects are noteworthy, which are worth keeping and which are too mundane and ordinary to bother with. This is why a three-year-old who is quite capable of talking about any aspect of her activities at nursery may be completely flummoxed when asked, at the end of a session, 'What have you been doing today?' It takes years to learn how to edit experiences down to retrievable memories because we have to learn how we can expect *other* people to feel about things that have happened to us. Life is too short to allow us to recall every detail of any experience. We can't spend a whole day remembering one day, so we have to edit our experiences down to the highlights and our decisions about what deserves to be kept are informed by our growing awareness of how other people will respond – what will be interesting, shocking, amusing or impressive. Our awareness of a shared, public concept of childhood is constructed even as this public concept informs the way we selectively edit the memories which will define our 'own' childhood.

Every year we ask our students to write a short account of 'What childhood means to me' and every year we are struck by the similarities between students' responses. While some students will write about difficult and dark memories, and we are careful to caution them that recalling their own childhood may be disturbing, the great majority of accounts feature the pleasure of freedom to explore outside, unsupervised by interfering adults, or special occasions, holidays, outings and time together with family. We then challenge our students to consider why they have these memories. Would they have any reason to remember them if they were ordinary events which happened every day?

We select and remember significant moments and moments which others remind us about and we forget the everyday experiences which barely required our attention. As a result our adult memories of our own childhood are inevitably more interest-filled (whether with happy or traumatic moments), rich and intense than our present-day experience of our own lives and the lives of today's children. Because we are usually comparing our 'edited highlights' experience of our remembered childhood with our 'live-streaming' experience of children's day-to-day lives it is not surprising that we should experience the feeling that something has been lost. Whereas we spent our time playing freely outdoors with friends, in the sunshine and on holiday, today's children sit indoors on their own, huddled over their computers, their phones or their homework, waiting for the rain to stop.

Although children do not think *about* their childhood in the same way that adults do, their childhoods are still shaped by adults' concepts of childhood. Particularly in affluent, minority world societies, every detail of a child's environment is considered, planned and managed, from her clothes, furniture and toys to the way people hold, feed, comfort and play with her. Even her attention to events in her environment is tutored by her shared interest in what other people find interesting. Before she is one year old she will be aware of what others find alarming, interesting, funny or disgusting and she will learn to use this growing social knowledge to inform her interactions (see Chapter 3). Although adult members of particular social groups are likely to share many aspects of their concepts of childhood, they will not agree on every detail and frequent, affectively charged disagreements, between mothers and fathers, between parents and grandparents and between parents and siblings, for example, help to ensure that we are often reminded about concepts of childhood.

We tend to claim ownership of our ideas in phrases such as 'my concept of childhood' or 'my views on parenting' but careful reflection will show us that these ideas are socially constructed and shared. Our feelings about how we 'ought' to behave or what we 'should' do are built out of our experiences of other people's behaviours, beliefs and arguments. We gradually become aware of what different kinds of people do, approve and expect and we internalise these intricate webs of mutual expectations and obligations in the form of our 'own' feelings about what we 'should' do. These social rules vary across different contexts and learning their subtle variations takes many years, establishing a widening distinction between adults, who know how they are expected to behave, and children, who are still learning.

Communities develop their own strategies for managing the inevitable disagreements about how adults should treat children and we may need to step back from our focus on individuals to recognise how roles and responsibilities can be distributed within and across social groups or figurations (Gabriel, 2010). In families, for example, traditional distinctions between gender roles have contributed to the construction of different role expectations for mothers and fathers (Hrdy, 2011; Gray and Anderson, 2012). Each family's ways of arriving at decisions about what children need, what they deserve and what can be expected from them will involve different dynamics of argument, coercion, subterfuge and appeals to members of a wider family or social group. Even within the same family, there are likely to be differences between what sons and daughters learn about the roles expected of fathers and mothers. In larger social groupings we can expect to find a different kind of dynamic in the arguments between members of social factions differentiated by variations including levels of economic, social or cultural capital. So when adults come together to form new families it is likely that they will bring with them different assumptions and expectations about childhood which may not become apparent until they have children of their own to argue about.

To say that our concepts of childhood are socially constructed is not to suggest that we are swept along by an irresistible force of social determinism. We are exposed to the richness and complexity of different attitudes and behaviours in our dealings with mothers, fathers, older brothers and sisters, grandparents, families of friends and media families in soap operas, sit-coms, films and 'reality' programmes. As we become more aware of the social appraisals associated with different patterns of relationships we are able, to varying degrees, to make choices about how we want to be seen by others. The names, clothes and hairstyles we choose for our children, whether and for how long we breast-feed, whether we carry them or put them in a buggy, the way we talk to them and the way we discipline them are all signifiers which we can use to tell other people who we think we are and how we want our children to be seen. We have space to shape our 'own' concepts of childhood within the wider context of alternatives which we choose not to adopt but our choices about how we should treat our children are always informed by our sociocultural knowledge about how *other* people will judge the choices we make.

Childhood v. Adulthood – an evolving dynamic

Acknowledging the subtleties of interactions between the *different* self-identities of individuals and the communities of *sameness* in which these identities are framed should make us cautious about attributing the *same* concept of childhood to whole social groups over extended periods of time. While the structures of authority in different families and communities will allow and forbid different kinds of challenges and disagreements, we have no reason to believe that any society has ever settled on a fully agreed and universally accepted approach to raising children. It can still be useful, however, to step outside the familiar disagreements of our own age to try to understand why people living in circumstances *more* different from our own may have developed *more* different ways of thinking about the relationship between childhood and adulthood.

Concepts of childhood are always shaped and defined in relationship with concepts of adulthood and as our understanding of adulthood changes we can expect this to influence our understanding of childhood. What we think of as changes in concepts of childhood may therefore sometimes be better understood as changes in concepts of adulthood or as changes in the relationship *between* childhood and adulthood. As our ability to travel and our access to information have grown, so has the threshold for attaining an 'adult' level of competence in an expanding range of social contexts. This has required changes both in the extent of childhood (there is just so much more to be learned) and in adults' attitudes to childhood and children (Heywood, 2001).

Throughout most of our recorded history we have assumed that learning to control our natural impulses, to subordinate our individual interests for the greater good of a tribe or family group, is a positive achievement. We have compared ourselves with other animals and prided ourselves on our ability to transcend our brutish nature. From this point of view, an adult is someone who has learned how to behave in different circumstances, understanding what will offend others, what will be admired and what will be punished. In the days of the great Persian, Egyptian, Greek and Roman empires, when large numbers of people were living in tightly packed cities, being civilised was an essential part of maintaining the social order. It is no accident that the words we still use to describe behaviour which acknowledges the interests of other people are drawn from words for large social groups; from *civis* we have civil and civilised, from *polis* we have polite, from *urbs* we have urbane and from *court* we have courteous. Of course in the days of empire only a few men, and very few women, would be in a position to manage their own behaviour. For most people, social order would be imposed on them by *others* and they would never experience the personal autonomy which we nowadays associate with adulthood. For example, in a Roman household, the *Pater Familias* had absolute authority over the behaviour of other men, women, slaves and children in the household, together with the responsibility to protect both the well-being and the reputation of the family.

Philippe Ariès (1962: 125) famously argued that 'in medieval society, the concept of childhood (*le sentiment de l'enfance*) did not exist'. Much has been made of the narrowness of the evidence on which this claim was based and other historians (Pollock, 1983; Hanawalt, 1986; Shahar, 1990; Hendrick, 1992; Crawford, 1999; Orme, 2001) have since shown that young children, certainly those under the age of about seven years, were clearly *not* treated like 'mini-adults' in the Middle Ages. Indeed the word 'adult' was 'not really naturalized' in English before the middle of the 17th century (OED, 1971: 129).

Norbert Elias (2000) focuses on the 'civilizing process' which resulted in the progressive internalisation of the mechanisms of social control, a process which might be described as the invention of adulthood (Kennedy, 2006). A growing belief in learning, reason and personal responsibility, rather than blind faith, can be traced back to the Renaissance but in England in the 17th century this focus on self-control was fuelled both by the puritan rejection of passive subservience to the authority of priests and by a radical political movement which rejected the authority of an overbearing and greedy nobility, resulting in civil war.

We tend to associate puritanism with the doctrine of 'original sin', the belief that children were born with the guilt of Adam and Eve which must be purged by thorough moral and religious instruction. Where Roman parents might have seen childish tantrums, wilfulness and stubbornness as evidence of children's uncivilised, 'natural' condition, puritans were more likely to construe this as evidence of children's inability to resist the temptations of evil. We should, however, remember that, just like today's news media and, indeed, our own memories, history has a tendency to focus attention on what is exceptional. The attitudes of 'mainstream' puritans, who would have condemned violent disciplining of children as a failure of adult self-control (Morgan, 1986 in Cox, 1996), are less likely to catch our attention than the 'fire and brimstone' sermons preached by more 'extremist' ministers. Careful examination of historical evidence shows that use of corporal punishment in the 17th century was broadly similar to practice in the 20th century (Pollock, 1983; Todd, 1987; Sommerville, 1992). Cox (1996) argued that the puritan emphasis on family life was driven by worries about the corruption of the 'civilised' world and a concern to protect children which is not so different from 21st-century withdrawal to the safety of the family home. Changes in how people lived with children led in turn to the development of a more personal, domestic approach to study and self-improvement.

John Locke (1690) argued that children's minds are shaped by the experiences imprinted on them and in his letters advising a friend on the private education of his son (Locke, 1693) he focused on the responsibility of fathers to guide their sons into a virtuous and reasonable adulthood by carefully managing the kinds of experiences to which they would be exposed. He advised fathers to watch their sons as they played, looking out for signs of 'Byass in their Natural Temper' (1693: para 139) which could be gently corrected by exposure to positive models. The challenge of education, as he saw it, was to preserve the 'Child's Spirit easy, active and free' (para 46) while introducing the habits of self-control and respect for others which are the hallmarks of virtuous adulthood:

> *All their innocent Folly, Playing, and Childish Actions, are to be left perfectly free and unrestrained, as far as they can consist with the Respect due to those that are present; and that with the greatest Allowance.' (para. 63, my emphasis)*

In the mid 18th century, Jean-Jacques Rousseau was deliberately controversial when he drew on popular accounts of the lives of native Americans to argue that the natural state of the 'noble savage' had been debased and corrupted by social affectations, leading to the absurd powdered wigs and elaborate costumes of the 18th-century gentleman and the dehumanising squalor of overcrowded cities. In 'Émile, or On Education', he issued a direct challenge to Locke's celebration of Reason:

> *To reason with children was Locke's great maxim. It is the one most in vogue today. Its success, however, does not appear to me such as to establish its reputation: and, as for me, I see nothing more stupid than these children who have been reasoned with so much. (Rousseau, 1762/1979: 89)*

Rousseau's romantic celebration of the natural condition of childhood saw education not as an introduction to the rules and manners of civilised society but as arrogant interference with nature's plan:

> *Everything is good as it leaves the hands of the Author of things; everything degenerates in the hands of man. He forces one soil to nourish the products of another, one tree to bear the fruit of another. He mixes and confuses the climates, the elements, the seasons. He mutilates his dog, his horse, his slave. He turns everything upside down; he disfigures everything: he loves deformity, monsters. He wants nothing as nature made it, not even man; for him, man must be trained like a school horse; man must be fashioned in keeping with his fancy like a tree in his garden. (Rousseau, 1762/1979: 37)*

Kennedy (2006) and Davis (2011) have shown that Rousseau's supposed invention of the romantic concept of childhood is actually grounded in a long tradition. In the 12th and 13th centuries St Francis and Bishop Anselm had argued that children are born in a state of pre-lapsarian innocence, like Adam and Eve before they were expelled from Eden, and the 17th-century poetry of Traherne, Vaughan and others celebrated the freshness and purity of children's immediate engagement with experience. Fogel (2001: 729) goes back even further, suggesting that pre-agricultural hunter-gatherer communities 'exemplify a primarily romantic culture'.

It is also important to remember that history tends to record the ideas of those who hold power and we should not assume that everyone shared the ideas advanced by those who had the time to write. Rousseau reminds us, for example, that mothers and fathers do not always share the same concepts of childhood:

> *Mothers, it is said, spoil their children. In that they are doubtless wrong –but less wrong than you perhaps who deprave them. The mother wants her child to be happy, happy now. In that she is right ... Fathers' ambition, avarice, tyranny and false foresight, their negligence, their harsh insensitivity are a hundred times more disastrous for children than is the blind tenderness of mothers. (Rousseau, 1762/1979: 38n)*

While throughout most of our history, writers and thinkers have focused on how children can be helped to acquire the knowledge and social understanding which will allow them to take their place among adults, they have also acknowledged what they would dismiss as 'blind tenderness' in the 'fondness' and 'coddling' demonstrated by the adults who spent more time with children.

Childhood *and* Adulthood: without contraries is no progression

Rousseau's *Émile* was particularly influential in England where it helped to inspire a radical Romantic movement at a time when revolutions in France and in America were challenging traditional assumptions about power and authority. At the heart of this Romanticism was the idea that difference and individuality were qualities to be nurtured and celebrated rather than flaws to be smoothed over by the uniform sameness of polite, obedient behaviour.

In his 'Songs of Innocence and Experience' William Blake (1794/1988) integrated words and images on his illuminated plates, weaving foliage through the text of his poems which contrast the phenomenological innocence of childhood and nature with the concept-bound experience of adulthood and the city. In 'London' he alludes to the strictures of the 'rational' social order:

> *In every Infant's cry of fear ...*
>
> *The mind-forg'd manacles I hear (1794/1988: 27)*

In 'The Garden of Love', a chapel has been built, 'Where I used to play on the green'. 'Thou shalt not' is written over the door,

> *And Priests in black gowns were walking their rounds,*
>
> *And binding with briars my joys & desires (1794/1988: 26)*

Unlike Rousseau, however, Blake did not represent innocence as a *higher* condition than experience. His assertion that 'without contraries is no progression' (1790/1988: 34) recognises the energy which comes from the dynamic tension *between* Heaven and Hell,

Innocence and Experience, or childhood and adulthood. Blake argued that progression depended on interaction *between* contraries, illustrated in the community of 'old folk' and 'little ones' who enjoy each other's company in 'The Echoing Green' (1794/1988: 8).

Romantic poets at the turn of the 19th century interpreted Blake's celebration of the energy of a diverse community into a more internalised, personal balance between the lyrical, ineffable energy of direct, unmediated sensation and the clarity of rational thought, reimagining childhood as a continuing feature of a balanced individual identity. Wordsworth explored memories of his childhood in an effort to find ways of communicating a 'sense sublime' (Wordsworth, 1999), which could capture in words the sublime feelings inspired by nature. Coleridge (1840: 497) defined 'Genius' as 'the carrying on of the freshness and feelings of childhood into the powers of man-hood' and Jane Austen wrote, in 'Sense and Sensibility' about two sisters, Elinor and Marianne, learning to balance the impulsive energy of 'sensibility' with the rational self-control of 'sense'.

In the mid 19th century this romantic effort to integrate some of the qualities of child-hood into adult life was diluted into a more sentimental 'cult of the child' (Coveney, 1967; Davis, 2011) as many adults looked back to their edited memories of a simpler time, freed from the burdensome responsibilities of adulthood. It was also challenged directly by evangelical moralists like Hannah More who objected to a 'spirit of inde-pendence and disdain of control, which characterise the times' (More, 1830: 109) and who sought to force children into a starchy uniform of 'good habits'. It was this desire to bring children under control, as much as the philanthropic concern to protect them from exploitation in factories or to protect their innocence from the depravity and squalor of life on city streets, which led to the introduction of compulsory education. By the early 20th century, Freud had developed the romantic internalisation of child-hood in his model of the childish *id*, the adult *ego*, and the parental/social *super-ego* but children had already effectively been removed from most areas of adult life.

Segregation of communities, whether on the basis of gender, ethnicity, age, (dis)ability or social class, reduces opportunities for encounters with difference. Adults who have become familiar with the reassuring sameness of the company of other adults may increasingly come to feel uncomfortable when they are faced with the different-ness of children. Children may then pose a double threat to adult equanimity, both because they don't yet know how they are supposed to behave around other people, especially unfamiliar people, and because they may provoke uncivilised behaviour (e.g. sexual and violent responses) in adults who are not used to their company.

A romantic vision of an alternative world, where adults and children can safely play together, is offered in recent accounts of the social structures of hunter-gatherer com-munities. Like Fogel (2001), Gray (2009) and Konner (2010) draw on ethnographic data from a wide variety of (just) surviving and recently studied hunter-gatherer socie-ties to highlight the sometimes surprising extent to which adults and children appear to enjoy and benefit from living alongside each other in small communities. Rousseau had compared the individual noble savage of the Americas with the sophisticated gen-tleman of 18th-century France but Gray and Konner focus on the social groups or bands which are a feature of hunter-gatherer life. They suggest that children benefit from opportunities to learn, at first hand and with no need for schools, about all the things that adults do but also that adults enjoy a relaxed, playful environment in which adults as well as children are largely free to choose how they will spend their time. In these communities the behaviour of adults can be directly influenced by the interests of children. When Mbuti children have had enough of the bad atmosphere caused by adults' arguments, they will perform the *molimo madé* ceremony, which involves them collaborating to imitate an angry elephant stamping through the camp, 'a playful means by which the young people, without blaming any individual adult, can influence the adults' behavior' (Gray, 2009: 512). It takes children to raise a village.

Conclusion: meeting with difference

We cannot simply turn back the clock to return to our hunter-gatherer roots any more than we can return to the imagined golden age of our own childhood. We can, however, learn something from stepping outside the social frameworks which have shaped our adulthood. Encounters with other ways of thinking can help us to develop a critical plurality which makes us more willing and able to see past the sameness of concepts and to meet with difference.

It is our shared concepts, learned from our participation in social interactions with other people, which allow us to communicate with people who do not share every detail of our own experience. But in order to meet with other people we must be prepared to look below the smooth surface which concepts offer and to notice differences in the ways in which sameness is performed. Instead of assuming that everyone does or should mean just what we mean, we can take the trouble to step outside our assumptions to *meet* and learn from the differences which other people have to offer.

David Kennedy (2006) argues that we can no longer understand the civilised adult as a discrete individual or *homo clausus* (Elias, 2000), instead we should acknowledge that we are *intersubjects*, who cannot be known, and indeed cannot exist, in isolation from the social figurations which shape us and are shaped by us. Kennedy argues that our existence and development as intersubjects depends on dialogue with others and that this dialogue can only take place when we are able to hold open space for difference. If the otherness of childhood is denied, repressed or absorbed by our adult self we cannot meet it in dialogue and benefit from the role that children can play as 'valuable strangers' (Harding in Kennedy, 2006: 142), helping us to trouble the surface of sameness.

ACTIVITY 1

Think back to your own childhood and try to recall some of the childcare issues which were contested in your family. This may take you back to arguments between your parents, between your parents and grandparents or wider family about how you should eat, dress, behave, talk, etc. or between you and your siblings over differences in how you

(Continued)

ACTIVITY **1** *continued*

were treated. You might also ask other members of your family about disagreements they can remember. (What childhood issues do your parents remember their parents arguing about?) What can you learn from these memories about different concepts of childhood within your own family?

ACTIVITY **2**

With a small group of friends, consider the opportunities open to different sections of society for spending time with a variety of people of different ages, backgrounds, beliefs and values. What factors, including personal preferences, resources and time, might influence these opportunities? Can you think of any ways of helping or encouraging people to get to know a wider variety of different people?

FURTHER READING

Cunningham, H. (2006) *The Invention of Childhood*. London: BBC Books.

This is an excellent introduction to the history of childhood from the Middle Ages to the 20th century. A CD or audio download of the BBC Radio 4 series based on the book is also available so you can listen while doing something else!

Gray, P. (2009) Play as a Foundation for Hunter-Gatherer Social Existence. *American Journal of Play*, 1(4): 476–522.

This article presents fascinating accounts of the ways in which adults and children live together and learn from each other in hunter-gatherer societies.

Kennedy, D. (2006) *The Well of Being: Childhood, Subjectivity, and Education*. New York: State University of New York Press.

Kennedy presents an extraordinarily rich picture of the place of childhood in our culture, history, psychology and sociology. This is not a light read but it is well worth the effort!

REFERENCES

Alderson, P. (2013) *Childhoods Real and Imagined: Volume 1: An Introduction to Critical Realism and Childhood Studies (Ontological Explorations)*. London: Routledge.

Ariès, P. (1962) *Centuries of Childhood* (trans. Robert Baldick). London: Jonathan Cape.

Blake, W. (1790/1988) The Marriage of Heaven and Hell. In D.V. Erdman (ed.) *The Complete Poetry and Prose of William Blake*. New York: Bantam Doubleday Dell Publishing Group. pp.34–43.

Blake, W. (1794/1988) Songs of Innocence and Experience. In D.V. Erdman (ed.) *The Complete Poetry and Prose of William Blake*. New York: Bantam Doubleday Dell Publishing Group. pp.7–32.

Brockliss, L. and Montgomery, H. (2013) Childhood: a historical approach. In M.J. Kehily (ed.), *Understanding Childhood: A Cross-disciplinary Approach*. Bristol: Policy Press.

Coleridge, S.T. (1840) *The Works of Samuel Taylor Coleridge, Prose and Verse: Complete in One Volume*. Philadelphia: Thomas, Cowperthwaite & Co.

Coveney, P. (1967) *The Image of Childhood: The Individual and Society: A Study of the Theme in English Literature*. Harmondsworth: Penguin.

Cox, R. (1996) *Shaping Childhood: Themes of Uncertainty in the History of Adult–Child Relationships*. London: Routledge.

Crawford, S. (1999) *Childhood in Anglo-Saxon England*. Stroud: Sutton Publishing.

Cunningham, H. (2006) *The Invention of Childhood*. London: BBC Books.

Davis, R.A. (2011) Brilliance of a fire: innocence, experience and the theory of childhood. *Journal of Philosophy of Education*, 45(2): 379–97.

Elias, N. (2000) *The Civilizing Process* (2nd edn). Oxford: Blackwell.

Fogel, A. (2001) The history (and future) of infancy. In G. Bremner and A. Fogel (Eds.) *The Blackwell Handbook of Infant Development*. Oxford: Blackwell.

Gabriel, N. (2010) Adults' concepts of childhood. In R. Parker-Rees and C. Leeson (eds), *Early Childhood Studies: An Introduction to the Study of Children's Worlds and Children's Lives* (3rd edn). Exeter: Learning Matters.

Gray, P. (2009) Play as a foundation for hunter-gatherer social existence. *American Journal of Play*, 1(4): 476–522.

Gray, P.B. and Anderson, K.G. (2012) *Fatherhood: Evolution and Human Paternal Behavior*. Cambridge, MA: Harvard University Press.

Hanawalt, B. (1986) *Growing Up in Medieval London*. Oxford: Oxford University Press.

Hendrick, H. (1992) Children and childhood. *ReFresh (Recent Findings of Research in Economic and Social History)*, 15 (Autumn): 1–4. Available at: http://www.ehs.org.uk/the-society/assets/Hendrick15a.pdf (accessed 21 February 2015).

Heywood, C. (2001) *A History of Childhood: Children and Childhood in the West from Medieval to Modern Times (Themes in History)*. Oxford: Polity Press.

Hrdy, S.B. (2011) *Mothers and Others: The Evolutionary Origins of Mutual Understanding*. Cambridge, MA: Harvard University Press.

James, A. and Prout, A. (eds) (1997) *Constructing and Reconstructing Childhood: Contemporary Issues in the Sociological Study of Childhood* (2nd edn). London: Routledge.

Kennedy, D. (2001) Parent, child, alterity, dialogue. *Philosophy Today*, 45(1): 33–42.

Kennedy, D. (2006) *The Well of Being: Childhood, Subjectivity, and Education*. New York: State University of New York Press.

Kennedy, D. and Kohan, W.O. (2012) Aión, Kairós and Chrónos: fragments of an endless conversation on childhood, philosophy and education. *Childhood & Philosophy*, 4(8): 5–22.

Konner, M. (2010) *The Evolution of Childhood: Relationships, Emotion, Mind*. Cambridge MA: Harvard/Belknap.

Locke, J. (1690) Essay Concerning Human Understanding. Available at: http://oll.libertyfund.org/titles/761 (accessed 21 February 2015).

Locke, J. (1693) Some Thoughts Concerning Education. Available at: http://www.bartleby.com/37/1/ (accessed on 7 October 2014).

More, H. (1830) *The Works of Hannah More. Volume V: Strictures on Female Education*. London: T. Cadell.

OED (1971) *Oxford English Dictionary* (compact edition). Oxford: Oxford University Press.

Orme, N. (2001) *Medieval Children.* New Haven: Yale University Press.

Pollock, L.A. (1983) *Forgotten Children: Parent–Child Relations from 1500 to 1900.* Cambridge: Cambridge University Press.

Rousseau, J.J. (1762/1979) *Emile, or On Education* (trans. Allan Bloom). New York: Basic Books.

Shahar, S. (1990) *Childhood in the Middle Ages.* London: Routledge.

Sommerville, C.J. (1992) *The Discovery of Childhood in Puritan England.* Athens, GA: University of Georgia Press.

Todd, M. (1987) *Christian Humanism and the Puritan Social Order.* Cambridge: Cambridge University Press.

Vygotsky, L.S. (1997) *The Collected Works of L.S. Vygotsky. Volume 4: The History of the Development of Higher Mental Functions.* New York: Plenum Press.

Wordsworth, W. (1999) *The Complete Poetical Works.* Bartleby.com. Available at: http://www.bartleby.com/145/ (accessed 20 February 2015).

14 The benefits of comparison: recent developments in the German early years workforce

Ulrike Hohmann

Introduction

Who we think children are, who we feel should be responsible for the care and education of the youngest members of a society and what skills we think are necessary to do this well are all questions which touch on wider social issues. Current shifts in thinking indicate changing relationships between children and adults and offer a rationale for new policy developments. This chapter explores the debate around the training and education of the early years workforce in Germany. It examines the drivers of demands to lift training and education of *Staatlich Anerkannte Erzieherinnen* (literally, 'state-approved (child) raisers' and the largest occupational group within this field) into higher education and identifies some barriers. This qualification and professional title is often shortened to *Erzieherin* (singular) or *Erzieherinnen* (plural). The discussions emerging in this process highlight the effects of demographic shifts observed in the developed world, show tentative signs of divergence in the experience of childhood across Europe and, in the tradition of comparative research, inform comparisons and contrasts with the development of Early Years Professional Status (EYPS) in England, displaced in 2015 by Teachers' Standards (Early Years). A cross-national, comparative perspective has a number of benefits. The 'difference view' and the 'import-mirror view' (May, 2001) refer to ways of analysing how other countries solve a particular problem, for example, how to meet changing demands for early years services. Exploring differences by taking 'insider' and 'outsider' positions aids the formulation of new questions and can pinpoint more precisely which conditions support or hinder particular developments. We can begin to ask questions about what would happen if we were to import a certain set of policies and practices into our national or local context. Related to this perspective, cross-national comparison acts as a mirror or lens which can sharpen our focus on our own positions and practices while inviting us to challenge background assumptions which are specific to our national context and which might otherwise be taken for granted.

The chapter is informed by a pilot study in one of 16 *Länder* (singular, *Land*) of the Federal Republic of Germany undertaken during autumn 2006, which accessed opinions of a number of stakeholders, qualified *Erzieherinnen* and students enrolled in one of the first German BA courses in pedagogy of early childhood in Freiburg and by recent developments in early childhood settings. I will begin by explaining and exploring some of the concepts used when reflecting on the relationship between parents, children and the early childhood workforce. Recent developments in early years pedagogy would not have been deemed necessary without the perception that childhood itself has changed, mainly due to socioeconomic and demographic developments which will be addressed briefly. This will be followed by a broad overview of the German care and education system for children before they reach compulsory school age, and then of the training and education of practitioners. The rest of the chapter will explore the debate about education and training issues in Germany and will extract three perspectives that contribute to a better understanding of early childhood services.

Erziehung, Betreuung and *Bildung* – raising children, care and education

On a formal level, relationships and responsibilities are defined and reflected by the legal framework, which sets out rights and duties connected to kinship and family formation and Acts which regulate childcare and education. The discourse of childhood in a society is powerfully expressed through language. For example, relationships are defined by making decisions about whether to talk about 'children' or 'kids' (defined in my dictionary as 'baby goats'); parents, mothers and fathers, or mums and dads; or addressing staff in early childhood settings as 'Auntie Jane' or 'Mrs Smith'.

In Germany understanding of childhood and the responsibilities of adults is reflected through the use and the definition of the words *Erziehung, Betreuung* and *Bildung*. In contrast to the new *Länder* (in what used to be the socialist German Democratic Republic, GDR, the old *Länder* (in what was West Germany) relied successfully on a particular definition of the traditional family with gender-specific tasks. Since this was generally accepted until recently, the structure and availability of childcare and education services appeared sufficient and congruent with people's expectations. The family is seen to be mainly responsible for *Kindererziehung* (literally translated as 'child-raising', sometimes translated as 'upbringing') reflecting primary socialisation tasks and *Betreuung* (best translated as 'care') during the earliest years of childhood. These expectations are discussed publicly and reflected in a number of family support policies. Around a child's third birthday attendance at a kindergarten or day centre has, at least until recently, been seen as beneficial in supporting parents in their task. A new Act (*Kinderförderungsgesetz*) provides the framework for extending early years provision and from 2013 has guaranteed a childcare place for all children aged one to three years whose parents need this. *Bildung* ('education') is the focus of school and to some extent of kindergarten, though relying on different forms of didactics. Recognising education as a distinct responsibility of the kindergarten was more pronounced in the former GDR. More recently the responsibility of early years services to provide educational opportunities has been emphasised and now all *Länder* have drawn up early childhood education and care (ECEC) frameworks, although with varying content and relying on a range of approaches (Jaszus *et al.*, 2008; Oberhuemer *et al.*, 2009).

The three different concepts *Erziehung, Betreuung* and *Bildung* are useful for the discussion of future challenges regarding the socialisation of children and planning of services. The 12th Children and Youth Report (BMFSF, 2005) states that the boundaries between childcare services and school ought to become more permeable. The aim is to move from viewing care, socialisation and education as a hierarchy of priorities towards approaches that integrate all of the three elements within all locations of childhood. For example, family has to be recognised as the basic and essential location of education and education has to have a firm place in early childhood services for the youngest children. School has to embrace an ethos that acknowledges that it provides care and socialisation as well as education.

The threefold definition of children's needs stands in contrast to the debates in English-speaking countries where differences between care and education are sometimes used to differentiate between the responsibilities of parents and the state in bringing up children.

Demographic changes

As in many European countries the fertility rate of women in Germany has declined, leading to more one-child households. Women's employment rates have risen and there is more demand for childcare for working parents in the old *Länder*. In the former GDR female employment rates were high, supported by the availability of free full-time childcare provision. However, 25 years after the unification of the two German states, marked differences remain, making it difficult to speak of one Germany. There are different perspectives on how to balance work and caring commitments and how to divide tasks within households. The economic situations of the old and new *Länder* and continuing differences in structures of early childhood services have led to heterogeneous experiences of children and their families. Although there is a general trend towards more one-child families and children growing up with one parent or in step-families, here too significant differences can be observed between the old and new *Länder*. Additionally over the past three decades the proportion of children with migration backgrounds has grown. Now just over a third of young children in Germany have some kind of migration background (at least one parent born in another country) and in the Western *Länder* 34 per cent of children who do not speak German at home attend daycare facilities where more than half of the children are in the same situation (Autorengruppe Bildungsberichterstattung, 2014). Closely linked to the changing face of childhood in Germany is the increasing proportion of children growing up in poverty. The pilot study shows that *Erzieherinnen* are acutely aware that this state of affairs imposes new demands on their skills and expertise. Growing knowledge about the long-term effects of disadvantages during childhood fuels the call for more and better institutional support for parents or even the demand to compensate for the lack of intrafamilial socialisation. A commitment to intervention during the early years is seen as an important step towards breaking the vicious cycle of lack of education and poverty.

The childcare system

In Germany, provision for children before they reach compulsory school age (at six years) is traditionally divided into two main sectors. Since 2013 children have had a legal entitlement to a place from their first birthday until they attend school. This entitlement covers only a part-time place and parents have to pay fees. Children up to the age of three years are cared for in what is called *Krippe* (literately translated as 'crèche') or they are looked after by a family daycare provider (childminder). Overall, 29 per cent of children under three years had a place in daycare in March 2013 (Statistische Ämter des Bundes und der Länder, 2013). Provision in the old *Länder* is still not meeting the Barcelona 2002 targets of 33 per cent (European Commission, 2014), with places catering for only 24 per cent of children, but continues to be good in the new *Länder*, with places for 50 per cent of this age group. The provision and take-up of places for 3–6-year-old children is high, with 94 per cent in the old *Länder* and 96 per cent in the new *Länder* in 2013. However, only 40 per cent of these places were full-time in the old *Länder* whereas three quarters of kindergarten places in the new *Länder* were offered on a full-time basis (Autorengruppe Bildungsberichterstattung, 2014). Places in *Krippe* and *Kindergarten* are subsidised but parents have to contribute, on average, 23.6 per cent of the cost. There are considerable differences between *Länder* and within *Länder* (OECD, 2006b). Only a relatively small proportion of children of compulsory school age have access to after school care (*Hort*); however, again there is better provision in the new *Länder*. Over recent years a softening of the rigid boundaries between these three sectors (*Krippe*, *Kindergarten* and *Hort*) has taken place, especially where these are housed in the same building under the same management (OECD, 2006a) and where some children are cared for in mixed age groups.

The workforce in day centres and kindergartens is overwhelmingly (96 per cent) female (Autorengruppe Bildungsberichterstattung, 2014), as in other European Countries (EGGE, 2009). The small proportion of men are most likely to be found in settings working with school-aged children or children with disabilities (Leu, 2005; Riedel, 2005; Autorengruppe Bildungsberichterstattung, 2008). There is growing awareness that a better gender balance in early years services could have benefits for the care and education of girls and boys and most staff would prefer to work with both men and women in the nursery (Rohrmann, 2009).

In general it is still the case that the younger the children, the lower the level of qualification held by staff working with them. About two-thirds (64 per cent) of the ECEC workforce (including administrators) hold the qualification *Staatlich Anerkannte Erzieherin*. Providing a translation of this qualification and status in a meaningful way is beset with difficulties. However, attempts to do so may help to explain some of the ethos of this profession and the early years sector. Literally translated, they are 'state-approved (child) raisers'. The noun *Erzieher* derives from the German word *Erziehung* (see above) and describes the tasks of taking care of children and of supporting the socialisation process which ends with the onset of adulthood. If the word 'pedagogue' did not have a negative ring in English, it would be appropriate to call them state-approved pedagogues. It would seem less appropriate to call them kindergarten or early years teachers, since the teaching profession is strongly protected by professional closure in Germany and driven by a quite different ethos. *Erzieherinnen* are also qualified to work with older children and adolescents.

After achieving lower secondary school qualification (corresponding to GCSEs) *Erzieherinnen* undergo three years' vocational training at a *Fachschule (FS) für Sozialpädagogik* (College for Social Pedagogy) including one year of work-based learning which is sometimes followed by a one-year internship. *Erzieherinnen* are qualified to work with children and young people of all ages in all kinds of settings. However, the training focuses on children between three and six years of age. The second largest group working in day centres are *Kinderpflegerinnen* (the name can be translated as 'child carers' – but also implies a suggestion of nursing). The professional title *Kinderpflegerinnen* is awarded after two years' vocational training and a one-year internship. Leaders of day centres are most likely to be social pedagogues who studied at a *Fachhochschule (FHS) für Sozialpädagogik* (university of applied science for social pedagogy). Social pedagogues are qualified to work with children and adults in all kinds of settings and can offer support in a wide range of adverse situations. Due to the federal structure of Germany and the education system, the content and more specific structures of the three training and education pathways vary from *Land* to *Land*.

The qualification framework of the early years workforce is considerably less fragmented than in Britain. One of the effects is that *Erzieherinnen* and social pedagogues have a professional habitus in common that is firmly grounded in the principles of social pedagogy. Both can be described as all-round professions because they work with people of all ages and personal situations (Prott, 2006). They base their work on a holistic understanding of children and adults, being aware of the complex interdependence of 'head, hand and heart' and the influence of historical and sociocultural context. *Erzieherinnen* draw much of their conception of their professional status from the approach developed by Friedrich Fröbel (1782–1852), viewing kindergarten as a pedagogical institution and utilising games and play to educate children (May, 2013; Hohmann, 2015). It is through play, art and everyday activities within communities that *Erzieherinnen* and social pedagogues build relationships and they are skilled in using group processes to support development and well-being (Cameron and Boddy, 2006; Eichsteller and Holthoff, 2011).

Demands on training and education

The context of demographic and socioeconomic changes and the debate about characteristics and skills to be held by the childcare workforce raised concerns about the levels of qualification. The *Erzieherin* of today has little in common with the *Kindergärtnerin* who educated and cared for children 50 years ago. Additionally, due to reforms of child and youth policies a much broader range of tasks and responsibilities has emerged for *Erzieherinnen* (BMFSF, 2013). The demands for more and better knowledge of child development are voiced frequently and the training and education of *Erzieherinnen* has been the focus of attention. The changing work context demands that the qualification *Staatlich Anerkannte Erzieher/Erzieherin* enables these women and men to engage successfully in continuous professional development, allowing them to base their daily work on the findings and insights of research. It was felt that modelling training too closely on school risked losing important elements of being able to apply theory to praxis and using theory to reflect on practice. Additionally, this form of teaching and learning did not promote self-study and self-development sufficiently. Although the deficit in the qualifications and training of *Kinderpflegerinnen* and *Erzieherinnen* has been repeatedly stated over the past 40 years (for example, Rauschenbach *et al.*, 1995) and the trade union GEW has demanded education at graduate level since 1993 (GEW, 2005), this had not led to any significant reforms and improvements in college courses or to a policy decision to entrust higher education institutions with the training and education of the early years workforce before 2004 when the Robert Bosch Foundation financed the pilot programme of higher education courses (Robert Bosch Stiftung, 2006; Thole and Cloos, 2006).

In contrast to Germany, the UK has a multitude of qualifications on a number of different levels. As in Germany, the demands for training of the early years workforce at graduate level emerged in the early 1990s and degrees in Early Childhood Studies have been offered in a number of universities in the UK since then (Abbott and Pugh, 1998). These degrees now form part of the highly complex National Framework of childcare qualifications. The British government contemplated whether improving the quality of the early years workforce should be achieved by increasing provision of early years qualified teachers or by developing a new profession along the lines of the continental 'pedagogue' model (HM Treasury, 2004). The Labour government introduced the Early Years Professional Status (EYPS) from September 2006. The coalition government replaced it with the Early Years Teacher Standards from September 2014.

Moving on: the Italian double momentum

In Germany, the impetus to reform the qualification path of *Erzieherinnen* stems from two separate developments not directly connected to the early years sector. Firstly, one strand of the German discussion was prompted by the unexpectedly negative results of the PISA (Programme for International Student Assessment) study. The ensuing soul searching emphasised the potential of very early childhood and raised concerns about the lost early years in the German system. The second factor was the Bologna process, which aims to standardise training and education across Europe and to make it more accessible by modularising and organising higher education as a coherent system of Bachelors and Masters programmes.

Some stakeholders in Germany are concerned that moving training into higher education institutions could exclude a group of young people, particularly women, from this education because they cannot meet the entry requirements. Instead of changing the location of qualifications, closer cooperation between the different institutions (*FS*, *FHS* and universities) and, for example, offering some shared core qualification for both *Erzieherinnen* and primary school teachers could be a more palatable compromise (Oberhuemer *et al.*, 2009). The dean of one of the *FS* for social pedagogy explained that this should not be regarded as a stance against change and different structures of teaching and learning; instead he is convinced that close cooperation with institutions training primary school teachers is a more realistic way forward. Since 2007/08 the teacher training college he had in mind has offered a BA course in early childhood and elementary education. The argument for integrating the training and education of *Erzieherinnen* and primary school teachers gains additional weight from questions about whether existing teaching staff at *FS* are able to teach at higher education level, and from the perception that staff at *FHS* are not involved in social sciences and education research and therefore cannot offer the whole university experience.

One of the major barriers to changing the level of qualification demanded of members of the early years workforce is the anticipation of increasing costs if core practitioners become graduates. It has been argued, firstly, that not all *Erzieherinnen* need initially to be educated to graduate level (Thole and Cloos, 2006); secondly that the costs of training are not higher than in *Fachschulen* and, thirdly, that the resources freed by a lower take-up of kindergarten places due to the declining fertility rate in Germany can be spent on increasing staff wages (Pasternack and Schildberg, 2005). This may calm the concerns of politicians, providers and parents but how, and how much, public money is spent on the care and education of children is still a political decision. Decisions like this should be driven by a belief in the content of a new qualification route and the possible effects on the quality of early childhood services and the outcomes for children (Rauschenbach, 2006). In England, similar concerns about the financial impact and rising costs of childcare due to the employment of graduate staff led to the implementation of the Transformation Fund (HM Treasury, 2004) later replaced by the Graduate Leader Fund (Mathers *et al.*, 2011).

Another aspect of the discussions (about whether the positioning of training and education within the higher education sector is a move in the right direction) is the question of what skills and characteristics are essential for people working with young children and how they are best acquired. Characteristics like patience, empathy, humour, openness, creativity and the ability to reflect, but also emotional stability and assertiveness, were listed as essential for their work by *Erzieherinnen* in the small-scale study. Many of these characteristics are sometimes described as 'female' and linked to caring attitudes and practices (Noddings, 1993; Tronto, 1993; Sevenhuijsen, 1998). In the German context they are often subsumed under the heading 'motherliness' and are seen to be strengthened, at least to some extent, by the experience of motherhood. The importance attached to motherliness, and the common agreement about ways to promote it, led to its being seen as a kind of 'natural' qualification, so that women who have children of their own are given easier access into some of the training colleges (Ahnert, 2005) and motherhood leads to higher professional status amongst colleagues in the ECEC workforce (Rabe-Kleberg, 2009).

Much of the literature positions caring skills and attitudes in the private, unpaid domain (Graham, 1991) and neglects the question of whether all aspects of care in the public domain could be taught and learnt. Motherliness could be seen as a dark side of the profession if it influences practice without reflection and if the requirement of motherliness means that the profession has a lower status (Rabe-Kleberg, 2009). The debate about the training and education of *Erzieherinnen*, and about the best location for it, may help to provide some answers. The *Erzieherinnen* in the pilot study explained that what proved to be useful in their work was knowledge and insight gained from psychology, particularly child development. Pedagogy and practical exercises, including those tapping into personal experiences, were valued. Other studies show that the current education and training at *FS* appears less suitable for fostering the ability to access academic knowledge and to make use of insight gained by research in the disciplines of psychology, pedagogy and other social sciences (Thole and Cloos, 2006). After all, colleges aim to make scientifically based knowledge accessible to their students in contrast to universities which are tasked with supporting the development of research skills and knowledge construction.

The debate around moving the training and education of Erzieherinnen into higher education institutions uses powerful arguments about improving the quality of services (Robert Bosch Stiftung, 2006), yet a closer look at the funded pilot projects shows that there is no agreement about the form this move should take. Courses vary regarding their location, teaching and learning mode, entrance qualifications, titles and final awards (GEW, 2005; Thole and Cloos, 2006). Ten years after the pilot project started, a search engine for interested students identified 97 BA courses and 18 Masters courses across Germany (Weiterbildungsinitiative Frühpädagogische Fachkräfte, 2014). This development may challenge the opinion that a general move to higher education is unrealistic. However, the range of variation already observed during the pilot stage shows that proposals to cooperate or to fuse *FS* and *FHS* and proposals to provide common core elements for the training of both *Erzieherinnen* and primary school teachers (Diller and Rauschenbach, 2006) have not been readily picked up. Considering the traditionally different training routes, differing professional identities and different purposes of early years care and education and school, this is not surprising. For example, elementary education (as the stage before schooling is called) is firmly grounded in inclusive ideas. In contrast to this value the German schools system has a strongly selective ethos.

The motivation of the first cohort of students on the BA Pedagogy of Early Childhood at the *Evangelische Fachhochschule Freiburg* arose from the perception that the previous qualification as *Erzieherin* was too superficial and did not allow them to acquire sufficient knowledge as a basis for their practical work. Students hoped for personal development and to increase their employability, both in Germany and abroad. They saw themselves as trailblazers and enjoyed their role, though they also had feelings of uncertainty (see also Fröhlich-Gildhoff, 2006). Now most *Länder* have established the occupation *Staatlich Anerkannte Kindheitspädagogin* which can be translated as state-approved childhood pedagogue (KMK and JFMK, 2010) and this term is used in official statistics, despite different titles awarded by universities and colleges. So far the move towards higher education has not resulted in a distinctive occupation with distinctive skills and competencies. Mischo (2014) compared child-related and environment-related competencies of people who trained either at college or at university and could not find any significant differences. Also acquired skills like research, multiprofessional cooperation and professional approaches decline when they are not part of the occupational role expectation (Kirstein and Fröhlich-Gildhoff, 2014b). There are concerns about how *Kindheitspädagoginnen* will integrate into the ECEC landscape, whether their higher education qualifications will enable them to achieve higher incomes and whether this is sufficient to keep them in this field of work. Part of the problem is that employers lack knowledge about this new qualification, that *Kindheitspädagoginnen* often work under the same conditions, including the same salary grade as *Erzieherinnen* and that only a minority take up leadership roles in ECEC settings (Fuchs-Rechlin, 2013; Kirstein and Fröhlich-Gildhoff, 2014a; Kirstein and Fröhlich-Gildhoff, 2014b). In 2013 *Kindheitspädagoginnen* made up 0.3 per cent of the workforce in daycare settings, compared to the 70 per cent who were *Erzieherinnen* (Statistisches Bundesamt, 2013).

In previous editions of this chapter I wondered whether in Germany *FS*, *FHS* and universities were competing against each other. Since then it has been agreed that courses at *FS* are at the same level as BA courses. Credits awarded in one institution (college or university) can be counted towards an award in another institution. The current challenge is how to train and educate more people quickly, to answer the rising demand due to the expansion of childcare places needed as a result of the legal entitlement to a place for even younger children. In this context colleges and higher education institutions cater for a range of basic training, continuous professional development and specialisation requests, creating more of a complementary pattern of courses than a competitive playing field.

The developments in Germany highlight three perspectives that can also be used to explore the state of affairs in other countries. Firstly, the debate about the purpose of childcare has not been resolved. The new balance of the three elements *Erziehung*, *Betreuung* and *Bildung* will depend on how the preferences and perceived requirements of parents, children and employers are prioritised. The German government has clearly expressed its intention to make ECEC accessible to very young children and to increase the focus on education in care settings. This is often perceived as downward pressure from school which risks introducing unsuitable ways of working with young children. It may also influence what is considered the best approach to help childcare workers or pedagogues to relate tacit, functional and professional aspects of their knowledge. When tacit and functional knowledge are emphasised, training can be offered currently by lower-level institutions and can be assessed by 'vocational-industrial qualifications'. A stronger emphasis on professional knowledge leads to demands for more professional academic education (Cameron and Boddy, 2006).

Secondly, do the proposed reforms lead to a greater specialisation of pedagogical roles and, therefore, the fragmentation of an all-round profession? This would work against the professional ethos of balancing *Erziehung*, *Betreuung* and *Bildung* – an ethos commended by the OECD (2004; Prott, 2006). For each of the possible solutions, either specialisation of roles or further integration of an all-round profession, new career and training paths will have to be developed. Observing the cohort of staff newly qualified as *Kindheitspädagogin* shows that changed structures of qualification have to be mirrored by a structure of ECEC roles in settings if acquired skills and knowledge are to be preserved and developed. Otherwise the status quo of established practice in settings may override innovative approaches, as seems to have happened with the EYPS in England (Roberts-Holmes, 2013).

Thirdly, the debate highlights questions about how to link theory and practice but has not provided answers. One could be forgiven for having the impression that this is a chicken-and-egg discussion. However, a preference for a particular sequence of development of practical skills and of theoretical knowledge will inform decisions about the level of education at which training and education are best situated, the role of work-based learning (a theme picked up in a special issue, June 2015, of the journal *Early Years*), as well as choices about the content and the structure of programmes.

An interesting twist in the debate about how theoretical knowledge and practical experience interlink is highlighted by tensions that emerged among the first cohort of the BA Early-Childhood Pedagogy degree in Freiburg. The group of students had to work through conflicting perceptions – for example that a qualified *Erzieherin* with work experience would already know all there was to know about the value of play. Opportunities to reflect on previously learnt theories in the light of experience, to examine newly learned theories from a number of angles and to share different students' perspectives allowed the group to develop new insights and to value this learning opportunity. Similar differences in perspective have been observed when people with and without previous work experience and/or vocational training study together on a degree course and it remains to be seen if this might lead to tensions in England when candidates for EYTS join higher education courses.

ACTIVITY 1

Access Early Education and Childcare: Statutory Guidance for Local Authorities *(DfE, 2014d) http://bit.ly/1qlHjhs*

What is the purpose of childcare services in England? Which elements of the standards suggest that they are 'vocational-industrial qualifications' and which suggest a requirement for 'professional education'?

ACTIVITY 2

How would you describe the interplay between Erziehung, Betreuung and Bildung in England and how do they link to different kinds of qualification?

ACTIVITY 3

Think about one of the overarching principles of the Early Years Foundation Stage (A Unique Child, Positive Relationships, Enabling Environments or Learning and Development) and explore your experiences of linking theory and practice in this aspect of your work with children.

Boddy, J., Cameron, C. and Moss, P. (eds) (2006) *Care Work: Present and Future.* London and New York: Routledge.

The authors critically examine current themes in care work and look at the changing face of care work and care occupations for those working with children, young people, adults and the elderly.

Gambaro, L., Stewart, K. and Waldfogel, J. (eds) *An Equal Start? Providing Quality Early Education and Care for Disadvantaged Children.* Bristol: Policy Press.

A collection of chapters describing ECEC systems in a number of countries, addressing country-specific issues around quality and the purpose of providing care and education for the youngest members of society.

Oberhuemer, P., Schreyer, I. and Neuman, M. (2009) *Professionals in Early Childhood Education and Care Systems: European Profiles and Perspectives.* Opladen and Farmington Hills: Barbara Budrich.

This text provides information on the social context of childcare and educational services in a number of European countries. Cross-national themes and issues on training, provision and policy have been emphasised for comparative analysis.

Scheiwe, K. and Willekens, H. (eds) (2009) *Child Care and Preschool Development in Europe: Institutional Perspectives.* Basingstoke: Palgrave Macmillan.

Public provision of care for children below school age is a pressing policy issue in European countries. This book traces the two competing approaches to childcare and shows historical and social roots. One focuses on facilitating women's paid involvement in the workforce. The other one focuses on the educational needs of children.

OECD reports on a number of countries and more recent projects can be accessed at www.oecd.org/doc ument/3/0,2340,en_2649_201185_27000067_1_1_1_1,00.html

Abbott, L. and Pugh, G. (eds) (1998) *Training to Work in the Early Years.* Buckingham: Open University Press.

Ahnert, L. (2005) Entwicklungspsychologische Erfordernisse bei der Gestaltung von Betreuungs- und Bildungsangeboten im Kleinkind- und Vorschulalter. In Sachverständigenkommission Zwölfter Kinder- und Jugendbericht (ed.) *Bildung, Betreuung und Erziehung von Kindern unter sechs Jahren.* Munich: Deutsches Jugendinstitut.

Autorengruppe Bildungsberichterstattung (2008) *Bildung in Deutschland 2008: Ein indikatorengestützter Bericht mit einer Analyse zu Übergängen im Anschluss an den Sekundarbereich I.* Bielefeld: Bertelsmann.

Autorengruppe Bildungsberichterstattung (2014) *Bildung in Deutschland 2014: Ein indikatorengestützter Bericht mit einer Analyse zur Bildung von Menschen mit Behinderungen.* Bielefeld: Bertelsmann.

BMFSF (Bundesministerium für Familie, Senioren, Frauen und Jugend) (ed.) (2005) *Zwölfter Kinder- und Jugendbericht: Bericht über die Bildung, Betreuung und Erziehung vor und neben der Schule.* Berlin: Bundestagsdrucksache.

BMFSF (Bundesministerium für Familie, Senioren, Frauen und Jugend) (2013) *Vierzehnter Kinder- und Jugendbericht: Bericht über die Lebenssituation von jungen Menschen und die Leistungen der Kinder- und Jugendhilfe in Deutschland.* BMFSFJ Bonn: Bundestagsdrucksache.

Cameron, C. and Boddy, J. (2006) Knowledge and education for care workers: what do they need to know? In J. Boddy, C. Cameron and P. Moss (eds), *Care Work: Present and Future.* London and New York: Routledge.

DfE (Department for Education) (2014) *Early Education and Childcare: Statutory Guidance for Local Authorities*. London: DfE.

Diller, A. and Rauschenbach, T. (eds) (2006) *Reform oder Ende der Erzieherinnenausbildung? Beiträge zu einer kontroversen Fachdebatte*. Munich: DJI Verlag Deutsches Jugendinstitut.

EGGE (European Commission's Expert Group on Gender and Employment Issues) (2009) *The Provision of Childcare Services: A Comparative Review of 30 European Countries*. Luxembourg: European Commission. Available at: http://ec.europa.eu/social/BlobServlet?docId=2803&langId=en (accessed 26 February 2015).

Eichsteller, G. and Holthoff, S. (2011) Conceptual foundations of social pedagogy: A transnational perspective from Germany. In C. Cameron and P. Moss (eds), *Social Pedagogy and Working with Children and Young People*. London and Philadelphia: Jessica Kingsley Publishers.

European Commission (2014) *Use of Childcare in the EU Member States and Progress Towards the Barcelona Targets: Short Statistical Report No. 1*. Brussels: RAND. Available at: http://www.rand.org/pubs/research_reports/RR185.html (accessed 26 February 2015).

Fröhlich-Gildhoff, K. (2006) Studiengang Bachelor of Arts (BA) 'Pädagogik der frühen Kindheit' an der Evangelischen Fachhochschule Freiburg – erste Erfahrungen. Kindergartenpädagogik – Online- Handbuch. Available at: http://www.kindergartenpaedagogik.de/1241.html (accessed 23 November 2014).

Fuchs-Rechlin, K. (2013) *Übergang von fachschul- und hochschulausgebildeten pädagogischen Fachkräften in den Arbeitsmarkt: Erste Befunde der Absolventenbefragung 2012*. Dortmund, Landau, Frankfurt: Projektgruppe ÜFA.

GEW (Gewerkschaft Erziehung und Wissenschaft) (2005) *Erzieherinnen Ausbildung an die Hochschule: Der Anfang ist gemacht*. Frankfurt am Main: GEW.

Graham, H. (1991) The concept of caring in feminist research: the case of domestic services. *Sociology*, 25(1): 61–78.

HM Treasury (2004) *Choice for Parents, the Best Start for Children: A Ten-year Strategy for Childcare*. London: HMSO.

Hohmann, U. (2015) Germany: parallel histories in ECEC. In V. Campbell-Barr and J. Georgeson (eds), *International Perspectives on Early Years Workforce Development*. Northwich: Critical Publishing.

Jaszus, R., Büchin-Wilhelm, I., Mäder-Berg, M. and Gutmann, W. (2008) *Sozialpädagogische Lernfelder für Erzieherinnen*. Stuttgart: Holland and Josenhans Verlag.

Kirstein, N. and Fröhlich-Gildhoff, K. (2014a) Wie stehen die Kita-Träger in Baden-Württemberg zu den Absolventinnen der BA Kindheitspädagogik-Studiengänge? *Frühe Bildung*, 3(1): 52–4.

Kirstein, N. and Fröhlich-Gildhoff, K. (2014b) Übergang vom Studium in den Beruf: Ergebnisse der AbsolventInnenstudie kindheitspädagogischer Bachelorstudiengänge in Baden-Württemberg. *Frühe Bildung*, 3(3): 155–68.

KMK and JFMK (2010) Weiterentwicklung der Aus-, Fort- und Weiterbildung von Erzieherinnen und Erziehern. Available at: http://www.kmk.org/fileadmin/veroeffentlichungen_ beschluesse/2010/2010_09_16-Ausbildung-Erzieher-KMK-JFMK.pdf (accessed 31 May 2014).

Leu, H.R. (2005) Kindertagesbetreuung – ein Feld in Bewegung. In B. Riedel, T. Gadow, E. van Santen, K. Fuchs, M. Schilling and H.R. Leu (eds), *Zahlenspiegel 2005: Kindertagesbetreuung im Spiegel der Statistik*. Berlin: Internetredaktion des Bundesministerium Familie, Senioren, Frauen und Jugend.

Mathers, S., Ranns, H., Karemaker, A., Moody, A., Silva, K., Graham, J. and Siraj-Blatchford, I. (2011) *Evaluation of the Graduate Leader Fund: Final Report*. London: DfE.

May, H. (2013) *The Discovery of Early Childhood* (2nd edn). Wellington: NZCER Press.

May, T. (2001) *Social Research: Issues, Methods and Process* (3rd edn). Buckingham: Open University Press.

Mischo, C. (2014) Early childhood teachers' perceived competence during transition from teacher education to work: results from a longitudinal study. *Professional Development in Education*, 41(1): 75–95.

Noddings, N. (1993) Caring: a feminist perspective. In K.A. Strike and P.L. Ternasky (eds), *Ethics for Professionals in Education: Perspectives for Preparation and Practice*. New York and London: Teachers College Press.

Oberhuemer, P., Schreyer, I. and Neuman, M. (2009) *Professionals in Early Childhood Education and Care Systems: European Profiles and Perspectives*. Opladen and Farmington Hills: Barbara Budrich.

OECD (2004) *Die Politik der frühkindlichen Betreuung, Bildung und Erziehung in der Bundesrepublik Deutschland: Ein Länderbericht der Organisation für wirtschaftliche Zusammenarbeit und Entwicklung*. Paris: OECD.

OECD (2006a) *Starting Strong II: Early Childhood Education and Care*. Paris: OECD.

OECD (2006b) *Education at a Glance: OECD Briefing Notes for Germany*. Available at: http://www.oecd. org/dataoecd/51/24/37392789.pdf (accessed 20 February 2015).

Pasternack, P. and Schildberg, A. (2005) Die finanzielle Auswirkung einer Akademisierung der ErzieherInnen-Ausbildung. In Sachverständigenkommission Zwölfter Kinder- und Jugendbericht (ed.) *Entwicklungspotenziale institutioneller Angebote im Elementarbereich: Materialien zum Zwölften Kinder- und Jugendbericht, Band 2*. Munich: Deutsches Jugendinstitut.

Prott, R. (2006) 30 Jahre Ausbildungsreform - kritische Anmerkungen eines Insiders. In A. Diller and T. Rauschenbach (eds), *Reform oder Ende der Erzieherinnenausbildung? Beiträge zu einer kontroversen Fachdebatte*. Munich: DJI Verlag Deutsches Jugendinstitut.

Rabe-Kleberg, U. (2009) Maternalism and truncated professionalism – historical perspectives on kindergarten teachers. In K. Scheiwe and H. Willekens (eds), *Child Care and Preschool Development in Europe: Institutional Perspectives*. Basingstoke: Palgrave Macmillan.

Rauschenbach, T. (2006) Ende oder Wende. In A. Diller and T. Rauschenbach (eds), *Reform oder Ende der Erzieherinnenausbildung? Beiträge zu einer kontroversen Fachdebatte*. Munich: DJI Verlag Deutsches Jugendinstitut.

Rauschenbach, T., Beher, K. and Knauer, D. (1995) *Die Erzieherin: Ausbildung und Arbeitsmarkt*. Weinheim: Beltz.

Riedel, B. (2005) Ausgewählte Daten zum Personal in Tageseinrichtungen für Kinder. In B. Riedel, T. Gadow, E. van Santen, K. Fuchs, M. Schilling and H.R. Leu (eds), *Zahlenspiegel 2005: Kindertagesbetreuung im Spiegel der Statistik*. Berlin: Internetredaktion des Bundesministerium Familie, Senioren, Frauen und Jugend.

Robert Bosch Stiftung (2006) *PiK - Profis in Kitas: Der Reformkatalog*. Stuttgart: Robert Bosch Stiftung GmbH.

Roberts-Holmes, G. (2013) The English Early Years Professional Status (EYPS) and the 'split' Early Childhood Education and Care (ECEC) system. *European Early Childhood Education Research Journal*, 21(3): 339–52.

Rohrmann, T. (2009) *Gender in Kindertageseinrichtungen: Ein Überblick über den Forschungsstand*. Munich: DJI.

Sevenhuijsen, S. (1998) *Citizenship and the Ethics of Care: Feminist Considerations on Justice, Morality and Politics*. London and New York: Routledge.

Statistische Ämter des Bundes und der Länder (2013) *Kindertagesbetreuung 2013 regional: Ein Vergleich aller 402 Kreise in Deutschland*. Wiesbaden: Statistisches Bundesamt.

Statistisches Bundesamt (2013) *Statistiken der Kinder- und Jugendhilfe: Kinder und tätige Personen in Tageseinrichtungen und in öffentlich geförderter Kindertagespflege am 01.03.2013*. Wiesbaden: Statistisches Bundesamt.

Thole, W. and Cloos, P. (2006) Akademisierung des Personals für das Handlungsfeld Pädagogik der Kindheit. In A. Diller and T. Rauschenbach (eds), *Reform oder Ende der Erzieherinnenausbildung? Beiträge zu einer kontroversen Fachdebatte*. Munich: DJI Verlag Deutsches Jugendinstitut.

Tronto, J.C. (1993) *Moral Boundaries: A Political Argument for the Ethics of Care*. New York and London: Routledge.

Weiterbildungsinitiative Frühpädagogische Fachkräfte (2014) Studiengangsdatenbank. Available at: http://www.weiterbildungsinitiative.de/studium-und-weiterbildung/studium/studiengangsdatenbank/ (accessed 23 September 2014).

15 Children's well-being in the Majority World: developing sustainable life patterns

Valerie Huggins

Introduction

If, as reflective practitioners, we are willing to widen our gaze to consider issues affecting the well-being of children in the Majority World it can prevent our thinking being constricted and shaped by beliefs, assumptions and taken-for-granted practice narrowly based upon our own personal and social experience (Paige-Smith and Craft, 2011), and enable us to take a more balanced and critically reflective view of education, care and child well-being in the UK.

One important aspect is to consider the varied experiences of children in Majority World countries and to recognise indigenous people's differing understandings of childhood (Kostelny, 2006; Penn, 2014). In the United Nations Convention on the Rights of the Child (UNCRC), childhood is taken to extend to the age of 18 (UN, 1989) but in many cultures childhood is considered to end much earlier. The roles and responsibilities that children take on also vary, sometimes because of their gender. Indeed, we cannot even assume that our taken-for-granted ideas about child development and well-being will necessarily apply to other regions of the world, based as they are on literature and research with an overwhelmingly Western perspective (Huggins, 2013; Westwood, 2014). For instance, our basic approach to a child is as an individual, exemplified in the English Early Years Foundation Stage framework (DfE, 2014), whereas in many cultures much more emphasis is given to children's roles as part of their family and community (Gottlieb, 2004; Morgan, 2013; Penn, 2014). Being aware of such differences can give us a better understanding of childhood globally as well enabling us to appreciate the diversity of children's experiences within our own communities (Nutbrown *et al.*, 2013).

A second aspect is to acknowledge the huge inequalities between Minority and Majority World countries. In 2000, eight targets, termed the Millennium Development Goals (MDGs), were identified by the United Nations, whose members agreed to address global inequalities in achieving them by the year 2015 (UN, 2008). They included MDG 1: eradicate extreme poverty and hunger, MDG 2: achieve universal primary education and MDG 3: promote gender equality. A 2014 UN report details the progress that has been made and argues that setting such targets has made a profound difference to people's lives (UN, 2014a), but acknowledges that there is still more to do. We have to appreciate the grinding poverty in which an estimated 1.6 billion of the world's population still live (OPHI, 2014), if we are to gain both a critical perspective upon our comparatively affluent lifestyle, and relate more sympathetically and intelligently to the needs of the significant number of poor people within our own communities.

A third aspect is to recognise that these issues are not narrowly economic. This is not about the problems of 'poor' people living in 'poor' countries with limited financial resources, but more broadly involves the opportunities and choices that people have to earn an income, reduce their vulnerability, recover from shocks, and enhance their life chances in a sustainable way. A child's well-being is very much affected by the assets that their family has, the political, social and environmental context in which they are growing up, and the strategies their families and communities can realistically employ to achieve sustainable livelihoods. The UK's Department for International Development (DfID) and other key governmental and charitable development agencies therefore have increasingly taken a so-called 'livelihoods approach', which puts people at the centre of any poverty-reduction initiatives, and demands that intervention is context-specific (DfID, 1999).

This approach considers that the key assets needed for a family to prosper are human capital, natural capital, physical capital, financial capital and social capital (DfID, 1999). Human capital has two major dimensions: the level of education, skills and knowledge that people have, and how healthy they are. Natural capital is the natural environment – assets such as unpolluted air and water and productive farming land that families rely on for food. Physical capital is the enabling infrastructure such as transport, good housing, sanitation systems and affordable, reliable energy supplies (e.g. electricity), all important for people in gaining employment, education and other opportunities. Access to information via good communication systems is also crucial, especially in ensuring that people can make well-informed decisions about how best to respond to challenges and take up opportunities.

Financial capital may include stocks such as cash, or liquid assets such as livestock or jewellery, which can be sold when times are hard. The poorest people struggle to build up even tiny amounts of financial capital, which limits their ability to set up small businesses or take other steps to improve their livelihoods. Social capital is the glue that binds communities together; it is the sources of support on which people can draw when times are hard, the networks, trust and reciprocal arrangements around childcare, for example, and the social structures and norms that dictate how people are treated within a given society. Some social structures make and keep certain sections of society poor, e.g. the caste system or social systems which deny education and employment opportunities to women.

These different assets are interdependent, and in different communities there will be different strengths and challenges; for example, social capital may be very strong in some poorer communities, but financial capital may be very limited. Ultimately solutions must lie in working with communities to enable them to develop workable and sustainable livelihood strategies, thereby improving economic well-being, and the ability to provide children with happy and productive lives. In the following sections we consider issues which may have a major impact upon this collaborative process, and the consequences for children's well-being.

Human capital: educational issues

The availability of educational opportunities is a key element in acquiring human capital. Pearce (2009) argues that education, literacy and lifelong learning are the key drivers of development, and education is seen by millions of families in the Majority World as the only way out of poverty, mirroring a similar pattern in the Minority World during the 19th century. Yet in some parts of West Africa, for example, despite the success of the Education MDGs, more than 40 per cent of people over 15 are still unable to read and write (UNESCO, 2012). This shortage of educated adults is a barrier to a country's political, social and economic progress and there are huge challenges for some regions in terms of creating a healthy, well-educated workforce, no longer reliant on subsistence farming, which will be wealth-generating in the modern globalised economy and will thereby provide health, education and other services for a growing population.

Significant progress has been made during the last decade towards MDG2, to achieve universal primary education, particularly in Sub Saharan Africa and Asia, where 90 per cent of children now potentially have access (UN, 2014a). However, further progress will not be straightforward. Firstly, there are huge problems to overcome in terms of resourcing education. The continuing increase in the birth rate in some countries, coupled with improving survival rates and better health, mean that there is an enormous demand for school places, for example in Ethiopia, where 42.2 per cent of the population is aged from 0–14 years (CIA, 2014). Thus, throughout the Majority World children are often taught in very large classes in mixed age groups, in broken-down classrooms or outdoors, and with minimal resources. Provision of school buildings, renewal of resources and staffing all require an ongoing stream of funding which many governments find difficult to sustain. Pearce (2009) notes that spending reforms driven by the demands of the International Monetary Fund (IMF) and the World Bank have actually led to a cut in the teacher workforce in some West African countries, confirmed by Urwick *et al.*'s (2012) discussion on Lesotho and Uganda.

Secondly, though observers from Minority World countries often comment on the powerful motivation of children in the Majority World to access educational opportunities, cultural attitudes and practices may present barriers. Within some communities there may be an ignorance about what is possible, linked to a fatalism arising from despair, poverty and poor nutrition, or there may be restrictions on aspects of access resulting from cultural or religious beliefs. A clear example is the reluctance to allow girls to attend school, whether because they are needed for childcare and other household duties, or because education is seen as unnecessary for girls who will shortly marry and raise children, or because of fears that they will be vulnerable to attack or abduction on their journey to and from school, a reality in areas of Ethiopia for example. However, given the limited resources, educating girls can be argued to be a priority since it can lead to huge capital increase in terms of family health and earning power (Harber, 2014). Educating women may be as important for the Majority World as the emancipation of women was for the Minority World in the 20th century.

Thirdly, financial factors still restrict many children's access to education. Families may have to make difficult choices about whether their child will work in order to contribute to the family finances, rather than attend school. Children living in rural areas often contribute towards their families' livelihoods, for instance, by engaging in herding cattle or helping on the family farm, whereas in urban areas children may be more likely to hawk goods or work in factories. The work that children engage in may further deplete their human capital if it is exploitative or dangerous, such as working with heavy machinery or toxic materials. The United Nations Children's Fund (UNICEF) estimate that more than 120 million children worldwide are engaged in hazardous work and girls in particular are at risk of being sent out to work rather than to school (UNICEF, 2006: 15).

Even where schooling is 'free', parents will often need to provide uniform, pencils and notebooks that they may not be able to afford for all or even some of their children (Harber, 2014). There are also difficulties in providing education in remote rural areas where pay, conditions and lifestyle are almost certainly inferior, not least because teachers who have trained in large towns or cities may be reluctant to go back to remote villages. Furthermore, even urban salaries are often less than teachers can earn abroad, where they can earn enough to be able to send money back to support their families. Harber (2014: 43) even argues, paradoxically, that education often 'reproduces the inequalities of the wider society rather than providing equal opportunities for all'.

This negative picture is lightened by some positive developments. The rapid spread of modern technology through the Majority World (Hankin, 2009) is beginning to overcome some of the resource difficulties. In particular the growth of wireless technology, linked to the spread of mobile phone use, offers to leapfrog the financial constraints on installing landlines and can give even remote communities the opportunity to connect to worldwide resources without the costs of sustaining libraries. Initiatives such as the GEM-Tech awards (ITU, 2014) show how e-learning tools can be used successfully to provide educational experiences, particularly for women and girls. But all this depends on the ability, at individual, local and national levels, to accumulate sufficient financial capital to support such developments.

Another major step forward is that the proposed Sustainability Development Goals embody a strong focus on early childhood education and care, an important shift in direction now that universal primary education is close to being achieved. From historical experience in the Minority World, this may reasonably be predicted to improve levels of academic achievement as well as to enhance children's well-being, However, in this area there is a real danger that governments may misguidedly look to impose Minority World early years 'solutions', backed by Western finance, a strategy, which although well-intentioned, may be inappropriate or unsustainable in the long term.

Models of education and developmentally appropriate practice grounded in the Minority World and shaped by its historical and political context are unlikely to be relevant or successful (Brooker and Yelland, 2005; Penn, 2014). As Taylor (2014) argues, education needs to be community-based, emerging from the developing needs of a community, and supported from within the community. This fits with the Education for Sustainability agenda with its focus on development that meets the needs of the present without compromising the ability of future generations to meet their own needs (Siraj-Blatchford *et al.*, 2010).

Human capital: health issues

The health of many children in the Majority World remains a deep concern, in stark contrast to that of the majority of children in more developed countries, and it is affected by a number of factors. For instance, despite the aim of MDG 1 to eradicate extreme hunger and poverty, this is still a reality for the 162 million young children who are suffering from undernutrition (UN, 2014a), while in the Minority World we are concerned about childhood obesity and unhealthy diets (Public Health England, 2014). A crucial aspect of improving human capital in the Majority World must be to help communities and families to feed themselves better, whether by enhancing their capacity to produce food or by improving their financial capital through opportunities for regular employment or for developing small-scale businesses.

In the Minority World, we take for granted our access to plentiful clean water and effective sanitation. However, almost half the world's population faces a scarcity of water; 783 million people do not have access to safe drinking water; 2.5 billion do not have access to adequate sanitation, with as many as 1 billion people still resorting to defecation in the open (UN Water, 2013). Such poor sanitation facilities are a major factor in contributing to water-borne diseases such as cholera and infant diarrhoea. Any proposal to construct major sanitation networks like those of the Minority World is totally impracticable even in the medium term. Instead, effective support must be in terms of small-scale community projects raising awareness of the issues and introducing intermediate technology, such as solar-pumped wells and composting toilets that can be constructed and maintained by the local people themselves.

The well-being of children is substantially affected by the parenting that they receive and maternal health in particular has an impact upon this. In the Majority World patterns of child-bearing and child-rearing are a significant factor. In many regions women experience large numbers of pregnancies; for example in Zambia there are 5.76 births per woman compared with just 1.42 in Italy (CIA, 2014). Multiple pregnancies, together with frequent stillbirths and deaths in infancy, put severe strain on mothers' physical and emotional health and increase their susceptibility to other widespread illnesses such as malaria and HIV/AIDS. Death in childbirth also remains common, given the shortage of obstetric and gynaecological health care services.

However, campaigns to reduce the birth rate are simplistic when a woman's status as a child bearer may be highly significant in terms of financial and social capital. Where life is uncertain, livelihoods precarious and where there is no welfare support for the elderly, having as many children as possible is often seen as one of the few strategies that may offer a family hope for the future. There are also advantages for the children from having a support network of siblings who, in many communities, play an important part in childcare. Thus, even where contraception is available, affordable and not proscribed by cultural or religious beliefs, efforts to control population may meet with considerable resistance. However, measures to improve child survival rates through improved health care and support may, over time, reduce pressures on women to bear many children.

Another key health issue is that of breastfeeding (Lucas *et al.*, 2008). Where bottle-feeding is dangerous because of problems with sterilisation and contaminated water supplies, early and exclusive breastfeeding is vital to infant health. It has the potential to prevent 12–15 per cent of deaths of children under five years in the Majority World and many organisations, such as UNICEF, actively promote it (UNICEF, 2014). However, many companies in the Minority World actively market formula milk to the Majority World, advertising it as being more beneficial to the children, more 'modern' and so of higher status – claims that are hard to resist.

HIV/AIDS has had a particular impact upon the well-being of children in the Majority World, especially in Sub-Saharan Africa. In 2004, in Botswana, a relatively affluent and developed African nation, 23.9 per cent of people aged 15–49 were HIV positive and 95,000 children had been orphaned through AIDS (UNICEF, 2004). Much progress has since been made, with 9.5 million people receiving antiretroviral therapy (ARP) since 1995, a process estimated to have saved 6.6 million lives, but the World Health Organisation (WHO, 2014a) estimated that in 2013 some 3.2 million children were living with HIV, with 250,000 newly infected each year and up to 190,000 dying from HIV-related illnesses. In Sub-Saharan Africa, children and their grandparents now constitute a majority of some communities and even more children are likely to have lost at least one close relative. The impact upon such communities in terms of human, financial and social capital is yet to be fully appreciated. The emotional cost is immeasurable.

All these health issues are compounded by the fact that many regions in the Majority World lack an adequate medical infrastructure. Even when medical treatment is available access to it can be difficult. The 2014 Ebola outbreak in Sierra Leone, Liberia and Guinea (WHO, 2014b) has recently demonstrated how quickly preventable diseases can spread when the infrastructure is not in place – unthinkable in countries where a variety of medical treatment is just a short trip or a phone call away.

Once again, it is unrealistic to attempt to remedy this by introducing the high-tech solutions of the Minority World. Instead, there is a need to develop affordable, sustainable, low-tech strategies to improve the situation. Lucas *et al.* (2008) argue powerfully that as the family is the frontline care system for children, strategies should focus on household- and community-based interventions. Local health-care provision should be provided wherever possible, e.g. many separate health centres in townships or slum areas rather than one large hospital in the centre of the city. In terms of enhancing human capital, cost-effective medical solutions may involve the limiting of sophisticated, Minority World approaches in favour of models that will reach far more people – paramedics instead of doctors, bicycle ambulances rather than cars or helicopters (Practical Action, 2015a), local people trained in very basic health care and the use of traditional healers within the community alongside more modern medical resources and personnel (Gottlieb, 2004).

A final concern in terms of human capital is that damaging and lethal conditions and diseases, which have largely been eliminated from the Minority World, are still prevalent in less affluent countries. In 2012, 122,000 children died of measles, 95 per cent of them in low-income countries with weak health infrastructures (WHO, 2014c). Solutions can be simple and relatively inexpensive; it costs less than £1 to immunise a child against measles and this has resulted in a 78 per cent drop in measles cases worldwide since 2000. Overall, steady progress is being made towards the MDGs. For example, the number of children dying before their fifth birthday was reported at 6.55m in 2012, compared to 9.7 million in 2006 and an estimated 20 million infant deaths in 1960 (UNICEF, 2007; UN, 2014c). But there is still some distance to go.

Children and conflict: the impact on children's well-being

Throughout much of the Majority World, family livelihoods, and so the well-being of children, are precarious. But the situation is worsened by the prevalence of armed conflict. Much armed conflict in the 21st century differs from our recent historic understanding of wars which have usually been fought for political reasons by soldiers, usually men in uniform, against soldiers from another nation state. The nuclear 'Doomsday Scenario' has made this pattern less likely, so that armed disputes are increasingly within, rather than between, countries, and are fought for a combination of economic, social, religious and criminal reasons (Singer, 2006). For example, during the conflict in the West Darfur region of the Sudan, which has continued since the 1970s, worsening periods of drought have intensified competition between different tribal groups for natural resources, such as water and grazing pastures, which they rely on for their livelihoods (Jaspars and O'Callaghan, 2008). When communities are in dispute over land and are violently attacked and displaced, even wiped out, the whole population, including children, is involved.

There are a number of internationally agreed protocols for the protection of children in situations of armed conflict, including the 1949 Geneva Convention and the 1989 Convention on the Rights of the Child (UNICEF, 2006). However, in many countries, especially in the Majority World, children continue to be adversely affected by violence. It is estimated that 1 billion children live in war-torn countries, including 300 million under five years old (ECHO, 2014) and up to 2 million may have been killed during armed conflict in the past decade (SOS Children's Villages, 2009). Alongside this, an estimated 7 million children are refugees, with possibly as many as 13 million displaced within their own country due to conflict with 2.8 million out of primary school (ECHO, 2014). Exposure to conflict is therefore a reality for a great many children and when considering issues of child well-being it is important to consider the impact this experience has on children, both immediately and in the longer term.

The immediate impact upon family livelihoods is obvious. It disrupts school attendance. It increases child mortality and incidences of injury, while displacement due to fighting increases the likelihood of children contracting diseases such as cholera and malaria, as families are forced into temporary housing or refugee camps with little or no provision of sanitation facilities. The damage to the physical capital of conflict areas disrupts life and impacts on the efforts that governments and other agencies make to provide adequate services for children and their families; the resulting damage to a region's infrastructure, such as roads, schools and hospitals, hinders the provision of the support that children need to achieve their potential and to stay safe. Though damage to natural capital may be less obvious, when families are vulnerable, conflict increases their vulnerability; for example, subsistence farmers who are reliant on their crops and animals to feed their family are at risk of severe malnutrition, even starvation, if conflict destroys these or forces them to flee their land, leaving jobs and possessions behind. Financial capital is at risk, since it does not reside in protected accounts but is embodied in the home and community environment, vulnerable to destruction or pillage. The social capital of the family in the community is all too often destroyed by bereavement, rape, forced separation and even kidnap and enslavement, with children in particular in increased danger of being inadequately protected from harm, or even co-opted into the violence (Child Soldiers International, 2012). The conflict against the government in Northern Uganda, led by the Lord's Resistance Army (LRA), has been raging since the late 1980s and has seen an estimated 10,000 children forced, through abduction and intimidation, into becoming child soldiers (SOS Children's Villages, 2009). The long-term effects on such children, who have often been forced to commit atrocities, and on the communities who are subject to LRA attacks, is difficult to appreciate fully. When children are coerced into such damaging roles, the post-conflict rehabilitation of communities is made all the more difficult. How can families recover and trust one another again? Violent conflict depletes social capital, destroying the social networks and sources of support that poor families in particular rely on for survival.

Conflict also creates even more complex situations. Children are often framed by the media and humanitarian agencies purely as victims, often by using phrases such as 'women and children'. Such language and imagery makes sense to many people, presenting stereotypical visions of mother and child, helpless and unequivocally non-participants in the conflict. Paradoxically, this may pose additional dangers to male children. For example, during the war in Bosnia in 1995, Serbian forces separated and massacred an estimated 8,000 boys and men in Srebrenica, on the grounds that males were potential combatants, and so legitimate targets (Gendercide, 2010). They sought to justify their definition by allowing humanitarian agencies access to women and younger children whom they constructed as 'innocents' or 'civilians', whilst depicting many children as actual or potential combatants, so not covered by international protocols such as the Geneva Convention (1949).

The issues around conflict and child well-being are therefore extremely complex and must be considered differently in each and every context, yet we must recognise that as victims, witnesses, even perpetrators of atrocities, children in war-torn countries are too often robbed of their right to a safe and happy childhood (UN, 1989).

The role of governments and non-governmental organisations (NGOs)

However strong our concern for the well-being of children in the Majority World, we can do very little individually to affect and enhance it. Overwhelmingly, it is shaped by world organisations, by national governments and by national and international NGOs. If we are to develop a critical professional perspective upon the issues, we need to be aware of some of the dynamics, conflicts and tensions involved.

Support for the Majority World functions at macro, meso and micro levels. At the macro level international institutions such as the World Bank and European Union have an extremely powerful role in providing aid, funding and loans to govern-ments in the Majority World, in coordinating humanitarian responses to crises, and in influencing (even controlling) world trade protocols. We need to be aware that the financial and technical support that they provide to Majority World coun-tries is almost always conditional on implementation of reforms and improvements to financial systems and governance which they dictate, and is often tied to trade or politically strategic agreements. These are often based upon the top-down impo-sition of a Western model of free-market democracy upon the Majority World and increasingly, there is an argument that such agreements often disadvantage poorer nations, and that loans serve only to lock them into debts that they can never repay. If there were a clear 'quid pro quo' with both parties clearly receiving their entitle-ment, such agreements would have validity, but Western governments' fulfilment of funding commitments to Majority World countries is still a contentious issue, with many wealthy nations failing to meet internationally agreed targets. In order to achieve the MDGs, in 2000 the United Nations Development Programme (UNDP) asked the world's richest nations to give 0.7 per cent of their GDP in development aid (UN, 2008). Caught in the spotlight of high profile events like the 2005 G8 Summit, which was accompanied by a groundswell of public concern to 'make poverty history' (Make Poverty History, 2005), a coalition of world leaders made this pledge to increase aid spending but only Norway, Sweden, the Netherlands, Luxemburg and Denmark have consistently met the agreed target (Penn, 2005: 35). Despite consid-erable political and public opposition from within the country, the UK government eventually achieved it in 2013 (Booth, 2014).

At the meso, or national government level, it is important to appreciate that each nation, whether in the Minority or Majority World, has its own set of strengths and challenges with regard to governance, infrastructure, natural and man-made resources and so on, and education, health and welfare services. In the Minority World there are increasing challenges to funding commitments to the Majority World, given the political tensions arising from recession and austerity policies, and growing demands that such financial and practical support be conditional upon receiving reciprocal benefits. In the Majority World, some countries, such as Botswana, Tanzania and Zambia, have been proactive in prioritising the needs of children by making primary education free for all, and have seen improved attend-ance and retention rates as a result (UN, 2008). Others have given priority to defence and security and the implementation of ideological imperatives. Robert Mugabe's driving through of land reforms in Zimbabwe, at enormous cost to the economic well-being of the country and its people, is a vivid example. But throughout the Majority World there will be many countries where governments cannot meet many of the needs of the population, and in such situations, NGOs are often particularly active in providing education, care and welfare services in the most disadvantaged communities.

NGOs are usually charities, working for philanthropic rather than profit-making or political ends. They often take up issues and deliver services that governments are unwilling or unable to tackle; as such, they can be seen either as indicative of the failure of states to provide adequately for ordinary people, or as a positive demonstration of humankind's commitment to helping those who are less fortunate. UK-based NGOs, such as OXFAM, Save the Children and Action Aid, are very active in providing welfare services throughout the Majority World, either directly or through a partner organisation based in the community that they want to support. They also take on a valuable campaigning role, seeking to improve the life chances of disadvantaged communities by challenging the structures and practices that make and keep countries poor. However, NGOs are not necessarily large, influential and international organisations but may be local, single-issue organisations working on a very small scale, or with a particular community.

NGOs are funded from a range of sources, including public donations, but may also be contracted by governments to provide services. They therefore have a number of lines of accountability to balance and they work hard to promote the work they do in a way that will generate continued support. There is a danger, therefore, that fundraising campaigns may accentuate the problems in order to generate income, thereby reinforcing the stereotypes of poverty in the Majority World, and/or focus upon situations and issues that are seen as having popular appeal, at the expense of arguably more important projects. It has often been commented that in the animal-loving UK, it can be easier to raise funds to help overworked and ill-treated donkeys than to help women and children overworked and exploited as sweated labour. There is also inevitable competition between NGOs for funding, but there are also examples of collaboration. The creation in 1963 of the Disasters Emergency Committee (DEC) has seen key international NGOs including the British Red Cross, Christian Aid and World Vision come together to coordinate a response to disasters such as the 2010 earthquake in Haiti, the war in Gaza and the Ebola crisis in parts of West Africa (DEC, 2014), but there is evidence that donor fatigue is growing.

Whilst large-scale, highly visible NGO responses to such disasters catch the headlines, it is arguable that the micro- or local-level work that NGOs take on in Majority World countries is even more important in the long term. To enhance well-being and to create sustainable livelihoods, disadvantaged communities must be enabled to build up and make the best use of their assets, and any external intervention needs to be sensitive to the local context. For example, when food aid is brought into famine-stricken areas to preserve life, humanitarian agencies need to be conscious of the risk of undermining the local economy, in particular local food producers, and of encouraging dependency.

Many NGOs, such as Exeter-Ethiopia Link (EEL, 2015) place great emphasis upon building the capacity of communities, enabling people to help themselves. NGOs look to bring additional resources into a community, to invest in local people's skills and knowledge, and to work with communities in a participatory way – poor communities should not just be recipients of aid monies but active agents in identifying and working towards solutions to their problems. A good example is the way that credit unions and small loan institutions like the pro-poor Grameen Bank in Bangladesh can make a huge amount of difference to people such as impoverished women who are traditionally unable to access credit (Grameen Bank, 2010), but with a small, repayable loan can create a business which lifts them out of extreme poverty.

Thus the old model of well-meaning Westerners going out to the Majority World to help is being increasingly replaced by local people being employed or trained to take on the design, implementation and maintenance of community development projects themselves, such as those promoted by Practical Action (2015b). As such projects are by definition context-specific, NGOs are very diverse, but a key word for all is 'sustainability', the aim being that any improvements can continue beyond the time span of a particular project. It is argued that an NGO can be said to have achieved its aims when it is no longer needed and can disband. However, many governments in the Majority World are not in a position, financially or in terms of expertise, to take over the work of NGOs, and need them to help to continue to prioritise the needs of children, the key to any country's future.

Conclusion

By considering the range of issues affecting communities in the Majority World, we can begin to appreciate the scale of the challenge involved in improving life chances for the millions of children worldwide who continue to live in poverty, especially given the current global economic climate and the ongoing presence of conflict and natural disasters. Understanding the interrelated and complex nature of the problems that families face in terms of sustaining livelihoods, educating their children and keeping them healthy and safe, reminds us that in order to be successful any interventions need to be people-centred and context-specific. Working with families, and children in particular, does not lend itself to a top-down 'one-size-fits-all' approach, but needs to be sensitive to innovative and different ways of identifying and implementing solutions. This principle can also be applied to the approach international institutions, governments and NGOs should take in helping the Majority World to help itself.

However, this demands of us much more than a well-meaning willingness to help. It also demands that we abandon assumptions that the answers to Majority World problems lie in offering (or even imposing) Minority World 'solutions' and open ourselves to hear, respect and support what local communities identify as their needs and wishes. To be able to do this we need to develop what are increasingly termed our 'intercultural capabilities' (Huggins, 2013), through critical reflection upon our beliefs and ideas leading to new understandings about the sociocultural and historical processes that shape the lives of children around the world.

As professionals looking to address the range of concerns about children's well-being we need to recognise that levels of human capital influence all other areas, and so issues of education and health are of paramount importance. People who are healthy and educated can make better decisions about managing their natural environment or finances and about keeping themselves and their children well. The UNCRC sees children as having universally applicable rights to an adequate standard of living, protection from harm and opportunities to participate fully in society (UN, 1989), yet we can see that the efforts to fulfil the aims of this convention and meet the targets set out in the MDGs still have a long way to go (UN, 2014a), not only in the Majority World but within Minority World communities too.

The new Sustainable Development Goals, planned to follow on from the MDGs in 2015, are based on the continuing desire to eradicate poverty (UN, 2014b). Having a well-informed, critical understanding of key global issues makes us more aware of provision here in the UK, the things we take for granted, and also of the continuing inequality in our own society. For practitioners interested in the care and education of young children, having an eye on the global context enables us to appreciate how far we have come in the UK, but also to acknowledge how much there still is to do.

Acknowledgment

Rebecca Carter Dillon, co-author of the version of this chapter which was published in the third edition, is gratefully acknowledged for her contribution to discussions about its revision.

ACTIVITY 1

Over the next month, look through newspapers and magazines for articles on children in the Majority World. What are the key messages that come across and which ones do not?

ACTIVITY 2

Research NGOs working in the Majority World. Choose one, and find out what its aims are, how it raises finance, what kind of projects it supports and how it involves local communities.

ACTIVITY 3

Organise a group to discuss the issues raised in the section on 'Children and Conflict'.

Some potential questions:

- *Are child soldiers victims or criminals? What might be some of the challenges involved in rehabilitating them into their communities?*
- *Why might civil conflicts, for example between different communities within the same country, be particularly difficult to resolve?*

FURTHER READING

Garcia, M., Pence, A. and Evans, J.L. (eds) (2008) *Africa's Future, Africa's Challenge: Early Childhood Care and Development in Sub-Saharan Africa*. Washington: The World Bank.

This collection of articles gives an in-depth perspective on children's lives in Sub-Saharan Africa, one of the most fascinating and significant areas of the Majority World.

Georgeson, J. and Payler, J. (eds) (2013) *International Perspectives on Early Childhood Education and Care*. Maidenhead: OUP.

The editors of this text have pulled together examples of ECEC practice and policy from a range of countries across the world to promote comparison and critical reflection.

Harber, C. (2014) *Education and International Development: Theory, Practice and Issues*. Oxford: Symposium Books.

The overall focus of this book is wider than ECEC, but the key issues discussed are just as relevant to the early years context. Harber provides a lot of useful background information on educational policy and the practical realities of educational provision in Majority World contexts.

Penn, H. (2005) *Unequal Childhoods: Young Children's Lives in Poor Countries*. London and New York: Routledge.

This book uses case studies from four different countries to illustrate the diversity of children's experiences, challenging Western assumptions about families and childhood.

Smidt, S. (2006) *The Developing Child in the 21st Century: A Global Perspective on Child Development*. London and New York: Routledge.

This book offers a fascinating insight into how ideas about childhood have changed over time and place.

REFERENCES

Booth, L. (2014) SN/EP/3714: The 0.7% aid target. *Economic Policy and Statistics*, 28 July. London: House of Commons Library.

Brooker, L. and Yelland, N. (2005) Learning to be a child: cultural diversity and early years ideology. In N. Yelland (ed.), *Critical Issues in Early Childhood Education*. Maidenhead: Open University Press.

Child Soldiers International (2012) *Louder than words: An agenda for action to end state use of child soldiers*. London: Child Soldiers International. Available at: http://www.child-soldiers.org/global_report_reader.php?id=562 (accessed 25 January 2015).

CIA (Central Intelligence Agency) (2014) *The World Factbook*. Washington: CIA. Available at: https://www.cia.gov/library/publications/the-world-factbook/geos/et.html (accessed 4 November 2014).

DEC (Disasters Emergency Committee) (2014) *Disasters Emergency Committee*. Available at: http://www.dec.org.uk/ (accessed 25 January 2015).

DfE (Department for Education) (2014) *Statutory Framework for the Early Years Foundation Stage: Setting the Standards for Learning, Development and Care for Children from Birth to Five*. London: DfE Publications.

DfID (Department for International Development) (1999) *Introduction to the Sustainable Livelihoods Approach*. Sussex: Institute of Development Studies ELDIS Document Store. Available at: http://www.eldis.org/vfile/upload/1/document/0901/section1.pdf (accessed: 5 February 2010).

ECHO (2014) *ECHO Factsheet: Children in Conflict 2014*. Brussels: European Commission Humanitarian Aid and Civil Protection.

EEL (Exeter-Ethiopia Link) (2015) Available at: http://www.exeterethiopialink.org/ (accessed 4 February 2015).

Gendercide (2010) *Case Study: The Srebrenica Massacre, July 1995*. Available at: http://www.gendercide.org/case_srebrenica.html (accessed 10 February 2010).

Gottlieb, A. (2004) *The Afterlife Is Where We Come From: The Culture of Infancy in West Africa*. Chicago: University of Chicago Press.

Grameen Bank (2010) Banking for the Poor: Grameen Bank. Available at http://www.grameen-info.org/index.php?option=com_frontpage&Itemid=68 (accessed 10 February 2010).

Hankin, L. (2009) Global citizenship and comparative education. In J. Sharp, S. Ward and L. Hankin (eds), *Education Studies: An Issues Based Approach* (2nd edn). Exeter: Learning Matters.

Harber, C. (2014) *Education and International Development: Theory, Practice and Issues*. Oxford: Symposium Books.

Huggins, V. (2013) Widening our awareness of international approaches to Early Childhood Education and Care: an imperative for 21st century Early Years practitioners? In J. Georgeson and J. Payler (eds) *International Perspectives on Early Childhood Education and Care*. Maidenhead: OUP.

ITU (2014) GEM-TECH Awards 2014. Available at: http://www.itu.int/en/action/women/gem/Pages/winners.aspx (accessed 4 November 2014).

Jaspars, S. and O'Callaghan, S. (2008) *Challenging Choices: Protection and Livelihoods in Darfur*. London: Overseas Development Institute.

Kostelny, K. (2006) Helping war-affected children. In N. Boothby, A. Strang and M. Wessel (eds), (2006) *A World Turned Upside Down: Sociological Ecological Approaches to Children in War Zones*. Bloomfield: Kumarian Press.

Lucas, J., Jitta, J., Jones, G. and Wilczynska-Ketende, K. (2008) Community-based approaches that work in Eastern and Southern Africa. In M. Garcia, A. Pence and J.L. Evans (eds), (2008) *Africa's Future, Africa's Challenge: Early Childhood Care and Education in Sub-Saharan Africa*. Washington: The World Bank.

Make Poverty History (2005) Make Poverty History. Available at http://www.makepovertyhistory.org/ (accessed 10 February 2010).

Morgan, J. (2013) International recognition of children's rights and its influence on early childhood education and care: the case of Zambia. In J. Georgeson and J. Payler (eds), *International Perspectives on Early Childhood Education and Care*. Maidenhead: Open University.

Nutbrown, C., Clough, P. and Atherton, F. (2013) *Inclusion in the Early Years*. London: SAGE.

OPHI (Oxford Poverty & Human Development Initiative) (2014) *Global Multidimensional Poverty Index 2014*. Oxford: University of Oxford.

Paige-Smith, A. and Craft, A. (eds) (2011) *Developing Reflective Practice in the Early Years* (2nd edn). Maidenhead: Open University Press.

Pearce, C. (2009) *From Closed Books to Open: West Africa's Literacy Challenge*. ANCEFA, Pamoja West Africa, African Platform for Adult Education, Oxfam International, Action Aid. Available at: http://www.oxfam.org.uk/resources/policy/education/downloads/closed%20books%20_west_africa_literacy.pdf (accessed 10 February 2010).

Penn, H. (2005) *Unequal Childhoods: Young Children's Lives in Poor Countries*. London and New York: Routledge.

Penn, H. (2014) The globalisation of early childhood and education. In T. Maynard and S. Powell (eds), *Introduction to Early Childhood Studies*. London: SAGE.

Practical Action (2015a) Bicycle Ambulance Nepali. Available at: http://answers.practicalaction.org/our-resources/item/bicycle-ambulance-nepali (accessed 25 January 2015).

Practical Action (2015b) http://practicalaction.org/ (accessed 25 January 2015).

Public Health England (2014) *Child Obesity. Public Health England.* Available at: http://www.noo.org.uk/NOO_about_obesity/child_obesity (accessed 4 November 2014).

Singer, P.W. (2006) *Children at War.* Berkeley and Los Angeles: University of California Press.

Siraj-Blatchford, J., Smith, K.C. and Pramling Samuelsson, I. (2010) *Education for Sustainable Development in the Early Years.* OMEP. Available at: http://www.327matters.org/Docs/ESD%20Book%20Master.pdf (accessed 4 November 2014).

SOS Children's Villages (2009) Child Soldiers. Available at: http://www.child-soldier.org/ (accessed 13 December 2009).

Taylor, J. (2014) Shaping the GAP: ideas for the UNESCO post-2014 ESD agenda. *Journal of Education for Sustainable Development*, 8(2): 133–41.

UN (United Nations) (1989) *UN Convention on the Rights of the Child.* Available at: http://www.unesco.org/education/pdf/CHILD_E.PDF (accessed 7 January 2010).

UN (United Nations) (2008) *The Millennium Development Goals Report.* United Nations. Available at: http://mdgs.un.org/unsd/mdg/Resources/Static/Products/Progress2008/MDG_Report_2008_En.pdf#page=44 (accessed 10 February 2010).

UN (United Nations) (2014a) *The Millennium Development Goals Report.* United Nations. Available at: http://www.un.org/millenniumgoals/2014%20MDG%20report/MDG%202014%20English%20web.pdf (accessed 4 November 2014).

UN (United Nations) (2014b) *Sustainable Development Goals.* United Nations. Available at: http://sustainabledevelopment.un.org/?menu=1300 (accessed 4 November 2014).

UN (United Nations) (2014c) *Child Health.* Office of the UN Secretary-General's Special Envoy for Financing the Health Millennium Development Goals and for Malaria. Available at: http://www.mdghealthenvoy.org/health-areas/child-health/ (accessed 14 November 2014).

UNESCO (United Nations Educational, Scientific and Cultural Organization) (2012) *Adult and Youth Literacy: UIS Fact Sheet September 2012.* United Institute of Statistics. Available at: http://www.uis.unesco.org/literacy/Documents/fs20-literacy-day-2012-en-v3.pdf (accessed 4 November 2014).

UNICEF (United Nations Children's Fund) (2004) *Botswana Statistics.* Available at: http://www.unicef.org/infobycountry/botswana_statistics.html#55. (accessed 10 February 2010).

UNICEF (United Nations Children's Fund) (2006) *Child Protection Information Sheets.* New York: UNICEF.

UNICEF (United Nations Children's Fund) (2007) Progress for Children: A World Fit for Children. *Statistical Review*, no. 6, December. New York: UNICEF.

UNICEF (United Nations Children's Fund) (2014) *Infant and Young Child Feeding.* UNICEF. Available at: http://www.unicef.org/nutrition/index_breastfeeding.html (accessed 4 November 2014).

UN Water (2013) *International Year of Water Cooperation.* United Nations. Available at: http://www.unwater.org/water-cooperation-2013/water-cooperation/facts-and-figures/en/ (accessed 4 November 2014).

Urwick, J. and Griffin, R. with Opendi, V. and Khatleli, M. (2012) What hope for the Dakar goals? The lower levels of education in Lesotho and Uganda since 2000. In R. Griffin (ed.), (2012) *Teacher Education in Sub-Saharan Africa: Closer Perspectives.* Oxford: Symposium Books.

Westwood, J. (2014) Childhood in different cultures. In T. Maynard and S. Powell (eds), *Introduction to Early Childhood Studies.* London: SAGE.

WHO (World Health Organisation) (2014a) Global Summary of the Aids Epidemic. WHO-HIV Department. Available at: http://www.who.int/hiv/data/epi_core_dec2014.png?ua=1 (accessed 4 November 2014).

WHO (World Health Organisation) (2014b) Six months after the Ebola outbreak was declared: what happens when a deadly virus hits the destitute? WHO Global Alert and Response. Available at: http://www.who.int/csr/disease/ebola/ebola-6-months/en/ (accessed 4 November 2014).

WHO (World Health Organisation) (2014c) Media Centre Fact Sheet No. 286: Measles. Available at: http://www.who.int/mediacentre/factsheets/fs286/en/(accessed 4 November 2014).

16 The research, policy and practice triangle in early childhood education and care

Verity Campbell-Barr

Introduction

The interplay between research, policy and practice can take many forms, from a linear relationship where research informs policy and policy informs practice to a more complex relationship where research, policy and practice can all inform one another and question one another. It is the latter that I want to focus on – in fact, the linear relationship feels more idealistic than one based in reality. I will begin with an overview of what is meant by social policy within the field of early childhood studies. I will then consider how research has interacted with the policy process before moving on to consider the implications of national policy for practice. Throughout the chapter I will talk of early childhood education and care (ECEC), a broad term that covers many different areas and services: preschool, nurseries, daycare, child-minders, out of school care, etc. For me the use of the term is about the fact that early childhood comes first, but I will question whether this is the case for policy. Within the chapter, I focus on understandings of quality in ECEC in research, policy and practice and how they interact with one another in both harmonious and contentious ways.

What is social policy?

The term social policy can take on different meanings depending on the context in which it is used, for example social policy as an academic subject and social policy as a process (see Dean, 2005). Even within social policy as process there are the policy-making processes at national, regional, local and practitioner levels and also the policy implementation process. For the purpose of this chapter I will be focusing on national policy-making processes. In this context, social policy is a statement of intention for social intervention that is designed to promote the well-being of citizens. Policies are developed to improve the life chances and social relations of society (Alcock, 2004), but as we will see they can also be about political ideologies and responding to wider social influences.

The formation of policy is a gradual (and messy) process.

> *At its most basic level the policy process has been described as a 'black box' into which are entered 'inputs' and from which emerge 'outcomes'. (Alcock et al., 2004: 58)*

Policy represents both a course of action proposed by those in power as a means to achieve the well-being of society and how they aim to achieve this (Forman and Baldwin, 2007). Policy will normally be developed by identifying a social problem and then finding a solution (that can be implemented) for it. However, there are a number of 'inputs' that will inform what are identified as social problems and what are the possible solutions, making the process of developing the policy complex (and long winded).

To develop the initial idea of a social policy, a social 'problem' has to be identified; this can be as a result of research, or it may be generated by lobby groups, the media, parliament or those working on behalf of parliament (civil servants), but often it will be a combination of these (each claiming to represent the views of the public). Having acknowledged a social problem, possible solutions will be identified and again this can involve a range of stakeholders (see Figure 16.1). There will then be a consultation on the potential solutions. Those consulted can include the general public and/or experts in the field and opposing political parties. The consultation process may involve several stages and could also involve the commissioning of, or reference to, research. The solutions will also be debated by parliament before any new legislation is passed. However, this presents a very simplified version of policy formation, as it assumes that all policy formation starts from a blank slate and this is rarely the case. Rather, an existing policy will be identified and the process outlined above will be followed to amend this policy in order to address the perceived social problem.

Policy developments can be in relation to all members of society, but often they will focus on a specific section of society, such as families or children, and even within these groups they will focus on sub-populations, such as lone parents or children living in poverty. Although a policy might be targeted towards a specific sub-population, the declared aim will always be to improve the well-being of the whole of society.

Policy developments inevitably have implications for the way in which we live our lives. Governments have made numerous decisions that impact on the lives of children, such as that they should be educated, but they should not work (Piper, 2008). Child-based policy developments impact on how lives are lived by representing children as a project, implying that they need to be controlled, regulated and surveyed to maintain the social order. Such policy developments contribute to a definition of what is deemed an appropriate childhood (see Chapter 13). Thus, policy becomes involved in the social construction of childhood (and adulthood, family life, etc.). For example, education policy imposes spatial and temporal constraints on children by stipulating when and where education takes place. Curriculum guidance also imposes a series of rules around what are deemed appropriate educational activities for children.

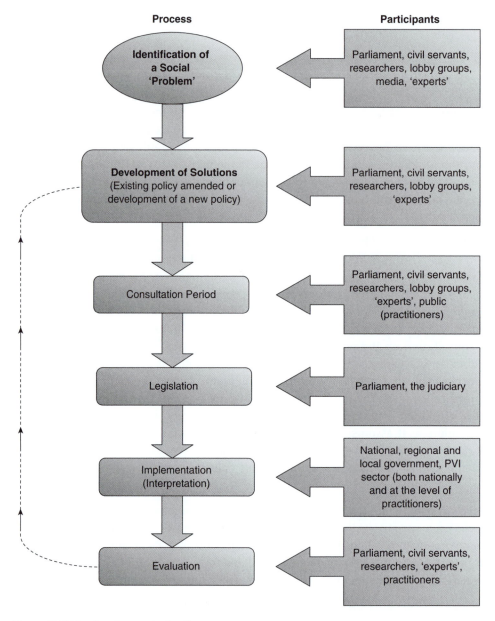

Figure 16.1 The development of policy

Education policy, therefore, becomes involved in the institutionalisation of childhood, having direct implications for the ways in which children live their lives (Moss and Petrie, 2002).

Where the outcomes of the policy are clear and relate to the group named in the policy (e.g. children), they are direct outcomes, but there will also be secondary and indirect outcomes for other members of society. Continuing with the example of education policy, the direct outcomes are that children become more educated (albeit in a particular form of education as defined by the state), but the secondary outcomes will include the social and economic gains of a more educated population that can compete in the global knowledge economy. Indirect outcomes are that parental time can be freed up (whilst the children are at school) enabling them to enter employment, further contributing to possible economic gains.

Equally, policies that are for other groups of society will have implications for children. The more obvious examples are in relation to *family* policy developments. For example, there have been numerous policy developments that can be referred to as 'activation' policies, whereby unemployed parents (primarily those who are dependent on the state) are incentivised to enter employment. The incentives can involve the offering of a reward for entering employment or they can specify tougher sanctions for those who remain on benefits for a long period of time. Under the rewards based approach, the UK has adopted a system of tax credits that offer support towards the costs of childcare based on family income. Under the sanctions approach, UK governments have increased the expectation that lone parents will look for work, adjusting the length of their benefits entitlement according to the age of their youngest child. The result is that once the youngest child reaches the age of five there is an expectation that a lone parent will look for work or enter training or they could find their benefits removed. Both tax credits and the tougher sanctions for lone parents have implications for the lives of children as they may find themselves having to attend an after school club, for example.

Early childhood education and care policy

Early childhood education and care policy is more clearly focused on childhood and therefore we can anticipate that it will have consequences for the lives of children. However, whilst policy may appear to be focused on children, secondary and indirect outcomes can lead us to question whether policy in the name of children is really about children and childhood. For many years children were largely invisible in policy, being referred to in relation to the family rather than having policy developments targeted specifically at them (Daniel and Ivatts, 1998). Education offers an exception to this invisibility, but only in relation to school age education. Through focusing on ECEC, I am considering services for children prior to school entry (e.g. nursery, daycare, preschool) and those that fit around school (e.g. holiday clubs). The provision of ECEC services can be regarded as a relatively recent policy phenomenon. Whilst Britain has a long history of philanthropic pioneers in ECEC, motivated by a desire to care for and educate (often disadvantaged) children, policy makers have been somewhat slower on the uptake (see Selbie *et al.*, 2015).

Prior to the 1980s there was little national political interest in ECEC, with some policy developments emerging in the 1980s and early 1990s (Moss, 2014). It was not until 1997 and the election of New Labour that ECEC could be seen as playing a core role in social policy provision. Building on emerging ECEC research and debates, New Labour developed a number of initiatives that arguably had ECEC at their centre. The Labour government's policy focus on ECEC presented a shift in political thinking that saw children as the direct focus of policy development and not just the secondary beneficiaries of family policy (Williams, 2004). The National Childcare Strategy focused on the quality, affordability and accessibility of ECEC, later introducing flexibility into the commitments (HM Treasury, 2004). The investment in ECEC services represents a social investment strategy, characterised by the dual aims of supporting parental employment and investing in children's futures. 'Childcare' services (such as those for children from birth to three years of age) were regarded as having an important function in supporting parental employment, whilst early education places were seen to provide the foundations for children's lifelong learning. Having been criticised for a split system of childcare and early education (see Bennett, 2003; Moss, 2006), New Labour attempted to bridge the divide by advocating a system of 'educare'. Examples include developing one curriculum for both services (the Early Years Foundation Stage) and having one inspection process (where previously there were separate childcare and early education registers). However, the relationship has never been an easy one due to persistent divides in how services are funded (early education is free, childcare is only partially subsidised) and the different qualification requirements (Baldock *et al.*, 2005; Moss, 2014).

In 2010 New Labour lost power to a Conservative-Liberal Democrat coalition. Initial policy decisions around ECEC for the coalition were in relation to cuts (see HM Treasury, 2010) as Britain, along with other European countries, faced a period of austerity in response to a global economic down turn (Campbell-Barr and Oakley, 2014). Following the cuts there was a period of silence from the coalition in regards to ECEC. Then in 2013 *More Great Childcare* (DfE, 2013a) and *More Affordable Childcare* (DfE, 2013b) were published. The publications continued the focus on quality, affordable and accessible ECEC (Paull, 2014). However, whilst New Labour advocated 'educare' there was a separate emphasis from the coalition, whereby *More Great Childcare* was focused on the provision of early years education services as a form of early intervention and *More Affordable Childcare* was centred on childcare to support working parents. In May 2015 the Conservatives won a majority. Their manifesto included increasing the number of hours of free childcare that parents would be entitled to, but it is yet to be seen whether this will be intended more as childcare to support working parents or as early intervention for the benefit of children.

Why invest in early childhood education and care?

The interest in developing policies targeted directly at ECEC was the result of a number of factors: research that resulted in greater knowledge about child development; research on the cost benefits of ECEC for national economies; research on the role of childcare in supporting family employment; feminism (more specifically changes in understandings of women's roles and motherhood); equality agendas (such as ensuring mothers had equality of access to the labour market and addressing child poverty); changes in family structures; the position of the economy; pressure from lobby groups (Randall, 2000); and the influence of supra-national organisations such as the European Union and OECD (Campbell-Barr and Nygard, 2014). In acknowledging the influence of each of these factors, we can begin to see how policy develops within the social and political context and can be a response to social changes and pressures.

One contextual feature that remains a strong influence on policy development is economics. I have already outlined how ECEC has been framed as a social investment strategy due to its function in supporting parental employment and the holistic development of the child. In economic terms we can see a relationship with parental employment, but child development has also become something to be monetarily valued.

The monetary value of ECEC has been conceptualised in relation to human capital theory, whereby ECEC supports investment in the knowledge, skills and competences of individuals for their individual success and that of the society in which they live (OECD, 1998). The economic persuasiveness of human capital theory has seen it gain a global profile, with supra-national organisations advocating an investment in ECEC to provide the foundations for lifelong learning (e.g. World Bank, 2003; European Commission, 2011). There are a number of high profile studies that are used as the justification for investing in ECEC: the Perry Preschool programme (also known as High Scope), the Abecedarian project and the Chicago Child-Parent Centers (see Penn, 2010 and Campbell-Barr, 2012). The studies provide claims that for every $1 invested, between $3.78 and $7.16 can be saved in the future through a reduction in public spending on, for example, additional education support, crime and teenage pregnancy. The notion of 'invest now, save later' is a clear example of the identification of a social problem and the development of an initiative to combat it. However, the use of the research evidence to support this investment needs to be carefully considered. The studies are all American and are largely targeted at African-American and Hispanic populations, raising questions as to their applicability to other countries and populations in the world. Also, the sample sizes for the projects are small (for example only 123 participants took part in the Perry Pre-school project) raising methodological questions about the study. Further, questions have been raised about the interpretation of human capital theory to conceptualise understandings of value in largely financial terms.

Heckman, a Nobel prize winner for economics and advocate of investing in early years education, has critiqued evaluations of investment in ECEC for being overly focused on cognitive test scores rather than the holistic development of children (Heckman, 2000). In political terms there is also the issue that the investment will not yield returns within the same parliamentary period. Despite the concerns raised around both the application of human capital theory and the research that underpins it (Penn, 2010; Campbell-Barr, 2012), the research has proved persuasive.

The quality of early childhood education and care

In England, The Effective Provision of Pre-School Education (EPPE) project (Sylva *et al.*, 2004) is contributing to the knowledge base on the role of ECEC in supporting child development. The EPPE project is a very good example of the interplay between research, policy and practice. Following the introduction of the National Childcare Strategy, New Labour (which upheld the notion of evidence-based policy making) commissioned the EPPE project – the first major study in the UK to focus on the provision of early education. The longitudinal study has tracked more than 3,000 children from attendance (and non-attendance) at preschool through to their GCSEs (under what is now the Effective Pre-School, Primary and Secondary Education, EPPSE, project). The findings from the project have supported claims for investing in early years education to support the lifelong learning of children, whilst shaping understandings of what constitutes quality in ECEC in England and beyond.

Supported by other research, both prior (e.g. Osborn and Millbank, 1987; Schweinhart *et al.*, 1993) and subsequent (e.g. Mathers and Smees, 2014) to the EPPE research, the evidence base is that the *quality* of provision will affect outcomes for children. I am not disputing that early years provision is a good thing for children and wider society, but I do want to question how understandings of quality and outcomes are being constructed. For quality to be determined it must correlate with a desirable outcome. In the US studies referred to above we see that their desirable outcomes were in relation to reductions in crime, teenage pregnancy and educational intervention. Within human capital theory we see a privileging of knowledge and skills – often associated with cognitive ability. The result is that quality is shaped by socially constructed understandings of specific desirable outcomes. However, we need to consider who it is that determines which outcomes are desirable and open ourselves up to the possibility of privileging other outcomes.

If we return to the understandings of social policy presented at the start of the chapter, we can see that policy is concerned with social problems and finding interventions that will provide solutions. In the case of ECEC, early intervention has become shaped by a view of what we want children to be in the future and the knowledge that we think they will need. Children become valued for what they will become rather than what they are. When government policymakers invest in the future they are gambling on what they see as the greatest potential risks (Piper, 2008). However, when deciding what to invest in, the government also has to make a number of assumptions, such as what knowledge the future workforce will need and how many jobs will be available to employ growing numbers of highly skilled people. Debates around school readiness indicate that we, as a society, are not comfortable with the notion that ECEC is just the path to the next stage of development and that we want to question/challenge understandings of value in ECEC (Campbell-Barr, 2012). Whilst we may wish to move assessments of value in ECEC beyond knowledge, skills and economic assessments, we have to be mindful of how research into the quality of ECEC is often conducted.

Research into quality privileges quantitative approaches as they are regarded as providing reliable, objective indicators of quality that are favoured in modernist societies (see Dahlberg *et al.*, 2007). However, such an instrumental approach to an assessment of quality runs the risk of losing sight of other important features. Often the aspects of quality that are difficult to measure are obscured in favour of more readily quantifiable indicators. The result is that features that are harder to value, such as emotions and relationships, may disappear from our evaluations (Held, 2002). Whilst concepts of quality and value for ECEC are culturally constructed, they interact with wider social and political structures such as the privileging of modernism and the neo-liberal underpinning of policy in the UK. Such structures are a powerful force in policy making and offer some explanation for why national policy may not feel relevant at a local level or why national policy does not seem to reflect practice.

The neo-liberal history of UK politics influences how policy has developed in ECEC (and other areas). The economic liberalisation and market economy focus of the approach is reflected in the reliance on a mixed market model in ECEC, whereby private, voluntary, independent and maintained (state) providers are all involved in providing ECEC (see Penn, 2012 for further discussion). Yet this brings with it a set of challenges when considering the quality of provision. In opting for a mixed market model, there is a need to ensure that the market is monitored in some way so as to ensure that it is meeting policy objectives. In the UK the monitoring is undertaken by requiring providers to meet set curriculum standards in order to be registered with their regional body, with only registered providers being eligible for funding. Within the UK there are four regional bodies that represent the four nations of the UK. Each body represents a centralised system of defining and monitoring the quality of provision. The consequences for practice are that ECEC practitioners find themselves subject to a national quality and curriculum framework that guides their practice. This view of quality is shaped by studies such as EPPE and helps ensure that all providers are working towards the desired outcomes (in this instance Early Learning Goals). Whilst monitoring in England is based on 'improvement through inspection' (Matthews and Sammons, 2004), there are concerns about the extent to which this is realised, due to variations in whether providers understand the regulation systems, the relationships between inspectors and providers (see Ho *et al.*, 2010), the frequency of inspections and the understanding of ECEC by inspectors (Campbell-Barr, 2009a). Further critiques are that ECEC providers find themselves operating in a managerialist system of accountability and performativity (Osgood, 2006).

Up-skilling the workforce

The managerialist agendas of policy makers have also been observed in the professionalisation of the ECEC workforce. Within the National Childcare Strategy there have been a number of policies that have looked at the skill level of the workforce (e.g. DfES, 2003 and DCSF, 2007). In 2007 the Early Years Professional Status (EYPS) was introduced as a Level Six qualification for those working in ECEC. The EYPS was a response to evidence that there was an association between qualifications and the quality of ECEC (such as was found in the EPPE study). In particular, the EYPS was targeted at the private, voluntary and independent sectors where staff had a history of lower level qualifications. Initial targets to introduce one Early Years Professional into every setting by 2015 were dropped following the 2010 Spending Review. In 2012 Cathy Nutbrown published her review, commissioned by the DfE (Nutbrown, 2012) looking at the current qualification structures of ECEC. The review reiterated the importance of quality in the provision of ECEC with clear recognition of the role that staff have in the provision of high quality services. However, the review questioned the rigour and depth of the qualifications on offer to ECEC practitioners. One result was that the EYPS was replaced with the Early Years Teacher Status (EYTS).

One of the criticisms of the qualifications in ECEC is that the training requirements have been imposed on those working in ECEC with little workforce engagement (Osgood, 2006; McGillivray, 2008; Miller, 2008). In particular, those who work in ECEC have not been consulted on the nature of the skills needed for this work. Nor is there a consideration of how professionalisation sits with historical constructions of the ECEC sector as requiring attributes such as being maternal, kind, warm, sensitive and liking children (McGillivray, 2008). Historical constructs of those working in ECEC are based on the assumption of philanthropic motivations to care for and nurture children. The notion of protecting children from the corruption of the adult world can be seen as the cornerstone of policy developments around children (Moss and Petrie, 2002). This desire to protect children can be associated with the romantic discourse (see Chapter 13) which argues that children need nurturing and protecting. Yet the romantic discourse is at odds with the managerialist agendas of ECEC policy initiatives (see Osgood, 2004; Campbell-Barr, 2009b).

Providers find themselves negotiating between their motivations for entering the ECEC workforce – to care for and educate children – and the motivations of policy makers. Systems of accountability are designed to ensure that those working in ECEC will work within policy frameworks. Professionalisation agendas advocate that practitioners should take responsibility for their actions, including their responses to policy, but this raises the question of whether policy makers know best. Should the research evidence that informs policy developments override the views and experiences of those who work in ECEC?

The developments around the professionalisation of the ECEC workforce demonstrate the fluid nature of policy. In an ideal world policymakers would be able to start from a blank slate, but instead they are involved in a process of political and social interaction where they make adjustments to existing policies to suit the political ideology of the party/parties in power (Alcock, 2004). Even where a political party has introduced policies, they will adjust them (as they see how they are applied in practice) to ensure that they continue to meet their political objectives. Given the fluid nature of policy development, and the role of social interaction in this process, practitioners must be involved in this interaction if their perspective is to be heard.

The interplay of research and policy: when ideologies collide

Above, I have used EPPE as an example of how policy makers have engaged with research findings to inform policy decisions. The interplay between policy formation and research can take one of two forms:

1. Social policy research can monitor, evaluate (and suggest changes to) existing policy.

2. Research can uncover findings that suggest a need for new policies or for changes to existing ones (see Alcock, 2004).

EPPE can be seen to represent both of these aspects as it evaluated the early years provision that was available at that time, but the findings have influenced many recent policy developments as well as informing subsequent research studies. More generally, evaluation research, which can range from quick literature reviews to extensive field research (Forman and Baldwin, 2007), looks at how policy is implemented, why it is implemented and whether it should be implemented at all. An essential question that is typically asked is whether the intervention (e.g. the policy initiative) has achieved the anticipated goals (Bryman, 2004). The connection between research and policy in evaluation research is relatively linear, but it might not always be transparent. For example, the research may be closely connected with the development of policy, but the relationship may not be politically neutral and objective.

Where research uncovers findings that have implications for policy, the relationship between policy and research is less clear. It can take time for research, such as that which demonstrated the benefits of ECEC, to result in policy changes (see Randall, 2000). Yet it is more than this; research findings are only likely to be acted on where they fit the political ideology of the policy makers (Alcock, 2004) and at times this can mean that the findings are interpreted to fit the ideology of the policy makers.

When *More Great Childcare* was published it drew on the EPPE findings in relation to ECEC's support for child development and progress at school, particularly for the most disadvantaged (DfE, 2013b: 15, citing Sylva *et al.*, 2004). *More Great Childcare* also stressed the importance of the quality of ECEC, referencing EPPE. Whilst these policies were allegedly informed by research, the proposals caused some alarm (e.g. Nursery World, 2013; NUT, 2013). Much of the concern focused on the proposed changes to ratios, the introduction of child-minding agencies and Ofsted becoming the sole arbiter of quality. In addition to the sector's response, Naomi Eisenstadt, Kathy Sylva, Sandra Mathers and Brenda Taggart – all well regarded academics in ECEC – published a document outlining their concerns about the proposals. Of particular interest for this chapter is that this document outlines their concerns on the misuse of research – including their own (Eisenstadt *et al.*, 2013). The outcome was that the government did a U-turn on the proposed changes to ratios whilst consultations on the other areas went ahead. Despite continued concerns, some features of *More Great Childcare* (such as Ofsted being the sole arbiter of quality) have been implemented. Whilst this may be construed as only being a partial victory for the sector, for me it represents the power of the sector's voice, but also the importance of knowing the research evidence. As a sector, our collective voice and expertise can be powerful, but ultimately it is those in the ECEC workforce who will put policy into practice and this is where it is important to have an understanding of research and also of the particular cultural context in which you work.

The research, policy and practice triangle

The implementation of policy into practice is an interpretative and playful process. How do we know this? Because all settings are different. The implementation of policy into practice reflects a process of micro policy development. Echoing the national level, at the practitioner level there are a series of inputs that shape practice: policy, research, children, parents, colleagues, etc. Reflection acts as a form of self-evaluation, enabling us to consider which inputs are effective in achieving the desired outcomes of supporting the children and families that we work with (see Chapter 17). This process of interpreting policies will enable practice to continue to develop as providers will (in theory) reflect on their practice and try new things. Allowing room for this playfulness is important as it helps to ensure that policy is not too restricting, but it can also develop a sense of ownership of the policy implementation process.

As we interpret policy and reflect on the inputs that are informing our practice, we have to be mindful that, just as at the national level, we can be shaped by our own ideologies. Reflecting on practice can help to develop an understanding of our ideologies (e.g. why we may not like some policy initiatives), but also it can provide the time to consider to what extent we act on the different inputs. We may critique policy for not considering the views of practitioners, but this highlights the importance of recognising all of the different inputs in our own practice. At a micro policy level, settings need to recognise the social interactions that inform their own policy development and implementation.

The relationship between research, policy and practice is complex and dynamic. Each can inform and shape the others, whether by providing support or challenges. Although (at the national policy level) the government has the power to create policies, it may not always be the most powerful contributor to the research, policy and practice triangle. Both researchers and practitioners can provide evidence that can inform policy. The response to *More Great Childcare* is evidence of the power of the expertise in ECEC coming together to challenge policy proposals. Whilst practitioners are in a position to interact with parents and children every day that their setting is open, at the national policy level the social interaction is more artificial, formal and mediated by processes of representation. Although the national policy process includes opportunities for interaction (e.g. research and consultation), practitioners have to ensure that they are actively involved if it is to reflect the level of social interaction that takes place at the micro level.

Figure 16.2 represents the interplay between research policy and practice, but the shape of the triangle can vary. We have to be mindful of the political ideologies of the party or parties seeking to introduce any policy, as unwelcome evidence from research or practice may have been ignored. Whilst policymakers seek to promote

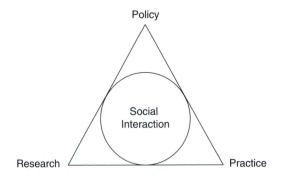

Figure 16.2 The research, policy and practice triangle

social well-being, different political parties will have varying views on how best to achieve this. Thus the importance attached to each corner of the triangle can vary.

What is evident is that despite a professed focus on social well-being, this is not the sole influence on policy making. Increasingly, economic factors determine the shape of ECEC policy. Neo-liberalism (as reflected in our market economy), the knowledge economy (as seen in human capital theory) and economic down turns can influence both the form and level of investment in ECEC. Such influences demonstrate how policies in the name of children and childhood and social well-being are frequently overridden by economics. Whilst I recognise that social and economic well-being will interact and need to be balanced against each other, my fear is that early childhood education and care policy has forgotten that its focus is children and childhood.

ACTIVITY

Visit the DfE's website and look at their consultation pages: https://www.education.gov. uk/consultations/ In a small group find a consultation that you feel is relevant. Discuss the consultation and develop a group response and submit it – remember, you have expert knowledge in Early Childhood Studies and can contribute to the debates taking place!

Issue for debate: The professionalisation of the ECEC workforce has raised debates as to what skills are needed to work with children. What are the skills that you feel are needed and how do they relate to those advocated by policy?

FURTHER READING

Eisenstadt, N., Sylva, K., Mathers, S. and Taggart, B. (2013) *More Great Childcare: Research Evidence*, available at http://www.ecersuk.org/resources/More+Great+Childcare+Research+Evidence+March+2013.pdf (accessed 18 September 2014).

This is a short but interesting piece as it demonstrates what the researchers feel are the important aspects around quality ECEC and how they relate to what has been proposed by government.

Moss, P. (2014) Early childhood policy in England 1997–2013: anatomy of a missed opportunity. *International Journal of Early Years Education*, 22(4): 346–58.

This article provides a comprehensive overview of policy developments in ECEC in England, picking up on many of the issues above. The article critiques the implementation of ECEC policy for building on what has gone before, rather than attempting to rethink the way we approach ECEC policy.

REFERENCES

Alcock, C., Payne, S. and Sullivan, M. (2004) *Introducing Social Policy*. Harlow: Pearson Education.

Alcock, P. (2004) Social Policy and Professional Practice. In S. Becker and A. Bryman, *Understanding Research for Social Policy and Practice: Themes, Methods and Approaches*. Bristol: Policy Press.

Baldock, P., Fitzgerald, D., Kay, J. (2005) *Understanding Early Years Policy*. London: SAGE.

Bennett, J. (2003) Starting strong: the persistent division between care and education. *Journal of Early Childhood Research*, 1(1): 21–48.

Bryman, A. (2004) *Social Research Methods*. Oxford: Oxford University Press.

Campbell-Barr, V. (2009a) Contextual issues in assessing value for money in early years education. *National Institutes Economic Review*, 207(1): 90–101.

Campbell-Barr, V. (2009b) Care and business orientations in the delivery of childcare: an exploratory study. *Journal of Early Childhood Research*, 7 (1): 76–93.

Campbell-Barr, V. (2012) Early years education and the value for money folklore. *European Early Childhood Education Research Journal*, 20(3): 423–37.

Campbell-Barr, V. and Nygard, M. (2014) Losing sight of the child? Human capital theory and its role for early childhood education and care policies in Finland and England since the mid-1990s. *Contemporary Issues in Early Childhood*, 15(4): 346–359.

Campbell-Barr, V. and Oakley, A. (2014) Providing choice? A comparison of UK and Ireland's family support in a time of austerity. *Journal of International and Comparative Social Policy*, http://dx.doi.org/1 0.1080/21699763.2014.951381 (accessed 15 April 2015).

Dahlberg, G., Moss, P. and Pence, A. (2007) *Beyond Quality in Early Childhood Education and Care: Languages of Evaluation* (2nd edn). Abingdon: Routledge.

Daniel, P. and Ivatts, J. (1998) *Children and Social Policy*. Hampshire: Macmillan Press.

DCSF (Department for Children, Schools and Families) (2007) *The Children's Plan: Building Brighter Futures*. Norwich: The Stationery Office.

Dean, H. (2005) *Social Policy: Short Introductions*. Cambridge: Polity Press.

DfE (Department for Education) (2013a) *More Great Childcare: Raising Quality and Giving Parents More Choice*. London: The Stationery Office.

DfE (Department for Education) (2013b) *More Affordable Childcare*. London: The Stationery Office.

DfES (Department for Education and Skills) (2003) *Every Child Matters: Green Paper*. London: The Stationery Office.

Eisenstadt, N., Sylva, K., Mathers, S. and Taggart, B. (2013) *More Great Childcare: Research Evidence*. Available at: http://www.ecersuk.org/resources/More+Great+Childcare+Research+Evidence+Ma rch+2013.pdf (accessed 18 September 2014).

European Commission (2011) *Early Childhood Education and Care: Providing Our Children with the Best Start for the World of Tomorrow*. Brussels: European Commission.

Forman, F. and Baldwin, N. (2007) *Mastering British Politics* (5th edn). Hampshire: Macmillan Press.

Heckman, J.J. (2000) *Invest in the Very Young*. Chicago, IL: Ounce of Prevention Fund and the University of Chicago Harris School of Public Policy Studies.

Held, V. (2002) Care and the extension of markets. *Hypatia*, 17(2): 19–33.

HM Treasury (2004) *Choice for Parents, the Best Start for Children: A Ten-year Strategy for Childcare*. London: HMSO.

HM Treasury (2010) *Spending Review 2010*. Norwich: The Stationery Office.

Ho, D., Campbell-Barr, V. and Leeson, C. (2010) Quality improvement in early years settings in Hong Kong and England. *International Journal of Early Years Education*, 18(3): 243–58.

McGillivray, G. (2008) Nannies, nursery nurses and early years professionals: constructions of professional identity in the early years workforce in England. *European Early Childhood Education Research Journal*, 16(2): 242–54.

Mathers, S. and Smees, R. (2014) *Quality and Inequality: Do three- and four- year-olds in deprived areas experience lower quality early years provision?* London: Nuffield Foundation. Available at: http://www. nuffieldfoundation.org/sites/default/files/files/Quality_inequality_childcare_mathers_29_05_14.pdf (accessed 13 January 2015).

Matthews, P. and Sammons, P. (2004) *Improvement through Inspection: An Evaluation of the Impact of Ofsted's Work.* London: Ofsted and Crown Copyright.

Miller, L. (2008) Developing professionalism within a regulatory framework in England: challenges and possibilities. *European Early Childhood Education Research Journal*, 16(2): 255–68.

Moss, P. (2006) Farewell to childcare? *National Institute Economic Review*, 195(1): 70–83.

Moss, P. (2014) Early childhood policy in England 1997–2013: anatomy of a missed opportunity. *International Journal of Early Years Education*, 22(4): 346–58.

Moss, P. and Petrie, P. (2002) *From Children's Services to Children's Spaces, Public Policy and Childhood.* London: RoutledgeFalmer.

Nursery World (2013) Childcare sector overwhelmingly oppose ratio changes. Available at: http://www.nurseryworld.co.uk/nursery-world/news/1106526/childcare-sector-overwhelmingly-opposes-ratio-changes (accessed 18 September 2014).

NUT (2013) *More Great Childcare Consultation – NUT Response.* Available at: http://www.teachers.org.uk/node/18045 (accessed 18 September 2014).

Nutbrown, C. (2012) *Foundations for Quality: The Independent Review of Early Education and Childcare Qualifications. Final Report.* London: DfE. Available at https://www.gov.uk/government/publications/nutbrown-review-foundations-for-quality (accessed 15 April 2015).

OECD (1998) *Human Capital Investment: An International Comparison.* London: OECD.

Osborn, A.F. and Milbank, J.E. (1987) *The Effects of Early Education: A Report from the Child Health and Education Study.* Oxford: Clarendon Press.

Osgood, J. (2004) Time to get down to business? The responses of early years practitioners to entrepreneurial approaches to professionalism. *Journal of Early Childhood Research*, 2(1): 5–24.

Osgood, J. (2006) Deconstructing professionalism in early childhood education: resisting the regulatory gaze. *Contemporary Issues in Early Childhood*, 7(1): 5–14.

Paull, G. (2014) Can government intervention in childcare be justified? *Economic Affairs*, 34(1): 14–34.

Penn, H. (2010) Shaping the future: how human capital arguments about investment in early childhood are being (mis)used in poor countries. In N. Yelland (ed.), *Contemporary Perspectives on Early Childhood Education.* Maidenhead: Open University Press.

Penn, H. (2012) Childcare markets: do they work? In E. Lloyd and H. Penn (eds), *Childcare Markets: Can they Deliver an Equitable Service?* Bristol: Policy Press.

Piper, C. (2008) *Investing in Children: Policy, Law and Practice in Context.* Devon: Willan Publishing.

Randall, V. (2000) *The Politics of Child Daycare in Britain.* Oxford: Oxford University Press.

Schweinhart, L.J., Barnes, H. and Weikhart, D. (eds) (1993) *Significant Benefits: The High/Scope Perry Pre-school Study Through Age 27.* Michigan: High/Scope Press.

Selbie, P., Blakemore, L., Farley, C. and Campbell-Barr, V. (2015) Britain: a complex mix of philosophy and politics. In V. Campbell-Barr and J. Georgeson (eds), *International Perspectives on Workforce Development in Early Childhood Education and Care: History, Philosophy and Politics.* Herts: Critical Publishing.

Sylva, K., Melhuish, E.C., Sammons, P., Siraj-Blatchford, I. and Taggart, B. (2004) *The Effective Provision of Pre-school Education (EPPE) Project: Final Report,* London: DfES/Institute of Education, University of London.

Williams, F. (2004) *Rethinking Families.* London: Calouste Gulbenkian Foundation.

World Bank (2003) *Life-long Learning in the Global Knowledge Economy: Challenges for Developing Countries.* Washington, DC: World Bank.

Part 5

Researching practice: developing critical engagement

17 In praise of reflective practice

Caroline Leeson and Victoria Bamsey

Introduction

An early years practitioner helps children to get changed for a gym session, assisting with zips and buttons. A colleague points out that she helped the boys far more than the girls and encouraged the girls to manage themselves. Both practitioners paused to think about what that meant, why it might be, what had been in her mind, what messages she was giving to the children and whether they had noticed. They decided to observe their own behaviour, and that of other colleagues, over the following days and explore the implications for their practice and for the children in their care.

A nursery offers Duplo bricks that have been disinfected in boiling water and thereby lost their shape and ability to click together. The fact that the Duplo has been rendered useless is not noticed and the practice continues over several years, with staff surprised that the children do not play with it. A practitioner who takes time to notice what is going on, who thinks about the implications of what she sees and who questions the practice, would suggest alternative ways of ensuring the bricks are kept clean without damaging their play value.

A social worker seems extremely keen to remove a child from an abusive household before she has fully engaged with the parents and established what might be done to remedy the situation. When encouraged to reflect, it becomes apparent that her own abusive background has caused over-identification with the child and failure to see the many positive signs suggesting that the family would benefit from active help rather than removal of the child. Working reflectively with colleagues becomes a social process, making decisions openly and honestly, questioning the influence of personal prejudice, social policy or current trends and examining issues critically and sensitively.

In this chapter, we argue that reflective practice should be regarded as an integral part of developing competent professionals in early years care and education and we link our argument to recent policy initiatives such as the Teaching Standards (Teaching Agency, 2013). We will look at different theoretical models of reflection and explore how reflective skills may be encouraged, achieved and maintained. In attempting to make sense of this area, we ask a number of questions – what is reflective practice, why should we engage in it, how do we actually do it, who can help with the process and what are the obstacles and opportunities that it presents? Through our discussions we hope to encourage you to try out some of the methods we describe, to value the importance of reflective practice and embed these ideas by using some of the methods we suggest.

Why should we engage in reflective practice?

Early years practitioners can potentially have a huge impact on the lives of the children they work with. The recent 'Effective Pre-School, Primary and Secondary Education' (EPPSE) Report (Sylva *et al.*, 2014) highlights that children who attend preschool have better outcomes not only through their primary school education but right through to and including their GCSE results; going to a high quality preschool showed the most positive effects. Critically reflective, well qualified staff, open to change and challenge (Hayes *et al.*, 2014), are a key element of the quality of what preschool can offer.

The role of the early years practitioner in a child's development is key as they build attachments, provide learning opportunities, understand child development and work with a child's family. The Children's Workforce Strategy recognised this, stating that 'the early years workforce is critical to … giving children the best start in life' (DfES, 2005: 24). As a result both the Teacher Standards (Early Years) (Teaching Agency, 2013) and the Early Years Educator Criteria (NCTL, 2013) highlight the need for reflection.

To ensure that children's needs are met there is an expectation that continuous improvement and adaptation of practice will be informed by ongoing personal development and reflection. This involves professional judgement, but what do we mean by this? Horwath and Thurlow (2004: 9) refer to Eraut's description of professional judgement as 'the interpretative use of knowledge' and they recognise that 'it also involves practical wisdom, a sense of purpose, appropriateness and feasibility'. It is vital to use systematic processes for collecting information, that show the steps taken to analyse and subsequently act, in order to better understand the basis of our decision making. Practitioners are then able to make open and honest professional judgements that acknowledge the needs and requirements of those they work with. It also means that decisions and actions are made from an informed position, making full use of the theory, knowledge and understanding available to us (Attard, 2008).

Focusing in more closely on the pedagogic role of the early years practitioner, Sylva *et al.* (2010: 149–50) described this as the set of 'techniques and strategies that enabled learning to take place … that provided opportunities for the acquisition of knowledge, skills, attitudes and dispositions'. Reflective practice should therefore recognise these professional and pedagogic roles; what techniques and strategies is the early years practitioner employing, and how is this affecting the child's acquisition of knowledge, skills, attitudes and/or dispositions? However, such reflective practice needs to mean something to the practitioner involved, to fit into daily life, to ensure valuable time is not unnecessarily taken up, and to make sense in the situation faced by each practitioner.

It is all too easy to work through the day following established routines, applying a standardised sequence of events and activities which have been designed to ensure that children have access to a range of resources to support learning across the EYFS as well as access to the outdoors. But how are children really benefiting from the activities offered? Are the Duplo bricks appropriate for children's developmental stage, meeting their interests and supporting their learning? What does the outside space offer? What about a child's well-being and involvement? How are characteristics of effective learning supported? As Ofsted (2013: 5) has stated, 'children's future success' depends on getting 'it right first time' for them, and giving them 'the very best start'. The key to making the right decisions for practice in settings is recognising the importance of reflection and that 'reflective practice is presented as an outlook for everyone' (Lindon, 2012: 1).

Reflective practice enables early years practitioners to mediate and adapt statutory frameworks, permitting innovative and creative practice to proliferate, thereby improving the quality of learning and the emotional climate that both the practitioner and the children experience (Pollard, 2002). Policy initiatives such as the National Professional Qualification in Integrated Centre Leadership (NPQICL) (NCSL, 2004) sought to promote the use of reflective practice. The new Teaching Standards (Early Years) include the need to reflect on and evaluate practice (Teaching Agency, 2013) and Early Years Educators are also expected to engage in CPD and reflective practice. Nevertheless, there still appears to be a preference in the workplace for having fact-based, routine responses to situations (Lam *et al.*, 2007) which can lead to greater anxiety and uncertainty among practitioners (Ruch, 2002; Attard, 2008) and a poor experience for children and families (Saltiel, 2003). Reflective practice can reduce uncertainty and enable practitioners to transfer knowledge and skills between different situations (Gould and Taylor, 1996). We argue that by engaging with our work in these ways we can begin to meet the requirements of our respective professions with confidence and remain alive to the many possibilities in our practice.

Indeed, Donald Schön (1983) suggests that the ability to reflect on action and thereby engage in a personal journey of lifelong learning is a defining characteristic of professional practice. Schön argues that a model of education in which students are given information as one would fill a glass and are sent into situations where they are expected simply to spill out that knowledge is not good practice and will lead to ineffective work. Rather, we should be encouraging the creation of opportunities to link theory to practice, to understand our actions and the impact of those actions, developing enhanced knowledge and skills that can be taken into subsequent situations. Therefore, as the demand increases for early years practitioners to be in the front line in improving the life chances for young children and their families (DfE, 2014), reflective practice would appear to be highly relevant and of great importance. We commend the policy attempts, indicated above, that acknowledge and promote the central position of reflection in effective quality practice.

Reflective practice should be available to all as a cultural mode of working. It should not be regarded as a 'bolt on', an optional extra or an indulgent 'navel gazing' exercise: it should be a conscious act, a way of being and a standard practice of examining the apparently routine and mundane, noticing new subtleties and making fresh connections for others and ourselves (Mason, 2002). If practitioners engage in reflective practice in this way the benefits include opportunities to: develop a greater understanding of ourselves and our own motivations; resolve past conflicts; develop new skills, knowledge and understanding in the workplace; and begin to question why we do things the way we do.

When decisions and actions are considered, creative, and informed by relationships with each person as a unique individual, there are also benefits for the people with whom practitioners work: other professionals, children, parents and colleagues.

What is reflective practice?

Reflective practice is taking the opportunity to think about the work that we are doing, either as we are doing it or after we have done it. This involves attempting to draw the lessons we can learn from our practice in terms of how our work has impacted upon us and others, and how it made or makes us feel about ourselves.

Reflecting *in* action (whilst doing something) and *on* action (following the action) (Schön, 1983) are critical skills that offer the opportunity to develop insight and understanding, especially in those professions, such as social work, teaching and health care, that have a substantial impact on the lives of others. It is our opinion that, unless we engage in this process, our work has the potential to be ill informed and possibly dangerous. We may perpetuate actions and decisions that no longer have relevance, simply because that is the way things have always been done.

The integration of knowledge and practice is a crucial aspect of reflective practice. Research has shown (Eraut, 1994; Ruch, 2002; Saltiel, 2003) that practitioners do not always see theory as related to real experience. Instead, theory is regarded as a sideshow; it is interesting, but not applicable to the situations that they work in and therefore feels remote and unusable. Schön (1983) talks about technical rationality, where knowledge is divorced from experience, where values underpinning prac-tice are never questioned and may not even be identified. This leaves practitioners unaware of how the context they work in liberates or constrains the decisions and actions they take.

Reflective practice should promote the application of theory when reflecting on experiences, events and situations, thereby encouraging a deeper understanding of the impact of one's work on oneself as well as on others. Schön would argue that reflection enables us to develop an understanding of the beliefs and principles that underpin our own practice. This is then articulated and explored with others through social processes as we learn to internalise challenges in our own thinking, and form a mutual understanding. The workplace should encourage and promote the develop-ment of the necessary skills, and create an ethos of reflective practice that ensures sensitive and effective actions are taken and risk is accepted as a necessary step in becoming self-aware.

Reflection is, therefore, not just thinking about what you do. Ghaye defines it as 'practice-with-principle': 'Being professionally self critical without being destructive and overly negative' (2011: 23). It is all too easy to become over-critical, to denigrate our own actions and doubt our practice. We should be very careful that we do not do this as it is personally damaging. This is often given as the reason why people do not reflect, preferring the less dangerous route of working by the book, on automatic pilot, or in our 'comfort zone', thereby becoming mindless practitioners.

Reflective practice demands that we go beyond simple observation (Brown and Rutter, 2008), challenging perceived wisdom, attempting to identify both the rational and the irrational. It involves moving to a place of understanding, acknowledging that every experience and every relationship is unique, worthy of reflection and note, rather than just another aspect of our working life. Reflective practice encourages us to find the creativity within uncertainty (Attard, 2008), allowing us to be alive to possibilities and to remain sensitive to the events and people around us (Mason, 2002).

How do we do it?

One of the difficulties we face when we engage in reflective practice is the myriad possible models available for developing the skills, which may lead to a confused attempt to identify which is 'best'.

Several writers on reflective practice identify cyclical models with stages frequently described as: having an experience, reflecting on this experience, taking learning from that reflection and using it to inform future practice (Lewin, 1946; Kolb, 1984; Gibbs, 1988). These stages are worked through systematically with equal importance given to each. These early models of 'experiential learning' (Kolb, 1984) have frequently been criticised as failing to emphasise the importance of reflection and because not all of the steps they identify will always fit with the ways in which people think (Pickles, 2003) or perform.

Seidel's model (1996, in Dempsey *et al.*, 2001) has similar stages, defined as looking backwards, looking inwards, looking outwards and looking forwards. Used to great effect on social work training courses this reflective approach has helped to improve the confidence and skills of many practitioners (Dempsey *et al.*, 2001). However, some may be uncomfortable with the highly personal and intimate questions which are asked in the promotion of such deep introspection and thought.

Seeking to address these criticisms, further models have been developed that encourage a different approach to deep reflection. For example, Pollard (2002) lists seven characteristics of reflective practice which encourage dialogue with colleagues and evidence-based reflections. Edward De Bono uses 'six thinking hats' to represent different ways of looking at a situation – focusing on the benefits, the difficulties, the facts, instincts, creativity, and the helicopter viewpoint (Lindon, 2012) each of which offers a different perspective. Similarly Stephen Brookfield (1995) recommends the use of 'critical lenses', looking at a situation from the viewpoint of others. All of these models offer clear frameworks and directions for reflection which are especially useful for those just starting a journey towards being a reflective practitioner.

We feel that the model developed by Ghaye (2011) gives excellent opportunities for reflection at different levels, enabling practitioners to improve and deepen their knowledge, skills and understanding as they become more proficient. This model sees reflection as a spiral of action, thought and understanding, rather than a closed circle, allowing for moving backwards to revisit steps and for development from one cycle onto another, similar in action to Dewey's model (1933). Ghaye emphasises the practice of placing any reflection within an organisational context, identifying how the workplace or society in which practitioners operate affects their actions and values and has the potential to exert power and influence over them. The underlying premise of Ghaye's model is that, at all times, practice is a value-laden occupation and that effective, reflective practitioners should make clear links between their values and their practice.

In the example at the very beginning of this chapter, the actions taken by the practitioner could have many underpinning values, grounded in their understanding of the respective positions of men and women in society. By reflecting, using models such as Ghaye's, an individual is enabled to develop both their personal and professional practice more deeply than if other, more closed, models were used. Such 'closed' models could be seen as suggesting that once one has extracted all the learning from an experience, that experience can be forgotten about and one can move on.

How do we actually do this in practice?

We have already seen the difficulties arising from practitioners not always appreciating the relevance of reflective activity and from the failure to create a culture of reflection *in* and *on* action. We have identified a number of potentially useful models, but how do we actually embody reflective practice in our work? First of all we should say that you need to find the model that works for you, given the requirements of your role, your setting, the parents and the children as well as the time available to engage in reflective practice. On a purely practical note, if it's too difficult it will not get done.

We should also acknowledge that reflection is not easy, the answers do not emerge instantly and one may exist in a state of uncertainty that is difficult to endure, especially when working in a culture that promotes certainty and precision (Attard, 2008). So we have to create an ethos in which reflective practice can flourish – a culture of trust, of working together in order for people to feel safe about opening up and examining their practice, to feel able to 'sink into your doubt and swim in your ocean of creativity' (Cadden, 2009: 38). Reflective practice requires a culture that respects the intrinsic value of each individual and promotes the belief that everyone has something worthwhile to say. The structure of the team and work context should offer containing and reflective spaces for practitioners to consider and share their ideas and practices (Ruch, 2007).

So time, space and the value placed on the activity are all important. What are you doing and why are you doing it? In a job that is carried out by people for people, it is important to consider what impact your actions may have on the children and on the setting.

Finally, we should think about the practical strategies available to us. One strategy is to write things down, engaging in an internal dialogue (Tsang, 2007) that allows us to think about actions for ourselves and then to share those thoughts and analyses with others, offering our experience to an individual or a group to be unpacked and investigated (Schön, 1983; Boud *et al.*, 1985; Gould and Taylor, 1996; Dempsey *et al.*, 2001;

Attard, 2008). Reflective journals are a popular tool for promoting engagement in internal dialogue. Practitioners are encouraged to write down general and particular experiences they have had throughout their day, reflecting on how events have affected them emotionally and intellectually (NCSL, 2004) before sharing their thoughts and emotions with others.

McDrury and Alterio (2000) advocate storytelling, where students engage with each other in narrative accounts, exploring what they have learned and understood. Eight different storytelling methods are identified, all of which use an informal setting with just one listener to a spontaneous story, an environment that they suggest offers the most learning and a sense of catharsis for the narrator:

> *One listener can provide undivided attention to the story and is more likely to focus on the affective domain. This pathway may also provide greater freedom for the teller to express unedited ideas, concerns and feelings. (McDrury and Alterio, 2000: 66)*

Statements of relevance have developed as an alternative way of encouraging reflection (Bourner *et al.*, 2002). A practitioner thinks about a learning event and writes down not only what they have learnt, but also how they might use that learning in the future. This work is shared with others for greater learning and understanding to take place. Statements of relevance are not simply descriptions and evaluations of the learning event, they are accounts that investigate feelings, current knowledge and procedures, and seem to correspond with the critical reflective stage of Ghaye's model.

Reflection can be encouraged through the use of 'sculpting', a family therapy technique which uses art as a medium for describing emotional situations and expressing associated feelings (Anderson, 1987), or through creative activities such as poetry or collage (Newton, 2004):

> *Taking time to make something, using the hands, gave people the opportunity to clarify thoughts or feelings, and to see the subject-matter in a new light. And having an image or physical object to present and discuss enabled them to communicate and connect with other people more directly. (Gauntlett, 2011: 4)*

What is evident in all of these strategies is the need for communication and discourse, a *'reflective conversation'* (Schön, 1983; Kolb, 1984) that offers a group of practitioners the opportunity to explore different perspectives, to become aware of the multitude of voices in each situation and to articulate the core values of respect, justice and equality (Tsang, 2007).

Who can help?

It would appear that we need other, likeminded people involved. We can only reflect so far on our own; we need the opportunity to co-reflect, to think about what we are looking at, to challenge our assumptions and prejudices and look at the things we are avoiding because they tell us things about ourselves which we would rather not face. Reflective practice gives us the opportunity to look at events or situations through the eyes of others or from different perspectives (Brookfield, 1995). Reflective practice is, potentially, a risky business, an interpersonal process that many are reluctant to engage in. Dewey (1933: 151) sums up this dilemma:

> *One can think reflectively only when one is willing to endure suspense and to undergo the trouble of searching. To many persons, both suspense of judgement and intellectual search are disagreeable, they want them to be ended as soon as possible. They cultivate an over positive and dogmatic habit of mind, or feel, perhaps, that a condition of doubt will be regarded as evidence of mental inferiority. We must be willing to sustain and protract that state of doubt which is the stimulus to thorough enquiry.*

Ruch (2002) discusses a state of confusion and anxiety that often prevents practitioners from taking these risky steps in analysis and reflection. She cites Papell (1996: 19, in Ruch 2002: 203):

> *Social work learners must perceive the human situation which they confront in their practice and recognise that their perceptions are filtered through their own thinking and knowing processes, through their own emotions and feeling processes and through the way they themselves integrate and regulate their own doing and behaving. Knowing the self is more than knowing how one feels. It is knowing how one thinks and acts.*

This raises considerable anxiety around the amount of personal exposure that may be required. Lindon (2012) explores how much personal risk is attached to different levels of communication and sees discussions about personal, peak experiences as the most risky of all. There is a danger that people will be less than honest if they perceive a risk they are not prepared to take, if there are considerable demands placed on them to cope with uncertainty, or if they are required to deal with grey areas. Those are the moments that offer the best opportunities for reflection, giving opportunities to develop self-knowledge as well as to reconsider decisions, interventions and actions taken (Gould and Taylor, 1996; Newton, 2004; Attard, 2008).

A supervisor who promotes and encourages this risk taking can also be helpful. Hobbs (1992) suggests that an effective supervisor is someone who:

- is able to give away control;
- can negotiate structure;
- can allow mistakes; and
- is able to cope with becoming redundant as the group or individual develops their own way of working.

The call for improved supervision for social work (DCSF, 2009) and early years practitioners (DfE, 2014) is to be welcomed as an acceptance that reflection cannot and should not be left to the individual; that engagement in a reflective process with a supportive 'other', whoever that might be, allows for greater quality, deeper understanding and thereby enhanced decision making. Implementing regular supervisory sessions in an early years setting provides a less formal space to reflect than that found in an appraisal meeting.

In a similar approach to that of McDrury and Alterio (2000), Susan Knights (1985) discusses working in pairs, giving each other 'free attention' to talk without interruption about their practice, ideas and feelings. This close relationship has the advantage of promoting greater honesty, although it could be criticised as having the potential for collusion and perpetuation of dangerous attitudes if there are no opportunities to share issues with others.

> *Meaningful, reflective conversations can sustain and nourish us. They can raise individual and collective consciousness. Above all else they involve a discussion of values. This is at the heart of the improvement process. (Ghaye, 2011: 189)*

Mentoring, formally recognising a role for an important 'other' to assist in reflection, is increasingly acknowledged as an important component of successful reflective practice (NCSL, 2004; Fowler and Robins, 2006; Pemberton, 2006). Reflection within a mutually supportive mentoring relationship can be a dynamic and creative way of learning for both parties:

> *Critical skills of reflection are crucial to all workers in the field of early years, as the importance of insight and understanding will shape and form not only immediate practice, but potentially the lives of children in our care and their families. Our role as effective mentors, supporting and teaching reflective practitioners, is vital to the ongoing maintenance and development of quality provision in our early years settings. (Fowler and Robins, 2006: 44)*

What are the obstacles?

But there are problems and obstacles to overcome, not least of which is the current climate of anxiety about the danger of taking risks. Such risks are inherent in creatively responding to a need within a culture that regards expertise as the ability to make an almost instantaneous assessment and to quickly put into action a plan to rescue, sustain or modify a situation (Fook, 1997; Saltiel, 2003). Reflection has not always been valued as a tool to enable the making of more considered decisions.

There is a danger of failing to look deeply into issues within our practice and ourselves, to work on them and to keep moving forward. Beck (1996, cited in Scourfield and Welsh, 2003: 403) argues that we need to ensure that our reflective practice involves 'critical appraisal and change' as opposed to reflexivity if we are to move away from just denying challenges to how we normally perceive the world, our workplace norms and culture. To really understand why we are working in certain ways, and how children and families are affected by the ways we are working, we need to engage in reflective practice. Without reflective practice there is a danger of early years education and care becoming a factory system 'designed to transform raw material (the children) into pre-specified products by treating it to a sequence of pre-specified standard processes' (Katz, 1993: 42).

Reflective practice is all too often not taken seriously. There is a

'real danger of reflective learning becoming a populist bandwagon which legitimates the abandonment of academic rigour' (Gould and Taylor, 1996: 74).

Again, the danger of reflection being perceived as navel gazing is great and practitioners need to establish a clear argument for its importance and to ensure it is given the priority it deserves (Newton, 2004). Early years practitioners need to see reflective learning and practice as an opportunity to contextualise and develop academic theory, rather than a soft option that allows people to talk about their work in unstructured, incoherent ways. This is no easy task in a world that seems to value convergent knowledge (fact gathering) as opposed to divergent knowledge (more creative and experiential) which is seen as being difficult to judge in terms of quality and relevance. We must ask whether supervisors can do what Hobbs requires of them (see above), to let go and allow the development of the individual rather than striving to perpetuate dogma. We need to look carefully at all our procedures and routines to ensure we promote reflective practice rather than discourage it.

The opportunities reflective practice offers us

It should be apparent that we feel strongly that the opportunities offered by reflective practice are sufficient to justify the effort required by practitioners to overcome all of the obstacles identified above.

Deep learning adds a rich quality to our practice (Boud *et al.*, 1985; Whalley, 2006), offering us the opportunity to develop more creative answers to difficulties (Gould and Taylor, 1996; Attard, 2008), enhancing our problem-solving skills and enabling us to recognise individual needs and devise individual solutions to meet them:

Reflective learning only has value if its effect is to deepen the complexity of practice; rather than rejecting the sphere of the intellect, the reflective paradigm actually requires an engagement with some of the particularly difficult debates within social theory. (Gould and Taylor, 1996: 74)

As reflectors, we are offered an opportunity to know ourselves and to study our motivations, needs, hopes and aspirations. We can explore the depths of our innermost being and bring our thoughts and feelings into the light for systematic observation and examination, allowing us to become rounded and grounded individuals, thoughtful, engaged practitioners and true advocates for those with whom we work (Tsang, 2007).

We have a plethora of possible models and methods to choose between to find the one that has relevance and resonance for us and for the children we work with. Reflective models such as those developed by Schön, Gibbs, Brookfield, Ghaye, Seidel, Lewin, and Kolb have been discussed and are all worth considering, but whatever reflective model we choose to use this should be further developed to meet our own needs and the needs of the children and families that we are working with:

'Every child deserves the best possible start in life and the support that enables them to fulfil their potential' (DfE, 2014: 5).

We have a window of opportunity at present. The current political climate and its spotlight on childhood offers us the chance to develop early years communities where practitioners from different disciplines can come together and reflect on the work they do, both separately and together, co-constructing a theory of good practice that all can relate to. For the last word, we turn to Attard (2008: 315):

> *If I thought I knew it all, I would not search for new understandings, but realising deficiencies in my own understandings makes me strive to better observe and better understand.*

ACTIVITY

Write a descriptive account of an incident or event from your practice and then share with another person. That person should listen to your account without interruption and then help you with the following stages as you further explore the incident/event.

1. *Exploring your feelings during the incident.*
2. *Considering the view of anyone else involved in the incident/event. This may be a colleague, parent or child.*
3. *Re-writing the incident from the perspective of the other person.*
4. *Asking: What? Why? How?*
5. *Creating links between what you have learnt from this incident/event and what you could do in the future.*
6. *Are there any concerns with established practice that you would like to address?*

Then, together, answer these questions:

- *Why is reflection on your effectiveness important?*
- *How has this task increased your confidence and self-esteem?*

FURTHER READING

Ghaye, A. (2011) *Teaching and Learning through Reflective Practice: A Practical Guide for Positive Action* (2nd edn). Abingdon: Routledge/David Fulton.

This book offers a full discussion on one of the most influential models of reflection.

Hayes, C., Daly, J., Duncan, M., Gill, R. and Whitehouse, A. (2014) *Developing as a Reflective Early Years Professional: A Thematic Approach.* Northwich: Critical Publishing.

This book offers a close look at the theory of reflective practice and demonstrates the practice through a series of themed chapters.

Mason, J. (2002) *Researching Your Own Practice: The Discipline of Noticing.* London: Routledge Falmer.

An inspiring read, giving many techniques and urging us to use a skill we already have, but take for granted: noticing what is happening around us.

REFERENCES

Anderson, T. (1987) The reflecting team: dialogue and meta-dialogue in clinical work. *Family Process*, 26: 415–28.

Attard, K. (2008) Uncertainty for the reflective practitioner: a blessing in disguise. *Reflective Practice*, 9(3): 307–17.

Boud, D., Keogh, R. and Walker, D. (1985) *Reflections: Turning Experience into Learning*. Ipswich: Kogan Page.

Bourner, T., O'Hara, S. and Barlow, J. (2002) Only connect: facilitating reflective learning with statements of relevance. *Innovations in Education and Teaching International*, 37(1): 68–75.

Brookfield, S. (1995) *Becoming a Critically Reflective Teacher*. San Francisco: Josey-Bass.

Brown, K. and Rutter, L. (2008) *Critical Thinking for Social Work* (2nd edn). Exeter: Learning Matters.

Cadden, C. (2009) *Peaceable Revolution through Education*. Carrboro: Baba Tree.

DCSF (Department for Children, Schools and Families) (2009) *Building a Safe, Confident Future – The Final Report of the Social Work Task Force*. London: DCSF Publications.

Dempsey, M., Halton, C. and Murphy, M. (2001) Reflective learning in social work education: scaffolding the process. *Social Work Education*, 20(6): 631–41.

Dewey, J. (1933) *How We Think*. Boston: D. C. Heath and Co.

DfE (Department for Education) (2014) *Statutory Framework for the Early Years Foundation Stage: Setting the Standards for Learning, Development and Care for Children from Birth to Five*. London: DfE Publications.

DfES (Department for Education and Skills) (2005) *Children's Workforce Strategy: A Strategy to Build a World-class Workforce for Children and Young People*. Nottingham: DfES Publications.

Eraut, M. (1994) *Developing Professional Knowledge and Competence*. London: Falmer.

Fook, J. (1997) *The Reflective Researcher*. London: Allen and Unwin.

Fowler, K. and Robins, A. (2006) Being reflective: encouraging and teaching reflective practice. In A. Robins (ed.), *Mentoring in the Early Years*. London: SAGE.

Gauntlett, D. (2011) *Making is Connecting. The Social Meaning of Creativity, from DIY and Knitting to YouTube and Web 2.0*. Cambridge: Polity Press.

Ghaye, A. (2011) *Teaching and Learning through Reflective Practice: A Practical Guide for Positive Action* (2nd edn). Abingdon: Routledge/David Fulton.

Gibbs, G. (1988) *Learning by Doing: A Guide to Teaching and Learning Methods*. London: Further Education Unit.

Gould, N. and Taylor, I. (1996) *Reflective Learning for Social Work: Research, Theory and Practice*. Bodmin: Arena.

Hayes, C., Daly, J., Duncan, M., Gill, R. and Whitehouse, A. (2014) *Developing as a Reflective Early Years Professional: A Thematic Approach*. Northwich: Critical Publishing.

Hobbs, T. (1992) *Experiential Training: Practice Guidelines*. Chatham: Tavistock/Routledge.

Horwath, J. and Thurlow, C. (2004) Preparing students for evidence-based child and family social work: an experiential learning approach. *Social Work Education*, 23(1): 7–24.

Katz, L. (1993) What can we learn from Reggio Emilia? In C. Edwards, L. Gandini and G. Forman (eds), *The Hundred Languages of Children* (2nd edn). Westport: Ablex Publishing.

Knights, S. (1985) Reflection and learning: the importance of the listener. In Boud D., Keogh R. and Walker D. (eds), (1985) *Reflections: Turning Experience into Learning*. Ipswich: Kogan Page.

Kolb, D.A. (1984) *Experiential Learning: Experience as the Source of Learning and Development.* New Jersey: Prentice Hall.

Lam, C.M., Wong, H., Leung, T.T.F. (2007) An unfinished reflexive journey: social work students' reflection on their placement experiences. *British Journal of Social Work*, 37(1): 91–105.

Lewin, K. (1946) Action research and minority problems. *Journal of Social Issues*, 2(4): 34–46.

Lindon, J. (2012) *Reflective Practice and Early Years Professionalism* (2nd edn). London: Hodder Education.

McDrury, J. and Alterio, M. (2000) Achieving reflective learning using storytelling pathways. *Innovations in Education and Teaching International*, 38(1): 63–73.

Mason, J. (2002) *Researching Your Own Practice: The Discipline of Noticing.* London: Routledge Falmer.

NCSL (National College of School Leadership) (2004) *National Professional Qualification in Integrated Centre Leadership (NPQICL).* Nottingham: NCSL.

NCTL (National College for Teaching and Leadership) (2013) *Early Years Educator (Level 3): Qualifications Criteria.* London: National College for Teaching and Leadership.

Newton, J. (2004) Learning to reflect: a journey. *Reflective Practice*, 5(2): 155–66.

Ofsted (2013) *Getting It Right First Time. Achieving and Maintaining High-quality Early Years Provision.* Manchester: Ofsted.

Pemberton, S. (2006) *Quietly Far Reaching: The Influence of the Mentor during the First Year of the NPQICL Rollout 2005/2006.* Unpublished thesis.

Pickles, T. (2003) Experiential Learning ... on the Web. Available at Experiential Learning: Articles and Critiques of David Kolb's theory: http://reviewing.co.uk/research/experiential.learning#axzz3M5U1OViG (accessed 16 December 2014).

Pollard, A. (2002) *Readings for Reflective Practice.* London: Continuum.

Ruch, G. (2002) From triangle to spiral: reflective practice in social work education, practice and research. *Social Work Education*, 21(2): 199–216.

Ruch, G. (2007) Reflective practice in contemporary child-care social work: the role of containment. *British Journal of Social Work*, 37: 659–80.

Saltiel, D. (2003) Teaching research and practice on a post qualifying child care programme. *Social Work Education*, 22(1): 105–11.

Schön, D. (1983) *The Reflective Practitioner.* New York: Basic Books.

Scourfield, J. and Welsh, I. (2003) Risk, reflexivity and social control in child protection: new times or same old story? *Critical Social Policy*, 23(3): 398–420.

Sylva, K., Melhuish, E., Sammons, P., Siraj-Blatchford, I. and Taggart, B. (2010) *Early Childhood Matters: Evidence from the Effective Pre-school and Primary Education Project.* Abingdon: Routledge.

Sylva, K., Melhuish, E., Sammons, P., Siraj-Blatchford, I. and Taggart, B. (2014) *Students' Educational and Developmental Outcomes at Age 16: Effective Pre-school, Primary and Secondary Education (EPPSE 3-16) Project. Research Report.* London: DfE. Available at: https://www.gov.uk/government/uploads/system/uploads/attachment_data/file/351496/RR354_-_Students__educational_and_developmental_outcomes_at_age_16.pdf (accessed 15 April 2015).

Teaching Agency (2013) *Teacher Standards (Early Years).* London: Teaching Agency.

Tsang, N.M. (2007) Reflection as dialogue. *British Journal of Social Work*, 37(4): 681–94.

Whalley, M. (2006) *Sustaining Leaders and Learners, Conference Papers.* Pen Green, March.

18 Research projects in Early Childhood Studies

Ulrike Hohmann and Christoforos Mamas

Introduction

Anyone interested in early childhood will come into contact with research. Advice given to you as practitioner, student or parent may be based on research studies; you may read about findings, you may be required to compare and contrast literature on any theme connected to the first years of children's lives and you will be required to undertake research for your undergraduate dissertation. You will come into contact with research both as a consumer, for example when writing assignments or changing your practice, but also as a producer, when you are asked to produce new knowledge by researching a particular topic or question. In this chapter we introduce you to some of the bigger and more theoretical questions around research in Early Childhood Studies and some of the methods employed in this type of research. We will highlight the implications for the design of your study, and the generation and analysis of data and we will outline the steps leading towards a written account.

What is research?

In everyday language research refers to a more or less systematic exploration of a topic or question by making use of information. Libraries, online portals and other repositories offer access to the material which can be used for research purposes. However, in this chapter we focus on empirical research, which means that information or data is collected from or generated with people. You may be asked to develop a research project and to write it up as your undergraduate dissertation. This opportunity allows you to follow up a question you have been interested in for a long time, a conundrum that niggles in the back of your mind, or to find a solution to a problem you encounter at work. Once you start formulating your research question, complex relationships between people, policies and structures become more visible. The quest for accurate expression of the research focus and sub-questions will reveal more than just interesting areas of inquiry.

Paradigms

The approach to research projects and the wording of questions is intimately linked to ontology, as it encompasses philosophical positions towards what there is to know about the world. Different schools of thought, also called paradigms, lead to different sets of ideas about how to gain knowledge about the world and how people relate to each other. Epistemology is concerned with what counts as knowledge and how people can know about the world. Social research, and with it educational research, has developed over time and can only be understood and evaluated in its historical context (Hammersley, 1995). For example, making use of modern information technology has thrown up new questions, involves working with novel forms of data and opens up fresh ways of conducting research.

It is useful to think about what you hope to gain through doing a research project and this process will point to a particular paradigm. Do you aim to uncover facts that ultimately result in 'correct' practice or are you more interested in gaining a deeper understanding of processes and meanings? The answer will lead you to the debate between positivist and interpretivist paradigms. The former relies on objectivism grounded in the assumption that the social world can and should be observed without interference by the researcher. The ontological implication is that meticulous observations of facts result in the discovery of 'truth'. People are studied like molecules observed by natural scientists. In experiments they are subjected to controlled conditions and consequently it is assumed to be possible to find consistent patterns in their reactions. The aim is to discover what causes particular behaviour. Here the starting point is a theory, which will be tested (deduction). The technical language involves hypothesis and null-hypothesis. It is also possible in the objective world to take a starting point from data. A careful analysis of a large number of observations will result in the discovery of patterns leading to a theory (induction). Both approaches rely on the world out there, regardless of how it is interpreted by people. Often these approaches to research involve quantitative data (data that can be expressed in numbers which can be further analysed by statistical tests).

There are two problems with the paradigm linked to objectivism. One problem is that people do not tend to react like molecules. Human beings do not form homogeneous groups of identical people and individuals have agency. The same or similar situations may not always trigger identical reactions. The meanings human beings attach to other people, things and situations are important. The second problem is that, according to the interpretivist paradigm, it is not possible to study the world outside directly. Instead of the wish to identify the causes of a certain kind of behaviour the interest moves to what kind of interpretations are possible, what processes and relationships are involved and how agency and power relationships influence behaviours.

Examples from past research by Ulrike (Gelder, 2002; 2003) serve to illuminate these two paradigms, moving from objectivism to interpretivism. With careful attention to detail, it is possible to work out how much money childminders earn. It requires information on fees and other financial contributions parents make, expenses and taxes paid, children enrolled and hours worked. Further analysis of these figures allows conclusions to be drawn about average 'take home' pay, which can be compared with the 'take home' pay of other early years practitioners. All of this is useful information. However, do these findings explain why, for a long time, childminding was the form of childcare with the majority of registered places in England? Can these figures now explain why there are fewer and fewer people setting up as childminders? The interpretivist lens reveals the meaning of the money to childminders and how they used it. For many it was an important contribution to family finances and was earmarked for food shopping or children's clothes. Only a minority of interviewed childminders treated it as 'pin money'.

The example shows that the differences between the above paradigms are not incompatible although each of them links to particular strategies influencing judgements about the quality of data, the approach to analysis, the relationship between theory and data and claims that can be made. The research focus and the way research questions are asked will link to one or the other paradigm and there may be instances of bridge building (Bryman, 2008; May, 2011). Research strategies may draw on methods loosely linked to one or the other paradigm (i.e. quantitative data and analysis are often linked to positivism and qualitative data and analysis to the interpretivist paradigm). However, starting with the research question itself can result in adopting one of the many research strategies, including surveys, case studies, ethnography and action research (Denscombe, 2014), each of which may include both quantitative and qualitative data. Any study may start with either a theory that can be tested or data that can be examined to form new theories, and the focus of interest can be found on a continuum from 'truths' to meanings. Many studies make use of mixed methods (Bryman, 2008) and the preparation of research projects often includes insights from qualitative pilot studies or is informed by the secondary analysis of statistical data.

Your decisions about how to conduct your research project will be guided by your interest and by the feasibility of conducting the study in the given timeframe with the resources available. Before you settle on a particular strategy and are in a position to fine-tune the research design you have to review relevant literature. The context for your unique study is what is already known about the phenomenon in question. In this way you can avoid simply repeating what has been done before and by critically engaging with literature you can identify unanswered questions, find new angles and perhaps then recognise the benefits of applying different methods. The topic of your interest may be well researched from the perspective of adults, like parents and early years practitioners, but may be barely informed by the perspectives of children. You will have to develop strategies for judging the quality of literature, for structuring the writing of a review and for addressing the conventions of academic writing (Oliver, 2012).

The review of the literature and your formulation of research focus and sub-questions may lead to research that emphasises the description of a phenomenon or a focus on the processes involved. Reading up on past research shows whether theory or data were treated as starting points and a closer look will show that these are like the two sides of a coin. What and how you observe (generate data) is influenced by theories you hold and, on the other hand, observations motivate you to revise your ideas and explanations. Keeping track of these links results in an iterative process employing both theory and observations and it supports a systematic inquiry which includes you as the researching agent.

Values and ethical behaviour

Every element of the research process is directly or indirectly influenced by value judgements. Values held by people guide and reflect social life and in this sense construct the issues that can be explored. Regarding the researcher, they span from dispositions and characteristics to practical considerations (Pring, 2000). Values you hold guide your research interest and inform what you view as a problem that deserves investigation. For example, an interest in two-year-old children in schools or in the effects of making corporal punishment of children illegal may initially be driven by the researcher's approval or disapproval of the current situation. These value judgements continue throughout the whole research process, influencing the questions asked, the analytical paths taken and ways of writing up. On the practical side, there are a number of ethical principles which guide the purpose of research and how people involved should be treated. Formal aspects include drawing up an ethics protocol, drafting consent forms and information for participants, obtaining permission to go ahead with your research from your tutor or an ethics committee. However, these cannot be treated as box-ticking procedures which can be forgotten once approved. As you proceed through the various stages of your research project decisions have to be made, often *ad hoc*, all working towards 'do no harm' and the potential to benefit participants, and all requiring continuous reflection on how personal and social values influence these decisions (Pring, 2000; May, 2011).

Tensions exist between the deontological or principled approach and the consequentialist approach to ethics (May, 2011). The former emphasises principles that should be applied in all circumstances. Principles include the right to informed consent, the right to withdraw without being penalised in any form and confidentiality. The latter approach emphasises the benefits of research findings that may sometimes outweigh discomfort felt by individual research participants or justify covert observation. Doing research with children sharpens the focus on particular dilemmas. How can you make sure that children understand what the project is about and why you are interested in it? How can children withdraw from research, when the research activity also places them in your care? Do parents have the right to learn what their child said in a research interview or would this breach confidentiality? Can parents or teachers *in loco parentis* withdraw children from research projects, even when children are keen to participate?

It is not always possible to gain an understanding of what is appropriately ethical research behaviour from past research. Concepts of childhood have changed considerably and research ethics in education have clearly moved to more principled and rights-based positions. Harm is not just understood as physical harm, but relates to psychological impact, like undue provocation of fear or embarrassment (Alderson, 2004). There is also more awareness of researchers' need for protection from harm, for example, when researching distressing aspects of social life (Wiles, 2013). To complicate things further, it is also not possible to plan for every possible situation or to rely on a fine-meshed net of rules specifying how to behave in the field. Ultimately it is the researcher who has to make tough ethical decisions based on their values and value judgements (Bogdan and Biklen, 2007) and discussing this process openly and honestly improves the quality of the research report.

Strategies

The combination of the purpose reflected in your research question, your value judgements and ethical considerations, and the availability of resources (including suitable research settings) will lead you towards the most appropriate research strategy. If your research project is the basis for an undergraduate dissertation it is likely that you will choose to conduct case study research, ethnography, mixed methods or action research. Other strategies may be less suitable because they require more time, equipment and skills, as is the case, for example, with large survey research. In this section we look at some important differences between various strategies.

Case study research

The case study strategy is particularly useful for small-scale research. The name indicates the focus on a distinctive case with clear boundaries in a natural setting (Yin, 2009). The boundaries are often physical and have to be well defined. You may be interested in a particular practice in one nursery room or you may want to investigate how Children's Centres support parents in the first few years of their child's life. This strategy allows you to take a holistic approach, observing many relevant factors within these boundaries. It is possible to concentrate on one case or to compare a small number of cases. The advantage lies in the flexibility to address suitable questions, the potential to reveal complex relationships and to uphold good research ethics. However, it may be more difficult to generalise findings.

Ethnographies

In contrast to a case study where the researcher may or may not participate, ethnographies rely on the gathering of information by participation in natural settings. The dilemma to be solved concerns how to get as close as possible to people, activities and meanings that are forming patterns of relationships without disturbing the normal dynamics of the setting. Ethnographic research can include covert observations, which demands carefully worked out ethical approaches. The question of whether and how the researcher may influence the phenomena in question by their presence in the context leads to a focus on reflection and the influence of personal values on data generated, analysed and reported. The advantages of these rich and often personal accounts may justify the challenges involved in getting access, dealing with ethical problems and recognising the potential risks involved in focusing on description instead of analysis and generalisable statements.

Action research

The role of the researcher changes drastically in action research (Chapter 19). Here the researcher does not aim to avoid influencing the behaviour and patterns under observation but purposefully takes action in order to improve professional practice. The advantages of this approach can include contributing to greater recognition of practitioners' knowledge and the democratisation of research

(McNiff and Whitehead, 2011). Reflection is a necessary part of this research process, especially in order to counteract effects associated with the researcher's inability to remain detached and impartial.

Mixed methods research

The three strategies introduced above are most likely to use entirely or mainly qualitative data and associated procedures of analysis. A stronger emphasis on quantitative data is introduced in the mixed methods approach, in which elements of qualitative and quantitative research approaches are combined in a single project 'for the broad purpose of breadth and depth of understanding' (Johnson *et al.*, 2007: 123). Mixed methods have particular value when a researcher is trying to approach a phenomenon or problem that is present in a complex educational or social context (Tashakkori and Teddlie, 2010). Likewise, because mixed methods designs incorporate techniques from both the quantitative and qualitative research traditions, they can be used to answer questions that could not be answered in any other way. The issue is not simply how to use methods from two paradigms alongside each other but how to integrate these methods into a coherent study (Tashakkori and Teddlie, 2003; Teddlie and Tashakkori, 2010; Bryman, 2012). The debates about exploiting the strength of both research paradigms are reflected in the terms used, such as integrating, quantitative and qualitative methods, synthesis, multiple methods, and multi-methods, although most writers have settled on the term 'mixed methods' (Tashakkori and Teddlie, 2010; Bryman, 2012).

Mixed methods include a variety of combinations of qualitative and quantitative approaches and the choice depends on the research question. Findings gained by different methods can be compared and may be strengthened by this triangulation, leading to improved accuracy from validation of findings, checking for bias and refining of research instruments. It is also possible to build up findings by a specific sequence of quantitative and qualitative methods. Richer findings are achieved through an iterative process of exploration and explanation. The rationale for these approaches is the enhancement of insights, which has made this research practice increasingly popular (Bryman, 2006).

The use of mixed methods can neutralise or cancel out some of the disadvantages of certain methods. For example, O'Farrelly and Hennessy (2014) employed structured observations of children, child consultations and parent interviews to research transitions of children within an early childhood education and care setting. By combining the methods in a particular study, we are able to 'broaden the dimensions and hence the scope of our project and obtain a more complete picture of human behaviour and experience' (Morse, 2003: 189). However, mixed methods are neither a panacea nor necessarily able to provide a full and multi-perspective picture of an educational phenomenon and there is a danger of diluting findings because available resources are spread too thinly (Bryman, 2012; Denscombe, 2014). The approach is tempting because it may seem to give students a fuller picture or because it gives the illusion of justifying not making firm decisions about methodological issues. Additionally the impact of this strategy on feasibility has to be considered. If you choose the mixed methods strategy you should be or become familiar with both quantitative and qualitative forms of research. Multiple sources of data require more time to collect the data, broader data analysis skills and an understanding about the integration of the different elements. You have to be aware that a greater number of methods does not automatically translate into a stronger study.

Methods

It is likely that you will use one, two or all of the three main methods of social research: interviews, observations and questionnaires. Despite some overlaps, each of them demands particular skills in data generation, handling and analysis.

Interviews

Interviews focus on what people say, what the researcher hears and, in face-to-face interviews, non-verbal communication plays a part, too. It is a flexible tool regarding the relationship between researcher and participant, the media used (face-to-face, online or by phone) and tools for analysis. Interviews enable participants to offer their interpretations of the world in which they live and to express their own point of view (Cohen *et al.*, 2011). Interviews can approximate how people communicate in their everyday contexts, 'one of the most common and powerful ways in which we try to understand our fellow human beings' (Fontana and Frey, 2000: 645). However, asking questions and getting answers in an interview is not an easy task because, as in any conversation, there is always room for ambiguity.

Decisions on the structure of the interview, choice of participants and formulation of questions aim to minimise the ambiguity inherent in human communication. At the same time care has to be taken not to tip the balance towards manipulating participants and affecting negatively the validity and trustworthiness of the data. Designs range from highly structured to completely unstructured. Structured interviews have a set of predetermined questions that are asked in a set order (Denscombe, 2014). The aim of this style of interview is 'for all interviewees to be given exactly the same context of questioning' and to 'ensure that interviewees' replies can be aggregated' (Bryman, 2012: 210). In a semi-structured or unstructured interview the focus is on the issues and interests of the research participant (Roberts-Holmes, 2014). The interviewer has a series of questions, commonly in the form of an interview schedule, but the sequence of questions may vary and follow-up questions may be asked by the interviewer. Unstructured interviews are supported by an interview guide, which typically consists of a list of topics or issues to be covered usually in an informal style of questioning or conversation. Being informal, freewheeling and not rushing participants into responding prematurely are useful practical strategies (Adler and Adler, 2002). A 'nonhierarchical, dynamic and fluid frame to the interviews' helps to establish rapport and trust with the interviewees (Levinson and Sparkes, 2005: 14) and open-ended interviews enable participants to show their unique way of looking at the specific phenomenon (Silverman, 2000). As the structure of interviews is reduced, the time and flexibility required (and the difficulty of analysing the resulting data) are likely to increase.

Good rapport between the researcher and participants and appropriate wording of questions can make interviews feel more relaxed, resulting in better data. Pitfalls to be avoided include asking about things people cannot possibly know or cannot be expected to remember, leading questions, confusing participants by asking two or more questions in one sentence, and not adapting language to the ability of participants. It can be tricky to create a space in which participants do not feel obliged to give socially desirable answers or the 'answers the researcher wants to hear' (Bryman, 2012; de Vaus, 2014). A trusting relationship between researcher and interviewee will be supported by appropriately ethical behaviour, setting out principles of confidentiality and the right to withdraw, without needing to give a reason, and outlining the structure of questions.

Practical concerns which may affect the quality of interviews include choosing a place that is comfortable and that allows confidentiality to be maintained. Interviews should not be overheard by others if this has been agreed. Sometimes it is useful to keep participation confidential, for example in research with several practitioners from one setting. The influence of the place on openness by participants ought to be considered. For example, children approached for participation on school premises may not feel able to decline, since this is not an appropriate response to an adult's request in this context (Mayall, 2002). A digital voice recorder can be used to record the interviews allowing you to obtain a more accurate account of what was said. You must inform all interviewees that you would like to record the interviews and ask for their informed consent.

Focus groups

Due to unequal power relationships, children and adults can feel intimidated when participating in an individual interview with a researcher (Roberts-Holmes, 2014). Focus group conversations with children may be more appropriate because the power imbalance between adults and children can shift in favour of children. As Folque (2010) argues, children are not used to their views and experiences being sought by unknown researchers, so developing rapport with them is necessary. To become familiar with the children (or adults) you hope to interview you should spend time with them ahead of the focus group meeting. In principle qualitative work with groups can range from heavily structured group interviews to unstructured focus groups and for research with children a flexible approach is appropriate (Scott, 2008). This kind of conversation can empower children by building up their confidence, supporting interaction between children and respecting children as experts in their setting (Lancaster and Broadbent, 2010 in Roberts-Holmes, 2014). Limitations of focus group work include that individual children may dominate the conversation and that the responsibility to maintain confidentiality is now shared with all participants. An additional practical aspect is that individual children may be hard to hear and transcribing recorded group interviews can be problematic.

Observation

Observation is a frequently used method of data collection for early childhood research. It allows you to explore familiar and routine events in early childhood settings in a new way (Roberts-Holmes, 2014) by 'looking critically, looking openly, looking sometimes knowing what we are looking for, looking for evidence, looking to be persuaded, looking for information' (Clough and Nutbrown, 2012: 54). Observations enable you to look at different aspects of children's development, including emotional, social, physical and cognitive development, as well as their relationships to other children and adults and include considerations of the natural context within which these occur. This form of data collection is attractive due to its directness, avoiding the transformations which occur when behaviour and emotions are described and explained in words to the researcher (Robson, 2011).

Specific forms of observations are characterised by structure, level of participation of the researcher and participants' knowledge about the research activities. Structured observations are systematic and may lead to the generation of numerical data. They are aided by observation schedules which set out, for example, the frequency and length of observations or require the observer to tick boxes indicating particular kinds of behaviour for each participant (Bryman, 2012). By contrast, unstructured observations do not have a tight focus. Early childhood researchers can take notes about different activities that are taking place in the setting, often before they begin to refine the focus of their study. These observations result in qualitative data, which are not easily analysed with statistical methods.

Another decision you have to make is whether you will participate in the activities you aim to explore and consequently seek to become a member of the observed group. This method is characterised by the researcher's immersion in the context and is closely linked to ethnography. It requires time to observe, listen and find opportunities to ask questions without disturbing people's normal behaviour (Bryman, 2012). However, not all participant observations have to, or can, involve the researcher so deeply. Forms of participation may include 'the complete participant', 'the participant as observer', 'the marginal participant' or 'the observer-as-participant' (Robson, 2011). For example, when observing children's interaction in a nursery context your participation as an adult will be different from your involvement in play with the children.

The most important ethical question is whether your observations will be overt or covert. A principled approach requiring informed consent does not allow covert forms of data generation. An emphasis on the benefits of the findings to the wider community and the attempt to avoid influencing the behaviour of the observed group may make covert research acceptable but you would have to have very good reasons to be allowed to undertake covert research. However, the grey area between the two poles overt and covert deserves attention. Are you able to explain to children why you want to listen in on their play? Do people who agree to be video recorded during activities understand fully that the researcher may replay sequences over and over again to capture every minute detail of their behaviour? Can we always inform everyone who may float in and out of research projects about our research aims (for example, the visitor to a children's centre)? It is also difficult to deny that researchers often hope that participants will forget that they are being researched and just behave as they would 'normally'.

Questionnaires

Questionnaires are a useful way to access a wide range of views, relatively quickly and in an economic manner. A popular form of questionnaire collects primarily quantitative data that cannot provide insights of the depth achievable with qualitative methods. They can be distributed in person, by post or other media, in paper form or electronically and answers can be returned by post, e-mail, as online response or in a face-to-face situation. This method is usually used with adults because questionnaires rely on participants' ability to read, comprehend and write. Yet the shift in concepts of childhood and research with children shows that often children's abilities to participate in research are underestimated and, with appropriate adaptations to research tools, they are capable of offering first-hand information on their lives and interpretations (O'Kane, 2008; Scott, 2008).

Questionnaires tend to offer a snapshot of a phenomenon in time. In combination with other methods, for example as part of a mixed methods strategy, they may support the fine-tuning of a research question or the testing of theories or they can help to identify people who are willing to contribute further to the research. However, it is common that after analysing your responses you end up with more questions, albeit different ones, than when you started your research project.

The nature of this form of data generation requires careful design. Once the questionnaire is distributed, participants cannot quickly ask for clarification if they do not understand a question, as they can in an interview. General format, length, ease of finding one's way through the questions, clarity of questions, space to respond and convenience of returning the completed questionnaire all influence the nature and fullness of answers and the return rate. The wording of questions deserves meticulous attention against the backdrop of your knowledge about the group of people you want to survey. Will they understand the questions and response forms? Will the chosen form capture the information you require? You will need to consider using closed and open questions. The former present a set of answers to choose from – and questions that can be answered with 'yes', 'no' or 'I don't know' belong to this category, too. The latter allow the respondent to answer in their own words and are likely to contain words like 'what', 'when', 'why', 'how', etc. Other possibilities are rating scales, multiple choice, ranking questions and more complex grids and tables (Bryman, 2012; de Vaus, 2014). Developing effective questions is a challenging process and we strongly encourage you to discuss drafts of your questionnaire with your peers and tutors and to pilot them.

In this section we have introduced you to the main methods of social and educational research. They can be used on their own or in combination with each other. Each of them requires a particular set of skills to generate data and to analyse it, each makes different demands on your (and your participants') time, each is more or less useful in doing research with children and each is likely to produce a certain kind of data. If you aim to access children's first-hand accounts and experiences, other forms of research, for example participatory methods, role play, drawings and photography, could be more appropriate (Christensen and James, 2008; Clark *et al.*, 2014).

Data analysis

Data analysis is a part of the research process which is often experienced by researchers as harrowing and exciting at the same time. Whatever type of data you are working with, analysis is a process of organising, summarising, describing and discussing your findings. The decisions you take about this process have to be informed by the underpinning paradigm guiding your research. In general, quantitative methods of data collection generate numerical data allowing statistical analysis, whereas qualitative methods require non-statistical techniques (Mukherji and Albon, 2010). Depending on your research instrument you may have to take decisions whether and how to use some qualitative data, for example, as remarks written into the margins of a questionnaire or answers to open questions, or you may feel tempted to examine the frequency of particular statements or phrases used across interviews.

As a first step you will organise and manage the raw data. For example, if you conduct interviews a transcript for each interview should be produced. Once transcription is complete, you can then begin to interrogate, read and re-read your data. Many researchers use thematic analysis, which is defined by Bryman (2012) as the process of examining the data to extract core themes that can be distinguished both between and within transcripts. These themes can be identified by careful coding of each transcript. Denscombe (2014) outlines a number of stages that can be useful, including becoming familiar with your data, coding the data, categorising the codes, identifying themes, and developing concepts that relate back to your research questions. You may also organise your data by groups of respondents, by individuals, by research questions or by research instruments (Cohen *et al.*, 2011).

A number of software packages can help you to manage and analyse your data and present your findings. The analysis of quantitative numerical data can be undertaken with the help of programs like Microsoft Excel, SPSS, SurveyMonkey or similar facilities, which also can create tables and charts. These programs allow you to run tests of data without understanding all the mathematics behind statistical methods, but it is advisable to be familiar with the principles of this kind of analysis. For most small-scale research projects a basic understanding of descriptive statistics is sufficient (Denscombe, 2014).

The analysis of qualitative data can be supported by NVivo, ATLAS.ti or similar software packages. They help you to keep on top of large amounts of data, to retrieve sections of text that have the same code attached and to annotate data with memos. They can replace paper methods (multiple copies, different folders, scissors and glue) or systems of colour coding of text. Apart from the insights you gain from analysing your data, you are also producing evidence for the claims which you will include in your written report. Data presented in tables, as figures or quotes illustrating your findings can bring findings to life and help readers to follow your arguments.

Writing up

No research project is complete until it has been written up. For most students, this is the longest and most challenging piece of writing they have ever been asked to complete. Writing is a craft and requires practice. It is important to continue to work on writing skills and manage your time well. Whether it is an assessed piece of work or not, you should make your findings available to other researchers, academics and fellow students and to people who are touched by the findings (Denscombe, 2014).

Each institution will have different requirements for how student projects should be written up and presented. The conventional structure divides the material into three parts: the preliminary part (title, abstract, key words, contents, list of tables and figures, acknowledgements, list of abbreviations), the main text (introduction, literature review, methods, findings, discussion and analysis, conclusions and recommendations) and the end matter (references, appendices). The main text will contain: a discussion of why you think the topic is important; the literature review, leading to the research question; a section on methodology, including a discussion of some ethical considerations; the findings and the conclusions you draw from them. Research projects based on quantitative methods and data may present findings and discussion separately. Ultimately, you should structure your report in a way that enables you to tell the story of your research in the most effective manner.

Institutions also differ in the required style of writing. For example, the Early Childhood Studies team at Plymouth University asks students to write in the first person. We believe that the use of the 'Royal We' or finding 'neutral' ways of setting out your position detracts from your ownership of your piece of research. You should be prepared to stand up for your findings and be proud of what you have achieved.

Ten top tips from Plymouth tutors

1. Research something you feel passionate about.

2. Choose a topic that will expand your professional horizon.

3. Decide on your focus, write it up as a provisional title and use it as a guiding light.

4. Draw up a timetable for your research, including some breaks from your work and buffer zones, for example, when there are delays in data collection.

5. Write a research journal.

6. Pilot your research instruments.

7. Ask yourself 'why': Why am I including this literature or choosing this methodology? Why do I want to know this, why am I discarding that?

8. Make use of your tutor and come to tutorials prepared with examples of your work and questions.

9. Draft and redraft sections – remember the report does not represent the order of writing.

10. Look after yourself: have time for your family and friends, sleep and exercise.

ACTIVITY

Choose one research article related to the topic of your interest and answer the following questions:

- *What is the underpinning research paradigm?*
- *What was the strategy of the study and which research instruments were employed?*
- *Which ethical questions had to be addressed?*
- *How was the data analysed?*
- *How accessibly are the findings presented?*

FURTHER READING

Denscombe, M. (2014) *The Good Research Guide for Small-Scale Social Research Projects* (5th edn). Maidenhead and New York: Open University Press.

Denscombe, M. (2010) *Ground Rules for Social Research: Guidelines for Good Practice.* Maidenhead: McGraw-Hill, Open University.

These books complement each other: *The Good Research Guide* sets out the practical steps and *Ground Rules for Social Research* explains the underlying principles.

Roberts-Holmes, G. (2014) *Doing Your Early Years Research Project: A Step by Step Guide* (3rd edn). London: SAGE.

This accessible book helps you to plan your research, providing a good overview of the whole research process from start to finish.

Christensen, P. and James, A. (eds) (2008) *Research with Children: Perspectives and Practices* (2nd edn). Abingdon: Routledge.

We encourage students to do research with children. Here you will find discussions of the shifts in the concept of childhood and how adults relate to children, leading to more direct involvement of children in research projects. The book offers a wealth of methods appropriate for work with children.

May, T. (2011) *Social Research: Issues, Methods and Process* (4th edn). Maidenhead: Open University Press.

If you are interested in deeper, theoretical engagement with social research you will find relevant discussion concisely presented here. It shows where bridges can be built between paradigms and how this impacts on various research methods. The book contains a useful chapter on comparative research.

REFERENCES

Adler, P.A. and Adler, P. (2002) The reluctant respondent. In J. Gubrium and J. Holstein (eds), *Handbook of Interview Research.* London: SAGE.

Alderson, P. (2004) Ethics. In S. Fraser, V. Lewis, S. Ding, M. Kellett and C. Robinson (eds), *Doing Research with Children and Young People.* London: SAGE.

Bogdan, R.C. and Biklen, S.K. (2007) *Qualitative Research for Education: An Introduction to Theories and Methods* (5th edn). Boston, London: Pearson.

Bryman, A. (2006) Integrating quantitative and qualitative research: How is it done? *Qualitative Research*, 6: 97–113.

Bryman, A. (2008) *Social Research Methods* (3rd edn). Oxford: Oxford University Press.

Bryman, A. (2012) *Social Research Methods* (4th edn). Oxford: Oxford University Press.

Christensen, P. and James, A. (eds) (2008) *Research with Children: Perspectives and Practices* (2nd edn). Abingdon: Routledge.

Clark, A., Flewitt, R., Hammersley, M. and Robb, M. (eds) (2014) *Understanding Research with Children and Young People.* London: SAGE.

Clough, P. and Nutbrown, C. (2012) *A Student's Guide to Methodology* (3rd edn). London: SAGE.

Cohen, L., Manion, L. and Morrison, K. (2011) *Research Methods in Education* (7th edn). Abingdon and New York: Routledge.

de Vaus, D.A. (2014) *Surveys in Social Research* (6th edn). London: Routledge.

Denscombe, M. (2014) *The Good Research Guide for Small-scale Social Research Projects* (5th edn). Maidenhead and New York: Open University Press.

Folque, M. (2010) Interviewing young children. In G. Mac Naughton, S.A. Rolfe and I. Siraj-Blatchford (eds), *Doing Early Childhood Research: International Perspectives on Theory and Practice.* Buckingham: Open University Press.

Fontana, A. and Frey, J.H. (2000) The interview: from structured questions to negotiated text. In N.K. Denzin and Y.S. Lincoln (eds), *The Handbook of Qualitative Research.* London: SAGE.

Gelder, U. (2002) Working for Women? Family Day Care Providers' Social and Economic Experience in England and Germany. Unpublished PhD thesis. University of Newcastle.

Gelder, U. (2003) Constrained entrepreneurship: the business of family day care in England and Germany. *Northern Economic Review*, 33/34: 118–33.

Hammersley, M. (1995) *The Politics of Social Research.* London: SAGE.

Johnson, R.B., Onwuegbuzie, A.J. and Turner, L.A. (2007) Toward a definition of mixed methods research. *Journal of Mixed Methods Research*, 1(2): 112–33.

Levinson, M.P. and Sparkes, A.C. (2005) Gypsy children, space and the school environment. *International Journal of Qualitative Studies in Education*, 18(6): 751–72.

McNiff, J. and Whitehead, J. (2011) *All You Need to Know about Action Research* (2nd edn). London: SAGE.

May, T. (2011) *Social Research: Issues, Methods and Process* (4th edn). Maidenhead: Open University Press.

Mayall, B. (2002) *Towards a Sociology for Childhood: Thinking from Children's Lives.* Buckingham: Open University Press.

Morse, J.M. (2003) Principles of mixed- and multi-method research design. In A. Tashakkori and C. Teddlie (eds), *Handbook of Mixed Methods in Social and Behavioral Research.* Thousand Oaks: SAGE.

Mukherji, P. and Albon, D. (2015) *Research Methods in Early Childhood: An Introductory Guide* (2nd edn). London: SAGE.

O'Farrelly, C. and Hennessy, E. (2014) Watching transitions unfold: a mixed-method study of transitions within early childhood care and education settings. *Early Years: An International Research Journal*, 34(4): 329–47. Available at: http://dx.doi.org/10.1080/09575146.2014.968838 (accessed 15 April 2015).

O'Kane, C. (2008) The development of participatory techniques: facilitating children's views about decisions which affect them. In P. Christensen and A. James (eds), *Research with Children: Perspectives and Practices* (2nd edn). Abingdon: Routledge.

Oliver, P. (2012) *Succeeding With Your Literature Review: A Handbook for Students.* Maidenhead: Open University Press.

Pring, R. (2000) *Philosophy of Educational Research.* London, New York: Continuum.

Roberts-Holmes, G. (2014) *Doing Your Early Years Research Project: A Step by Step Guide* (3rd edn). London: SAGE.

Robson, C. (2011) *Real World Research* (3rd edn). Chichester: John Wiley & Sons.

Scott, J. (2008) Children as respondents: the challenge for quantitative methods. In P. Christensen and A. James (eds), *Research with Children: Perspectives and Practices* (2nd edn). Abingdon: Routledge.

Silverman, D. (2000) *Doing Qualitative Research: A Practical Handbook.* London: SAGE.

Tashakkori, A. and Teddlie, C. (eds) (2003) *Handbook of Mixed Methods in Social and Behavioral Research.* Thousand Oaks: SAGE.

Tashakkori, A. and Teddlie, C. (eds) (2010) *SAGE Handbook of Mixed Methods in Social and Behavioral Research* (2nd edn). Thousand Oaks: SAGE.

Teddlie, C. and Tashakkori, A. (2010) Overview of contemporary issues in mixed method research. In A. Tashakkori and C. Teddlie (eds), *SAGE Handbook of Mixed Methods in Social and Behavioral Research* (2nd edn). Thousand Oaks: SAGE.

Wiles, R. (2013) *What Are Qualitative Research Ethics?* London: Bloomsbury.

Yin, R.K. (2009) *Case Study Research: Design and Methods* (4th edn). London: SAGE.

19 Action research

Ulrike Hohmann and Karen Wickett

Introduction

A defining feature of a popular version of action research is a clear focus on one particular aspect of practice, initially contained in one location, for example a nursery. Individual practitioners identify a problem or an area where improvements can be made, introduce changes to their practice, reflect on subsequent observations and discuss these with their colleagues (for example, Burgess-Macey and Rose, 1997; General Teaching Council for England, 2003: 123; Nind, 2003; Mac Naughton and Hughes, 2009).

The term action research originates in the social experiments in natural settings designed by Kurt Lewin in the 1940s. As part of this work Lewin developed the model of action research as a spiral of steps that repeats cycles of planning, action, observation and evaluation. In this respect action research is reminiscent of Kolb's (1984) experiential learning or Dewey's (1938) experiential education and Piaget's theory of cognitive development which represents children as weaving between assimilation and accommodation as they make sense of the world. However, a number of other influences can be traced, for example from liberationist thought, pragmatism and feminism (Reason and McArdle, 2004). For some, action research offers an answer to Marx's appeal to change the world. We will return to this aspect of action research later.

The family of approaches to action research that emphasises changing professional practice (Mac Naughton and Hughes, 2009; Cohen *et al.*, 2011) has been found to be particularly useful in education, health care (Koch and Kralik, 2006) and organisational research. Many research methodology books contain chapters or sections on action research (see Coles and McGrath, 2013; Denscombe, 2014; Mukherji and Albon, 2015; Roberts-Holmes, 2014) and new books which focus exclusively on action research are published every year (for example, Altrichter *et al.*, 2006; Taylor *et al.*, 2006; Koshy, 2010; McNiff and Whitehead, 2011; Baumfield *et al.*, 2013; McAteer, 2013). Despite the frequent use of subtitles such as 'a step by step guide', there is general agreement that action research is not so much a methodology as an orientation to inquiry.

> *Action research is a participatory, democratic process concerned with developing practical knowing in the pursuit of worthwhile human purposes, grounded in a participatory worldview ... It seeks to bring together action and reflection, theory and practice, in participation with others, in the pursuit of practical solutions to issues of pressing concern to people, and more generally the flourishing of individual persons and their communities. (Reason and Bradbury, 2001: 1)*

Three interdependent strategies of action research

To achieve these aims action researchers use three interdependent strategies. The first-person research/practice level relies on the ability of an individual to inquire into his or her practice and to act purposefully, being aware of and interested in the effects of these actions on the outside world. The second-person action research/ practice level addresses questions of collaboration and cooperation in small groups of practitioners/researchers who share an interest in particular areas in which change should take place. This level of inquiry is most amenable to the emergence of cycles or spirals of action and reflection by a small group of cooperating peers. Third-person research/practice develops broader networks and draws together a number of inquiries (Reason and McArdle, 2004).

In addition to the description of the persons involved in action and research we have to consider the kind of research that is possible with this approach. Action research can be of a technical nature, undertaken by practitioners under the watchful eye of an academic researcher, or of a practical nature, when the practitioners take on a more pro-active role to improve their own practice. It may also take a more eman-cipatory form, linked to political action, striving for collaborative learning, allowing people to understand themselves as agents. Conceptualising this kind of research as a form of social action and social movement aiming to change the social world for the better can connect the micro and the macro levels (Kemmis, 1993).

In this chapter we explore how action research can enable those working in the field of Early Childhood Studies to strengthen the integration of theory and prac-tice. Sometimes integration of elements of theory and practice is described as 'praxis' which refers to tacit knowledge, things we can do without having to be aware of every decision along the way. Action research can help practitioners to raise their knowledge and practice into the light of conscious examination so that new forms of praxis can be developed. Everything we do is informed by theories, even if we are not aware of them. Every time people act or decide not to act they also adjust their theories of the world. Sometimes unsettling experiences, both negative and positive, motivate us to talk with colleagues or read up on a topic and they may change our understanding and judgement of a particular explanatory model.

Denscombe (2014) summarises the common features of action research as follows: action research is practical, it introduces change, it is a cyclical process and it relies on participation. In the following section we will explain these characteris-tics, relate them to particular forms of action research and explore their strengths and weaknesses. We will illustrate each section with reference to the relevant fea-tures of one example of action research (Wickett, 2006) which took place in a day nursery which was part of a children's centre. Karen's role, as children's centre teacher, was to oversee and support the development of teaching and learning within the setting.

Action research is practical

Practical nature: It is aiming at dealing with real-world problems and issues, typically at work and in organizational settings. (Denscombe, 2014: 123)

Practitioners in early years settings and academics appreciate the fact that action research addresses issues that are of real concern to people, or in other words that it is a form of living inquiry (Wicks *et al.*, 2008). However, a preference for action research can also imply disillusionment with theoretical thinking and this form of research may also be attractive to those who are cynical about the value of theoretical or academic forms of inquiry. Ideally, however, decisions about research questions and about actions to be taken will emerge out of collaboration between practitioners and those who engage with early childhood issues at more theoretical levels. Some researchers argue that questions should initially be identified by practitioners (for example Somekh, 2003). There may, however, be questions that practitioners are unlikely to ask, because they have not noticed a problematic side to particular practices, because there is a concern about highlighting less than perfect practice or to avoid exposing latent conflict (Elliott, 1991). Another threat to the idea of linking knowledge to practice, leading to empowering praxis, is the temptation to concentrate on raising standards, or on demands for evidence-based practice (Campbell *et al.*, 2004). It is useful to look closely at the motivation to engage in action research: who formulates research questions; the wider context of a setting and how willingly participants move on from their initial ideas. It may reveal that interests other than improving practice for the sake of children, their families and practitioners are prominent. These difficulties have led to criticism of the partisan nature of action research.

Some of these problems can be avoided if action research is informed by theoretical understanding and academic insights. For example, deconstructing contemporary perceptions of childhood can lead to a better understanding of existing practice and may help to explain strong feelings about the best ways of educating and caring for young children. If children are seen as weak and dependent on very close relationships with a very small number of significant adults – one interpretation of Bowlby's (1953) work on attachment – then the implementation of key person systems in Children's Centres is reasonable. However, armed with other ways of understanding children's ability to thrive in different contexts it is possible to develop models of learning and spending time together that are less focused on trying to emulate the mother and child relationship (Dahlberg *et al.*, 1999).

Karen's research: The context

Children have a right to a place, as do teachers and parents. All of us have a right to spend our days in school, surrounded by places and spaces that enhance our lives, support our growth and hold us in respectful ways. (Cadwell, 2003: 117)

(Continued)

(Continued)

Although my role was to develop the teaching and learning I perceived it as more than just developing systems for planning and assessment for children's learning and development. I aspired to develop the children's centre as a learning community (Whalley, 2006), so I wanted us to establish an ethos and culture of learning. Within this community of learners it would be recognised that all participants, children and adults alike, were learners. Therefore I embarked on an MA to model learning and to show that although I was a teacher there was still much I had to learn. It was a requirement of the MA to undertake a piece of research. As well as being the researcher leading this study I was also the children's centre teacher.

During 2005, the year before the research question was identified, the practitioners within the nursery spent a day reflecting and considering the beliefs about children and their families which underpinned the team's principles. This day resulted in the team agreeing their guiding principles for the setting. One of our principles was 'we recognize that all adults and children are capable learners who can use the opportunities provided to develop their own learning' (Circles Nursery Team, 2006). Before the principles were written there had been many changes within the setting, for instance children had access to the outside throughout the session, a café-style system had been put in place, the routine had evolved and these changes had resulted in practitioners developing their understanding of an appropriate learning environment for children. By the time we wrote our principles the team was beginning to be aware that they were learners alongside the children. The ethos of a learning community was gradually gaining momentum.

After articulating our principles, we, the team, reflected on our practice and whether it was in line with our principles. Another of our principles was 'we recognize and cater for the needs of individuals, valuing their experience and promoting their personal development' (Circles Nursery Team, 2006). In order to gain an insight into the children's experiences and interests, so we could plan for the next steps in their learning, we needed to ensure that we actively listened to them and that our documentation systems provided opportunities for children to be heard. At this point we regularly wrote short observations, analysed these to find repeated patterns (schemas) in the children's actions/play and used this information to plan children's next steps. This practice was inconsistent and not rigorous. Therefore I embarked on a piece of action research to facilitate change and development of this practice. I wanted to explore how an 'in-house' workshop on 'Documenting Children's Learning' affected practitioners' understanding and use of documentation within the setting.

Action research introduces change

Change: Both as a way of dealing with practical problems and as a means of discovering more about phenomena, change is regarded as an integral part of research. (Denscombe, 2014: 123)

This aspect of action research may give it an optimistic appeal. Practitioners can critically reflect on their practice and work out ways of implementing changes and it is possible for managers, academics and researchers to support this kind of professional engagement (Schön, 1983). As in the previous section, there may be concerns about whether the chosen change of practice masks other, more necessary, changes or highlights the need for structural modifications which are beyond the practitioner's responsibility or influence. Additionally, a constant demand for change may take attention away from good practice that ought to be protected and continued.

Before introducing changes in practice it is useful to engage with accounts of the historical development of structures and practice and to work out how similar challenges have been addressed elsewhere, perhaps in other countries. It would be a waste of practitioners' time and energy to 'reinvent' practice which has already been developed by others and which can serve as a good starting point. A good understanding of why current practice has taken a particular form and how it is based on particular explanations and insights can help to ensure that change is more effective. A careful approach can also help to avoid the temptation to embark on arbitrary experiments. Professional commitment to the well-being of children, the need to 'get things right the first time' and a broadly ethical approach all caution against experiments in which practitioners are not reasonably confident that changes are likely to produce better outcomes.

Karen's research: More changes in practice and attitudes

During the in-house workshop on 'Documenting Children's Learning' (2006) practitioners shared that they had noticed that the children's behaviour had improved since we had started to do short observations, record repeated patterns (schema) in the children's play and use these for planning the next steps in their learning. Therefore they could see the benefits of developing the documentation systems. The content of the workshop included an introduction to the analytical framework of 'levels of involvement' (Laevers *et al.*, 1997), practice in writing narrative observations and exploring other approaches to documenting children's learning. These included Learning Stories from New Zealand (Carr, 2001), documentation from Reggio Emilia (Giudici and Rinaldi, 2001) and children's profiles from Pen Green (e.g. Whalley and the Pen Green team, 2001).

After the workshop there was much enthusiasm and excitement about our new learning. In order to maintain the enthusiasm and excitement certain systems and strategies were put in place by the leadership team. Resources were provided – digital cameras, camcorders, a computer and printer – and practitioners were also timetabled for non-contact time each week and had a pedagogic support session with me every half term. During the pedagogic sessions there were opportunities to discuss the learning stories and consider individual children's possible learning. When appropriate I would also introduce other theories to them such as levels of

(Continued)

(Continued)

well-being (Laevers *et al.*, 1997), Maslow's (1970) Hierarchy of Needs, the principles of free flow play (Bruce, 1991) and learning dispositions (Katz, 1995).

The impact of the workshop was evident during each pedagogic support session. I observed:

- More learning stories were used to document the children's learning – practitioners were more confident when sharing their documentation with me during their pedagogic support sessions. The learning stories were used as a starting point to discuss a child's learning. At the same time I would introduce theory which would link with the practitioner's interests.
- Practitioners were more likely to document learning when a child was highly involved during an activity. This resulted in them providing an increasingly challenging learning environment for the children, in which children were more likely to become highly involved in their play.
- Practitioners were more confident about discussing a child's learning with their parents/carers.
- Practitioners were more confident and enjoyed documenting children's learning and then planning next steps.

As practitioners became more confident in observing children during high levels of involvement and using the learning story framework, I interviewed them and asked them about their changing understanding and attitudes to documentation. These are a few of the comments that I recorded:

- Sophie: 'I used a more "tick box" approach to observation in the past, identifying whether children have acquired certain skills and knowledge. But now I realise they provided a limited snapshot of a child and didn't provide any insight into a child's thinking.'
- Rachel: 'I no longer use observations to tick boxes. In the past, [doing] observations I would have been used to ticking developmental milestones, for example I used to look to make sure they could cut with a pair of scissors. After the workshop I understand that observations and documentation can be used to inform the planning, building on children's interests or schema.'
- Fiona: 'I used to think observations were used so we could see where the child was in their ability so we could help them to extend their abilities. My understanding now has changed. I now understand that they can be used to find out their interests and patterns of learning.'

Action research is cyclical

Cyclical process: Research involves a feedback loop in which initial findings generate possibilities for change which are then implemented and evaluated as a prelude to further investigation. (Denscombe, 2014: 123)

Researching one's practice, introducing change, reflecting and sharing this information, can be rewarding although it does cost time and energy and sometimes these costs mean that practitioners are only able to go through one cycle. Also, when the motivation to embark on action research arises from an assignment task for college or university it may be difficult to continue an enquiry beyond what is required to complete the task. However, the full benefits of action research come from repeated revisiting of research questions. Forward planning can include identifying strategies to pass on insights to colleagues and to create opportunities for further cycles. Practitioner networks can form a good supporting system that allows members to pool insights and develop new research questions in collaboration, sometimes leading to spirals on spirals, as illustrated by McNiff and Whitehead (2011). An approach allowing for evolving research spirals also highlights the creative messiness of action research. On the one hand this can make it difficult to justify research projects but on the other hand it does allow emerging questions to be followed up.

These research spirals and possible networks can also help to develop sustainable practice. To illustrate this point we can refer to the multitude of television series in which an expert (on childrearing, cooking or fashion) advises practitioners (from parents to restaurant proprietors) on good practice but leaves after one cycle. When the expert returns after a few weeks or a year it often turns out that people have returned to their old ways.

Although at times action research may look like the individual exercise of reflective practice (think – do – think), the difference lies in a greater emphasis on theory which fuels the progression of the cyclical process once the research question has been developed. For example, Denscombe (2014) builds into his representation of the action research cycle the element 'Research: systematic and rigorous inquiry' before practitioners are invited to start their action. Most books on action research include a chapter on literature review. Another difference compared with reflective practice is the expectation that findings will be disseminated to other practitioners and interested academics and researchers, ideally generating further questions and further cycles of action research projects.

Karen's research: The next part of the journey – entering the second cycle

The changes in practice and practitioners' attitudes and understanding meant we had completed the first cycle. When this new learning and practice became embedded within the practices of the setting we entered the second spiral of the action research.

Not only were the practitioners increasingly skilled and confident in documenting children's learning, analysing the documentation and then planning the next steps for the children but they were also becoming familiar with past and current theorists and their theories. All of us were gaining a deeper insight into our children as learners. We were excited about our new learning community. During pedagogic

(Continued)

(Continued)

sessions practitioners and I would document our own learning and this helped us to gain a deeper understanding of both the children and ourselves as learners. However, during several discussions with the practitioners I sensed there was a need to further develop the documentation systems. It was agreed by the team that there should be a consistent framework for analysing the documentation.

Another INSET day was planned for the following academic year, 2007/2008. During the day the team considered what was important to them and which theorists had influenced our practice. Again other systems and frameworks, such as Learning Stories, were looked at and discussed. These discussions led to the team identifying the headings and concepts which they wanted to use and develop when analysing the documentation. Inspired by Margaret Carr's (2001) work, the first heading was 'Taking an Interest'. The next came from Laevers *et al.* (1997) – 'Well-being'. As a team we were very aware that children needed to be feeling good about themselves and the world in order for them to learn and reach their full potential, so we wanted to make sure that the children's well-being was at the forefront of our minds. 'Challenge' was the third heading. As a team we were unsure what challenge would look like in a learner-led learning environment, so this was an area for further investigation which could develop into a third cycle. Finally, as our principles focus on the importance of valuing and recognising the links between the home, setting and community the last heading was 'Relationships'. This would recognise the many relationships that a child has within the setting and beyond.

Action research requires participation

Participation: Practitioners are the crucial people in the research process. Their participation is active, not passive. (Denscombe, 2014: 123)

Action research makes two demands on the practitioner: firstly, that he or she is an active researcher and secondly, that the focus is on his or her own practice. If only the first demand is met, this kind of research is called practitioner research and can be research on any issue, for example the practice of others, but undertaken by the practitioner. However, what is actually meant by 'the practitioner as researcher' is not always quite clear. Often the researcher role includes collaboration with non-practitioner researchers, students or academics and, of course, fellow practitioners (Kemmis and McTaggart, 1988). One condition of successful action research is that those involved are clear about, and agree on, who is doing what. It seems to work well if there is recognition and acceptance of different roles and skills, for example, an academic researcher can be used as a 'reader', an 'interpreter' of academic knowledge and summariser of research reports (Nind, 2003).

However, it is not always clear how the democratic expectations concerning participation are played out. Participation may be constrained by the setting (Elliott, 1991; Burgess-Macey and Rose, 1997; Edwards, 2004; Wilkie, 2006), colleagues may be less willing to participate, or may feel threatened by the research questions and a head teacher may be reluctant to support research. Here the diplomatic skills of researchers and the willingness of practitioners are important. These challenges highlight the fact that action research is not necessarily emancipatory and that expectations about collaboration can hinder the research trajectory of individual practitioners and prevent research on controversial issues (Burgess-Macey and Rose, 1997).

It is often unclear whether everyone is expected to participate on the same level. For example, when action research is conducted in a nursery, do practitioners, the manager, parents and children have the same responsibilities for working out the research question, changes in practice, data collection, reflection and initiation of the next cycle? Contemplating possible scenarios arising from this question shows how challenging the demand for participation is and highlights the potential for conflict. An emphasis on collaboration may mean that areas of potential conflict are not addressed, only topics where there is already agreement, leaving more sensitive areas untouched even though these might benefit most from exploration and change.

Obtaining informed consent is a necessary precondition for ensuring that action research is ethical. Löfman *et al.* (2004) show the difficulties potential participants may experience in giving consent because part of the nature of action research is that we cannot foresee where the project will lead. Employees in a setting may also feel they have limited choice in whether or not they participate in a programme of action research when managers are clearly keen to promote it. When children and/or vulnerable adults are also involved, which is quite likely in projects suitable for action research, ethical considerations require much care and attention.

Karen's research: Reflections on participation in action research

When embarking on my role as teacher within the setting I had the vision of establishing an environment where all participants were learners, children and adults alike. For all of us the initial cycle of action research had scaffolded the development of our documentation practices. Although I initiated the first cycle of the action research, the relationships and my role in the team (teacher/researcher) enabled me to reflect on existing practice and sense the next area of development. My inside knowledge and understanding of the team and our practices ensured I was able to identify an aspect of practice to research which would make sense to others and enable them to be participants in the research. For instance during the first spiral of the action research the team realised the benefits of using short observations to inform the planning of activities for the children, so they were willing to develop the documentation systems. However, the second cycle was initiated by the team. Many members of the team realised that we needed to develop our own framework of analysis for documentation, so the second INSET day was planned and carried out. Throughout this day practitioners were able to discuss the issues, theories and practices they believed were relevant and important to themselves, children and families.

(Continued)

> (Continued)
>
> My studies gave me opportunities to deepen my understanding of some theorists and theories and to learn about new theories and research. Not only was I modelling to the team that I was learning but I was also able to share my new understanding about children's learning during pedagogic support sessions. When sharing the learning stories each practitioner had the opportunity to consider what the stories revealed about the child's learning but we were also able to link this to theory. For instance a practitioner had documented a child playing in the sand tray. To begin with she thought this child was involved, but when we analysed the learning story we realised the play was at a routine level. We referred to other observations of the child and to levels of well-being. We decided this child seemed to have low levels of well-being so we planned for the practitioner to spend more time with this child in her role as key person.
>
> Linking theory with practice helped us to plan for children's learning but it also provided common frameworks and vocabulary which enabled practitioners to share their own theories and ideas. For instance, when deciding on the themes for our learning story analytical framework they were able to enter into dialogue with each other. Their new learning and vocabulary enabled them to participate as practice was being developed. They also owned the systems that we developed, making our practice more sustainable. Linking theory with practice enabled practitioners to make sense of statutory and non-statutory expectations and guidelines from the DCSF and to engage critically with these in order to implement requirements in ways which would suit this setting's children, families and practitioners.

For most of the chapter we have concentrated on action research which aims to change practice at the micro level. However, there are hints of links to macro issues, for example the way national policies regulate and influence early childhood services. It is useful to remember that action research has its roots in social movements (Kemmis, 1993). The term action research implies dynamic and exciting activities with greater personal engagement by the researcher than is normally attached to traditional approaches which use established methods like observing children, interviewing parents and surveying practitioners. It is associated with the invigorating feeling of rolling up one's sleeves, balancing concerns about objectivity with passionate commitment to a cause and putting one's research skills at the disposal of people who may need them. This approach is exemplified by research on childminding in the 1970s by Jackson and Jackson (1979). Their work was political, aiming to improve the situation of children and childminders and they combined research with action.

From the beginning of the project we have tried to provoke action by others (issuing an Action Register, calling national conferences, making television programmes, urging blueprints from the research) [and by] ourselves (The Children's Centre in Huddersfield, The Drop In Centre in Manchester, courses for childminders).

This has the virtue of getting something done, instead of having impotently to wait for years for possible government action; and action breeds action. (Jackson and Jackson, 1979: 14)

Their research activities included the dawn watch (researchers spending time on English streets in the early morning hours, observing children being taken to child-minders), interviews, observations and organising play and safety equipment for childminders and the project led to the founding of the National Childminding Association. Many of their action research activities provided blueprints for services to support childminders. For example, the childminder networks, toy libraries and start-up packs they encouraged are still in place in many local authorities. Even more pressing needs for social change were identified by a study which found authoritarian forms of behaviour management in post-war Guatemalan parenting (Schrader McMillan, 2007) and several cycles of action research aimed to develop sustainable ways of reducing the child abuse associated with this.

Conclusion

In this chapter we have highlighted some of the characteristics, benefits and challenges of action research. This form of inquiry has promoted a number of qualitative methods, raising the status of small-scale research on day-to-day practice. However, action research does not exclude quantitative methods but like any well organised research, it requires researchers to identify the approaches which are most appropriate to the questions asked. There are a number of people who criticise small-scale action research projects and accuse them of being unscientific and lacking in rigour. They argue that research should avoid political issues and that researchers should remain neutral. We, however, see in action research a useful opportunity for practice to be explored from perspectives which are not easily accessible to the more remote, visiting researcher.

When practitioners combine their daily work with the role of researcher it can lead to development in two areas. Firstly, they improve their own practice by making better use of theory and, secondly, they contribute to new knowledge which, in turn, can help the wider community of early years practitioners, children and their families. Additionally, dissemination of findings from action research means that academics can receive insights into a world they could not access by themselves. A benevolent cooperation between academics and early years practitioners leads to theory and practice informing each other, removing unhelpful barriers. In practice it could mean that early years practitioners gain confidence in talking about and sharing their practice and learning. The emerging dialogue may shift hierarchical structures towards a more democratic way of relating to each other. For instance, taking reflective practice and engagement seriously will change relationships between managers, teachers and early years advisors. The participatory approaches developed during action research can influence policies and wider structures from the bottom up. In the political tradition of action research, practitioners and researchers can become effective advocates for children.

ACTIVITY 1

Action research in the nursery

Katrina is a new member of staff in a nursery. In the resources room she finds a large set of giant wooden building blocks, which has been purchased by the previous head of the nursery. It emerges that some of her colleagues value the opportunities these building blocks offer to children but others worry about health and safety issues, space and noise levels, and question whether plain wooden building blocks are stimulating enough. At a meeting the staff agree that it would be a shame to leave these expensive resources in the cupboard and they start to plan how they can be introduced, beginning a cycle of action research.

The following questions may help you to consider how such a project might demonstrate the four characteristics of action research: being practical, introducing change, being cyclical and encouraging participation:

- *What could be the different stages of this giant wooden building blocks action research?*
- *What can be done to develop and maintain everyone's participation?*
- *What outside experts could be useful and what should be the focus of negotiations around their involvement?*
- *What kind of research cycles could you see emerging?*
- *How can insights and findings feed back into practice?*
- *What are the advantages and disadvantages of insider knowledge in the project?*
- *What ethical matters have to be taken into consideration?*

ACTIVITY 2

Action research at university

Think about the seminars and group work meetings you have attended. Are there any practices that puzzle, amaze or annoy you? What could you do to explore how these could be changed? How can you ensure that your inquiry is practical, introduces change, is cyclical and participatory? Adapt the questions listed above to consider how this student action research project might be conducted.

FURTHER READING

Mac Naughton, G. and Hughes, P. (2009) *Doing Action Research in Early Childhood Studies: A Step by Step Guide.* Maidenhead: Open University Press and McGraw-Hill Education.

This book contains a wealth of practical advice and theories about the different approaches to action research. Examples are projects in early years, often conducted by students. The book addresses many concerns of potential researchers and offers useful suggestions about how to approach the challenges in this form of inquiry.

Baumfield, V., Hall, E. and Wall, K. (2013) *Action Research in Education: Learning Through Practitioner Enquiry* (2nd edn). London: SAGE.

This book offers a wealth of action research in a wide range of education settings and contains many examples of how different methods can be employed to generate relevant data.

Chapter 8 in **Denscombe, M.** (2014) *The Good Research Guide for Small-Scale Social Research Projects* (15th edn). Maidenhead/New York: Open University Press.

Here you will find a good overview of action research and links to other research approaches. Denscombe highlights ethical issues, advantages and disadvantages and provides a checklist which is useful when developing an action research project.

The journal **Educational Action Research**, published by Routledge, offers accounts of action research and related studies, reviews of literature on action research and a forum for dialogue on methodological and epistemological issues.

REFERENCES

Altrichter, H., Feldman, A., Posch, P. and Somekh, B. (2006) *Teachers Investigating Their Work: An Introduction to Action Research Across the Professions*. London: Routledge.

Baumfield, V., Hall, E. and Wall, K. (2013) *Action Research in Education: Learning Through Practitioner Enquiry* (2nd edn). London: SAGE.

Bowlby, J. (1953) *Childcare and the Growth of Love*. Harmondsworth: Penguin.

Bruce, T. (1991) *Time to Play in Early Childhood Education*. London: Hodder & Stoughton.

Burgess-Macey, C. and Rose, J. (1997) Breaking through the barriers: professional development, action research and the early years. *Educational Action Research*, 5(1): 55–70.

Cadwell, L.B. (2003) *The Reggio Approach to Early Childhood Education: Bringing Learning to Life*. New York: Teachers College Press.

Campbell, A., McNamara, O. and Gilroy, P. (2004) *Practitioner Research and Professional Development in Education*. London: Paul Chapman Publishing.

Carr, M. (2001) *Assessment in Early Childhood Settings: Learning Stories*. London: Paul Chapman Publishing.

Circles Nursery Team (2006) *Setting's Principles*. Taunton: Acorns Children's Centre.

Cohen, L., Manion, L. and Morrison, K. (2011) *Research Methods in Education* (7th edn). Abingdon: Routledge.

Coles, A. and McGrath, J. (2013) *Your Education Research Project Handbook* (2nd edn). Abingdon: Routledge.

Dahlberg, G., Moss, P. and Pence, A. (1999) *Beyond Quality in Early Childhood Education and Care: Postmodern Perspectives*. London: Routledge Falmer.

Denscombe, M. (2014) *The Good Research Guide for Small-scale Social Research Projects* (5th edn). Maidenhead and New York: Open University Press.

Dewey, J. (1938) *Experience and Education*. New York: The Macmillan Company.

Edwards, A. (2004) Understanding context, understanding practice in Early Education. *European Early Childhood Education*, 16(1): 85–101.

Elliott, J. (1991) *Action Research for Educational Change*. Buckingham: Open University Press.

General Teaching Council for England (2003) *Researching Effective Pedagogy in the Early Years*. London: General Teaching Council for England. Available at: http://www.learning-concepts.co.uk/research/repey.pdf (accessed 27 February 2015).

Giudici, C. and Rinaldi, C. (eds) (2001) *Making Learning Visible: Children as Individual and Group Learners.* Reggio Emilia: Reggio Children.

Jackson, B. and Jackson, S. (1979) *Childminder: A Study in Action Research.* London: Routledge & Kegan Paul.

Katz, L. (1995) *Talks with Teachers of Young Children.* Norwood NJ: Ablex Publishing.

Kemmis, S. (1993) Action research and social movements: a challenge for policy research. *Education Policy Analysis Archives,* 1(1): 1–6. Available at: http://epaa.asu.edu/ojs/article/view/678 (accessed 27 February 2015).

Kemmis, S. and McTaggart, R. (1988) *The Action Research Planner* (3rd edn). Geelong, Vic: Deakin University Press.

Koch, T. and Kralik, D. (2006) *Participatory Action Research in Health Care.* Oxford: Blackwell.

Kolb, D.A. (1984) *Experiential Learning: Experience as the Source of Learning and Development.* New Jersey: Prentice Hall.

Koshy, V. (2010) *Action Research for Improving Educational Practice: A Step-by-Step Guide.* London: SAGE.

Laevers, F., Vandenbussche, E., Kog, M. and Depondt, L. (1997) *A Process-oriented Child Monitoring System for Young Children.* Leuven: Centre for Experiential Education.

Löfman, P., Pelkonen, M. and Pietilä, A.-M. (2004) Ethical issues in participatory action research. *Scandinavian Journal of Caring Science,* 18(3): 333–40.

McAteer, M. (2013) *Action Research in Education.* London: SAGE.

Mac Naughton, G. and Hughes, P. (2009) *Doing Action Research in Early Childhood Studies: A Step by Step Guide.* Maidenhead: Open University Press and McGraw-Hill Education.

McNiff, J. and Whitehead, J. (2011) *All You Need to Know about Action Research* (2nd edn). London: SAGE.

Maslow, A.H. (1970) *Motivation and Personality* (2nd edn). New York: Harper and Row.

Mukherji, P. and Albon, D. (2015) *Research Methods in Early Childhood: An Introductory Guide* (2nd edn). London: SAGE.

Nind, M. (2003) Enhancing the communication learning environment of an early years unit through action research. *Educational Action Research,* 11(3): 347–64.

Reason, P. and Bradbury, H. (eds) (2001) *The Handbook of Action Research: Participative Inquiry and Practice.* London: SAGE.

Reason, P. and McArdle, K.L. (2004) The theory and practice of action research. In S. Becker and A. Bryman (eds), *Understanding Research for Social Policy and Practice.* Bristol: The Policy Press.

Roberts-Holmes, G. (2014) *Doing Your Early Years Research Project: A Step by Step Guide* (3rd edn). London: SAGE.

Schön, D. (1983) *The Reflective Practitioner.* New York: Basic Books.

Schrader McMillan, A. (2007) Learning at the edges: action research and child-maltreatment in post-war Guatemala. *Bulletin of Latin American Research,* 26(4): 516–32.

Somekh, B. (2003) Theory and passion in action research. *Educational Action Research,* 11(2): 247–64.

Taylor, C., Wilkie, M. and Baser, J. (eds) (2006) *Doing Action Research: A Guide for School Support Staff.* London: Paul Chapman Publishing.

Whalley, M. and the Pen Green Team (2001) *Involving Parents in their Children's Learning*. London: Paul Chapman.

Whalley, M. (2006) Children's Centres: the new frontier for the welfare state and the education system? Conference paper, Early Interventions for Infants and Small Children in Families at Risk, 27–28 April, Oslo. Available at: http://webarchive.nationalarchives.gov.uk/20140719134807/http://www.nationalcollege.org.uk/download?id=17124&filename=childrens-centres-the-new-frontier.pdf (accessed 27 February 2015).

Wickett, K. (2006) How does the workshop 'Documenting Children's Learning' impact on practitioners' understanding and practice of documentation within the setting? Unpublished assignment for MA Integrated Provision for Children and Families. Pen Green, Leicester University.

Wicks, P.G., Reason, P. and Bradbury, H. (2008) Living inquiry: personal, political and philosophical groundings for action research practice. In P. Reason and H. Bradbury (eds), *The SAGE Handbook of Action Research* (2nd edn). London: SAGE.

Wilkie, M. (2006) Benefiting from action research. In C. Taylor, M. Wilkie and J. Baser (eds), *Doing Action Research: A Guide for School Support Staff*. London: Paul Chapman Publishing.

Index